VOLUME ONE

BROWN
— OF —
THE GLOBE
VOICE OF UPPER CANADA 1818-1859

J.M.S. Careless

To my wife

VOLUME ONE

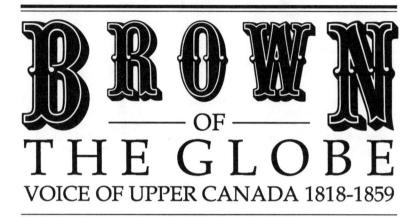

BROWN
— OF —
THE GLOBE
VOICE OF UPPER CANADA 1818-1859

J.M.S. Careless

TORONTO & OXFORD
1989

Cover Design: Andy Tong
Printing and Binding:Gagné Printing Ltd., Louiseville, Quebec, Canada

The publication of this book was made possible by support from several sources. The publisher wishes to acknowledge the generous assistance and ongoing support of **The Canada Council, The Book Publishing Industry Development Programme** of the **Department of Communications, The Ontario Arts Council.,** and **The Ontario Heritage Foundation,** an agency of the Ontario **Ministry of Culture and Communications.**

Care has been taken to trace the ownership of copyright material used in the text (including the illustrations). The author and publisher welcome any information enabling them to rectify any reference or credit in subsequent editions.

J. Kirk Howard, Publisher

Canadian Cataloguing in Publication Data

Careless, J. M. S., 1919-
  Brown of the Globe

Includes bibliographical references.
Contents: Vol. 1. The voice of Upper Canada, 1818-1859 —
v. 2. Statesman of Confederation, 1860-1880.
ISBN 1-55002-050-1 (v. 1) ISBN 1-55002-051-X (v. 2)

1. Brown, George, 1818-1880. 2. Canada — Politics and government — 1841-1867. 3. Politicians — Canada — Biography. 4. Journalists — Canada — Biography. l. Title.

FC471.B76C3 1989   971.04092   C89-090670-X
F1032.B76C3 1989

Originally published by Macmillan of Canada.

Dundurn Press Limited
2181 Queen Street East, Suite 301
Toronto, M4E 1E5
Canada

Dundurn Distribution Limited
73 Lime Walk
Headington, Oxford
OX3 7AD
England

Contents

Illustrations

Illustrations at chapter endings are reproductions of engravings which appeared in *The Globe* with the exception of Malcolm Cameron's broadsheet of 1851 (p. 98).

Preface

This is the first of two volumes on George Brown, 1818-1880, Canadian journalist, Liberal leader, and maker of Confederation. The present volume carries him from Edinburgh boyhood to the proprietorship of the powerful Toronto *Globe*, traces his connection with the all-absorbing contest of the 1840's over responsible government, and describes his entrance into parliamentary life amid the hot religious disputes of the early 1850's. It records his strenuous advance through the jarring sectional politics of the fifties to become the dominant voice of an angry and aggrieved Upper Canada; his successful reconstruction of a defeated, shattered Liberal party, and his winning of that party to policies of north-west expansion and federal union that clearly forecast the subsequent development of Canadian Confederation. The second volume will examine Brown's critically important role in the actual achievement of Confederation, and his later career in the new Dominion, where he still stood high as a Liberal elder statesman, if no longer party leader, chiefly because of the unrivalled power of his *Globe*.

Almost half a century has passed since the last full-length biography of Brown appeared: that written by John Lewis and published in the *Makers of Canada* series in 1910. Indeed, before Lewis's book, there had been only a stilted memoir and party tract, *The Life and Speeches of the Hon. George Brown*, produced in 1882 by Alexander Mackenzie, Brown's loyal follower and heir as Liberal leader. One could contend, therefore, that such a prominent figure in Canadian history decidedly deserves another look. At least we might reasonably contrive to re-examine the great men of our past every fifty years or so. But there is more ground than this for a new biography of Brown.

A substantial number of his private papers have only recently come to light. Used in conjunction with other manuscript collections that are now available in Canadian archives, they pro-

vide a basis of primary material for the study of Brown, which
was virtually lacking before. It was the present writer's very
good fortune that his search for resources of this kind led in
1955-6 to his being given access to a trunkful of George Brown's
papers in Scotland, at the residence of Mrs. G. M. Brown and
Mr. G. E. Brown, Ichrachan House, Taynuilt, Argyll, the
daughter-in-law and grandson of George Brown respectively.
The discovery of these documents permitted the filling of gaps
in Brown's story and the re-assessment of the man and his many-
sided activities in a way previously impossible. The whole
valuable collection has now been deposited in the Public
Archives of Canada as the Brown Papers, thanks to the generous
understanding of Mr. G. E. Brown, the present head of the
family.

I have to thank Mr. Brown and Mrs. G. M. Brown, ahead
of many others on a long list, not only for their all-important
consent to allow me to enter their home and use the papers, but
also for the warm and unflagging hospitality they displayed on
my repeated visits to Ichrachan, surely one of the most attractive
places in the beautiful western Highlands. I also owe my thanks
for a variety of aid to other members of the Brown family,
including Professor Katharine Ball of the University of
Toronto, Miss Bessie Ball of Woodstock, and Mr. Stuart
Brown, Q.C., of Toronto.

My gratitude is great to Dr. W. Kaye Lamb, Dominion
Archivist, who did so much to make essential source materials
readily available to me, and to members of his staff at the Public
Archives of Canada, particularly Mr. W. G. Ormsby. I am
equally grateful to Dr. G. W. Spragge, Provincial Archivist
of Ontario for his constant helpful interest and numerous acts
of assistance. I feel a special debt besides, to Mr. J. A. Edmison,
then of Kingston, who most willingly lent me rare records and
his own knowledge of matters pertaining to the penitentiary
question. Others who kindly furnished useful leads or documents included Mr. Leslie Grey of London, Mrs. Frank Yeigh
of Toronto, and Dr. Peter Waite of Halifax.

I am most happy to acknowledge grants from the University
of Toronto which assisted me in this work, and especially that
from the Rockefeller Corporation, received through the University of Toronto committee administering Rockefeller funds,
which above all enabled me to carry out my basic researches in
Scotland. Finally, I should like to make particular acknowledg-
ment to my wife, who had to put up with a great deal while this
book was being finished.

October 1, 1959   J. M. S. Careless

VOLUME ONE

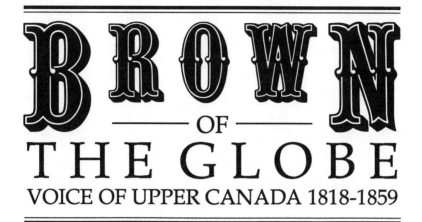

BROWN

— OF —

THE GLOBE

VOICE OF UPPER CANADA 1818-1859

J.M.S. Careless

Ambitious Emigrant

I

For brief minutes the ships lay restlessly alongside, while several bags of potatoes and fresh meat were passed from the *Eliza Warwick*, eight days out of Liverpool, to the *Collingwood* inbound from Calcutta.[1] For the British emigrants aboard the New York-bound craft it was a last chance to send a message home. As they scribbled notes to put aboard the *Collingwood*, Peter Brown pencilled a few hurried words to the family left in Scotland: "Monday, 8 May, 1837. At sea for 8 days, made only 400 miles. All well—not a minute to spare. Every good wish attend you. God bless you."[2] Then with a rattle of blocks and the boom of filling sails the vessels drew apart. Their wakes stretched out between them. The *Eliza Warwick* continued on her slow way westward, crammed to the legal limit of two passengers for every five tons of ship's burden: among them, the former Edinburgh merchant and his eighteen-year-old son, Peter and George Brown.

They watched the other craft slip back toward the empty eastern horizon where, far beyond, lay all that they had left: the clatter of Edinburgh, the tall grey house in Nicholson Square, and the warm family circle that it held. There Marianne the mother, the four girls, and nine-year-old John Gordon would wait until they had established themselves in America—whenever that might be.[3] They knew that their venture was but one among thousands in that era when Britain was pouring out her people to the United States, to British North America and other colonies across the seas. But each venture had its separate story of frustration and ambition, defeat, distress, and dreams of new beginnings. And the Browns were conscious only of their own.

Peter Brown had been a prosperous wholesale merchant in his native city, proprietor of a leading Russian and Manchester warehouse in North Bridge Street, Linen Draper to the King.[4] As a burgess and guild brother of Edinburgh, he had been a respected member of the city's influential business and professional community: a stout, deliberate man of strong opinions, relieved, however, by the kindliest of natures.[5] Yet he also possessed a wide-ranging, cultivated mind, and it had led him further, into distinguished literary circles in the metropolis. He had moved with John Wilson, poet, Tory essayist, and professor of moral philosophy at the university—the famed "Christopher North" of *Blackwood's*. He knew J. A. Lockhart, sparkling satirist, later editor of the *Quarterly Review*, the biographer and son-in-law of Sir Walter Scott. He knew the great Sir Walter himself, and other lesser figures in that swift northern flowering that helped to merit to the Scottish capital, with its smoke and mist-hung Greek Revival architecture, the illustrious title of Athens of the North.[6] But in particular, his wide reading in British constitutional history and political thought had brought him to the Whig-Liberal side in politics, making him friend and intimate of the writers and politicians behind the *Edinburgh Review*—men like Henry Cockburn, eloquent advocate, who became Solicitor-General for Scotland in Grey's government of 1830, and the brilliant Francis Jeffrey, founder and editor of that mighty Whig journal.[7]

Furthermore, Peter himself had plunged into local politics, striving for borough reform in his city's close corporation, and sharing in the victorious struggle for the Great Reform Bill of 1832.[8] When the Reformers broke through the oligarchy in Edinburgh, he was named Collector of Assessments for the new municipal administration.[9] He flourished as a trusted civic official—and then in 1836 came sharp disaster. Suddenly he was involved in the withering loss of nearly £2800 of municipal funds: no inconsiderable sum today, but a great deal larger in that earlier time.

Ill-starred business speculations that actually went back ten years to the inflated times of 1825-6 had ended in abrupt failure, and in their collapse carried away the public money that had been mixed up with his own accounts. Dishonesty was not imputed; but plainly such a confusion should never have occurred.[10] Though relatives and friends who had gone surety for Peter Brown made good the £2800, he deeply felt the loss and the responsibility.[11] He faced no legal charge or obligation. Yet to his mind the debt must be settled and his name restored. He could hardly have found a worse time to try to make restitution. That autumn, a financial crisis broke in London, and the next year, 1837, saw trade prostrate and depression spreading over Britain and the world. Money dried up; he could not realize cash from his own debtors. At length, after a fruitless struggle, there seemed to be but one answer left to him, the ever-present answer of the age. Emigrate—go to America, the land of new fortunes and fresh starts.

He would sell out his interests, pay what he could, and leaving funds to support the family while it remained in Scotland, take the rest to America to start again with a little draper's shop. Peter Brown discussed the plan with his wife and elder children, and staunchly, affectionately, they pledged to do their full share.[12] George, his nearly adult son, would go with him. The rest would move from the big house in Nicholson Square to less expensive quarters. And he and George would journey to Liverpool to find a cheap passage across the ocean. So it was that on April 17, 1837, father and son turned away from friends and family to take the mail coach "on the cold and barren road to Glasgow", en route to Liverpool and whatever ship awaited them there.[13]

A few nights later, in the bleak loneliness of a port-side lodging-house, Peter set down some of his yearning thoughts that welled up at parting. "My Beloved Marianne," he wrote desolately, "who has had so much to endure on my account and has borne it all with such patience and fortitude—nothing but a firm conviction that God in whom you have for so many years placed your trust will support and guide you—nothing but that feeling could make me regard our situation and the trials and difficulties you may yet have to surmount with any degree of composure. And my dear girls, who were so willing to leave their comfortable situations and take the fate (it may be of much hardship) of their family, how my heart warmed when I thought of their attachment! My kind and affectionate Isa and my beloved Phasie and Gordie—all were often before me, and dear, oh dear beyond all calculation did every one of you appear to me."[14]

Many emigrants would know these feelings. Some would leave far more misery behind, and face greater hardships ahead. Yet once more, each case was individual; and for the Browns the wrench of parting was real and bitter enough. Their lives had been so secure, so comfortable, and up till now the family fortunes had seemed only to improve. Peter himself, almost from birth in 1784, had known a steady rise in circumstance. His father, James Brown, sprung from farming stock in the village of Athelstansford in nearby East Lothian, had prospered in Edinburgh as a wright and builder,[15] and had even become a General Commissioner of Police there—for which service the grateful inhabitants of the Southern District presented him with a massive silver cup, suitably inscribed in recognition of his conscientious performance of "arduous duties".[16] And while the elder of James' two sons had continued in the building business, the younger, Peter, had successfully struck out on his own to become a merchant.[17]

By 1809 he had started as a linen draper near the Cowgate, where the narrow wynds and closes of Old Edinburgh plunged to the bottom of the city's crowded hill.[18] His wholesale business had grown with the rise of steam-powered Scottish textile industry, and the development of Edinburgh's port of Leith that traded eastward to the Baltic. Then he had extended his interests into another growing industry, glass-making, and shared in the direction of a glassworks in the little town of Alloa, some twenty miles westward up the placid Firth of Forth, to which the new-fangled steamboats had been running from Leith since 1812.[19] He was, in fact, at Alloa off and on through much of the 1820's; but towards their close his Edinburgh business demanded full attention. For now he owned a fine large wholesale warehouse in North Bridge Street, which led to Edinburgh's stately New Town, and dealt in general merchandise as well as textiles through agents as far away as London and New York.[20]

Peter Brown had married well besides, in 1813 wedding Marianne, the only daughter of George Mackenzie, gentleman, of Stornoway in the Hebridean isle of Lewis, who could proudly trace her ancestry back seventeen generations to Kenneth Mackenzie I of Kintail, not to mention John Baliol, John of Gaunt and John and Edward I of England.[21] From their marriage the couple's domestic surroundings had reflected Peter's steady advance in the world. There were moves from quarters over the draper's shop to the (then) suburban charms of Hope End Park, and on to the austere but affluent dignity of Buccleuch Place, that had been founded to rival the fashionable New Town. There was the country-like residence in Alloa as well, and finally the four-storey town house in bustling Nicholson Square, where now substantial burgher families were replacing the aristocrats who had earlier dwelled there.

Children had come in fairly regular succession, to be duly baptized at St. Cuthbert's Chapel of Ease: Jane in 1814, Catherine three years later, and George at Alloa in 1818. Isabella arrived in 1823, Marianne, nicknamed "Phasie", in 1826; and the next year John Gordon was born at Alloa, like his brother. The Browns had known tragedy as well, for three other little boys, two in turn hopefully called James after their grandfather, and one named Peter, had all died in infancy.[22] But by the 1830's they were a thriving, contented and close-knit family, in no want of material goods, friends and society, or standing in the Kirk with minister and congregation. They were, in short, prominent yet typical members of Edinburgh's highly regarded burgher community—and that was ground for satisfaction in itself.

2

It was into this community that George Brown was born on November 29, 1818. He actually spent his earliest years in Alloa, a peaceful little port where the slow River Forth spread from its broad valley into the silver sheet of the Firth, while behind the stone cottages and blossoming May gardens the hills swelled softly into blue-brown velvet crests. He played along the waterside, rambled the hills, and began his education in the small parish school kept by Mr. Brodie.[23] But with his family he belonged to the larger realm of Edinburgh; and there they all returned by the time that he was eight. It was only natural that he should then be sent to the city's famous High School, school of great Scotsmen like Hume, Cockburn, Brougham and Adam Smith, where dukes' sons and the children of cobblers, boys from Germany and from the West Indies and America, mixed with the solid core of Scottish burgherdom. Here, in the unpretentious grey stone building of the Second School on Infirmary Street, George had as schoolfellows many whom he would meet again in later life: young William and Thomas Nelson, for example, sons of Thomas Nelson, the rising publisher, who would one day be his brothers-in-law; or David Christie, who would become his political associate in Canada and a Senator besides; and Daniel Wilson, a future president of the University of Toronto, and ally of George Brown in university battles that lay far ahead.[24]

But George did not remain at the High School. He always knew his own mind, and very often won his way. He succeeded in persuading his family that the new Southern Academy of Edinburgh, taught by the estimable Dr. William Gunn, would be far more suitable for him.[25] And he seemed to be right, for throwing himself earnestly to work, he gained top distinction in his classes there. The sort of volume deemed suitable for encouraging the young fell to him as school prizes for arithmetic and algebra, penmanship and composition: Archdeacon Paley's *Horae Paulinae* in his twelfth year; *Virgil's Works*, handsomely bound in green-tooled, gold-stamped leather, in his thirteenth, with Southey's *Life of Nelson* as lighter relief.[26] At the Academy's closing exercises he was chosen to declaim. And in introducing his prize pupil Dr. Gunn was led to say (significantly, and perhaps with some evidence of strain), "This young gentleman is not only endowed with high enthusiasm but possesses the faculty of creating enthusiasm in others."[27]

Young George's driving vigour did not flag thereafter. Peter Brown wanted him to enter the University and study for a learned profession; but his son had determined from his talent for mathematics and a liking for the noisy life of the market place that commerce was the proper field for him.[28] There were lengthy arguments with his equally decided father, yet again George won. He entered Peter's business, and was briefly sent to the fascinating great world of London, to gain experience with the firm's agents there, before settling down to the wholesale trade in Edinburgh.[29]

His victory in this question of a career, however, was by no means merely the result of stubbornness and persuasive ability. Peter Brown respected the opinions of his keen-minded offspring no less than the son revered his father's thought and learning. Very soon, indeed, they had come to seem almost senior and junior partners to one another, as they discussed politics, books and ideas—Mr. McCulloch's lectures on political economy, Dr. Paley's proofs of Christian dogma—in evening hours by the fire or long Sunday afternoon walks through the pleasant countryside south of Edinburgh. George recalled those walks especially: the steady pace, the fluent conversation of the sturdy, amiable man at his side—the day they met the venerable gentleman whom his father greeted with such deference, whispering that this was the great Sir Walter Scott.[30] The Mid-Lothian land was green and vivid, the curving crest of Arthur's Seat stood high above them, and over all was the ceaseless play of sun and shadow through cloud-swept Edinburgh skies.

No doubt George's background was hardly conducive to making him a retiring character. For some time he was the only surviving boy in the family, and then was nine years Gordon's senior. He was surrounded by adoring sisters; his mother, though firm-willed, idolized him; and his father increasingly turned to his company. Hence it was almost inevitable that natural high spirits and forceful intellect should in him be moulded into a powerful and dominating personality. But much as well he derived from his parents. From his father came the tireless mental energy that shredded and digested ideas until the conclusions reached seemed almost demonstrated propositions. To him, besides, he owed the physical vigour and resilience of hardy Lowland forebears. From his mother came the idealism and generosity, the long memory for friends and enemies, the

swift temper and passionate emotions of her Highland stock.
On the Mackenzie side George was descended from warriors
and adventurers as well as land-holding gentry. Were not the
warlike Mackenzies of Red Castle among his direct ancestors?
Perhaps it was this that gave him the spark of daring—even
reckless boldness—that was lacking in the cautious Peter Brown.
Yet at times, also, he could be dour and tenacious, endure and
endure again: and this, similarly, he surely owed to his steadfast
paternal inheritance.

There were other forces also that shared in the early moulding of George Brown. One was his father's ardent Liberalism,
his zeal for reform and progress, the revelations of Adam
Smith and his heirs, and for the destruction of every aristocratic
privilege and hidebound Tory prejudice. Peter, in fact, was of
the type acidly depicted by his Tory contemporary, Lockhart:
"that glorious compendium of all reason and knowledge—that
spirit extract—that oil essential of the universe—*the Scottish
Whig!*"[31] His political saints were Henry Brougham and Lord
John Russell, bright stars in the Whig-Liberal parliamentary
firmament. George must have heard of them often—how Peter
had actually watched Lord John address the House of Commons[32]—of lesser luminaries like Joseph Hume and George
Roebuck, and soon, of a brilliant new star ascending, John
Lambton, Earl of Durham.

Whig-Liberal doctrine infused the Brown household, where
the *Edinburgh Review* lay on the table, and its writers were
welcomed to the parlour. And George grew up amid the rising
clamour for parliamentary reform, the torchlight processions,
the vehement speeches. His earliest political memories were of
the excited campaign for Scottish borough reform, while at
thirteen he had witnessed the triumph of the forces of truth
and light over ancient darkness, when the Reform Bill of 1832
finally passed into law.[33] Possibly, too, he was present at the
great Reform Jubilee celebrated in Edinburgh in August of
that year, when on a magnificent summer day 15,000 Reformers
gathered on open Bruntsfield Links to march in ordered ranks
with banners and music before a crowd of 40,000 ranged on the
slopes about. Together they sang "Rule Britannia" and "Scots
Wha Hae", "God Save the King" and old Scots hymns—for
it was almost a religious occasion. There were many boys in the
Reform procession, and one group carried a banner inscribed
"We have gained it in our youth, we will maintain it in our
manhood."[34] It might almost have epitomized the shaping of
George Brown's Liberal creed.

Yet there was another force, perhaps even stronger, that

stamped him from the start: the deep-rooted religious convictions of his family. The Browns were thorough-going members
of the Church of Scotland, Presbyterians of the old independent
breed that looked with much disfavour on the temporal connections and lay patronage that had grown up in the Kirk over
the previous century or so. In truth, however, the spirit of their
religion was not so much the austere and rigorous Calvinism of
an earlier age as it was the more emotional, outgoing faith of
the nineteenth-century evangelical movement. Family prayers,
Sunday-school teaching for George, charitable work among the
poor for his mother and elder sisters, all were an essential part
of their lives. Moreover, Peter's Liberalism was thoroughly
related to his religious tenets. He warmly believed, and taught
his son, that political liberty was grounded on religious freedom;
that victory over authority in the church had led to the conquest
of despotism in the state; and that the right—nay, duty—of
each man, to worship and serve God as his conscience dictated
made necessary the freedom of religion from state interference,
the citizen's freedom from clerical domination, and all those
other freedoms that combined to produce free speech, civil
liberties and self-government.

There was nothing very new in these doctrines descended
from the Puritan tradition; but they were none the less real for
Peter and George Brown. Much of the latter's political career
in Canada would be governed by his belief in the vital need to
keep religion free from political intervention and politics free
from clerical influence. Much of the "bigotry" and "fanaticism" with which his efforts would be charged could be traced—
paradoxically—to the concept of religious freedom that was his
from the first awakening of understanding. And certainly, his
whole life was influenced by the strong faith that supplied almost core and foundation for the unity of the Brown family.

A later generation, far too ready to dismiss nineteenth-century
moral and religious beliefs with adjectives like "smug" or
"sanctimonious", might also assume that the devoutness of the
family would induce a sombre or priggish note in the character
of its members. But the lively, cheerful Browns were no prigs,
and above all George was not. Rather he was good-humoured,
buoyant and boisterous; by his eighteenth birthday late in 1836,
a ruddy, big-framed, and red-haired youth, already over six
feet tall, with feet that seemed to grow more rapidly than anything else, large hands that he waved expansively on powerful
arms, a ready laugh, and a friendly, vivacious manner that
earned him popularity among contemporaries and older folk
alike. His enthusiasm, as Doctor Gunn had said, could arouse

enthusiasm in others. He early discovered and enjoyed using this gift, whether in organizing the production and sale of rabbits among his friends (the rabbits alone failed to respond, and died off unhappily),[35] or in debating societies where his ringing voice and electric energy swayed his listeners—possibly on a favourite topic, the denunciation of Negro slavery, for Peter had made him a strong abolitionist as well.[36]

Thanks to his interest in public speaking (he intently followed the reports of debates in Parliament), George at eighteen joined the Philo-Lectic Society of Edinburgh, a typical gathering of earnest young men of the period who sought to instruct and entertain themselves by conducting parliamentary discussions on current leading topics.[37] On an evening early in 1837, the weighty question before the Society was the value of phrenology, the popular pseudo-science of the day that claimed to read character by exploring bumps on the human skull where, allegedly, different traits had conveniently lodged themselves. Young George marched out on the negative side, and attacked the so-called science with a will. As a result he was favoured with a special reply by a self-styled phrenological expert, one Mr. Alexander Bryson, who claimed the most extensive knowledge of the topic, and mocked at and deplored his immature opponent's grievous ignorance of the teachings of phrenology— for had he understood them, said patronizing Mr. Bryson, he could not possibly have argued so foolishly in opposition but would immediately have bowed before their truth.

It was perhaps the first time that anyone made the mistake of trying to wither George Brown in public. Many others besides the unfortunate Bryson would live to regret it. George rose, blue eyes snapping, to make the kind of retort that he would develop to the full in later days of politics: a bit ponderous, perhaps; but the battle-axe is no less effective than the knife for one strong enough to use it—and may be a good deal more thorough.

"Now, Sir, although I cannot by any means pretend to have written as much on Phrenology as any inhabitant of Edinburgh, nor yet to have composed an essay on that subject so deep that nobody could understand it without a particular bump for the occasion, yet, Sir, I cannot conceive how this gentleman makes out my ignorance to be a disadvantage to his side of the question! The only reason I *can* conceive for it is that Mr. Bryson has a bump situated within less than one hundred miles of Self-Esteem. I think, destitute of all intellect though I be, it might have been possible with a learned gentleman of Mr. Bryson's capacity to have turned all my silly effusions and weak arguments into a means of increasing the aforementioned bump. Why not set up his bumpless opponent as a butt for the display of Mr. Bryson's huge powers of criticism and his refined and biting sarcasm—or for showing how large his bump of wit was? But no, Sir! Although there cannot be the least doubt that Mr. Bryson possesses all these learned bumps in the utmost perfection, yet—as he has never been in the habit of exercising them— it was not to be expected that they should all start forth at a moment's notice—even to oblige so eminent a phrenologist!'"[38] And so on, to beat at phrenology no less than Mr. Bryson, until both had been battered flat.

So much for forceful speaking: it may possibly seem strange that George Brown's equal talent for forceful writing, which through journalism would make his name in Canada, remained quiescent during his Edinburgh days. Yet the kind of mind that quickly responded to public controversy, and thrived on constructing arguments to sweep an audience, would be no less qualified for the fiery, contentious press of the day than for the debating platform. In any case there was little to take George into journalism in these early years: later opportunities in America would do that. And as it happened, he had scarcely begun his career in business with his father when the calamity occurred which led the latter to decide to emigrate.

As a dutiful son, a necessary aid, and a devoted partner also, there was no question that George would accompany his father on the venture. In fact, his optimistic youthful spirit let him break far more readily than the older man from the world that they had known so far. Much would he take with him from his Scottish past, but far more lay ahead. Despite the pains of leaving, in April of 1837 George Brown eagerly and confidently set his face westward. After all, ambitious eighteen seldom looks back.

3

Finding a ship at Liverpool was not as easy as expected. There were many choices, but the regular packets were far too dear, the merchantmen offered little more than steerage. Finally they hit on a smart-looking American brig, the *Eliza Warwick*, whose captain, after a bargaining battle of giants—Scots *versus* New Englander—agreed to take them in the second cabin for five pounds apiece; not seven as first asked.[39] Then they gathered their little luggage, bought a mattress and sea stores, and brought them on a pony-cart through the noisy tumult of the dockside streets. George strode manfully behind with a cudgel over his shoulder, guarding their possessions. Already he was taking on increasing responsibilities, as his father, half-dazed, worn out, and sick at heart, leaned on "faithful George, kind George, my dear George". He it was who first scoured the port for ships while Peter rested; who insisted they should not be overcharged by the "sharks" vending the sea stores; who raced back from the wharf to buy a forgotten lantern—and returned just in time to jump aboard as the *Eliza Warwick* was being hauled out into the Mersey.

The second cabin proved a bitter disappointment. When the ship set sail on April 30, nearly ninety had been crowded into its shed-like space. Carpenters were still erecting extra tiers of rough wooden bunks down the centre, amid a chaos of mounded bags of potatoes, biscuits and chests of luggage. Yet the milling, unhappy inhabitants were still better off than the hundred and more steerage passengers down below, the English small farmers from Huntingdonshire, the Irish labourers, and the bewildered Welsh colony who knew little English and still dressed in their traditional folk costume, the women in tall black steeple hats. In the second cabin the Browns were lucky enough to have an upper berth to themselves, a bare wooden shelf, but even here some lay five and six to a bed: "Sexes mixed in some cases most indecently," Peter ruefully commented.

Food too was a problem, for while the ship's galley provided fires, passengers apart from the few in the relative luxury of the first cabin must cook their own, or pay the cook to do so. The terms were high; hence George took charge of cooking and managed their supplies—the salt beef and mutton ham, the biscuit, oatmeal and potatoes, and the oranges and six gallons of ale. Bleary-eyed with smoke, he would triumphantly appear in the cabin bearing puddings concocted with borrowed raisins: "It would do Catherine good to see George making a pudding—and then, how he praises it!" He took charge as well of tending bedding and fetching the water, and watched over his father with unremitting care. And at first his care was most necessary, for Peter Brown was miserably seasick in the cramped and airless cabin, loud with the creaking timber of the wallowing ship, the squalling of pent-up children, the groans of the sick, and the shouts and squabbles of the drunken.

Wallowing was the word for the *Eliza Warwick*, despite her deceptively trim lines. Besides her capacity load of emigrants and their effects, she had 600 tons of pig iron stacked aboard;

in all, some 900 tons of cargo, though her registered burden was but 530. As a result, she staggered heavily through the seas, shipped a great deal of water, and made practically no headway except with a good following wind. And so the voyage was tedious and wretched, and at times perilous too. On the stormy night of May 19, the waves washed right over her decks, and the passengers lay down in their clothes, expecting to hear at any moment that the straining masts had carried away. The seas calmed; but the weather remained dismal and blustery. The vessel tacked back and fore interminably. Sickness spread; six bodies went over the side before the infection abated; and though they had been out nearly a month they were still 900 miles from New York.

Peter Brown, however, had recovered his strength by this time, while George was in rousing good health. He was clambering up the rigging with other youths, and joining in their rowdy practical jokes, such as snaring one of their number by the foot with a loop of rope run from a yard-arm to the deck—so that he could be hauled aloft, struggling and yelling, and entirely upside down. The long voyage wore on from May into June. Food was beginning to run low, and they messed with three friendly young Irishmen, one of whom had land in the fast-growing British province of Upper Canada, pooling their provisions in a common stock. And daily now the Captain promised a landfall for tomorrow. They had almost ceased to believe it would ever come, when on Saturday, June 10, at seven in the morning, the long-awaited cry resounded from the mast-head, and the rounded outline of Sandy Hook rose slowly into view. "Blessed be God in his goodness!" exclaimed Peter, on deck with his son since first light, as a pandemonium of cheers, tears, prayers and oaths broke out among passengers and crew. By three o'clock they were off Staten Island in waters dotted with ships. They heard the joyous sound of the anchor cable running out. The six-weeks' voyage was over.

The Browns gazed avidly at their first prospect of America, shimmering in the sunlight. On one side lay the fresh, green cultivated fields and white clapboard farm-houses of Long Island, and the heavy red masonry of the fort on Governor's Island; on the other were the rising slopes of Staten Island with its "many showy villas", rich foliage, and rambling summer-houses. But New York proper still lay ahead. The ship was anchored in quarantine; it might be some time before they could proceed. In the meantime, however, they could go ashore to Staten Island. They went eagerly, for beer and beefsteak and a good bed that did not rock. Yet although two days on the

Island passed pleasantly, the Browns were anxious to go on. Once more George rose to the occasion, by contriving to extract a pass through quarantine from the port authorities. Taking a high-built river paddleboat, that seemed to their wide eyes like a many-storeyed house on the water, they crossed to New York city, lodging at last in the Philadelphia Hotel. The next day George had to go back for the luggage; he spent a night sleeping beside it on the deck of a harbour schooner before he brought it safely to the hotel. But at last they had really arrived, and could begin the task of establishing themselves in their new surroundings.

There were a number of friends from home to visit, letters of introduction to present to persons who might aid in getting them placed, and there were business premises to examine. Hence father and son roamed about New York, generally pleased and impressed with what they saw—though at times it was good to be with Scots friends in the privacy of their homes, so that "we can get a laugh at the Yankees without looking around the room to see who is there". "This is a large and very fine city on the whole," Peter observed. "Brick houses chiefly, with grey slate roofs; marble steps in some places, but ill regulated streets—repairs constantly going on and all left loose. Stones and planks, on which the legs may be broken, not removed at night, pavements in shocking bad order. The authorities are so much Jack-fellow-alike that they rarely complain on one another, unless it be a black man and an Irishman. The Scots are favourites.—Hem!! So far well."

Weeks passed in the search for a suitable shop, for in their "weak and almost helpless state" they had to choose warily. Also the selfsame depression that had affected Peter Brown in Edinburgh had in New York gravely curtailed the flow of credit. Gradually, however, he found wholesalers in linens and woollens ("dry goods", he learned to call them) who were willing to open accounts with him on four to six months' credit. Deciding on a store was rather harder. The Broadway was a most desirable location, a fine, busy main street of more than 800 numbers, but here competition might be too stiff. A cross street, Maiden Lane, might be better; yet some said it was falling off. Then there was Fulton Street, on an angle to Broadway, which was improving because it had been widened and ran down to a butchers' market and a ferry to Brooklyn. But there they were asking $1000 for a year's rent of a store: too steep for Peter's resources. The Browns even thought of leaving New York altogether to go up-country; they did make a reconnaissance by Hudson River night-boat as far as Kingston on the Hudson, a hundred miles away. Yet they decided against it, because in New York the elder girls, Jane and Catherine, might be able to find work to assist the family, as they could not so easily in a smaller place.

The advice and sympathy of kind friends helped, especially that of Mr. Boyd, who had been New York agent of Peter's firm in the old days. His house was always open to them, and he lavished hospitality. There, at least, George's enormous appetite was fully satiated—with pies, tarts and ice-cream, and "a delicious West India fruit called Banana". Mr. Boyd strongly recommended the Broadway. Here at last they decided to make their stand, with "a *moderate* concern and for ready money only".

It was a modest shop; but, as Peter said, "we must creep up by degrees". At any rate, conceived in modesty it thrived on caution, and the merchant found that the business acumen that had once done well in Scotland had not wholly deserted him. Perhaps he even had some advantage as a newcomer, for while American competitors, used to a roaring boom and easy money, were floundering in what they bemoaned as dark depression, the Scottish emigrant considered that "now it is like Edinburgh in good times!" Thrift kept their costs low. George was the only shop assistant; they moved to Mrs. Wilson's boarding-house for bed and board at $3 a week each; they saved and went without. Accordingly, they were able to meet their accounts promptly, enlarge their credit as a result, and see their way brighten ahead. By the end of the year—gloriously—they could even look forward to bringing out the rest of the family before another summer had passed.

Accordingly, in the early months of 1838, letters went busily back and forth across the ocean: inquiries from Edinburgh, instructions from New York. Passage for mother and children was arranged, more comfortably this time, in the first cabin of the *Roger Stewart*, sailing from Greenock.[40] On May 2, in their turn, Marianne and the others left Edinburgh, amidst many tearful farewells—though Jane, as befits a responsible elder sister of twenty-four, "argued myself into composure and made my face *fit to be seen*".[41]

Their voyage was almost as long as that of father and son, and at times as stormy. But the *Roger Stewart* was less crowded, the accommodation far better. Marianne, the mother, who had dreaded the passage the most, was not too ill; while the rest came through nicely, except for poor Catherine who had seemed to recover in time for her birthday celebration aboard, and then, sadly enough, had suddenly to rush out and abandon her special dinner. Jane, on the other hand, quite as energetic as her brother, was up and doing throughout, distributing to bewildered sailors the chestful of tracts that she had so thoughtfully brought with her, or prevailing on a reluctant captain to hold proper observance of the Sabbath at sea. The weather cleared and grew hot. They now were all in excellent spirits: the children, Isa, Phasie and Gordie, dashing about the deck, their mother looking on benevolently, while chatting with a Mrs. Grey who knew their friends in Edinburgh, and the girls, Jane and Catherine, deriving "mischievous amusement" from watching the antics of some of the Scots emigrants in steerage.

Then on June 16 they too cast anchor off Staten Island; and it was sweet to sniff the strong scent of birch and cedar on the land breeze, drowning even the pervasive smell of tar. Very soon a stout-looking, excited George came bobbing alongside in a rowboat. He could not come aboard because of quarantine restrictions: only by favour had he been allowed to come this far. But he shouted that their father was anxiously waiting on Staten Island. And Catherine and Jane jumped down into the boat, bonnets and all, to be rowed across and run headlong into Peter's arms.

By this time the privileged cabin passengers had been cleared of quarantine. In just a few hours they were all together in New York, in the house on Varick Street that Peter had rented in anticipation of their arrival. And then—as Jane wrote later to her Edinburgh friends—"Then there was such a meeting and kissing and hugging, there never was the like, some laughing and some crying—it was worth a twelve-months separation!" The family was reunited, re-established. The long migration was over.

4

The next few years went quietly but satisfactorily for the Browns. The shop continued to prosper, though it was not piling up a fortune. The family was comfortably settled in the large, airy house on the corner of Varick Street, a white wooden house with green doors and shutters, greatly pleasing to the female members after the grey stone drabness of Edinburgh dwellings. Marianne Brown had brought out furniture and treasured household possessions to complete what her husband had provided and make the place home. The children were at school, while "the Misses Brown", Jane and Catherine, had begun a school of their own for young female persons, which kept them occupied and added usefully to their family income.[42] And with the growth of the business George had begun to travel for his father, along the coast into New England, up the Hudson, and even on into Canada.[43]

As for Peter Brown, he had found a most agreeable part-time occupation in writing articles for the New York *Albion*, the weekly journal of the British emigrant community, founded in 1822.[44] It was not to be expected that a man of his cast of mind would drop his interest in public affairs. In close contact still with informed opinion in Edinburgh, and urged on by his widening circle of friends in New York, he had begun to send an article or two on British politics to the *Albion*. His clear, logical writings soon attracted attention; and thus he became a fairly regular contributor.[45]

He was, moreover, taking a growing interest in American political developments. The turbulent tide of Jacksonian Democracy was still running high in the United States, notably in New York. In fact, a new Democratic radicalism had taken shape there in the depression of 1837, the so-called Locofoco movement, strenuously egalitarian and firmly opposed to banking monopolies and money power.[46] In Peter's first year in the city he had witnessed the tumult caused by Locofoco-ism, and had found party spirit "risen to an unexampled height".[47] Three years later the frenzied "log cabin and hard cider" presidential campaign of 1840 swept the country. It was a heady atmosphere for a man of his ardent political instincts, and it was increasingly reflected in his writings for the *Albion*.

One might think that Peter Brown's devotion to reform and progress would make him sympathetic to the democratic ferment in his new home. But he was a constitutional liberal, not an egalitarian democrat. He stood for freedom secured by a balance of forces in government; and to him the rule of equality and universal suffrage in America meant simply domination by the overwhelming power of the mere majority, rule by the passions and ignorance of the multitude—an attitude he passed on to his son. Furthermore, as a business man and a believer in the divine rule of natural economic laws, he was opposed to the radicals' demands for the state control of banking and for legislative intervention in the sphere of business. Finally, as an unreconstructed and very sturdy Briton, he reacted strongly to the anti-British sentiment then prevalent in the United States, and especially in Democratic radical ranks.

All these sentiments urged Peter into publication on a scale that he had never before considered: nothing less than a book, which circulated not only in the United States but in the British North American colonies as well. Indeed, he must have made some impression in Britain also, since he later won the honour of mention in the renowned *Dictionary of National Biography*; and this specifically as the author of a noted work, *The Fame and Glory of England Vindicated.*[48]

His book was conceived as a reply to an American volume attacking British life and institutions, C. E. Lester's *The Glory and Shame of England*, which was published in New York in 1841. It was but one more salvo in the Anglo-American battle of travel books that began before Charles Dickens' *American Notes* and went on long afterwards. Transatlantic cousins crossed the ocean to the one country or the other, presumably for the purpose of attacking it in print on their return. Mr. Lester, sometime American consul at Genoa, had gone to England and did not like it. He found it loud with the groans of the poor, riddled with aristocratic corruption, and staggering under monarchial tyranny. To say the least, it compared unfavourably with the great American democracy, freedom's true home. His book was agreeably received in New York; but in Peter Brown it brought the simmering champion of British freedom to full boil. All his political sensibilities were aroused, as the following autumn and winter he scribbled feverishly to produce a crushing reply. He arranged to publish it under the meaningful pseudonym of "Libertas", and early in 1842 *The Fame and Glory of England* appeared. It was almost a page-by-page critique of Lester's work, full of statistics and detailed political argument —and a resounding testament as well of Peter's British Liberal creed.

With mighty sarcasm his study dissected the *Glory and Shame*, to prove that the author of that reprehensible tract knew little about England, that much of what he did say was fabricated, and that that which was true had been copied from other sources—leaving the impression that Mr. Lester had not got far beyond the Staten Island steamboat. Besides this, Peter put up a stout defence of British institutions and government, and attacked American, decrying "the silly attachment" to universal suffrage in the republic, denouncing "the tyranny of the majority", and, particularly, condemning slavery in the United States, which, he said, had resulted in the gagging of liberty and made mockeries of American boasts of freedom and equality.[49] To top it off, he analysed liberty into various components, and proved to his satisfaction that Britain had virtually all of these and the United States practically none.[50] It was an impressive performance; but it was not calculated to endear Peter to his new country; nor did it give much indication that he would ever feel at home there.

The stimulus, however, of this venture into the literature of opinion and public debate led Peter Brown to a bold decision. He would go further, and publish a journal of his own. He knew from his contributions to the *Albion* that he could write effectively for the press, and after his book he felt quite capable of editing a newspaper for himself. The warm response to his volume among the British emigrants in New York and the Northern states (his authorship was no secret), suggested that a ready audience might be found.[51] For though there was the *Albion*, it was more a literary periodical than a journal of opinion. Besides, the Scottish element in the British community could be catered to more fully, since the *Albion* tended to give its attention to the English.[52]

It would mean giving up the shop, but that no longer seemed a matter of much interest to Peter Brown. He had begun anew before, and he could do it again. Perhaps, at the age of fifty-eight, he had found what he really wanted to do in life. Again he discussed his project with the family, and won their ready support. George, of course, was to come in with him; and there is reason to think that he came easily. He shared his father's political views and interests, while everything in his make-up suggested that a journalist's life would prove more agreeable to him than that of a dry-goods clerk. At any rate, after canvassing their friends and acquaintances in New York, father and son received sufficient promises of support to begin a new weekly newspaper, christened the *British Chronicle*.[53] It was truly a momentous step, for this little paper was the lineal forebear of the powerful *Toronto Globe*, and the means whereby George Brown opened a career that wrote his name across the nineteenth-century history of Canada.

The first issue of the *British Chronicle* appeared on July 30, 1842, with Peter Brown's name at the masthead as editor. The opening number announced decidedly: "The Subscriber who will conduct the editorial department of the *British Chronicle* has been long and intimately acquainted with the politics of Britain and with many of its leading political characters. . . . He is deeply convinced that the power and even the safety of the British Empire can only be preserved by an adherence to those principles which produced the Reform Bill of 1832 and for ten years guided the counsels of the Whig Ministers. He further holds that, whatever ministry is in power, they must on the one hand avoid that executive Tory misrule which in times past . . .

trampled on the rights of the people, and that, on the other, they must resist to the death the encroachments of Radical and Chartist violence which would sweep away the institutions of the country and destroy the rights of property and of individual freedom."

The statement well expressed the British, Whig-Liberal character of the new journal. To every intent it was an emigrants' newspaper, of the sort that still flourish today in Canada and the United States among the foreign-language press. It looked primarily to the homeland and its politics, furnishing as well many local British news items, especially on church affairs, together with detailed obituaries, classified under "England", "Scotland" and "Ireland". Gradually, however, the paper's horizon widened, and it began to pay a degree of attention to events in the neighbouring British territory of Canada. No doubt this reflected the spreading of circulation in that direction, for by December 1842, the *British Chronicle* was printing a list of Canadian agents. Among them was a certain John Sandfield Macdonald, M.P.P., who would one day be George Brown's somewhat prickly colleague in a Canadian Liberal party.[54]

Under the regular heading of "Canada", the *British Chronicle* watched with interest the progress of the union established in 1841 between the provinces of Upper and Lower Canada, now Canada West and Canada East, the former English-speaking, the latter largely French. It spoke approvingly of the system of responsible government which the late Lord Durham had advocated for the Canadas, and considered that, thanks to the "noble-minded, liberal and lamented Durham", the new plan would solve the problems of government that had caused the unfortunate rebellions of 1837.[55] Moderately but sympathetically, the *Chronicle* commented on the course of the Reform ministers who had taken office in the young United Province in September, 1842, chief among them, the Upper Canadian, Robert Baldwin, and the French Canadian, Louis Lafontaine. And it shared a widespread assumption (premature as it turned out) that responsible government was now in full working order in that country.[56]

Meanwhile the junior Brown was playing an increasing part in the *Chronicle*. It was in March, 1843, that his name for the first time began to appear beside his father's on the masthead, which henceforth denominated them "P. Brown, Editor; G. Brown, Publisher".[57] With his usual energy the young publisher set about the task of increasing the circulation, making tours for that purpose through New England, up-state New York, and finally through Canada.[58] He had already taken an interest in the last-named province, and was quite probably writing the articles on Canadian affairs for the paper. Now his interest and knowledge were enhanced, as he talked with leading politicians and editors in provincial centres such as Toronto, Kingston and Montreal on visits in the spring of 1843, or stayed with friends there among the local Scottish communities.[59] In Toronto he dropped in on Samuel Thompson, editor of the *Herald*, who found him "a very pleasant-mannered, courteous and gentlemanly young fellow".[60] In Montreal, chief city and commercial heart of Canada, he met a shrewd young merchant in the forwarding trade, Luther Holton, who years later would become a close political ally and personal friend besides.[61] One thing more: a series of descriptive articles now began to appear in the *British Chronicle*, entitled "A Tour in Canada", written in a lively, graphic style that would long be characteristic of George Brown's journalism.[62]

5

The "Tour" Series never proceeded far, however, for in that same spring of 1843, grave events in Scotland were starting to crowd all but the most important North American reports from the pages of the *British Chronicle*. A crisis was developing in the established Church of Scotland, and to Peter Brown, hardly anything could be of more significance, nor to the mass of his largely Scottish Presbyterian readers. The original question at issue in the homeland had concerned the right of a lay patron to "intrude" a minister into a parish contrary to the wishes of the congregation there. With the upsurge of evangelicalism in Scotland, a zealous Non-Intrusionist party had arisen to contend against this temporal interference with the freedom of the Kirk. Led by the redoubtable Dr. Chalmers, they had even brought the General Assembly, the great annual parliament of the Church of Scotland, to restrict the power of patronage. Now, however, the courts of the land had upheld the patron's right to name a minister; and in May of 1843, the General Assembly was faced with a fundamental decision: whether to submit or separate; whether to accept the ruling of state authority, or perforce abandon the very position of a state-established church.

The Non-Intrusionists argued fervently against accepting secular dictation. As evangelicals who stressed the freedom of the individual conscience and the simplicity of a warmly per-

sonal religious faith, they foresaw nothing but baneful consequences stemming from submission to the state: a bureaucratic
church of empty forms, a church based not upon the teachings
of the Bible but on the edicts of men, and—worst of all—a
church already on the downward slope toward the ancient
errors of Rome. Nevertheless, the majority of the Assembly
did not heed their urgings nor share their fears. The issue was
lost. The Non-Intrusionists saw only one course left to them.
On May 18 they solemnly withdrew from the Assembly, re-
nounced the state connection and the funds of the establishment,
and set about creating the Free Church of Scotland. Thus came
the memorable Disruption, that carried close to 500 ministers
and a large part of the Scottish population out of the Auld Kirk;
that sent reverberations through Presbyterianism around the
world, and made the Free Kirk a living testament to a powerful
religious and political principle, the separation of church and
state.

Certainly the reverberations rang through the *British Chronicle*. The Browns' own spirit and opinions were so similar to
those of the Non-Intrusionists that all their sympathies lay with
them. For months their paper had anxiously followed the events
in Scotland, hoping against hope for settlement, but clearly on
the side of the evangelicals. When the news of the Disruption
finally arrived, Peter Brown wrote in mingled sorrow and
pride: "The noblest branch of the visible Church is in ruins. On
Thursday, 18th of May, was exhibited at Edinburgh one of the
most sublime scenes of Christian self-denial and devotion to
the cause of truth that the world has ever seen. The Evangelical
Party on that day left the Church of Scotland."[63]

Reverberations were also being heard in Canada, among the
Presbyterians of that province. There the issue of temporal
interference could not really arise, since the Church of Scotland
was not an established state church in the colony, though it did
receive a certain amount of state support—far less than the
Church of England—from the clergy reserves endowment of
Upper Canada. Nor was the colonial Scottish church under the
jurisdiction of the parent body. Yet so strong was the tie of sentiment with the home country that Scots Presbyterians in Canada
took up the dispute as if it were their own. They too began to
divide, one party endorsing the position of the Scottish established church, the other condemning it and approving the separation of the Free Kirk. Conflict was looming, since resolutions on
the question would surely be put before the Synod of Canada and
congregations would then have to declare themselves decisively.

The Free Church sympathizers, however, in readying themselves for battle, recognized that they lacked any organ to present their views to the Canadian Presbyterian community. But there was the New York *British Chronicle*, already well known among Scotsmen in the province for its support of the Non-Intrusionists at home. Could they persuade its editor to remove to Canada? It was early in June, most likely, that forty-five leaders of the Free Church party in the neighbourhood of Toronto, both lay and clerical, signed an offer to induce Peter Brown to bring his journal to Toronto and issue it there in the Free Kirk cause.[64] They put up a bond to the extent of $2500, guaranteeing a minimum circulation.[65] And through the Reverend William Rintoul, a former moderator, they presented their proposal to George Brown, who was then on his way through Toronto, still on his travels for the family paper.[66]

George was interested, very interested. He had himself already half formed the notion of coming to Canada. He had told Samuel Thompson in May that they might move their newspaper to Toronto, since New York was so hostile to everything British. He had added, in fact, "It's as much as a man's life is worth to give expression to any British predilections whatsoever."[67] And in Kingston, then the capital of the United Province, he had met Samuel Bealey Harrison, Provincial Secretary in the government of the day. Harrison had been astonished at the knowledge of Canadian affairs displayed by this young stranger of twenty-four, and had introduced him to other members of the government, including its two chief Upper Canadian figures, Robert Baldwin and Francis Hincks.[68] These resolute Reformers were watchfully eyeing a new and strong-willed Governor-General, Sir Charles Metcalfe, anticipating further difficulties in their efforts to achieve fully responsible government. They were more than willing to see another newspaper friendly to their cause established, and the feasibility of moving the *British Chronicle* was discussed. No actual negotiations were begun; yet George Brown was left with the impression that Canada could offer a very congenial future for a journalist, especially if he might look for some official support.[69]

Consequently, once he was armed with the definite proposal from the Free Kirk group in Toronto, he hurried back to New York, eager to convince his father of the benefits of a change of scene. But the cautious Peter Brown saw a fair prosperity before him in the United States and was none too ready to move again.[70] His son argued hard for the merits of Canada. "The country is young," he urged. "There are few persons of ability and education. There is no position a man of energy and character may not reasonably hope to attain—if his will be strong and his brain sound!"[71] New York, he went on confidently, offered a competence, nothing more; while Canada promised wealth— and possibly fame besides.[72]

These were compelling arguments for an ambitious young man, but they had less appeal for one approaching sixty. Yet George had others to put forward. He could point out that, despite every effort, the *British Chronicle* still faced powerful competition from the long-established *Albion* in New York, while in Canada, as the Free Kirk organ, their paper would have a field all its own. He could wave the definite financial guarantee before his father, and note besides that friends among the Canadian Presbyterians had just secured his own appointment as chief agent for a new series of church publications.[73] And on quite a different level, he could appeal to his parent's strong feeling for the Free Church cause, to which the latter could devote his best efforts in Canada. Persuasions of this sort, aided by Peter's distaste for the American political scene, finally brought the decision. The Browns and their journal would go to Toronto. George had won his way again.

On July 22, 1843, the *British Chronicle* made its farewell bow, just one year after its first appearance, and in that final issue the editor announced that his paper was moving. This was not for any want of success, he said, but because it could best fight the battle for religious liberty in a new setting. In Canada it would be renamed the *Banner,* and would advocate the views "of the Presbyterian portion of this part of the empire". It would be "a useful Family Paper", not one of narrow sectarianism or political partisanship; yet on all great questions it would hold to "Reform principles". Thus the *British Chronicle* backed off stage, flourishing a prospectus of the new Toronto *Banner*. Its part had been brief, but none the less important.

There was not much equipment to move, apart from a small hand-press. The Browns' journalistic enterprise was carried mostly in their heads. It remained to uproot the family once more, though saying good-bye to New York was far easier than leaving Edinburgh. The eldest sister, Jane, would stay behind, however. She had recently married George Mackenzie, a likeable young Scots shipping merchant and a distant connection who had often visited their house. The second Marianne, now seventeen, would also stay in New York for a time, to live with the Mackenzies and keep her sister company in the separation from the family.[74]

As for the rest of them, early in August they took the boat up the Hudson to Albany, and from there travelled overland to Niagara. A brief steamer trip across Lake Ontario then brought them to Toronto, and back once more to British territory.[75] As it turned out, New York had merely been a stopping-place. Only now had the emigrants reached their final destination. And George Brown had come to the city that would be his home for the rest of his life: years to be spent in building the strongest newspaper in British North America, in moulding a powerful political party, and in helping to shape the destinies of an emerging Canadian nation.

6

They watched it spreading out before them, as the Niagara boat neared harbour on that sunlit August afternoon—Toronto, the former capital of the old province of Upper Canada and still the administrative head of the western section of the United Province: the chief commercial centre and the largest city in Canada West. Uneven ranks of red-brick, roughcast, and weathered wooden buildings stretched out along the low-lying shores of bright Toronto Bay. Beyond them, yellow fields rose gradually to a line of dark green pine forest that crowned the heights to the north. A few church towers stood out above the huddle of roof tops, against the rather sombre back drop of the heights: there was St. Andrew's, Presbyterian, and the rebuilt Anglican cathedral of St. James, quite imposing in a manner reminiscent of the later imitators of Wren. To the east, the mouth of the Don River and the out-thrust arms of Mr. Gooderham's windmill marked the limits of the town. In the centre sat the plain, uncompromising brick mass of the market buildings and city hall. And at the western end, beside the entrance to the Bay, was the "not very fierce-looking Garrison", the Union Jack floating over it.[76]

As the *Chief Justice Robinson* thrashed into the Bay they could see handsome private residences dotted eastward along its bank; beyond them, the long, low, red-brick edifices that had been the Upper Canadian Parliament Buildings, and which now temporarily housed the newly opened provincial university of King's College. A little to the rear, above a thick plantation of trees, rose the chimneys and flagstaff of the former Government House. Not far away the white block of Osgoode Hall, home of the Law Society, shone in the warm sun. And now, as they sailed still eastward, they were opposite the commercial heart of the city, marked by an irregular line of warehouses, the bustle of carts along the water front, and the tall, reeking smoke-stacks of the soap works near Queen's Wharf. They moved in to dock through a swarm of graceful schooners, darting cutters and self-important steamboats, to land at six in the summer afternoon.

This was Toronto when the Browns arrived in 1843. It was a rapidly growing town of some 16,000 inhabitants, its motto, "Industry, Intelligence, Integrity"—in declining order of importance, rivals said sourly. Charles Dickens, pausing briefly there the year before, had found its situation uninspiring but the place itself full of "bustle, business and improvement", and had commented approvingly on the paved and gas-lighted streets, the large houses, the opulent display of the shop windows—and the "good stone prison".[77]

Essentially, the city lay along the shore between the Don River and the Garrison, a slowly crumbling 1816 fort, though new stone-walled, tin-roofed barracks had been erected a little beyond it for the regular British troops still stationed at Toronto. On the north, the real boundary was Lot Street, later Queen. There were only scattered rows of houses and a few neighbouring hamlets beyond this limit, such as Yorkville, up above the sandy Bloor Street track. On the south, along the Bay, Front Street boasted such amenities as the commodious North American Hotel (whose flat roof, four storeys up, afforded a splendid view of the metropolis) and the Royal Floating Baths, now little used, however, except by the Baptists, who conducted immersions in the Bay below.[78] But the main east-west artery was King Street, home of important business houses and the finest shops. Its central stretch looked quite impressive, lined as it was with substantial brick office blocks of generally uniform height, relieved by the row of Lombardy poplars before St. James, and fairly thronged with cabs and carters, hurried business men, and promenading shoppers "doing King".[79] The principal north-south street was Yonge, and it had an importance all its own. For while its lower reaches were largely taken up with the drab storehouses of wholesale merchants, and its upper with undistinguished dwellings, this was the great highway to the north. Stages went daily up Yonge Street to the fast-spreading settlements around Lake Simcoe, some forty miles away. And from there the way beckoned on to the Georgian Bay, the Upper Lakes, and even beyond, to that distant, vast North West of the lonely fur trade.

East of Yonge, not very far above Lot Street, were wheat-fields, swamps, and Allan's Bush, at times the haunt of dangerous gangs of ruffians. To the west of Yonge, and paralleling it,

broad College Avenue (now University) had just been opened
up. Otherwise there was but sketchy development in this quarter.
The Avenue ran to the new King's College buildings, rising in a
tract to be called Queen's Park, and was landscaped and planted
with shade trees, as the citizens were proud to point out. Elsewhere, however, the streets were bare of adornment. Sidewalks,
if any, were of planks, even in King Street, and few roads were
surfaced outside the central area. Pigs might roam residential
streets to scavenge, despite repeated and heated newspaper protests. Rough board shanties disfigured the laneways; within
them, drunken brawls and knifings were a not infrequent occur-
rence. The city had inadequate water supply, five regular police
constables, and more than a hundred taverns and licensed premises, from the *Erin go Bragh* to the *William III*, the *Rob Roy*
to the *George and Dragon*. It was in many ways uncouth, untidy,
and ill-built, a town still close to the frontier, both in character
and geography.

Yet Toronto was something else as well, for all its raw, unfinished look. Somehow it held a consciousness of dignity and of
mission—"delusion", perhaps its rivals would prefer. Toronto
saw itself as an imperial city, a bastion of Empire deep in the
heart of the American continent. It had been founded in the
1790's both as the capital of the new province of Upper Canada
and as a British arsenal to guard against attack from the United
States. It had known that attack in the War of 1812; even
briefly undergone American occupation; and, in consequence,
those marks of imperial devotion and antipathy to Yankee republicanism, which dated from first settlement by officials, sol-
diers and Loyalists, had been stamped all the more firmly on
the town. Then too, as capital, it had continued to be a centre
of imperial authority, as well as the seat of the long-dominant
local Tory oligarchy, the so-called Family Compact. And since
the 1820's British immigrants had been pouring in, notably the
hyper-loyal Protestant Northern Irish, the Ulstermen, who
further ministered to a spirit that had positively appalled
Charles Dickens—"the wild and rabid Toryism of Toronto",
he termed it.[80] But rabid or not, the years had only confirmed
Toronto in the belief that it was a veritable garrison of Empire:
its duty to maintain all that was British in the face of ever-
spreading American power in the continental interior.

No doubt the vociferously British protestations of Toronto's
citizens often did not accord too well with the physical facts of
their North American way of life. To most appearances, their
city was like any comparably-sized American Great Lakes port,
Buffalo or Rochester, for instance. And yet there was an un-

deniable air about this busy and expanding western community; a certain determined, earnest attitude, derived from consciousness of duty, which set it apart; and which visitors found comfortingly solid or depressingly dull according to their own habits of mind.

There were other facets to Toronto's earnest sense of mission; the religious and moral, for example. Its population was more than four-fifths Protestant and this markedly drawn from various sects that had sprung originally from the zeal of Puritanism. The results could be seen, some might say, in Puritanical narrowness and intolerance, or in the political influence of the Orange Society, brought from Northern Ireland and dedicated to the defence of Protestant Christianity and the Empire. Others might point to the strength of the city's religious feeling and its decent, responsible, law-abiding population. True, there were crimes of violence, but these could largely be dismissed as due to a few drunken reprobates (probably Irish Catholics); and, indeed, by contemporary North American standards Toronto was an orderly community. Its actual character doubtless lay between the extreme versions of tight-lipped bigotry and shining moral rectitude. But doubtless as well, the fervour of evangelical Protestantism helped to shape the city's personality and give it further purpose: in this case, to guard zealously in Canada the Reformation heritage of Protestant freedom. Toronto, in short, was not only a bastion of Empire; it was Derry Walls besides.[81]

A final and quite different side of the city's sense of mission lay in its economic aspect. Nature seemed to have promised much to Toronto. It had a spacious, sheltered harbour, easy routes of access to the fast-developing settlements that lay to north and west, and its own fertile hinterland as well. Furthermore, it stood at the foot of a portage route between Lake Ontario and the Upper Lakes, in use since before the coming of the white man, a route by trail and waterway that cut off hundreds of miles in the journey from the Lower Lakes to the far reaches of the North West. Yonge Street had further developed that ancient trail, and already there was talk of a railway from Toronto to the Georgian Bay that would pour down a wealth of western traffic into the city.

Canals were also increasing Toronto's trade and wealth. From its strategic position athwart the rich Ontario peninsula, it was in touch with the sea either through New York and the Erie Canal, finished in 1825, or *via* Montreal and the St. Lawrence, where canal improvements, already under way, would by 1849 provide a continuous route for shipping through the shoals and rapids of the Upper River. As yet, Toronto was merely one of the more prominent western commercial towns; but it could envisage great things ahead. In fact, the next decade would see it embarked on a rise to truly metropolitan status, seeking to control the trade of other Upper Canadian towns and competing with the older wealth of Montreal for economic dominance over the western half of the United Province. Ten years hence a new metropolis would be taking shape here in Canada West, based on the coming of railways, the beginning of industrial concentration, the city's geographic advantages and political precedence; and not a little on the energy and initiative of Toronto's citizens themselves. For this, too, they came to feel as a mission: that their community was destined to rule over the inland British settlements, and to extend its influence far into the great North West beyond.

7

To the Browns their new environment was congenial from the start. Earnestness and sense of purpose they entirely understood. They shared Toronto's strongly British predilections, its dislike of American republicanism. They were readily at home in its religious atmosphere; and George Brown in particular would soon identify himself with the city's drive for commercial expansion. It was true that father and son were far from being Tories of the kind that still largely dominated Toronto. Yet they were just as far from being radicals in their political thought; and their reaction to American democracy during the New York years had clearly made them more conservative in outlook. Had not George even told Samuel Thompson of the Toronto *Herald* in May of 1843 that they intended to found "a thoroughly conservative journal" in the city?[82]

The Browns would actually discover that British Liberal principles which had seemed almost conservative in republican America looked a good deal more advanced in colonial Canada. Even in Tory Toronto, however, they now could find a growing element of middle-class Liberalism that was much like their own, resident chiefly in the rising commercial classes, who looked askance at the resolute defence of privilege and the "first-family" exclusiveness of old Compact Tories. In any case, there was little trace of radicalism to be seen in Toronto. Once, indeed, there had been, despite the evident power of Toryism. It had even helped the bitterest Reform foe of the Compact, William Lyon Mackenzie, to become mayor in 1834, and had backed the agitation that ended in his ill-fated rebellion three years later. But since the ruin of Mackenzie's cause, radicalism—in reality, always a minority force in the city—had remained leaderless and submerged. The Reform party that was now headed by Toronto's Robert Baldwin purveyed a much more moderate Liberalism in politics, although inveterate Tory foes still insisted on branding it no better than rank republicanism.

Peter and George Brown would come quite naturally to support this Baldwin Reform party. As their *Banner* prospectus had made evident, they had at first intended to uphold liberal or reforming principles only in a general sense, without any specific party commitment.[83] But they were soon to find that a detached non-partisan course was impossible for anyone of strong convictions in the Canada of 1843. Political tempers simply were too high. One must declare where he stood, or others would do it for him—"litterally", as George would say.[84] At least Tories would quickly decide the new Presbyterian *Banner* was nothing but a Reform sheet, and the Browns would prove about as quick to agree. So much, then, for the "thoroughly conservative journal" amid the vehemence of Canadian politics.

For Canadians in that day were in the midst of a strenuous ten years' struggle to work out the system of responsible government in their country. In the Union of the Canadas, launched in 1841, the power of old oligarchies in government had been broken, and the Governor-General was ruling through ministers who could command a majority in the provincial assembly. Yet it was not at all certain that this change denoted responsible government as it was practised in Britain, with the ministry formulating policies for which it took responsibility in parliament. Rather, the Governor-General still dominated his ministry, and the policies it carried out were his own. Some Tories looked back yearningly to the simple golden days of oligarchy; others, who would call themselves Conservatives, accepted the existing half-way house, and were even willing to see it as the final destination. But the Reformers under Baldwin and Lafontaine insisted that the responsible system would not be truly established until the Governor-General was but a constitutional monarch, as in Britain, and his Canadian ministers made and carried out their own designs in government.

Accordingly, Canada's political future hung on the edge of a definition, the meaning of that vague term, responsible government. Could it mean, essentially, government by a Canadian

ministry, without bringing separation from the Empire? Did it
somehow mean conjoint responsibility to the imperial authorities, who appointed the governor, and to the local legislature
elected by the people? Or must not real responsibility remain
with the Governor-General while Canada continued—as it
wanted to continue—under Britain's sway and protection? In the
circumstances, the widespread sentiment of loyalty in English-
speaking Canada supplied a powerful source of strength for
Tories and Conservatives. Rallying round the Governor-General, they could hotly attack Reform opponents as disloyal con-
spirators, and defend the prerogative and responsibility of the
Queen's Representative with a nice blend of sincerity and self-
help.

Reformers, with as nice a blend, could appeal to hallowed
traditions of the Briton's fight for liberty against despotism,
and against the rallying call of loyalty raise the counter-cry of
British freedom. In truth, there was nothing disloyal about
their ardent demand for a fully British pattern of parliamentary
institutions within the Empire. And if some eclipsed radicals
on the fringe might harbour thoughts of moving on eventually
to Canadian independence, Reform leaders like Baldwin saw
the granting of responsible government as the very means of
safeguarding and preserving the British tie. Reformers were
briefly in office when the Browns reached Canada; but in a few
months a quarrel with Governor-General Metcalfe brought
their resignation and intensified the angry quarrels over loyalty
and British attachment. Within their first year in the province
George and Peter Brown would see the storm over responsible
government mount to gale force—and learn, too, just how
complex was the tumult in their new country.

Canada, then, was little more than a narrow, straggling band
of settlement stretched out for a thousand miles along the grand
St. Lawrence water system, from rugged Gaspé in the east to
the fertile western peninsula that lay between Lake Huron and
Lake Erie. To the north, the forbidding granite mass of the
Precambrian Shield thrust down upon the province. Its southern
limits were set plainly by the wilderness crests of the Appala-
chians, the line of the upper St. Lawrence and the waters of
the Great Lakes. It was an immensely elongated valley-plain,
with only about two million people scattered down its length,
chiefly near the water lifeline. Even in the busy little world of
Toronto, the limits of settlement were never far away, and in
the western peninsula the ancient forest still soared a hundred
feet above the newest backwoods clearings. And yet this out-
lying, immature community was constantly exposed to forces

stemming from the world without. The great valley spread open at both ends. Eastward, the broad St. Lawrence-Atlantic water highway linked it to Great Britain, brought it trade and settlers, tied it to ideas and policies emanating from the heart of Empire. Westward, deep in the continental interior, there was easy access from the American states below the lakes, and the Canadian community lay profoundly influenced by American connections, examples, and common patterns of life.

Winds from the sea and the American land-mass met and mingled over Canada. Issues and animosities carried from across the ocean added to the turbulence on the provincial scene. With Irish emigrants there came the feuds of Orange and Green, to embitter religious feelings in a country already divided between largely Protestant English-speaking settlers and wholly Roman Catholic French Canadians. The Irish helped to raise the heat of politics as well, for if Ulster Orangemen were militant Conservatives and often Tory bully boys at elections, Catholic Hibernians could be no less belligerent Reformers, ready to break a few heads for freedom from British Tory oppression. Then from Scotland came the passions of the Disruption and the fervour of the Free Kirk movement, to pour into local quarrels over the relations of church and state and intensify sectarian differences. England, perhaps, conferred a double measure of trouble, by sending officials and upper-class migrants with engrained belief in privilege, and hostility to "levelling", while at the same time conveying vehemently opposed sentiments from the popular liberal and democratic movements then everywhere at work in the homeland.

American contributions were at least as potent. The burgeoning power and wealth of the United States, so close at hand, inspired in Canada a strange mixture of envy and admiration, distrust and desire to emulate. In almost the same political argument a Canadian could urge the American model of material progress and condemn the republic's lawlessness and mob-rule. Yet whatever its faults might be, the United States supplied a glittering example of the possibilities of self-government. Canadians, neighbours across an open border, could hardly be contented with less. The influence of American equality, democracy, and closely similar ways of life, pulled powerfully in one direction. Anti-republican sentiment and fear of an aggressively expansionist American Union pulled as strongly in the other. The result was only to sharpen conflicts in Canadian affairs.

And there were grave conflicts sprung from Canadian sources themselves. Quite apart from the vexed question of responsible government in the colony, there were disputes over the claims of the Church of England to privileges of establishment: the contest over the rich endowment of the Church in clergy reserve lands; the mounting argument over the provincial university, King's College, still under Anglican control. Yet the most significant strain of all—for it ran through so many issues in Canada—was the ever-present friction between two cultures, the problems induced by joining English-speaking Upper Canada with predominantly French-speaking Lower Canada in one uneasy union. These two sections, now Canada West and East (though the old names were still broadly applied), had really maintained their separate and distinct identities within the United Province. They held equal representation in its legislature; a dual party structure was taking shape there, with dual leadership for East and West. Politics thus threatened to become no more than the endless balancing of widely different contingents from the two sections, the one inclined to dark suspicions of the backward, papist French, the other as quick to fear the greedy, heretic English. When this basic sectional problem was weighed with all the other sources of provincial discord, then Canada's prospects could look dark, indeed.

And yet, despite everything, the country was steadily advancing in population, material development and wealth. In Canada West, the end of the raw frontier era was in sight; the last good lands below the infertile Shield were being occupied during the 1840's. In Canada East, the drive of the powerful Montreal metropolis to complete the chain of the St. Lawrence canals, and thereby attract the commerce of the continental interior, was a clear sign of the coming new age. It would be a time of rapid trade expansion, extending communication systems, and ever-growing commercial capitalism. The railway locomotive, already transforming life below the American border, would be heard throughout the length of Canada. With it would come the onset of the industrial revolution, a flood of British investment, mounting prosperity and strength—and even the dazzling prospect of uniting to form a new nation with the other scattered British American colonies that were now so far away, still almost unknown to the people of the Canadian province.

These were the outlines of the future, already rising over the horizon when George Brown arrived in Canada in 1843; this was the land that he had come to. It offered him challenge and promise, side by side. There was excitement and battle, the call of righteous causes to which his whole background and experience committed him: causes of political liberty, religious freedom, and the defence of British institutions. Here was the very place for energy and ambition. Here he would set his roots.

Reform Journalist

I

The Browns had rented a little shop at 142 King Street, Toronto, with just enough space for a combined business and editorial office in front, a press-room and a store-room behind.[1] In the cramped front office of the new *Banner* Peter Brown conducted editorial operations, increasingly aided by his son. George, the man of parts, was also named publisher once more, and besides that held the post of General Agent in charge of vending suitable publications for the Presbyterian Synod of Canada.[2] In the rear, a third member of the family worked with their single printer. Fifteen-year-old Gordon, who had already shown aspirations as a journalist by offering articles to the *British Chronicle*, now began a down-to-earth apprenticeship by turning the hand crank that operated the *Banner*'s flat-bed press.[3]

Friends from the city's Scots community came in to offer encouragement and advice. In particular, there were frequent visits from the portly, somewhat pompous Isaac Buchanan, recent Liberal member of the Legislative Assembly for Toronto, and one of the wealthiest and best known wholesale merchants in the province.[4] The formidable Isaac was taking a leading part in the Free Kirk movement. Indeed, he was one of twenty substantial sympathizers approached by the first Moderator of the Free Church in Scotland for individual contributions of £1000 towards the establishment of a theological college for the new body: and he had agreed to put up such a sum, provided that it was applied to the Free Church cause within the colony.[5] His brother and partner, Peter Buchanan, had been one of the subscribers to the original guarantee for the *Banner*; this while Isaac was home in Scotland on business.[6] And since his return, he had shown the new journal benevolent if slightly patronizing attention, freely offering its editors the benefit of his ten years' experience in Canada, and lending it his not inconsiderable influence with Presbyterians in the province.

At any rate, the *Banner* was assured of a good audience when the first number of the little weekly came out on Friday, August 18, 1843. It was a single sheet folded over to make four pages, after the practice of the press of the day, and was much like the *British Chronicle* in appearance, with six crowded columns of small type to a page. On the first were reports of Canadian Presbyterian activities; on the last, advertisements—notably for patent medicines and *The Fame and Glory of England Vindicated*. The real meat of the journal lay inside. Here were the British, European and local news items, and the all-important editorials. Those dominating page two, which bore the caption "Religious Department", were the prime responsibility of Peter Brown; those on page three, the "Secular Department", would be George Brown's particular concern.

Straightway the Religious Department plunged into the sectarian controversies in the province, not only setting forth the Free Church argument within Presbyterianism, but also generally upholding the evangelical churches of the colony in their protests against the privileged position of the Church of England. The editor turned sharply on the *Church*, the local High Anglican journal, which had deplored the pernicious sectarianism of "the Dissenters". He answered emphatically, "There is *no established church* in Canada, and, of course, there can be *no Dissenters*."[7] The *Banner*, Peter declared, would resist such usurping claims to the utmost. Darkly he pointed to the Romish trend in the Anglican establishment at home, displayed in England's current Oxford Movement; the evil of state interference in the Church of Scotland; the growing pressure of the Roman Catholic Church in Ireland and the United States upon civil society. And he called for "a friendly Christian union" of evangelical Anglicans, Independents, Baptists, and Methodists, together with the Presbyterian supporters of the *Banner*, to stand guard against similar dangers arising in Canada. Plainly, Peter Brown stood ready to wage war for religious freedom, as he saw it. His new standard-bearing journal would live up to its name.

The *Banner*'s Secular Department started out more mildly, with an exposition of political principles that amounted to a eulogy of the British constitution. No other was so admirably adapted for securing individual rights and property, thanks to "its happy medium between absolute monarchy on the one hand and the tyranny of a democratic majority on the other".[8] This, the paper announced, was the belief it would sustain in Canada. Surely this was safe and moderate doctrine. Yet the fact was, that while it was permissible for colonial editors to praise British parliamentary and cabinet rule in Britain, to advocate its full extension to Canada as the system best suited for free men everywhere, might still be deemed dangerous radicalism by Tories and self-proclaimed friends of the Governor-General.

For the first few months, however, there was no open joining of battle on the political front. While the *Banner*'s Religious Department continued to preach strong gospel, its secular editorials simply showed a tendency to speak favourably of measures brought forward by Reform leaders in the provincial legislature and government—though Tory journals grew increasingly suspicious of the alleged non-partisanship of the new Presbyterian paper. But then came a decisive issue. In mid-November the rising strain between the Governor-General, Sir Charles Metcalfe, and his Reform ministers burst into an open quarrel over patronage, the highly significant power to control the appointments to public service. And on this question, with his father's full accord, George Brown made his lasting choice of sides in Canadian politics.

The devoted, resolute, and rigid Metcalfe had proved an able administrator in possessions like India and Jamaica. But he was about as much at home in the blasts of popular Canadian politics as a rhinocerous in a blizzard. He had come to Canada determined to yield no more of what he regarded as the essential rights of the Crown. When, therefore, his Reform ministers had protested his filling of official positions without consulting them (such as offering the Speakership of the Legislative Council to one of their opponents), Metcalfe had firmly declared that patronage must remain part of the Governor's prerogative. They had as firmly insisted that they could hardly act as his advisers without possessing his full confidence. No doubt past practice and Colonial Office policy supported the Governor-General. No doubt as well, Reformers could be charged with greed for power, or with favouring the debased American spoils system, whereby a victorious party rewarded its faithful with jobs throughout the public offices. Yet it was just as true that a Governor might effectively undermine ministers supplied to him by an uncongenial Assembly through maintaining his own faithful in the government service. And it would come to be clearly recognized that a necessary attribute of the responsible system was the ministry's ability to command full obedience from its own subordinates.

In any case, Metcalfe stood obdurately to his ground, whereupon, on November 26, Baldwin, Lafontaine, Hincks and their

colleagues resigned from the government. There was an exchange of ministerial and gubernatorial explanations—or contentions—before an excited Assembly, and the result was an
emphatic, two-to-one vote of confidence in the retiring ministers. It was a flat rejection of Metcalfe's stand. Hence, on
December 9, he prorogued the legislature, in order to gain time
to patch up a new ministry that might somehow bring him parliamentary support. Meanwhile he ruled virtually on his own,
with but one minister still beside him, and in opposition to the
plainly expressed opinion of the people's representatives.

Canada was in crisis. As public feeling mounted, the two
editors of the *Banner* anxiously debated the course that they
should follow in their journal. At first, they had hoped that the
differences between the Governor and his advisers might be
amicably settled, and in their paper had acknowledged the former's right to share in the management of patronage.[9] But the
prorogation decided them. Sir Charles Metcalfe had refused
the advice of ministers who held a parliamentary majority, replaced them with a government—if it was a government—that
did not enjoy the Assembly's confidence, and made plain his
readiness to rule in spite of parliament by this high-handed
prorogation. It was a blow against the British constitutional system; it was a dire step backward into a despotic past.

All the Browns' Liberal sympathies were aroused and
quivering, as George drafted an editorial for their next issue,
December 15, that openly declared war upon the Governor-
General. But while condemning him, the young editor did not
yet intend definitely to endorse Baldwin and the other former
ministers. He still felt too new to the country, and to the Reform leaders, to back them out of hand. His primary concern
was with a question of principle, the responsibility of government to parliament. In fact, it was Isaac Buchanan, who came
bustling in at the proper moment to read the proof sheets, who
persuaded him to add a few words favourable to the Reform
ex-ministers themselves.[10]

The central argument of the decisive *Banner* article was this:
that while the "distinguished individual" who was Governor-
General had an undoubted right to his own view of the Canadian
constitution, he could not alter that constitution without the
consent of the contracting parties.[11] The "contract" here implied
lay in the celebrated Resolutions of September 3, 1841, passed
by the legislature on the one hand and sanctioned by the Governor-General on the other, which had declared that members of a
provincial administration should possess the confidence of the

Assembly. The resolutions had been purposely amended into vagueness by supporters of the Governor-General. But the Browns held the view widespread among Reformers, that their "solemn and deliberate" acceptance had inevitably incorporated the principle of parliamentary responsibility into the government of Canada. Thus, by repudiating ministers who held the confidence of parliament, Metcalfe, Brown charged, had upset the established constitution and endangered his own office. Here was a conviction, based on the Resolutions of 1841, that remained with George Brown throughout the struggle over responsible government; and his feeling that Tories and friends of the Governor-General sought to ignore or destroy a binding constitutional agreement simply added moral fervour to his own part in the conflict.

Opinions of this sort reached their natural conclusion soon enough. From defending a principle in the issue of December 15, the *Banner*'s political editor readily moved on to defend the ex-ministers themselves against the charge that it was they who had threatened to subvert the constitution. Within two weeks he had made their cause his own, and it was in outright, vigorous support of Baldwin, Hincks, and the Reform party. Now the *Banner* openly attacked those elements who were rallying to Metcalfe as "foes of free government". It strenuously denied that Reform leaders were republicans in disguise; and it called for the maintenance of party unity above all, so that the Governor could not detach sufficient Liberals to form some new ministerial combination with a working parliamentary majority.[12]

Indeed, a movement did begin among "moderate" Liberals to join in supporting the Governor for the sake of British loyalty, a movement backed by men who claimed to uphold the principles of responsible government, but who felt that the Reform leaders had gone too far, and in an aggressive demand for more personal power had actually endangered the bond with Britain. This viewpoint was pressed upon the Browns—and did not convince them in the least. As George described it later, "we had all the old horrible arguments summed up to our inexperience by our 'moderate' friends; we were told Mr. Baldwin was a rebel, Mr. Hincks was a 'fiend'; that there were but two parties, a monarchical and a disloyal, in the country. Our answer was simply that all this might be very true for what we knew, but there was a great constitutional principle in dispute—the men we knew not and cared not for, but the principles they advocated we should adhere to, the ground they had taken up we should heartily support them in—come what might."[13] Come what might. There would be no turning back now.

2

So it was, by the beginning of 1844, that Peter and George Brown had decisively allied their journal with the Baldwin Reformers. It would be no ineffective ally. Already the *Banner*'s pungent, closely-reasoned political editorials were gaining wide attention, and its circulation was steadily expanding. Furthermore, it was doing useful service in meeting the loyalty cry of the moderates who would split the Reform party, making nonsense of their charges that the party captains had turned republican, offering instead lucid expositions of what responsible government properly involved. And in this regard, most significantly, George Brown met and repelled the unexpected onslaught of Mr. Isaac Buchanan on Messrs. Baldwin, Lafontaine and Hincks.

By the end of December, Isaac had undergone a notable change of heart from that time earlier in the month when he had urged George Brown to add some commendation for the Reform leaders to the *Banner*'s first outspoken editorial on the Metcalfe crisis. For now Toronto's ex-member was sending long pronunciamentos to the city press, declaring that he, Isaac Buchanan, tried friend of responsible government, felt compelled to dissociate himself from the disaffected clique led by Hincks and Baldwin whose real goal was separation from the Empire, and proclaiming as well the need for a moderate Liberal party that would work with Metcalfe in the staunch defence of every British tie. "SIR CHARLES METCALFE AND BRITISH CONNECTION!" he resoundingly held forth.[14]

There was serious danger here for the Reform party, since Buchanan's name carried weight with the large element of Scots Presbyterian voters. It was, therefore, a matter of some public note when the Browns brought the *Banner* out against him, making bold to differ with their self-constituted patron, whose Free Kirk sympathies they still completely shared. George wrote the necessary article for the *Banner* of January 12, 1844, commenting at length on Buchanan's public letters.[15] He regretted having to dissent "*in toto*" from the views of a man who had been one of their first and most valued supporters—"but we hold that the Press never ought to occupy an equivocal position, but should speak out honestly and fully the views of its conductors". Buchanan, he went on bluntly, while professing responsible government would actually destroy it, by throwing unrestrained power into the Governor-General's hands. That might not be his intention, but it would be the sure effect—especially since the

main content of his contributions to the press seemed to be attacks on the reputations of those who had left the government
in protest. This was forthright criticism. It brought a quick
response.

Buchanan set down a copious answer for publication, sending
a copy to the *Banner* as well as to the Conservative *British Colonist*. He coupled pained fatherly rebuke with much stronger
indictment, renewed the attacks on the ministers, and then struck
at the Browns themselves. They had regrettably involved a
religious paper in political controversy, even though he had
distinctly *warned* an inexperienced George Brown to keep clear
of party tangles, as had "other friends who kindly offered the
same advice".[16] In fact, the Browns had broken the agreement
which had brought them to Canada; for, as Isaac cuttingly reminded them, it had been Free Church interests, not politics,
"which led us to induce you to leave New York".[17] The *Banner*
printed the scorcher in full; but alongside it George Brown ran
one of his own, addressed to "Isaac Buchanan Esq., late M.P.P.
for the City of Toronto". The two long documents together
made a thoroughly engrossing exchange, and surely no one
minded that they occupied practically all the news space in the
Banner for January 26.

Once again, as in the case of Mr. Bryson, the self-recognized
expert on phrenology, young George Brown proved not at all
abashed by the weight of an opponent, and quite capable of
pulling down a superior attitude. His reply to Buchanan vigorously denied that an agreement had ever been made to bind the
Banner's political views. It was an independent journal making
its own way, supporting the Free Church cause but by no means
the mere tool of a group. "We write to please no man," he declared emphatically. Conditions made at its inception to publish
Presbyterian church material had and would be kept, but the
real friends who had brought the journal to Canada—"the whole
forty-five of them"—were well aware that they had no control
over its politics. Incidentally, it was mere impertinence on Mr.
Buchanan's part to talk as if he himself had shared in bringing
the *Banner* to Canada, since he was across the ocean at the time.
(Indeed, he had never since even bought a subscription to the
paper!) Nor would he be allowed to arrogate the Free Kirk
movement to himself, nor make Free Churchmen "loyal" to
the extent of displaying docility to any sort of government. And
as for his reference to past warnings not to let the *Banner* meddle
in politics, did he not recall *who* had urged its secular editor to
do justice to the Reform leaders only the month previous—
before his own opinions had been so marvellously transformed?[18]

There were several columns more, refuting Buchanan's charges against the late ministers, but the most significant note in George Brown's whole letter was its declaration of journalistic independence—"we write to please no man". He would say much the same thing on later occasions in his career. In short, his views were his own; and though they might coincide in many respects with those of a group or party, it did not follow that he should not speak his own mind as he saw fit. His letter, besides, was an effective rebuttal of Buchanan's attacks on Baldwin and his friends, effective because it was carefully detailed and documented, and, while lengthy, remained lively and commanding throughout. Above all, his performance won attention in high Reform circles. Francis Hincks enthusiastically wrote to Robert Baldwin that "Brown's letter in reply to Buchanan is admirable",[19] while the austere Canada West leader informed his eastern partner, Lafontaine, in his usual circumspect way, "The new paper, the *Banner*, will I hope prove a valuable auxiliary. I am rather afraid to place dependence in new hands, but I am rather prepossessed in favour of the man as far as manner goes, and there is no doubt the paper, if it does keep right, will have a powerful effect in keeping the Presbyterian section of our friends so also."[20]

The force of political circumstance, however, would soon bring the cautious Baldwin and his friends to place considerable reliance on George Brown. In these opening months of 1844, the Reformers were girding themselves for a crucial test with Metcalfe's supporters when parliament next met. There was a grave need to counter their enemies' appeal to loyalty, and its always effective influence on public opinion. For this a powerful Reform press was essential, especially in Canada West, which was so full of loyal British sentiment. Yet in Toronto, particularly, which might be called the focal point of western politics, the main established Reform organ, the *Examiner*, was far from flourishing. In fact, that February, its proprietor, James Lesslie, was complaining to Baldwin that his journal had only six or seven hundred subscribers on its list—although he had to admit that the recently founded *Banner* had some 1700. It was lamentable, he thought, that not one in twenty among Reformers who could afford to take a paper did so. Really, it should be a party duty.[21]

Here was a serious consideration to keep in mind, when Reformers were planning a campaign to win a following so wide that Metcalfe would be forced to yield. Public meetings were being held and a new Reform Association projected, with branches throughout the countryside to organize support. But what of the press that would beat the drum and bring the people in? Reform leaders meditated. It was decided that a new party journal was needed in Montreal (to which the capital was to be transferred from Kingston), since the English-speaking press there was strongly Tory. Francis Hincks, the skilful party promoter who had worked to bring Upper and Lower Canadian Reformers together, would go to Montreal to run the publication; he was well qualified by his experience as editor of the *Examiner* before Lesslie had assumed control. As for Toronto, where the *Examiner* now was slipping, an approach would be made to the political editor and publisher of the *Banner*, who had shown his worth to the Reform cause not only by the force of his writing but also by that newspaper's obvious ability to sell copies.

Accordingly, in mid-February, a group of prominent local Reformers applied to George Brown to found a new political journal, promising some measure of financial aid. Four of them —Skeffington Connor, Joseph Morrison, Shuter Smith and R. P. Crooks—stood ready to provide £250 of immediate capital by furnishing him with notes for £62 10s each.[22] Yet their strongest appeals were to his sense of enterprise and his attachment to the cause of responsible government. They found a ready listener. The *Banner* at best could give only a partial attention to political questions, tied as it was to but one section of the community, and that involved in a religious issue as intense and absorbing as the political controversy itself. Its senior editor, Peter Brown, for all his agreement with his son's opinions, was supremely interested in the dispute within Canadian Presbyterianism, now coming to a head in demands for formal condemnation or approval of the Disruption in the Church of Scotland. But George, on his part, despite every sympathy for the Free Church movement, was by this time wholly taken up with politics.

With a journal of his own he could indulge his interest to the full. He could champion free government with undivided effort, joyfully pitch into his newspaper opponents, rouse public feelings like a swelling sea. He could do these things to which the last few months had brought him—and which he now wanted to do, perhaps more than anything else in the world. Perhaps also, he saw opening before him, in the conflict of the time, that opportunity which he had once told his father lay in Canada— the chance for a man to rise to any heights, if he had sufficient energy and character. He would seize the chance. In March of 1844, there would be a new Reform weekly published in Toronto: the *Globe*, George Brown editor and publisher. And this when he was not yet twenty-six.

3

The *Banner* of February 23 printed the prospectus of the new journal, setting forth once more its editor's attachment to the British Constitution and the British tie, and his faith that "the limited Monarchy of Great Britain is the best system of Government yet devised by the wisdom of man". But this time George Brown added pointedly, "It is usual in such announcements as the present to declare against all political partisanship; the undersigned, however, is convinced that no strong Government has ever existed—no great measure has ever been carried— without a combination of persons holding similar views. THE GLOBE will therefore strenuously support the party which shall advocate the measures believed best for the country." (There was no doubt which party that should be!) He explained besides: "The wide circulation of the *Banner* has brought its political views generally before the public, but in a paper in which so large a part is devoted to religious and ecclesiastical information, it was impossible to do justice to those views. The same political opinions will be maintained in the *Globe*, and a wider field afforded for the expression of them, as it will be entirely devoted to secular subjects."

Peter Brown, cautious still, at first had not been too enthusiastic about his son's branching out with another newspaper. Yet he could see that the decision to found the *Globe* need not involve a great deal of new expense. It would be published at the same King Street premises as the *Banner* and use the same equipment, coming out on Tuesdays while the Free Church journal continued to be issued on Fridays. He, Brown senior, could help to write for it, while George's *Globe* editorials could be reprinted in the *Banner*'s Secular Department. On occasion too, when a ship arriving from Europe brought important transatlantic news, joint *Banner* and *Globe* extras could be published. Hence the establishment of the second paper would chiefly mean more work for both of them, and perhaps a better use of their press, with Peter continuing to take prime responsibility for the *Banner* and George for the new enterprise.

The money came through from the four friends; Robert Baldwin lent £50 more later.[23] They laid in more printing stock, secured more type. And on March 5—with no public awareness that this was a noteworthy occasion—the first of the new Toronto *Globes* was issued. There was little to distinguish the paper at first glance. Like the *Banner* it was typical of the small provincial journals of its day. Four pages of plain, close print again, six columns wide: fivepence a copy; subscription, £1 currency, *per annum*—"No paper will be discontinued until all arrears are paid up, unless at the option of the Publisher." Page One normally presented lengthy non-political articles lifted from the British or American press, and, during sessions, even closer-packed reports of the Canadian and British parliamentary debates. On Page Two were the editorials, and an up-to-the-minute, or rather, month, digest of world events ("Latest News By the Steamship *Hibernia*!"). Page Three, as a general rule, furnished local news, commercial intelligence, and short excerpts from British, colonial and American contemporaries. And Page Four supplied the advertisements characteristic of that era: "Dalley's Magical Pain Extractor—the Wonder and Blessing of the Age", "William Henderson, 48 King Street, Toronto, keeps constantly on hand a general assortment of Groceries, Wines and Liquors. He also offers for Sale—20 Barrels Port Hope Whisky; 20 Barrels Good Common Whisky."[24]

Mr. Thomas Teasdale suggested traffic hazards of an earlier day, as he testily announced, "Strayed into the Premises of the Subscriber—A LIGHT RED COW". Even the firm of Isaac Buchanan ran an advertisement to herald "Dry Goods Spring Shipments by the arrival of the English Steamer", and took the opportunity "of intimating to their connections and the Trade generally that for variety and nicety they have never on any former occasion held superior assortments".[25] All this, however, might similarly be found in any of the other Toronto newspapers. Yet the fighting tone that won the *Globe* attention from the first was well indicated in the motto which George Brown selected for it from the letters of *Junius*, that sharp-tongued champion of liberty against the government of George III: "The subject who is truly loyal to the Chief Magistrate will neither advise nor submit to arbitrary measures." There, blazoned across the head of page one, was the answer to the "loyal" adherents of Metcalfe. More than a hundred years later, in very different circumstances, its successor, the Toronto *Globe and Mail*, would still carry that sentence.

Aside from denominational papers like the Methodist *Christian Guardian*, the *Globe* had five competitors as a political journal in Toronto: the Reform *Examiner*, of course; the *Mirror*, organ of Irish Roman Catholic Liberals; the *Herald*, the Orange Tory mouthpiece; the even higher Tory *Patriot*; and the able and more moderate Conservative *British Colonist*. The last was the most vigorous of the five. Its Scots editor, Hugh Scobie, was congenial to the Browns in many ways, although he upheld the Church of Scotland side in the Presbyterian controversy. Considering this competition, and this in a city still predominantly Tory, one might expect the *Globe* to have a fairly meagre future. But not with the personality of George Brown glowing through its pages. He threw his paper lustily into the political conflict, assailing, combating and refuting to such effect that even political opponents could hardly forbear buying the *Globe* to see what (or whom) Brown was demolishing today. He rapidly began to build a following for his forceful new journal.

A later age might tend to regard much of this forcefulness as mere invective; but to a great extent George Brown was simply handing back what he and his fellow Reformers received from the other side—and doing it superlatively well. In that era of belligerent, partisan journalism, readers expected their press to speak out ardently on every public issue. Perhaps, as a result, they found engrossing entertainment in their editorial pages, whereas a tamer generation must look to the vicarious warfare of the sports section, the pontificating of the columnist, or the fantasy world of the comic strips. For this was the era when an opposing journal could finish dissecting the *Globe* with the pungent comment, "such a mass of putridity—we feel as if we have been cutting up a dead dog",[26] and when the *Globe* could refer incisively to its distinguished contemporary, the *British Colonist*, as "the literary common-sewer of Toronto".[27]

At any rate, Brown soon proved himself a master of denunciation, returning two strong words for every one received. Consequently some adversaries began to take the high line—of retreat—deploring the incendiary language and abusive character of the *Globe*, which was lowering the whole moral tone of the provincial press. Thus began the legend, added to over the years by every devastated politician who matched himself against the paper, that George Brown had introduced journalistic terrorism into Canada. Examining the contemporary press, however, reveals that this was simply not true. George merely outplayed his rivals at their own well established game; though Girondins trundling to execution could not be expected to appreciate the Jacobin who had supplanted them.

Yet there was far more behind the *Globe*'s rising influence than a mere talent for invective. George Brown's arguments were carefully considered, exhaustively supported. Moreover, his was no mere sensation-hunting sheet, concerned with scandal and popular excitement for their own sake. Charges were made on public issues, and sincerely made, expressing the editor's burning sense of justice. If the *Globe* set forth accusations of corruption or political double-dealing, it usually had more than a little to go on, in an era of shadowy political morality, and its own air of assured conviction gave it almost irresistible force—especially when evidence was attached. Here was further reason for the exasperation of its enemies, and for the steady expansion of its following. Here too was additional cause for the violence of reactions against it. Indeed, the *Globe* itself characterized these reactions rather well: "...all we get is just some such reply as this—'You poor, paltry, villainous, foul-mouthed, ignorant, blaspheming ruffians—why do you call names? Why do you not maintain the bearing of gentlemen and simply argue as we do?' The *Globe* has given from day to day not abuse but the most damaging statements that could be made against public men. It has given particulars, dates, facts and figures. It has said these things are so ... it has brought charges such as no public man in England would be under for a single hour—which would be prosecuted as libel forthwith. It has dared any of those concerned so to prosecute. ... And what is the answer? 'You are a set of low, mean scoundrels!' "[28]

Writing of this sort could hardly help but catch the public eye. *Globe* editorials were not fine-drawn and polished. They were hastily poured forth, in a style that was often ungainly but always lucid; and above all, trenchant and provocative. George Brown set the pattern by his own habit of writing: first of all, a meticulous gathering of information on scraps of paper; next, the jotting of headings and topic sentences, crossed out and re-written; then, when the heat of composition had risen sufficiently, the drafting at full blast of the whole editorial—so that it was cast as a single, molten whole. Revision with stumps of black lead pencil followed later in the proof sheets, but chiefly to stress vital facts and sharpen arguments, not to alter the nature of the full-length production, which kept the merits and defects of the manner of its making.[29]

Beside the power of its editorials, however, the *Globe* rapidly won support because it was a good newspaper in a fundamental sense; that is, it energetically went after the news, and presented it fully.[30] Even convinced foes would grudgingly admit that its information—if not its interpretation—could usually be trusted. Hence it came to circulate among far more than faithful Liberals in Tory Toronto. Indeed, as time went on, politicians of both camps came regularly to use the *Globe* as a ready reference for the contemporary history of Canada. And Brown strove constantly to increase his paper's circulation by still more news coverage and better services. He was anxious always to have it printed and distributed as fast as possible: out on the streets, off to subscribers first thing in the morning. "The early bird gets the early worm," he once remarked, "—and so does the early newspaper."[31]

He was well aware, moreover, that if he could offer advertisers a wider audience than his competitors, the *Globe* would gain a larger share of a lucrative source of revenue. Profits from advertising could then be fed into more press improvements, for still more circulation—and so on up, in influence and prestige besides. Nowadays there is nothing very startling about this doctrine, but to the shoestring Canadian journalists of this time, investing in expansion in advance of paid-up subscriptions was regarded as a wildly speculative gamble. But for the *Globe* it worked, and showed results in steadily improving facilities and in the ever-mounting circulation figures that accompanied them.[32]

As early as May of 1844, a mere two months after the paper had started, George Brown was down in New York to buy for the *Globe* the first cylinder press used in Upper Canada, one that could throw off 1250 copies an hour, whereas the old Washington hand press could produce only 200.[33] It was an example of the rotary press but recently invented by Richard Hoe of New York: Brown became Canadian agent for Hoe's firm.[34] This new equipment permitted the establishment of a book, card and job printing business, which brought further returns to the Brown enterprise, and in June made necessary a move to larger quarters in Mr. Sutherland's new brick building on Yonge Street, between King and Market.[35] Two years later the printing office had to move again, to still larger premises at 63 Yonge.[36]

George Brown was quite conscious that the rapid growth of his journal did not necessarily indicate an equal growth of fervent Liberal partisanship in Toronto. It was rather the result of appealing effectively to the uncommitted "general reader" no less than the good party man. Brown made that point himself, in the pages of the *Globe*. Until now, he declared, Reform papers in the city had been read only by party followers for political articles. The general reader had gone to the Tory press, almost by default. But the *Globe* meant to earn his patronage by offering him a wider and more varied fare, the latest news, local, American and European, and the most correct commercial information, all without weakening its political character.[37]

"The Publisher of the *Globe*," he proclaimed, "is determined that, at whatever cost, he shall at all times receive THE ENGLISH NEWS, at the earliest possible moment."[38] In pursuit of this policy, when the new electric telegraph reached Toronto, and the city was linked by wire with the seaboard via Buffalo and New York, Brown joined with his most energetic com-

petitor, Scobie of the *British Colonist*, to share the considerable
expense of buying use of the telegraph for news messages from
Atlantic shipping.[39] Soon a wire to Montreal was similarly employed.[40] A different kind of innovation—"a new feature in
Canadian newspapers"—was the republication of full-length
novels by instalments in the *Globe*. Charles Dickens' latest,
Dombey and Son, was the first of these, announced late in
1846;[41] and a number of other notable Victorian novels came
to a rapt Canadian audience through the pages of George
Brown's journal.

Another feature of expansion was the issuing of more frequent editions. In September, 1846, the young *Globe* announced
that it would become a semi-weekly, noting proudly that no
Reform newspaper in the Conservative stronghold of Toronto
had ever before been published more than once a week.[42] Two
years later it enlarged the dimensions of its sheet "to the utmost
our presses will permit", and took to smaller type to crowd in
an increased budget of news and, above all, more advertisements.[43] The agreeable pressure on space continued; to lead the
next year, 1849, to the *Globe*'s being issued three times a week.[44]
At the same time, "to meet the widening demand for newspapers
in the country districts", the weekly *Globe* was instituted, containing a selection of articles printed in the *Globes* of the week
preceding.[45] Altogether, the journal now claimed a circulation
of nearly 4000, three times that of its nearest rival, the *British
Colonist*.[46] Here one might reasonably allow for some element
of newspaper exaggeration: claims and counter-claims of circulation in that era were highly inconclusive. None the less, it was
plain enough that within its first five years George Brown's
Globe had grown with surprising speed to become a leading, and
quite probably the leading, member of Toronto's press.

In every way these early years of the *Globe* made evident
the journalistic skill and enterprise of its publisher and chief
editor. As one result, the financial position of the Brown family
improved. They moved from lodgings in Church Street to a
house on Queen Street East, in a better residential area.[47] Yet
it would be a mistake to think that they were becoming wealthy.
Peter was still striving to reduce his Scottish debts; George was
assisting him to do so.[48] More than that, the son's hard-driving
policy of expansion meant that most of his receipts immediately
went back into the *Globe*. Then there were always subscribers
in arrears, and there were always sizeable accounts to meet.[49]
The cylinder press, for instance, was not paid for in a day.
As the paper grew there were reporters and pressmen whose
salaries had to be found. Besides, the Browns had to pay back

(and they did) the funds advanced them to aid in launching and developing the *Globe*.[50] But further, any assistance that the journal had received from party friends was soon very much outweighed by expenditures on the party's behalf: for broadsides, pamphlets, handbills, and extras printed for free distribution at Reform meetings, or to aid in canvassing.[51] Consequently it was not entirely to amuse themselves that the girls of the family set up their finishing school anew in Toronto: young Marianne replacing her married sister, Jane, and joining with Catherine and Isabella to teach "Music, Drawing and all other branches of a complete Female Education".[52] As it had in New York, the school added usefully to the family income.

Nevertheless, through journalism, George was obviously making his way as a business man, increasingly known and respected in the most exalted circles of King Street commerce and finance. But far more important, through journalism he was making himself a force in provincial politics. The power of the *Globe* was raising him high in Reform ranks, bringing him into closer and closer contact with the leaders of the party. He was taking a prominent part in political meetings now, speaking to toasts at Reform banquets, even receiving suggestions to run for parliament.[53] The first few years of the *Globe* did more than shape a great Canadian newspaper. They also led George Brown towards a masterful political career.

4

Brown had spoken briefly at a dinner to the former Liberal ministers in Toronto at the end of December, 1843; but his first real address from the political platform was made at a grand party rally in March of 1844, less than three weeks after the *Globe* first came out. This was the opening general meeting of the Reform Association of Canada, which set the all-out campaign against Metcalfe and Co. officially in motion.[54] By now the Governor-General had acquired three rather varied ministers. There was "Perpetual Secretary" Dominick Daly, a vestige of antique bureaucracy who had cheerfully stayed on in office when his late colleagues had resigned, as he had ever since 1827. There was the ex-radical D. B. Viger, who had come some distance from past connections with the Lower Canadian rebellion of 1837, but brought along no following. And there was the undoubtedly talented William Draper, a former Attorney-General and a moderate Conservative who did have some backing in Upper Canada, but by no means enough to give the government a majority. Indeed, Metcalfe had the latter two sworn in as executive councillors only, without salaried ministerial offices, so that they need not yet withdraw from parliament to face by-elections. With this incomplete, anomalous ministry he was governing, while still negotiating manfully to detach some Reform support for a patriotic "no-party" administration, through which alone he could hope to carry on his rule for any length of time.

In consequence, it was in a mood of both real and calculated party indignation that Reformers gathered in full force at Toronto's leading hotel, the North American, on Monday evening, March 25, to expose the patriotic project for what it was, and to expound some home truths on the nature of responsible government. The large ballroom was packed by 6:30, a buzzing, eager crowd settling down for five full hours of speeches.[55] Three Upper Canadian ex-ministers sat on the platform that night: Robert Baldwin himself, his cousin and now his close supporter, Robert Baldwin Sullivan, and the former Solicitor-General West, James Small. Francis Hincks was absent in Montreal, managing his new paper, the *Pilot* (begun, incidentally, the same day as the *Globe*), but there were other prominent Reformers on hand, to place an impressive series of resolutions before the meeting. Henry John Boulton came first, an experienced politician who had once been a leading Compact Tory, until his removal from the Attorney-Generalship by the Colonial Office in 1833, and subsequent inadequate consolation prize of five years as Chief Justice of Newfoundland, had turned his mind decidedly to the left. Then there were James Hervey Price, member for First York, and William Hume Blake, brilliant barrister and orator, both of whom would become Reform cabinet ministers. Beside them on the speakers' platform were Blake's law partners, Joseph Morrison and Skeffington Connor, who had lent money to start the *Globe*, old Jesse Ketchum, the greybeard of the city's Reformers, and James Lesslie, the editor of the *Examiner*, and still a force to be reckoned with. And joining this shining panoply of Reform leadership, to introduce the sixth of the intended resolutions, was the youthful editor of the new party journal in Toronto: George Brown, not yet a year in Canada.

Robert Baldwin was put in the chair, of course. From there he gave the opening address: a typical Baldwin product, somewhat pedestrian, based on a long series of quoted passages from Durham's Report designed to show that Metcalfe's refusal to be advised on matters of patronage contradicted the very words of the great imperial authority on responsible government. The whole was sonorously delivered with little colour, grace or touch of emotion. Yet, as always, there was something about this broad-shouldered, stooping figure with the stolid features and pale grey eyes that inspired profound respect and the closest attention: the utter integrity of the man, the driving force of his ideas unaided by any personal magnetism, his cold but unimpeachable logic. When he sat down amid a roar of applause, he had renewed his ascendancy over the Reform party; and in George Brown confirmed a trust in his leadership that lasted as long as Robert Baldwin remained in active politics.

Boulton came next, with an aggressive, stirring speech; then Blake, Price, Sullivan, and Connor. The sharp-witted Sullivan spoke lengthily but effectively, ridiculing the charges that the late ministers had sought unwarranted power and suggesting instead that the Governor-General's notions of the rights of British subjects might have been formed in his years of ruling conquered East Indians. But the speaker who most aroused the audience was William Hume Blake. His tall, handsome presence and flowing oratory brought loud acclaim, especially when, after an eloquent apostrophe to British freedom, he concluded: "And I hesitate not to declare that, much as I glory in the power of Britain, much as I admire her unparalleled greatness, I had rather see them mouldering in the dust than supported by an infringement of those Constitutional principles of liberty upon which they were founded—and with which I even dare to hope that they will fall!"[56] So the meeting grew in keen intensity, faces aglow beneath the flaring gas jets, as the men of note one after another came forward to make their ringing declarations. And then it was time for Resolution Six and that still half-unknown quantity, George Brown.

As the audience watched expectantly, he rose rather stiffly from his platform seat to move a long pronouncement that appointments recommended by a ministry must be deemed to be for the benefit of the Governor-General's own government, and could not be viewed as favours to the ministers themselves. This, he pointed out, with a degree of nervousness and hesitation, was the established doctrine of the British cabinet system. A bit laboriously he analysed that system, "the surest preservative of the principle that Governments must rule for the good of the people".[57] Then he began warming to his subject. "The Cabinet Minister of England is no hireling—he is not the head clerk of a public office whose advice is asked when wanted, to be unheeded when it is given—he is not the plastic nonentity con-

descendingly to be consulted on matters of *'adequate* importance' [Metcalfe's words], but he is the life, the moving power
of every wheel in the whole machinery of government—he is
the very Government itself. Still, the minister does not one
single act in his own name or for his own benefit—all is in the
name of the Sovereign. The Cabinet Council as a party or as a
power in the State is perfectly unknown—it is the executive of
the Crown—the mouthpiece of the Sovereign."[58]

Now he was well away, nervousness forgotten. In Canada,
he declared, to mounting response, the Governor-General had
struck "a deadly blow" at the British cabinet system by drawing
a line between the late Reform ministers and himself as the
representative of the Sovereign, and refusing to surrender government patronage to them for "their" purchase of parliamentary support. But they *were* the "mouthpiece of the Sovereign",
his very government! How, then, could he have made appointments without consulting them? How could he have made appointments prejudicial to his own Government—prejudicial to
himself!

"What would Sir Robert Peel or Lord John Russell have said,
if they found Her Majesty had made important political appointments without even consulting them, and on their remon-
strating had been told that Her Majesty would not consent to
make appointments which would secure (of course, indirectly)
'parliamentary support'? Either of them would have at once
resigned the seals of office! They would have laughed at the
idea of a Ministry not giving vacant offices to such of their
supporters as were competent to fulfil the duties required, in
preference to a political opponent. Is the Governor of Canada
to assume a position which the Sovereign of Great Britain could
not maintain? Is then the chasm so much wider between his
Excellency and his Administration than that which divides Her
Majesty and her Secretary of State?"[59]

He was conscious now of sweeping his audience with him as
he cried, "The Governor-General, it is evident, is determined
to rule alone and without restraint—if he can. Already has he
appointed Cabinet Councillors who are not heads of Departments—heads of Departments who are not in Parliament nor
in the Executive. Four months have nearly all the offices of
State been unfilled up—and now it wants but to carry out the
new scheme that the Cabinet and the Crown are not one and
the same thing—that the Cabinet Councillors are only the head
clerks of the Departments to be consulted on cases of 'adequate'
importance. And then may the people of Canada bid adieu to
the title of Freemen!"[60]

They were cheering him on, and fully, happily, at ease, he drew a deft and ludicrous sketch of the ultimate in the "no party" rule envisaged by the Governor's supporters—one in which Robert Baldwin was seated at the council table with "Sweet William" Draper, Francis Hincks placed beside arch-Tory Sir Allan MacNab, the unyielding High-Church Bishop Strachan across from Methodist leader, Dr. Egerton Ryerson—and "his Excellency at the middle of the table, on a chair raised above the warring elements below". "The most delightful picture of bickering would be presented which any self-willed Governor could possibly desire! His Excellency might let the Council fire off on one another—he could not, of course, adopt the advice of *all*, and so to keep the peace among the belligerants, he would kindly decide the point for them and carry out his own ideas. Where is the man who would accept office under such an absurd and anti-British principle? Sir, I trust he is not to be found in the ranks of the Reform Association of Canada!"[61]

As he ended there was sustained and vigorous applause, loud shouts of approval from every quarter of the crowded room. It was not a great speech, nor yet a practised one; but George Brown had made his mark. The journalist had shown what he could do in person as well as through his paper, and henceforth there would be more and more demands for his voice at political gatherings. He had, moreover, set a pattern for his speeches that would seldom vary; the slow, almost halting start, the gradually rising tempo as he and his hearers took fire together—the ardour of his words in full flight, when speaker and audience seemed to merge in one zealous, glowing whole. He would still have far to go, but already the Brown that could hold two and three thousand spellbound for four or five hours at a stretch was forecast in the novice of 1844.

5

The proceedings of this important party gathering were turned over to him to issue as a *Globe* extra, first, and then as a forty-page pamphlet, the opening manifesto against the followers of the Governor-General.[62] An "Address of the Reform Association to the People of Canada" was also drawn up for publication. It came out in the *Globe* in May, where without undue restraint the editor lauded it as a State Document worthy to be bound up with Lord Durham's Report. "Less ambitious in its composition than the letters of Junius, it is not less elegant and its reasoning is greatly superior."[63] Brown even appealed to the Tories to read the Address, to forget their old monopoly of power, and go with "the thinking, sober-minded people". "We do so because in their ranks there is honour and sincerity and principle, though clouded by local prejudice and want of political knowledge."[64] Who could say fairer than that?

By now a war of words was raging between the Governor's side and Baldwin's adherents, as Metcalfe, still striving to form a viable ministry, repeatedly postponed the reassembling of parliament by proclamation—eleven times in all. The Reform Association had launched a widespread press agitation. And this, late in May, led the eminent and influential Reverend Dr. Ryerson to announce that he would take the field on the Governor's behalf through a series of letters to be published in Hugh Scobie's *British Colonist*.

Egerton Ryerson, then Principal of Victoria College, was the strongest voice in Canadian Methodism, a potent force in Canada West. A man of much ability, energy and will, he had an often aggravating zeal for setting other people right. Those who admired him beheld a fearless and far-seeing champion of causes he believed in. Those who did not, found a somewhat sanctimonious controversialist. Ryerson already had a notable public career behind him, as editor of the Methodist *Christian Guardian*, a vigorous foe of Anglican religious ascendancy, and as the leader who had helped to turn Methodist opinion away from Reform during the height of Mackenzie radicalism in the early 1830's and into paths of moderation. Now he would preach moderation again; warn the people against what he considered the dangerous extremism of the Toronto Reform Association. "In the same manner," he wrote portentously, "I warned you against the Constitutional Reform Association formed in 1834. In 1837 my warning predictions were realized to the ruin of many and the misery of thousands. What took place in 1837 was but a preface of what may be witnessed in 1847."[65]

No doubt his sincere feeling for constitutional monarchy and his strong dislike of narrow political partisanship led Ryerson to take this course once more—despite the difference between Baldwin's stand in 1844 on approved British cabinet practice and Mackenzie's sweeping demand ten years previous for elective institutions on the American model. Perhaps, also, the cordial interview held at Metcalfe's request in Kingston back in January, and the Governor's offer of the post of Superintendent of Education for Canada West, had affected Egerton's judgement as well. Not that his was simply purchased support, as Reformers subsequently alleged; for Ryerson had stipulated that, while the offer would be announced, he should not take up the post until the principles he meant to advocate on the Governor's behalf had been accepted by a parliament.[66] Nevertheless, in his own case interest and principle were obviously conjoined; and thus it was that his pontifical letters were so irritating to Reformers, in their chaste spirit of disinterested patriotism and their moral superiority to mere desire for office. They were irritating, too, because of Ryerson's wide influence—and they had to be taken very seriously. The *Globe, Examiner* and *Mirror* did so; the last particularly fiercely: "A BASE UNHOLY CAUSE IS TO BE DEFENDED BY A BASER, UNHOLIER ADVOCATE!"[67]

George Brown greeted Ryerson's first missive in the *Globe* of June 4: "The astonishing flourish of trumpets with which the mailed glove of the doughty champion of the Governor-General has been thrown down, has been followed by the reverend combatant careering into the ring. He has pushed aside with contempt the crowd of imbeciles who have hitherto guarded the prerogative at Kingston, and burst into the arena shouting: 'Ring the alarum, blow wind! come wrack, At least we'll die with harness on our back!'" The tone was bantering; but from here on Brown answered the letters with the closest attention. The note of raillery continued, however; it was an effective attack on Ryerson's rather pedantic manner of imparting knowledge to those less fortunately endowed.

Thus on June 11 the *Globe* fastened on his exposition to the unlearned as to why the ex-ministers had not been correct in the mode of their resignation. Canadians, it noted brightly, need no longer trouble with "odd, unsophisticated notions" about parliamentary control of government, when they could learn instead the most approved methods of transacting official business or retiring from a ministry. "What a benefit to a country to know the exact rule for carrying on such important operations by which light is conveyed to 'one who has little knowledge of the science of government and legislation'!" Some rustics might have thought the central point at issue was the known and practised British doctrine of responsible government. But, the *Globe* conceded gracefully, "It is well that those who have 'little knowledge' can drop such minor lights as Chatham, Temple and Granville and substitute the weighty authority of the Reverend Egerton Ryerson, Principal of Victoria College."

Yet Ryerson was plainly having his effect. Men like Isaac Buchanan were rallying to him from one side, George Duggan, prominent Toronto Orangeman and Tory M.P., from the other. A "moderate" alliance between former foes indeed was taking shape. To counteract it, the Reform Association called on one of their best polemicists, Robert Baldwin Sullivan. His penetrating wit and thorough knowledge were thrown into a series of letters in reply to Ryerson, published in the *Examiner* and *Globe* under the signature of "Legion"—for we are many. Sullivan took up the sobriquet of "Leonidas" for Ryerson (which had been applied by Brown in the *Globe*, in response to the Doctor's classical allusion to his stand at the Pass of Thermopylae)[68] and neatly pointed out that, at one and the same time, this Leonidas who announced his headship of the gallant Spartan few claimed to have the whole weight of the Empire at his back.[69] The battle of letters continued through the summer, George Brown adding his own answers in the *Globe* to those of "Legion", publishing as well the Reform Association's *Tracts for the People*, and even ascending—or descending—to poetry with the "Songs of the Moderates". The first, allegedly by Leonidas, ran in part:

> *Hurrah for political power!*
> *No matter how we may attain it.*
> *And although it may last but an hour,*
> *Stick at nothing, "my brethren" to gain it!*
> *When liberty's voted a bore,*
> *And religion an engine of State,*
> *Indulgence may enter the door,*
> *So that decency stands at the gate. . . .*
> *Oh these will be glorious times!*
> *When each one of our set is a hero,*
> *Our fame shall be blazoned in rhymes*
> *And attuned to the fiddle of Nero!*
> *Hurrah for political power!*[70]

Now it was September, and at last Metcalfe had completed a ministry, thanks largely to the success of the "moderate" tactic. At least, he had brought in the middle-of-the-road Liberal, William Morris, highly regarded among Scots Presbyterians for diligently pressing their claims against Anglican privilege, W. B. Robinson, an Anglican Conservative, D. B. Papineau, brother of the principal leader of the Lower Canadian Rebellion, who provided a largely false note of French-Canadian support, and James Smith, a Canada East nonentity who had never yet sat in parliament. But Metcalfe would not attempt to have this mixed team meet the existing Reform-dominated legislature. On September 23 he dissolved parliament, without recalling it, and writs were issued for general elections in late October.

George Brown was quickly caught up in his first Canadian election campaign. The *Globe* worked industriously for the party, running lists of approved candidates throughout the country, printing their election addresses. "Every man to his post," urged Brown. "A short, hard struggle and victory is ours."[71] He put out a stream of editorials, not only on the central constitutional issue but on other significant concerns as well: especially the university question, which the *Globe* and *Banner* had been canvassing off and on for some time now. In this regard, Baldwin the year before had introduced a bill in parliament to end Anglican control of Upper Canada's state-supported university by transferring its public endowment to a new secular institution, the University of Toronto, with which Victoria and other denominational colleges could be affiliated as divinity halls. This Bill of 1843 had been much approved by the Browns themselves, since it separated public higher education from church authority. But it had never been put to a decisive vote, because of the resignation of Baldwin and his colleagues and the prorogation that had followed. Now George Brown recalled the measure in the *Globe*. "Electors!" he proclaimed on the eve of the local contest for Toronto's two seats, "never forget that King's College will be only a hot-bed of Sectarianism unless you return Liberal members of parliament!"[72]

But this appeal and all Brown's others failed to check a Tory upsurge in the city which returned two supporters of Metcalfe. "The spirit of freedom is yet in the bud in Toronto," the *Globe* remarked tartly.[73] There were other seats to be won, however, and its editor threw himself into the task. Not only did he write, but he also travelled into neighbouring constituencies on missions for his party, and took a leading role in settling serious difficulties in the nearby county of Halton. Here three Reform candidates had put themselves forward, when only two could have the party nomination. George Brown was sent out from Toronto, along with Thomas Ewart, another speaker at the March Reform Association meeting, to bring one of the three to resign, and so avoid splitting the party vote. The most desirable candidate was John Wetenhall, Warden of Gore District. The man to remove, above all, was Caleb Hopkins, the sitting member and an old Reformer, yet one who had once been associated with radical William Lyon Mackenzie—a dangerous association in an election loud with loyalty cries. It was a ticklish mission, but it succeeded, despite Hopkins' strong local following.

Brown had gained first-hand experience of the problems of campaign management, when he afterwards reported back to Baldwin: "We had very hard work to put matters to rights in Halton, but I think we have managed it. It is unnecessary, I presume, to enter into particulars, but in a word, we found it necessary to blackball Mr. Hopkins. Not until every other measure had been tried in vain; and when at last it came to this result, the onus of throwing him overboard came not from us but from a large meeting of Reformers. We think the party is now so united on Mr. Wetenhall that he may possibly go in, in spite of Hopkins."[74] But to clinch matters he was anxious to have a conciliatory message from the leader to put before the Halton people. He sent a rough draft of one to Baldwin, which the latter accepted and sent back for distribution, with only minor amendments in Brown's judiciously worded screed.[75]

The young lieutenant was proving competent, and decidedly useful to the party. Indeed, because of his obvious talents, he had already been considered as a possible parliamentary candidate.[76] Yet he refused to stand because his journal was still too newly rooted a plant to leave in someone else's care, and because he had too many financial commitments, both to the *Globe* and to his father's debts, to turn his attention away from business.[77] He preferred to give his best to the party behind the scenes and through the pages of the *Globe*, as he worked and strove wholeheartedly throughout the heated election month of October.

So much energy expended—and yet to no avail. By early November, when election results were in, it was plain that the Reformers had suffered disaster in Canada West. They had lost severely in parliamentary seats: Francis Hincks himself had failed of re-election. In Canada East, on the other hand, the Reformers had gained a long lead, largely because the French Canadians had voted as a solid block for Reform and responsible government, which they saw essentially as a means of winning home rule for their own culture. Hence Metcalfe's new government held an over-all majority of only three supporters in the House. But that, at first, was little comfort to the crusaders of the Toronto Reform Association. What had happened in the western section? One of the answers was that their opponents' loyalty cries had worked all too well. The popular sentiment of Upper Canada had gathered strongly about the beleaguered British Governor, to meet the threat of rebels and republicans in disguise. In fact, it was reported that in some places votes had actually been cast for Metcalfe himself. The *Globe* described a conversation heard at a York county poll: "Whom do you vote for?" "I vote for the Governor-General." "There is no such candidate. Say George Duggan, you blockhead." "Oh yes, George Duggan—it's all the same thing."[8]

In any event, goaded by the disloyalty charges against them, Reformers had undoubtedly gone to foolish extremes in name-calling themselves. R. B. Sullivan's reference to Metcalfe as "Charles the Simple", when carried away by his own eloquence at a county meeting, was only one of the milder expletives used against the Governor.[9] These were boomerangs in the bitter election contests. They could be used to demonstrate that Reformers were so infatuated by a mad desire for power as to attack the very symbol of the imperial tie: that, whether they knew it or not, they were moving, as Ryerson had said, to "a practical declaration of independence".[80] Then too, antagonism to some of the measures of the late Reform ministry took a toll in Upper Canada: for instance, their act to remove the capital to Montreal in Lower Canada, or Baldwin's University Bill, to which many supporters of church colleges, otherwise Reformers, were opposed. And finally, there was the Moderates' patriotic appeal against narrow partisanship ("Loyal Hearts and Liberal Measures!") that worked to divide the Reform vote in Upper Canada—a tactic to be repeated more than once during the next three decades.

It doubtless carried away numbers that had previously added to Reform strength, aligning them instead with groups of definite Conservative or Tory sympathy. For example, though many Methodist church leaders objected to Ryerson's intervention in politics, lay opinion was inevitably influenced by the weight of his name on the Governor's side.[81] William Morris must have had a similar effect among Scots Presbyterians generally; and even staunch Free Churchmen may well have been affected by the Moderate stand of Isaac Buchanan. It was quite enough. Whatever Baldwin, Hincks, George Brown and the rest could do, a people in the majority favourable to responsible government—though as yet they did not wholly comprehend it—were, for the moment, sufficiently divided to produce a strong check to the outright advocates of that idea, and to return a loose combination of old-guard Tories, vague Conservatives and even vaguer Moderates. Three years later the election verdict would be overwhelmingly different. Brown and the *Globe* would have more than a little to do with public re-education during the interval.

6

Meanwhile what of the *Banner* and Peter Brown? They had been as actively engaged on the religious front, for the debate within Canadian Presbyterianism had finally led to the rupture of the colonial church itself. Since the middle of 1843, the two groups that had backed opposing sides in the Scottish Disruption had increasingly moved apart, and open quarrels had begun to grow between them. Then in the spring of 1844, a Free Church deputation had arrived from Scotland to explain their cause in detail and raise subscriptions for it. The mission, which included the learned and contentious Dr. Robert Burns, effectively fanned the Free Kirk flames in Canada, as they preached to Presbyterian congregations throughout the province, including the Browns' own church of St. Andrew's in Toronto.[82] Free Kirk sympathizers set up committees to receive them and to collect funds, Isaac Buchanan being named the general treasurer, while the *Banner* warmly welcomed the whole enterprise.[83]

The Church of Scotland partisans in Canada as warmly resented this Free Church intervention. Though the mission departed for the Maritime Provinces in May, it left a forest fire burning in its wake. It was plain that the approaching meeting of the Canadian Synod that summer would see a decisive struggle between the two factions. The *Banner*, in the meantime, was working as ardently against the "Residuary Church influence" as the *Globe* was against Metcalfe, and in this respect took a rather different view of Buchanan from its own political partner, treating him as a most sincere friend of the cause.[84] When the Synod met at Kingston in early July, George Brown himself went down to report it for the *Banner*, taking time off from the *Globe* and the long debate with Ryerson, for the religious question was so seriously regarded.[85] The Reverend Mr. Chalmers was there too, the Scottish Free Kirk Deputy to America.[86] The Canadian dispute was taken that seriously in Scotland as well.

The result was much the same as in the mother country. A motion in the Synod affirming a connection with the established Scottish church produced 56 in its favour, 40 against. The minority then earnestly withdrew to found the Presbyterian Church of Canada, as distinct from the "Presbyterian Church in connection with the Church of Scotland". "We rejoice," said the *Banner* simply,[87] while Isaac Buchanan wrote to William Morris, who was on the other side at Kingston, to insist that the rent in the body of Presbyterianism would be the salvation of its spirit. "This will be a great church extension."[88]

Now the work of organizing the new church proceeded. At Toronto, Peter Brown was busy supporting a Free Kirk secession from St. Andrew's that set up the new congregation of Knox Church. At Kingston, similarly, George Brown for a short time sat as a member of a committee which sought to help the seceding Presbyterian minority in that city to establish a new congregation of their own. But they found it a difficult task, because "peculiar local circumstances" made Presbyterians in the neighbourhood of Kingston strongly hostile to Free Church principles.[89] Quite probably these circumstances included the Conservative character of the Kingston Scots, whereas those in Toronto and farther west were largely Liberal in their sympathies. Kingston, moreover, was the seat of Queen's, the Presbyterian college, whose controlling clergy were strongly Church-of-Scotland in their outlook. At any rate, that eastern Upper Canadian city remained the virtual capital of the Church of Scotland, while Toronto, where Knox College was shortly established as the Free Kirk's divinity school, became the headquarters of the new church body. It was notable, too, that the Free Church made little headway among the Highland Scottish stock from Kingston eastward in Upper Canada, whereas it spread rapidly among the more recent Scottish settlers—many of them Lowlanders—from Toronto to the western extremities of the province. And in the years to come it would be notable as well that George Brown and his political associates made small inroads in Kingston and the east, even though they swept the western half of Upper Canada.

Late in the fall of 1844 Knox College opened in Toronto, and, in December, the new Knox Church on Richmond Street. A committee of the congregation that included Isaac Buchanan and Peter Brown brought the energetic Dr. Burns to return to Canada as its minister.[90] He arrived in Toronto in the spring of 1845, to become professor of theology at Knox College besides. Naturally the *Banner* was in close touch with all these developments, hailing them with the enthusiasm to be expected. That journal, however, had fallen in circulation, now that Presbyterianism had been definitely divided, even though it still had several years of life ahead of it in the service of the church which it had helped significantly to build.

Yet its interest for George Brown had passed away. The *Banner*'s secular editorials now were largely just brief reprints from the *Globe*, and frequently there were none at all. The latter journal kept up political interest sufficient for two papers, however, in no way downcast by the recent Upper Canadian election defeats. Instead, during the first session of the new parliament, which was held in Montreal from the end of November, 1844, to late March, 1845, it gleefully remarked the weakness of the ministerial ranks in the Assembly as a whole. The fact was, that after every effort, after pulling out all the stops on the antique Tory loyalty organ, and after using to the hilt the patronage instrument indignantly denied to their foes, the allies of the Governor-General had achieved an ill-assorted ministry so feeble that it could do almost nothing except manoeuvre to stay in office. The capabilities of its leader, Draper, were wasted in a fruitless effort that within three years gave him his fill of political life forever. Apologists might point to Sir Charles Metcalfe's courage and high purpose in the election struggle, to a sharply uncompromising spirit among Reform leaders, and to the understandable fears of Upper Canadians but seven years past a rebellion. Nevertheless mountainous labours had produced a very sickly government mouse. The *Globe* had little enough to dread here: merely to look for Metcalfe's replacement in due course of time, and, meanwhile, work to re-organize the Reform vote for the next election contest.

Accordingly, George Brown was busy early in 1845, warning against the "minor host called the Moderates" who claimed to offer "practical" measures, not "abstract principles" like responsible government, and who would offer half a slice of university reform in order to gain Liberal support.[91] The proper answer was that Reformers would still hold to Baldwin's University Bill of 1843, and to real responsible government, paying no heed to those who had sold out to Tories and High Churchmen. Furthermore, Brown could note with satisfaction that when Draper did introduce a compromise University measure in March, on which the ministry pledged itself to stand or fall, he let it lapse ignominiously after the second reading, rather than undergo certain defeat. The government did not resign, but its prestige was gone at the start—as both the *Globe* and *Banner* observed with relish.

7

When the summer of 1845 arrived, the *Globe* editor set off for the West—leaving Peter Brown in charge—in order to see what could be done in this promising fast-growing region to strengthen his paper and his party: to him their interests were synonymous. The West is where you find it, and for Torontonians of that era

it lay essentially in what is now the broad south-western peninsula of the Province of Ontario. Beyond, of course, stretched
the American West of the prairies, the Far West of dry plains
and mountains, of California and Oregon, and the illimitable
North West of the fur trade. But the West, pure and simple,
then lay between Toronto and Lake Huron, between Hamilton
and the Detroit River: it was that area and portion of Upper
Canada nearest to the frontier stage of settlement. Here in the
"Peninsula" Brown first came to know the people who would
give him years of political support. He learned their views and
wishes as he stayed in their squared-log cabins or proud new
frame farm-houses. He sensed the future of the rich tract of
country, even as he travelled its execrable back roads and saw
the forests still standing close about the hopeful little hamlets.
Galt, Brantford, Woodstock, London, Chatham, he grew to
know them all, and found friends everywhere, with his eager
interest in crops and improvements, his sympathy for the farmers' problems, and his lively enjoyment of their homes and
firesides.[92] George Brown, the farmer's friend, was in the making. And he was gaining a warm affection for rural life that was
his till the end of his days.

He met problems of his own, too, in the West. From the
start he had sought to circulate the *Globe* as widely as possible
among western Reformers. Yet he found that his journal faced
stiff competition here from Hincks's *Pilot*, sent all the way from
Montreal, but far cheaper in subscription because of an effective
subsidy from the party that actually allowed it to be sold below
cost. Admittedly the *Pilot* needed regular annual contributions
to keep it going. In Montreal, where the mass of the Reformers
spoke French and the mass of the English-speaking inhabitants
were Conservatives, it could hardly hope to thrive unaided,
and it was none the less important to have an English-speaking
party organ at the new seat of government. But these facts,
George Brown felt, should not justify its circulating so far west
as well at such an artificially low price. On July 10, he sent a
long letter of carefully worded protest from London, in the
heart of the Peninsula, to party leader Baldwin, reporting that
his efforts to push *Globe* subscriptions among western Reformers
had met with the reply that they had to assist the *Pilot* by dona-
tions as well as subscribe to it, and could hardly do more than
that.[93]

"Letters have been sent to the leading Reformers throughout
the West pressing them for assistance, and they are exerting
themselves to increase the circulation of that paper even at the
expense of the *Globe*, *Examiner*, *Banner* and other papers. The

great argument is:—'the *Globe* is $5, the *Pilot* is only $2. You had far better take it and save your money! It will go down if you don't.' Now Sir, I know well the great benefit which the *Pilot* confers on the Reform party, and no man in Canada would more seriously regret its going down than I would. Not only for the sake of the party, but from *self interest*. If the party thrives, the party press will at once feel the benefit of it. If it does not prosper, the press will sustain certain damage. I have therefore no *jealousy* as to the *Pilot* being sustained in this way; but I feel that in one particular, gross injustice is being done to the other Reform papers."

He went on to explain that Hincks's price of $2, or ten shillings, was far lower than anyone could charge and make ends meet. "If we had 5000 subscribers at 10/- we could not make money out of it. Now, we hardly get a subscriber who does not grumble at the price in comparison with the *Pilot*. 'Why can't you sell as cheap as Hincks?' is constantly put to us." The whole standard of value of the Upper Canadian press was being lowered, he asserted, and the effects on it would be disastrous. "The answer is clear. Let Mr. Hincks put the price of the *Pilot* at a fair rate—at a rate which will remunerate a man who earns his bread by it—and then let the party help him as much as they like. They will do no injustice to others.

"I allude to this subject with some little feeling," Brown admitted wryly. "In addition to the expediency of a newspaper editor journeying among his readers occasionally to feel the pulse of the country people, I have been *under the necessity* at present of doing so—and I confess I have felt annoyed at the half-patronizing air which I met in some localities when I only asked for the money which I had worked hard and waited long for. I think if Mr. Hincks had heard some solemn fool whispering most consequentially to me, under the strictest pledge of secrecy, that he had subscribed 5/- or 10/- to keep the *Pilot* from going down, he would think with me that the system is utterly destructive to the best interests of the press. Such creatures look on us as a better sort of paupers. A newspaper can only be of efficient service if it stands on a perfect footing of reciprocity with its readers. Value for value—and the moment the subscriber thinks he confers a favour, half its influence is gone with him."

This forthright statement of the rights and wrongs of the press gained Baldwin's prompt attention. He wrote to Brown, sending him part of a letter from Hincks in which the latter was opportunely talking of having to raise his rates, and subsequently spoke both to Brown and to Hincks besides.[94] But it is more than likely that the *Pilot*'s editor was annoyed by the incident. He was already bemoaning his paper's financial losses in the stony soil of Montreal. His complaints of losing money and of not receiving sufficient party aid grew in number and intensity over the next few years.[95] Hincks, in fact, might well have envied the *Globe*'s far more fertile environment in Canada West; and certainly a coolness, or even a distrust, grew between him and the aggressive young editor of the Toronto journal. If the direct, impetuous Brown resented Hincks's journalistic tactics, the complex, introspective Hincks suspected Brown's political intentions. But two months later, while still uncertain what to do about his paper's rates, the *Pilot*'s editor was informing Baldwin that Brown was "a thorough scoundrel", who cast greedy eyes on his, Hincks's, former seat in the Assembly, the western county of Oxford where there were many Scots and Free Churchmen, especially in the township of Zorra. "I have been much *disgusted* at recent information from Oxford. George Brown has been through exerting himself *not only against the Pilot* but against me personally. His object is to unseat me for that county and as my friends think *to substitute himself*. He proposes also to substitute Blake for you as leader. My information *can be relied on*."[96]

It is most unlikely that it could have been, if for no other reason than Brown's reluctance to seek a place in parliament, and his evident respect and admiration for Baldwin. Two years later, moreover, he would contest Oxford in Hincks's behalf, and do much to win for him in the latter's absence. And on the present occasion, when Brown heard of Hincks's suspicions, he sent him an emphatic answer direct. "As to my going into Parliament, I never for a moment harboured such a thought. I am not so vain as to think I could carry the county of Oxford. If I could, I have not an acre of land—if I had, I should not contradict the opinion I have ever had that Parliamentary honours should only be the reward of long political service. If I changed from that, I would not go into Parliament while a newspaper editor—if I overlooked that, I would not, for it would ruin my business prospects for life. And if I overcame even that, I would not—for I dislike the thing itself. So you see if you have no other opponent but your humble servant, you may sit for Oxford long enough."[97] But though the trouble was patched over, it left lasting results in suppressed hostility between the two men that affected the whole future of the Reform party.

There was another, more immediate result. George Brown decided that if he was going to make headway in the West, his best chance lay in publishing a special regional edition of his paper. That autumn, accordingly, he was in London again, making arrangements for a *Western Globe*, setting up a sub-editorial office on Ridout Street and arranging for a full supply of local correspondence to deck its pages.[98] The march of modern progress had made possible this early Canadian venture into the syndicated press. The completion of the Toronto-Hamilton plank road had so speeded communications with the London District that local reports could leave London on Monday night, be in Toronto on Tuesday, for printing by the next morning, and the completed paper could be distributed first thing Thursday "over the whole Western Country".[99] Truly a marvel of modern speed—and George Brown's enterprise. Furthermore, since there was no other Reform paper in the western districts, the new journal stood to prosper by combining authentic local flavour with a robust diet of *Globe* editorials.[100]

On October 16, 1845, the first issue of the *Western Globe*, or *London, Western and Huron District Advertiser*, reached a ready public. The *Globe*'s empire was rising. As its editor journeyed back and forth to London and beyond in search of still more business, riding the farm tracks and forest trails in that crisp, golden western fall, he could look back with pride on but two years' accomplishment in his new country. A leading Toronto newspaper, its influence spreading far to the West beyond; readers, too, eastward to the St. Lawrence and Montreal. A prominent place in the Reform party, his presence known and respected on the public platform—business growing, the family content, his father's dearest cause prospering. Definitely, his time of apprenticeship in Canada was over. As for a temporary political set-back—what of that? Only a battle still to win, for a man born to combat and full of the confidence of victory.

Party Stalwart

I

Late in 1845 it was announced that Metcalfe was leaving. He was going home to die, his life eaten away by cancer: a gallant, tragic figure, though his embittering effort at government had been all too reminiscent of the inflammatory career of Sir Francis Bond Head, the promoter of rebellion. It was a dull November Saturday when George Brown hastily brought out a *Globe* extra to celebrate the news. "We heartily congratulate the country on the departure of Lord Metcalfe," he wrote exultantly. "Out of Canada, we wish every blessing may attend him."[1] The tone was none too sympathetic, yet in fairness one might note that Brown was not aware of the fatal extent of Metcalfe's illness. Indeed, he added that if, as some asserted, the Governor's state of health was the cause of his retirement, then it was to be hoped he would recover in England—still, it was far more likely that he had been recalled for his ruinous policies. Decidedly unsympathetic, but understandably so; and really not a violent attack on the departing Governor-General. Certain Toronto Tories, however, saw fit to regard it as an outrageous slander on a great man. In fact, it almost cost George Brown membership in that august fraternity of all true Scots, Toronto's St. Andrew's Society.

That year, St. Andrew's Day, November 30, fell on a Sunday. Hence the Society met on the night of December 1, at old Government House, to hold its annual patriotic banquet. The President, Mr. Justice Maclean, a vintage Tory, was in the chair; the room seemed shining with good fellowship; and all went cheerfully until the time for the toasts of the evening. The regular round began—the Queen, the Prince Consort—the band blaring out as each was drunk by the well satisfied sons of Scotland, until the President rose to give the usual toast to the Governor-General.

Suddenly he swung into a political eulogy of the departing Metcalfe—and added a heated denial that the saviour of Empire had been recalled, "as certain persons have most *impertin-*

ently and *untruly* assumed and set forth."[2] Everyone knew who was the principal person intended. He was present, his own Scots temper quickly blazing. Amidst excited clamour, young George Brown flatly refused to drink a toast offered in this fashion, and, when the rest had done so, rose angrily from his place to crave the right of reply. "It cannot be possible—" ("Order, order." "Hear him—Chair, chair!") "I have been publicly insulted from the chair." ("Kick him out!") "I asked the simple favour to say a few words in reply. It is denied to me, and I retire from this room unheard—to the lasting disgrace of the Society and of those present—as Scotchmen!"[3]

Somewhat alarmed at this storm—as some gathered around Brown and others yelled, "You'll be put out!"—the President hurriedly ruled that any member had a right to be heard: "But all are expected to conduct themselves like gentlemen." Brown vehemently seized his chance. "I beg it may be distinctly recollected that up to this moment I have not said one word further than asking to be heard. I asked that in justice, Sir, in order that I might say a few words in reply to what fell from you in introducing the last toast. I perfectly understood your allusion, Sir, and your epithet of 'impertinent' as applied to myself. I throw it back on you with contempt—and will content myself with saying that your using such language and dragging such matters before this Society was highly improper! This is not the place to discuss Lord Metcalfe's administration. There is a wide difference of opinion on it—but I refrain from saying one word as to his conduct in this province. This is not a political but a benevolent Society, composed of persons holding every variety of political sentiment; and such a toast ought never to have been brought here. Lord Metcalfe is not now Governor-General of Canada, and I had a right to refuse to do honour to him or not as I saw fit, and that without any disparagement to my character as a gentleman—even though the person who is President of this Society thinks otherwise!"[4]

Maclean's only reply was a brief further eulogy of Metcalfe, and a rapid call for the next toast. Order returned as this was drunk, while the band doggedly played on. The affair passed off, but it was far from settled. In the next week or so the city buzzed with the story, and many professed deep shock at Brown's gratuitous insult of so elevated a personage as the Honourable Mr. Justice Maclean. But, as the *Globe* put it crisply in response, "The only apology for his conduct which his friends offer for him is that—he was *elevated*! Even that will not avail: it was only the fourth toast."[5] It went on to charge that Maclean had altered the original plan of toasts when he had heard of Metcalfe's departure. Instead of giving the ordinary health to the Governor-General (which now would have referred to the Administrator replacing him, the commander-in-chief, Lord Cathcart) he had omitted any reference to that distinguished soldier, but given the ex-Governor twice; even though the banquet managers had warned that any political allusions would only cause a commotion in the assemblage. Maclean, in short, by his unmannerly, partisan conduct had damaged not only the Society but the dignity of the Bench. "He may puff about in his official peacock's feathers, he is but a jack-daw after all, and everybody knows it."[6]

The foes of George Brown saw in these assertions against the very majesty of Justice a splendid opportunity to pass public condemnation on a bumptious and overbearing editor. They made their plans. There was an unexpectedly large turn-out at the next quarterly business meeting of the St. Andrew's Society, which was usually ill-attended. It was notable that most of these diligent members were Tories, and remarkable that friends came along with them, eager to join that night of March 1, 1846. In the absence of Brown and most of his supporters, a series of resolutions were easily put through, censuring the *Globe*'s statements, sharply characterizing their writer's conduct as "highly indecent and improper" and bringing in a motion to lay before the next general meeting that George Brown's actions were unworthy of a member of the Society—a declaration plainly calling for him to resign.[7]

But the object of censure was not ready to take these proceedings lying down. Instead, he asked for a special meeting, which was called for the evening of March 9. When it met, it was the largest the Society had ever seen, some 90 strong; and this time the Brownite faction among its members was out in force. Political allies like Morrison and Ewart spoke on his behalf. So did John McMurrich, a prominent city wholesaler whose word carried independent weight. And Brown himself made a bold and stormy speech ("I am not here to vindicate the *Globe*: the *Globe* can vindicate itself!"), urging that they should then and there vote on his worthiness for membership. Challenged thus directly, his opponents backed away from an open test of strength; though not before accusing the abstemious but not teetotal Brown of having been drunk on the fatal night. Those moderate elements who were anxious to save the Society from a deep political division contrived at last to have the entire question held over until the next regular meeting, some months away.[8] By that time, of course, it had been conveniently forgotten.

The whole affair was really a storm in a teacup; and Brown did not achieve decisive success, although he frustrated the designs against him. Still, the incident had not been without significance. For one thing, it showed what an angry political legacy Metcalfe had left behind him, when the benevolent brotherhood of St. Andrew's could erupt so strongly. For another, it displayed the undoubtedly prickly spirit of George Brown, his sharp reaction to personal affront, his insistence on having it out and settled forthwith. Some might call him stiff-necked and bellicose; others, straightforward and unflinching. Political sympathies would have much to do with the qualities selected—but surely he was a mixture of them all. In any case, the aspects of Brown revealed in the somewhat unusual transactions of the Toronto St. Andrew's Society of 1845-6 would be exhibited in far weightier personal encounters in politics to come.

After this initial skirmish, 1846 was almost a quiet year for Brown and his journal. The latter continued to thrive—became a semi-weekly in the autumn—but there were no great battles now that Metcalfe was gone. Cathcart, his successor, was obviously just a *locum tenens*, and the Conservative ministers led by Draper could only manage to survive by evading major issues. As Canadians marked time to see what changes might come with a new Governor-General, the university question, much discussed by the *Globe*, remained virtually the only active issue in the western section of the province. In February, indeed, Reformers had held a "Great King's College Meeting" in the Congregational Chapel in Toronto, with Peter Brown and his Free Kirk pastor, Dr. Burns, among the speakers.[9] The meeting had passed resolutions opposing either the continued church control of King's College or the division of its endowment between various church colleges, and upholding Baldwin's plan for one non-sectarian provincial university. The whole question came up again when parliament re-assembled that spring. Draper's compromise University Bill was re-introduced, a measure that sought to couple a secular, state-endowed teaching and examining university with church-controlled and state-aided residential colleges. This time the double opposition from friends of Baldwin's unified scheme and from the defenders of the existing Anglican King's College brought it outright defeat.[10] The government, however, had prudently declared beforehand that it would not stand committed to the Bill. Draper and Co. were glad enough to last at all through the short session, until its close in early June brought them a breathing-space once more.

Accordingly the *Globe* was almost complacent when in August it declared, "Though not in *office*, our friends have been in *power*."[11] The ministers had no bond of union, no aim but office: and to keep it, had above all been making full use of patronage on their own accord. The Reform principle once denounced as revolutionary had now become the practice of its foes. The right of the ministry to try to strengthen itself through the making of appointments, and hence to be consulted for that purpose, was now tacitly admitted. The Reformers need only hold firm. The day of a new election could not be far distant. Hopefully, eagerly, the *Globe* and its master looked forward to the reckoning.

2

As early as July, 1846, Reformers were beginning to think of elections. It was with this in mind that Hincks, ever the shrewd party strategist, wrote to Robert Baldwin, urging him to make a tour of the West to prepare foundations for the Reform reconquest of Upper Canada.[12] The next few weeks brought the news of the fall of the Conservative Peel ministry in Britain, and the beginning of a new regime at the Colonial Office under the Whig-Liberal, Earl Grey. Here was sound reason to prepare for change. The Peel government had fully backed Metcalfe, had regarded him as the preserver of imperial authority in Canada, and honoured his services with a peerage. Their Whig opponents might be expected to act differently on imperial issues, especially since they were now committed to the potent doctrine of free trade, which logically implied the lifting of old controls over colonial economic and political affairs. Moreover, Grey had certainly not approved of Metcalfe's policy, but believed instead that it had perilously entangled the Crown's representative in the antagonisms of local Canadian politics. Given a fair field and no favour, unprejudiced by the opposition of the Governor and charges of disloyalty, Reformers might reasonably hope for far better results in an election contest.

The announcement that autumn that the Earl of Elgin, an able, liberal-minded statesman, would be the next Governor-General, aroused Reform anticipations further (still more when he married Durham's daughter in November). And Elgin's first speech on his arrival in Canada led the *Globe* to remark comfortably, "There is a candour and frankness in his language which no dissembler could assume."[13] Early in 1847 he came on to tour Canada West, receiving enthusiastic welcoming addresses everywhere in his progress. The citizens of London met at the courthouse on March 4, to draw up a loyal address of their own; and George Brown was there to second its adoption.[14] Meanwhile, more business-like county Reform conventions were also being held, to draft party appeals for presentation to the electors. Again Brown was found in London, writing the manifesto of the convention for the surrounding county of Middlesex, to be published, of course, in the *Western Globe*: "Our cause is the cause of Canada, and it must prevail!"[15]

At the same time, with much foreboding, the unhappy ministerial legatees of Metcalfe were making final desperate efforts to reconstruct the government. The attempts proceeded during April and May, while the *Globe* helpfully reported every rumour of the ministry's travails. Among other things, the changes brought into the cabinet a bright young Kingston lawyer, a Church of Scotland Presbyterian and Conservative member of the Assembly. This was John A. Macdonald, the new Receiver-General, whom George Brown's journal (with singularly clouded vision) dismissed blandly as "a *harmless* man".[16] As well, Henry Sherwood, a High Tory, replaced the more moderate Draper as Attorney-General, while the latter thankfully escaped to the secure haven of the judicial bench.

The rebuilt but still shaky ministry met parliament in June of 1847. Once more it proved virtually unable to transact business. Another University Bill was introduced, this time by John A. Macdonald, making provision for the wholesale carving up of the state endowment between the church colleges, the lion's share to go to the Anglican King's. Yet the open bid to all sectarian interests did not please the Anglican Conservatives sufficiently, and outraged the Baldwin Reformers far more by abandoning any central and secular university whatsoever. Again this double opposition forced the measure to be dropped.[17] Almost at once parliament was prorogued. The intense heat in Montreal and the spread of "immigrant fever" there supplied convenient reasons—while the *Globe* swiftly announced the news "by magnetic telegraph from Prescott", in an extra of July 30 that scooped its Toronto contemporaries.

Far into the autumn, the Tory-Conservative ministers worried over their course: whether to face still another dismal session, or try to find a better parliament. Either way looked dark enough; but eventually they decided to gamble on a general election. Reports that elections were at last definitely impending appeared in the press early in November, 1847. That month, Reform preparations rose to their height. The western party leader, Baldwin, was deep in correspondence regarding the prospects of candidates in the Upper Canadian constituencies:

hearing from A. J. Fergusson, son of old Adam Fergusson, prominent Liberal, regarding his candidacy in Waterloo;[18] asking the advice of John Sandfield Macdonald in Cornwall as the chief Reform authority on the easternmost counties along the St. Lawrence;[19] and charging George Brown in London with "putting the machinery in motion" in the southwestern constituencies of Middlesex and Kent.[20]

One nagging problem was the absence of Francis Hincks, Baldwin's second-in-command in the Upper Canadian party. He was still away in Ireland, on his first visit there in fifteen years. Could he be elected for Oxford, if he did not return to Canada in time to campaign—elected for a county he had won in 1841, but had failed to carry in 1844? Baldwin even asked Sandfield Macdonald if an eastern Upper Canadian seat might be found for his colleague; for while the news was generally good for the West, it was not so good in Oxford county— "That is, not for Mr. Hincks."[21] The trouble was that Hincks had little influence with the powerful Scottish vote in Oxford, centred mainly in the townships of East and West Zorra. In fact, the numerous Free Kirk element in Zorra were not sure he was sound on the cardinal doctrine of "non-intrusion" in church and state, and feared that he would come to terms with sectarian influences in politics for the sake of office. Hincks himself had admitted early in 1847 that "an influential body" in Oxford would oppose him, but support any other Reform candidate.[22] And party friends were writing to T. S. Shenston, his chief election agent in the county, expressing their grave uneasiness as to Hincks's chances there.[23]

Baldwin passed on his own concern over Oxford to George Brown, already recognized as a knowledgeable man in the West. From his London newspaper office in the heart of the western peninsula, Brown on November 12 sent a long reply.[24] First he reported on Middlesex, where William Notman would run again. "We had a meeting of the London Central Committee on Wednesday night which went off famously. It was agreed that the hurrah system, and not the quick style of canvassing was the best, and that a mass meeting should be held at the Junction next week, and township meetings in every section of the county. I have written all the delegates, 34 in number, calling on them to form Township Committees as agreed upon at the Convention." Next he took up Kent, Middlesex's western neighbour, where Malcolm Cameron would stand, a powerful Port Sarnia lumber merchant who had been a Reform member since 1836. "From all I hear," he asserted briskly, "his Sarnia influence in the north, his stave-purchasing influence in the south, and the selfishness of Chatham and the middle townships—and their fear of Cameron as a Railroad Contractor and a probable member of the new government—will altogether secure his return."

Then George Brown turned to Oxford, on the eastern side of Middlesex. This was a ticklish problem that he was reluctant to handle because of Hincks's declared suspicions of his own intentions there, and because of his inherently strong feelings of pride. "In the circumstances," he wrote, "I think it is better that I should keep clear of Oxford entirely and if you have not already done so, perhaps you will write to parties in the county." He supplied a list of the best names; then went on anxiously: "Has Mr. Hincks left his qualification papers behind him? Will he be here in time for the election? There is an absolute necessity for some decided step being taken—if we hang fire we are lost —and I am much afraid that if the county is left to decide for itself our difficulties will be increased." Sense of urgency overcame reluctance, as he added, "Of course I am prepared to aid in any way in my power, but I will do nothing unless by the request of our friends. A tour through Zorra and a mass meeting in favour of Mr. Hincks might be of advantage just now."

He waited with concern for Baldwin's answer. But when it came he found it a typical Baldwin product, so circumspect as to be indefinite, "Scotch-fashion", really leaving the problem to his own initiative.[25] Now what to do? Brown made up his mind with a swift and characteristic snap. Remarking that "It would be absurd to risk the loss of a county like Oxford for a little petty feeling,"[26] he suggested to the Middlesex candidate, Notman, a fellow Free Church Scot, that "we should run together and see the leading folks"—and within half an hour had them both galloping up the road to Woodstock, the chief Oxford centre.[27] Brisk riding brought them to the village at eleven o'clock that night. They knocked at the doors of Hincks's main allies and fetched them yawning from their beds to a midnight meeting. Then they laid before them a proposal that someone else should run in Hincks's stead, someone loyal enough to step aside, if the absent statesman should return before the election, or to yield him the seat if elected.[28]

"They snatched at the idea," Brown reported to Baldwin the next day.[29] Robert Beattie of Toronto was proposed as the best man. "He will, of course, have all the assistance I can give him personally in Zorra, and in the *Globe* and *Banner*. Mr. Notman will also give him a hand in Zorra and he can do much." But if Beattie would not run? "It would be mere affectation in me to omit saying that my name was mentioned as the next best: that I could carry the Zorra people I think is likely; but as to the rest of the county, if I could, it could be only as Mr. Hincks's friend, and even then, I doubt it. Of course you are aware how ill situated I am to go into Parliament. Moreover, you must see how disagreeable the position would be—as a mere *locum tenens*—and for Mr. Hincks. But at the same time I go all for my party, and if my coming forward as a temporary candidate will save the county, I'll put my pride in my pocket and do a magnanimous thing—even in favour of friend Hincks." He hesitated, striving to make plain his intentions. "I hope you will not misunderstand what I say. You must know that I am not such a *fool* as to wish to go into Parliament, even for a day—much less to receive the abuse of a contest without its reward. My whole inducement will be to serve the party, and if any other man can be had, of course you will not ask me to do it." Surely nothing could be clearer than that?

Again he waited. This time Baldwin answered more definitely and fully: to propose instead that Hincks's name should still be put up as Oxford Reform candidate, but that in his absence Brown should conduct a campaign in Zorra on his behalf.[30] It was not an easy suggestion for a man of Brown's temperament to accept. Yet he did so, for the sake of the larger cause: this man so often to be charged with putting his own grievances and his personal taste for electoral triumphs ahead of everything else. As for his offer to run for Hincks, it was best to forget it, Brown told Baldwin: Hincks would not thank him. "It was an offer which tells against one's dignity sadly," he asserted wryly, "and I am as proud as my neighbours."[31]

It was still hoped that Hincks might return to Canada in time to make at least a token appearance in Oxford. Actually, he set sail for home in early December, about the same time that the election writs were issued, and was in Montreal by the 15th. But there he ran into urgent business problems that gave him little chance of reaching the western county in time to share in the campaign.[32] He sent up his qualifications to his agent, Shenston; and wrote gloomily about his prospects, noting the number of Oxford townships that he might expect to carry—"but can they *against* Zorra succeed?" His presence, Hincks declared, could do little good in any case. "It all depends on Zorra."[33]

And that must be George Brown's job. It called for all his energy, even with the help of Joseph Lesslie, brother of the owner of the *Examiner*, since besides canvassing Zorra, he had still to attend to the *Globe* and the *Western Globe*; and they, of course, were fully engaged in the wider contest for public opinion throughout Canada West. Fortunately a good deal of the newspaper affairs could be left to his father in Toronto. There his younger brother, Gordon, was also coming along usefully as an editorial assistant. And so George Brown could find the time for arduous travels on the winter roads between Toronto, London and Woodstock, for journeying up and down the iron-hard mud ruts of Zorra, to speak at hotels and inns, schools and farm-houses, or even to huddled little groups at crossroads.

Late that December it was biting cold, although there were only light falls of snow and the roads at least were clear and frozen hard for fast travel. It was a good thing, too; for on the morning of the 27th, just as Brown had returned to Toronto from attending Baldwin's own election contest in the Fourth Riding of York, he learned that he was needed back in Oxford almost at once. Hincks, it seemed, would not even be able to come up in time for the important county nominations meeting on the 28th.[34] Someone must substitute for him. At once George Brown set out with Lesslie by sleigh for Woodstock. Bundled in robes and straw, they drove the rest of that day, all night, and again the next morning, to reach Woodstock's new courthouse for the meeting at one p.m.[35] They arrived in time, to find the local magistrates presiding over some six hundred people jammed standing into an overheated room and overflowing down the stairs and out into the lobby. They heard the opposing candidates officially nominated and seconded, and make their addresses in reply. Then Hincks's name in turn was duly proposed. Brown rose to answer for him since "Mr. Hincks finds he cannot be present in this county."[36]

He spoke on Hincks's behalf for three forceful hours, despite the strain of his journey; moreover, held his audience, despite the heat and their tedious standing position. He told his father afterwards, "Some slight attempts at interruption were made, but it was merely temporary, and I must give our opponents the credit of having behaved wonderfully well for Tories!"[37] The show of hands for the rival candidates came at the close, a preliminary test considered highly indicative of ultimate results at the polls. It produced "a perfect forest" for Hincks, Brown reported happily.[38] The nominations successfully concluded, he and Lesslie took on a final round of meetings for Hincks across Zorra and into neighbouring areas: in Woodstock, Embro and Blenheim, and the centre of Nissouri—sixteen miles back, over frightful roads.[39] He managed six meetings and six long speeches in the last four days of December. The next day, on January 1, 1848, came the polls.

Their outcome was a grand majority of 384 for Hincks, and a triumphant Reform dinner for Brown and Lesslie afterwards, at Gross's Hotel in Woodstock.[40] Their work had effectively complemented that of Shenston and Hincks's other friends in the rest of the county to bring complete victory. "Zorra did nobly," a jubilant Hincks wrote to Shenston from Montreal. "I have publicly acknowledged my obligation to Messrs. Brown and Lesslie who appear to have done wonders."[41] And this success in Oxford was only one in a Reform sweep across Canada West that finally gave Baldwin's followers 26 seats to their opponents' 16. This time, the appeal of "moderates" against "extremists" had proved as hopelessly dead as the old loyalty cry. An electorate impatient with three years of havering futility had now determined to establish responsible government by returning its wholehearted advocates.

George Brown as journalist had played an important part in the victory at large, quite apart from his personal politicking in Oxford. The *Western Globe* had been the main Reform voice in the Peninsula. The *Globe* itself had devoted nearly two months to party bulletins and addresses, to long articles on the leading issues, and to producing extra copies of the paper for election meetings. Brown, for example, was writing Baldwin on December 15, "I send you 100 *Globes* to keep you going—lots of the *whole* on Friday." As for payment, he averred, "if I can get money enough to buy the paper I will run the risk. It is no time to stick on trifles."[42] Nearly 20,000 *Globe* extras were thus printed and distributed throughout Upper Canada at Brown's own expense, with the understanding that Baldwin would circularize Reformers after the election to try to raise funds to meet the sizeable cost of £200.[48]

For services thus rendered as the chief party paper in Canada West, the *Globe* would be made official Upper Canadian government organ by a new Reform administration. The winter campaign, however, had already done much for its proprietor, in making him better known than nearly any other public figure across the West and giving him valuable experience on the hustings besides. Indeed, one might almost say that George Brown had won an election before he ever stood for parliament. But there was another consequence. Gratitude is a sometime thing in politics. Once his momentary flush of joy had subsided, Francis Hincks could hardly take pleasure in the thought that he largely owed his seat to a man whom he had earlier termed "a thorough scoundrel": a party newcomer who had risen so fast; an editor whose Toronto journal, founded at the same time as his own *Pilot*, had had brilliant success, while his Montreal venture had remained on the brink of failure. Brown, for his part, could scarcely help feeling that a good deal was owed to him for swallowing his pride and successfully campaigning for his detractor—who had not even appeared in the whole election. Perhaps, too, despite his declared unwillingness to enter parliament, he felt of Hincks that there, but for the grace of George Brown, might go George Brown. At any rate, an ominous rift between two powerful party figures had not really been closed. If anything, it had been widened.

3

By mid-January, 1848, the full extent of the Reformers' triumph stood revealed: a large majority in Canada West, almost total extinction of their opponents in Canada East. The old government chose to remain in office to meet parliament in February. Thereupon it was emphatically defeated, and on March 4 gave up its rather reluctant ghost. With the new impartiality of the Governor-General, Elgin now called on the leaders of the Reform majority to form the ministry: thus giving clear and effective recognition to the principle of responsible government. Four days later the Lafontaine-Baldwin ministry was announced—Lafontaine the senior partner in the double-headed administration because he had the larger parliamentary following. It contained all the chief Reform talents; for Canada West, comprising Baldwin, Hincks, Sullivan, Price, Blake, and Malcolm Cameron. Shortly afterwards parliament was prorogued, in order to give the new cabinet time to prepare a full programme of reform legislation for its next meeting.

George Brown, of course, was not of the exalted ministerial circle. Yet he had considerable access to it, as editor of the Upper Canadian newspaper authorized to publish the government's pronouncements, charged with presenting its policies, and enjoying its printing contracts. These were useful advantages, but as official western ministerial organ the *Globe* did face a certain inevitable restriction on its freedom of expression that might in time grow irksome. The new position also brought a change in the Brown press enterprise, since the very eminence of the *Globe* placed still larger demands upon its managers. Peter and George Brown decided to cease publication of the *Banner*. On July 7, 1848, they brought it to a close, while the *Globe* explained that the elder journal was not being dropped through any lack of readers. Its circulation had actually increased in the first six months of 1848; the decision had been "a mere matter of business, chiefly connected with the editorial department of our office".[44]

There seems no reason to doubt this statement. The *Globe* by now was obviously the all-important enterprise, and its needs had to come first. They must have been particularly exacting during the hectic election period that had preceded. George Brown had then been compelled to leave the office repeatedly, for a week or more at a time; yet he had had to know that the *Globe* would go on speaking his mind while he was gone. His father understood that mind better than anyone else; but it was no easy task for a man of sixty-five to edit and manage both the powerful political journal and the church paper during any extended absence of his son. And so it was decided to furl the *Banner*, its Free Kirk mission largely realized, and to concentrate wholly on the *Globe*. Henceforth Peter Brown would devote all his effort to the latter as its deputy editor; that is, during the years of active journalism that still remained to him.

Furthermore, there was a special reason to make the change early in July of 1848, since a week or two before George Brown had received an appointment that would keep him out of Toronto for further lengthy periods at a time.[45] He had been named secretary of the commission set up by the new Reform government to inquire into the affairs of the Provincial Penitentiary at Portsmouth, just outside Kingston; and though he might return to the *Globe* office on occasion, he would have to attend the hearings in Kingston and sit with the commissioners in the capital, Montreal, while they drew up their report. There had long been signs of trouble at the penitentiary. In fact, complaints of maladministration and harsh treatment of prisoners had mounted in the press over the two preceding years, and led to the government's decision to conduct an official investigation. Brown's inclusion on the commission of inquiry was probably an acknowledgement of the *Globe*'s activity on the penitentiary question, as well as recognition of his stature in the Reform party. In any case he was very much interested, and stood prepared to give his best to the work ahead.

No doubt party bias had played some part in newspaper criticisms of the penitentiary and in the appointment of a Reform commission, since the institution was controlled by a Warden and Board of Inspectors who had been good friends of the late Tory-Conservative government. Nevertheless, it was obvious that conditions at the prison were far from satisfactory and fully justified investigation. The storm-centre there was Warden Henry Smith himself, a captious, difficult individual, to say the very least against him. His basic shortcoming was an inability to get on with immediate subordinates, which had led to constant friction, charges and countercharges, and the cleavage of the prison staff into hostile factions. This in turn had brought all sorts of evils—favouritism, intimidation and indiscipline—resulting further in the staff's neglect of duties and in waste and corruption, while the ill-regulated prisoners met with laxity at one moment and extreme severity the next.

Smith had been placed in charge when the penitentiary opened in 1835. In 1836 a series of quarrels had begun between him and his Deputy Warden, which only ended when he had his assistant removed in 1840, though the supervisory Board of Inspectors split over the decision.[46] More quarrels and exchanges of charges had followed between Smith and his next deputy, whom he also had removed in 1845.[47] By now the Warden had gained a useful parliamentary champion in his son, Henry Smith, Conservative member for Frontenac, the county surrounding Kingston. Smith Junior had originated a Penitentiary Bill, put through by the Conservative ministry in 1846, that helpfully increased the power and salary attached to the Warden's post, while decreasing those of the Deputy Warden.[48] The Board of Inspectors had taken umbrage and resigned at this, whereupon the government had obligingly set up a new Board favourable to Warden Smith.[49] And Smith, in full enjoyment of his new authority, had promoted a favourite follower to be his Deputy, replacing him as Kitchen-Keeper with a second son, Frank Smith, who happened to be available since he had not long left the post of Deputy Sheriff of the Midland District—over certain "irregularities of conduct".[50]

A number of keepers were now abruptly dismissed, while reports of mismanagement and maltreatment began to spread from Kingston. As to these reports, the records showed that the yearly rate of punishments inflicted on inmates of the prison had risen from 750 in 1843 to 3445 in 1846; and while an increase in the convict population supplied some explanation, it could not explain the further fact that punishments jumped to 6003 the next year, even though the number of convicts had remained the same.[51] As many as thirty or forty men and women were now being flogged each morning.[52] Even a supposedly hard pioneer age could find that excessive. Furthermore, Kitchen-Keeper Smith, an unlikeable lad, was not only running an open market in prison stores, but was indulging in pranks such as sticking pins in prisoners, pelting them with potatoes and stones, and using them as targets for archery practice with blunt arrows, through which one convict lost an eye.[53]

But the episode which finally took the lid off at the penitentiary was the Warden's ill-advised quarrel with James Sampson, M.D., a bluff, strong-minded, hot-tempered Irishman, a former British Army surgeon who would become first Dean of Queen's Medical School and a founder of Kingston General Hospital. As the prison doctor, Sampson had medical authority over the convicts which the Warden could not override. Clashes inevitably occurred, but came to a head in October, 1847, when the Doctor complained to the Board of Inspectors regarding Kitchen-Keeper Smith's abuse of prisoners.[54] The Warden's faithful Board found no grounds for the complaint, however, whereon Sampson forwarded it to the provincial government. In the meantime there were more dismissals of keepers who had backed up the Doctor; and quarrels as well over prisoners whom he pronounced insane and unfit for punishment, while the Warden in his wisdom deemed them to be shamming. Finally, in February, 1848, with Smith's connivance, a prison matron accused Sampson of "improper conduct" with female convicts, furnishing details in stiffly suggestive Victorian terms that left little to the imagination.[55] Fiercely resenting this infamous slur on his character, the Doctor communicated directly with the Governor-General, rejecting any further Board inquiry and demanding a full-dress, outside investigation of penitentiary conditions—while the Board for its part diligently transmitted evidence against him.[56]

This, then, was the chaotic situation which the Lafontaine-Baldwin government faced at Kingston on assuming office. Given the public unrest over the penitentiary, there was no doubt that they would soon comply with Dr. Sampson's strenuous demand. They moved to organize a Commission of Inquiry: composed of Adam Fergusson as Chairman, an elderly, wealthy and highly reputable Reform member of the Legislative Council, Narcisse Amiot, a Montreal barrister and justice of the peace, Cartwright Thomas, the Sheriff of the Gore District, William Bristow, the editor of the Montreal *Times*, which had first exposed "the atrocious usage of the unhappy inmates",[57] and George Brown—in what he quickly made the key position of Secretary.

The Commission were broadly instructed to examine the past management of the penitentiary and report their findings; and further, to recommend changes in the penal system. Towards the end of June they opened their proceedings at the Kingston courthouse. George Brown was there, of course. The party journalist faced a new kind of task in the service of the government, one that called forth administrative ability and powers of

constructive suggestion which as yet he had had little opportunity to display.

4

The Commissioners began with preliminary public hearings
at 10 a.m. daily in the City Hall, to which they invited anyone
with complaints or information to present, from the Roman
Catholic Bishop of Kingston to the editor of the local *Chronicle*
and *News*.[58] As well, they interviewed the Board of Inspectors,
the Warden, other members of the prison staff, and even some
of the convicts. Then they removed to the privacy of a suite in
Kingston's best hotel, the British American, drew up a regular
list of charges, and began taking sworn evidence upon them.
From the start Mr. Secretary Brown was busily occupied, writing late into the hot summer night upstairs at the British American, transcribing information and framing charges for the Commission to pass on before their presentation at the formal exam-
inations, to be held *in camera*.

They had carefully decided on procedure for these vital private sessions. Anyone involved in the list of accusations would
be presented well in advance of his hearing with a copy of all
testimony for and against him, in order to give him an ample
opportunity to have witnesses recalled for cross-examination or
to summon more in his own behalf. It was a time-consuming
method, but it enabled considered defences to be prepared;
even though political foes would later charge that the Commission had been unjust and peremptory in its procedure. The first
case of importance was that of Kitchen-Keeper Frank Smith.
But when that high-minded worthy was presented with a set of
charges, he refused to meet them and resigned his post indignantly—far too proud to brook examination.[59] Then, as for Dr.
Sampson's alleged carryings-on, the matron who had accused
him now withdrew the charge and gave very different evidence,
admitting that Smith and his wife had pressed her into it.[60] The
keepers were next examined. Several who had been recently
dismissed were reinstated; for of ten who had supported Dr.
Sampson's protests against Kitchen-Keeper Smith, the Warden
had had five removed, reported three, and brought one to
resign.[61]

Yet the chief problem was obviously the conduct of Warden
Smith himself. Early in September, Brown sent him 301 pages

of copiously documented charges, while the Commission adjourned to allow him time to prepare his defence. When they reassembled on the 29th, however, the Warden sought another month's postponement, claiming that he needed further time to arrange for legal counsel.[62] With some sign of impatience the Secretary answered for the Commissioners, "As a large proportion of the charges rest on evidence of parties on the spot, or upon books and papers in your possession, they cannot see why you should require twenty-nine days before entering your defence. The Commissioners are still more at a loss to know in what way legal advice can be necessary to you in answering truly questions of fact."[63] Nevertheless, Brown added, to avoid any appearance of pressing him they would give him until October 9 before calling for his defence.

They would also permit him to bring his son, Henry Smith, Junior, to the hearings to advise and keep his own record, although he was not to serve in his professional capacity of lawyer.[64] But when the sessions at last got under way on October 9, the Warden introduced a long written protest against the whole proceedings, stating in part that the evidence against him was drawn from witnesses personally hostile to him, and many of them convicts with desires for revenge. Convict testimony would only be used for corroboration, replied the Commissioners; no charge would be established by it alone.[65] Yet from the Warden's protest would spring another accusation to be freely purveyed, in future, against the whole inquiry: that its findings were based on the words of convicted criminals; a claim as sweeping as it was unfair.

For three weeks Smith's defence went forward, through increasingly stormy sessions in the crowded second-floor corner suite of the British American that had been rechristened "the Commission Rooms". Brown in particular waded into the cross-examinations, while his colleagues about the long table blinked and nodded sagely. His pressing manner, and his habit of tracing out each detail in order to reason from it, soon reduced the unhappy Warden to a mass of confused admissions, damaging retractions and total exasperation. At last Smith sought a second lengthy postponement. He was reluctantly awarded another week. For the Commissioners were uneasy over these delaying tactics, chiefly because of the unsettled state of the penitentiary, where the Warden and his partisans were actively spreading reports that the inquiry would eventually blow itself out, leaving the old captain still in command to reward and punish. Hence Chairman Adam Fergusson wrote to Robert Baldwin to announce that it was clear that the prison management had been "vicious and unsuccessful", and to urge that the government earnestly consider the necessity of replacing Smith.[66]

The government, however, hesitated to make a possible martyr out of the Warden. His defence was resumed on November 6; but new trouble soon arose. He demoted two gate-keepers who had testified against him, despite the pledge he had made not to interfere with anyone giving evidence. At this Fergusson requested the government to support the reinstatement of the guards and the suspension of Smith.[67] Furthermore, the Chairman had the latter removed from his comfortable quarters within the prison, as the only way to ensure independent testimony from other members of the prison staff.[68] This time the government agreed. On November 19 they sent a temporary Warden, D. A. Macdonell, who later became Smith's permanent replacement.

George Brown was not on hand for this critical development, also the source of later attacks: of charges of Commission tyranny, and heart-rending pictures of white-haired Warden Smith wandering homeless in the snow. On November 6 he had left with his fellow-Commissioner, Bristow, to visit American penal institutions and gather information on changes that might be recommended in the Canadian prison system.[69] It was an extensive tour that took him to Albany, Boston, New York, and as far south as Washington. He inspected the Capitol critically, studied the mysteries of the "congregate" and "separate" types of prison, and returned to Kingston, brimful of information, on December 10.

There he found Smith still vigorously defending. In fact, the hearings went on with little pause throughout December and into the new year, 1849. Then on January 19 the embattled Warden tried a new tack. He asked that Mr. Secretary Brown himself be sworn in, and when that was done, sharply questioned him on the manner in which the Commission evidence had been collected and presented. Brown answered coolly; but Smith went on to imply that the testimony against him had been inaccurately or even falsely drawn. He launched a fierce personal onslaught on the man he evidently regarded as his chief tormentor. "Quite irrelevant," exclaimed Chairman Adam Fergusson, calling him to order. The Warden was furious. He would not continue. Emphatically he closed his defence, and stamped out vowing "to apply to another quarter" for the justice denied him; yes, to parliament itself.[70] One may understand his anger, but after reading the closely documented record can scarcely help but conclude that here was an application of that fine old legal dictum, "No case—abuse the plaintiff's attorney."

Now as the Commission retired to the government offices in Montreal to deliberate on their findings, the testimony against the Warden seemed overwhelming. The penitentiary's own records alone spoke volumes, even if other evidence were dismissed. But judging from the total mass that had been gathered, the Commissioners found every charge against Smith substantiated: from neglect of duty and palpable favouritism, to keeping inaccurate accounts (never balanced since the penitentiary opened) and to buying his private carriages at the penitentiary's expense.[71] Needless to say, they recommended his permanent removal.

But the gravest charges against the Warden concerned the maltreatment of prisoners, ultimately his full responsibility, and again well documented by the prison books. There were revelations of rations largely composed of stinking, maggoty meat and wet, mouldy bread; rations still so inadequate that half-starved convicts had stolen the kennel bones or eaten from the hog troughs.[72] There were long lists of punishments so excessive that one prisoner had received 168 lashes in twenty-eight days and others had been goaded into insanity, one following six years of 216 applications of the rawhide and 966 of the cat-o'-nine-tails.[73] And there were records of punishments so brutal that a boy convict of ten had received six lashes for laughing, twelve for whistling and twelve more for turning round at the table, while an incorrigible monster aged eight had earned the lash, solitary confinement and the dread "box"—a veritable coffin for the living—for such high crimes as staring, shouting in his cell, and losing his handkerchief.[74]

"We can only regard this as a case of barbarity disgraceful to humanity," Brown wrote forcefully, as he settled down at Montreal to the Secretary's task of drafting the Commission report.[75] "Most frightful oppression—revolting inhumanity": phrases like these came burning from his pen. Indeed, they did the document credit, for the state of the penitentiary was a reproach to the whole Canadian people. He prepared a second report besides, covering the changes to be recommended in the penal system. Its proposals are far from new today, but when George Brown set them forth they represented a long leap forward in penal practice.

"In Canada," he noted, "little progress has been made towards introducing the ameliorations and improvements which the wisdom and philanthropy of other countries have tested and approved."[76] First offenders were mixed with hardened criminals. There was no separate provision for juvenile prisoners, treated at the penitentiary as the confirmed evil-doers they would almost certainly become. There was only one institution whose supposed aim was reformation, and "the little success" of this, the Provincial Penitentiary, was all too evident. The only attitude there had been was one of detention and punishment—"physical force alone has been kept in view".[77] Yet, "the great object of all penal institutions is the prevention of crime", and that demanded the reclamation of criminals wherever possible, through using the minimum amount of force and making every attempt at rehabilitation.[78]

With this in view, the Secretary outlined plan after plan. "Houses of refuge", projects designed to rescue juvenile offenders, classification of convicts, to prevent contamination by confirmed criminals; the closing of the penitentiary to casual visitors, where prisoners had been on public view like so many beasts in a zoo; a plan of after-care (well in advance of the age), because so many discharged convicts were driven back to crime through harshness, poverty and despair; and the appointment of permanent, salaried government inspectors, since the unpaid amateur Board at Kingston had performed so badly. All in all, Brown's second report stood as a milestone in Canadian penology, even though most of its bold recommendations would wait long years for implementation.[79]

Nevertheless, the Commission's work at the penitentiary was far from wasted. It resulted in a sharp decline in corporal punishments, efficient administration under the new Warden, and the elimination of laxity and waste.[80] Moreover, it led to legislation in 1851 establishing permanent salaried inspectors. In any event, when George Brown at last finished his writing in mid-April of 1849, and passed the final report to the other Commissioners to sign, he had good cause to feel satisfied with three busy months of literary effort and the six months spent on the inquiry beforehand. But he was quite wrong if he thought his part in the penitentiary question was concluded. Not five years, or ten, would see the end of it.

For ex-Warden Smith was far from finished. Even before the official reports had been drafted he had taken his cause to a friend of the family, the former Conservative Receiver-General and the member for Kingston, John A. Macdonald. From January on, Smith had bombarded him with letters chiefly denouncing Brown and Bristow as "errant scoundrels" [sic] and "unblushing liars", accusing the former of everything from personal vilification and re-writing evidence to exhibiting anti-Catholic bias and running up "enormous" postal bills as Secretary.[81] He also prepared a lengthy refutation of the charges against him, and submitted a memorial to the government. But his chief hope lay in Macdonald, who conceivably could bring other Conservative members as well to take up the Commission proceedings in parliament.

Macdonald was interested. The Smiths, father and son, were good friends, Kingston affairs were his special concern, and he readily came to the conclusion that the inquiry had been unjustly handled. Undoubtedly it had not been conducted according to the legal forms followed at courts: they had not been considered necessary where questions of law were not involved. Undoubtedly too, George Brown, for his part, had shown impatience during Smith's delayed defence, and at the same time, feeling certain of the Warden's culpability, had worked to pile up overwhelming evidence against him. Here Brown had revealed a congenital flaw in his own make-up: a propensity, once convinced of a case, to shut his ears to anything against it, and to push his views so hard that he might actually weaken sound arguments by making them seem extreme and arbitrary. Yet in this instance, whether or not prejudice had influenced Brown's course against the Warden—and whether or not the latter was as black as painted in the Commission's report—there were plain and plentiful matters of record to make clear the shocking state of the penitentiary under Smith's administration. But Macdonald had a trait somewhat comparable with Brown's: at times forgotten, while the other's is remembered. He too could shut his ears firmly to inconvenient arguments, letting himself be ruled by feelings and intuitions, especially if a friend were involved. Wholly ignoring the facts of Smith's disreputable regime, Macdonald saw only the presumed faults in the Commission's proceedings, and the dominant role played there by George Brown. And he quickly convinced himself that Brown was chiefly responsible for a malicious persecution, based on wilfully distorted evidence.

For the present, nothing much happened. In the parliamentary session that began in January, 1849, issues of far greater moment soon pushed the penitentiary question aside, and Macdonald did not press Smith's cause. But he did not abandon it, and would bring it up repeatedly at future sessions. In the back of his mind his largely emotional conviction persisted against Smith's most outspoken opponent. It would bring him ultimately to make violent personal charges against Brown in parliament, never retracted, which the latter in turn could never forget. None of this could be foreseen in 1849. At that time, for Brown, the penitentiary inquiry had chiefly meant another successful episode in an advancing public career, and a useful contribution made to penal reform. Yet from it would spring one of the most significant forces in his life: the deep-seated personal enmity between John A. Macdonald and himself.

5

The hard-worked and turbulent parliamentary session of 1849 had opened in Montreal on January 19, two weeks before Brown came down from Kingston to begin writing his reports.[82] From the Commission offices close by, he no doubt found time to visit the Assembly chamber, to watch the progress of the impressive budget of reforms that the Lafontaine-Baldwin ministry had constructed for this, their year of greatest achievement. There was Baldwin's new University Act, for instance, whose passage Brown would observe with particular approval, since it embodied the principle of the separation of church and state that was basic in both his political and religious opinions. The Act finally replaced the Anglican-dominated King's College with a wholly secular University of Toronto, endowed with the public funds that King's had enjoyed. In short, it realized Reformers' demands that the state university of Canada West should be non-denominational, and that public money for university support should not be divided up among church colleges. Yet if George were pleased with this successful ending to a Reform campaign second only in importance to that for responsible government, he could be sure that his father would be even more delighted: after the years that Peter had spent on the *Banner* arguing for a public university free from sectarian influences, one which left religious matters wholly to the churches that men joined according to their own freedom of conscience.

Another government measure, however, was causing far more popular excitement—rousing Tory-Conservative members of parliament to fierce oratory and angry denunciations that must have made Brown clutch at the railing of the press gallery, and long to join in the hot debate on the Assembly floor below. This was the Rebellion Losses Bill, introduced by Lafontaine to compensate those who had suffered damages in the Lower Canadian Rebellion of 1837. Payment for losses in the Upper Canadian rising had been arranged as long ago as 1840 and 1842; the measure for Lower Canada had largely been forecast by a commission appointed by the late Tory ministers themselves, to consider the indemnity that would be needed here as well. As Lord Elgin reported, it was "nothing more than a strict logical following out of their own acts . . . though now they tell us they never intended to go further".[83]

But things were different now. The Tories were out of office, embittered by their weakness in the House, their traditional anti-French prejudices stimulated by the triumphant power of Lafontaine's massed French-Canadian following. The trouble was, moreover, that any attempt to pay Lower Canadian losses was bound to bring in the bedevilling factor of "French" *versus* "English" in Canada. The damages incurred in Lower Canada had generally involved the activities of English-speaking regulars and militia in suppressing rebellion among French-speaking inhabitants; and thanks to the *nationaliste* colour of that insurrection, it had apparently attracted wider support, or at least sympathy, from the French-Canadian population than had Mackenzie's corresponding movement from the people of Upper Canada. Consequently it was possible for Tories to invoke the old sweeping charge of French-Canadian disloyalty, to raise again their vehement anti-French cries, and to assert that the broad compensation offered by Lafontaine's bill really concealed payments to rebel sympathizers and actual enemies of British rule. This would be the veritable rewarding of treason!

Yet the French-Canadian majority, at last in control of their own section of the country, were determined to right the wrongs of what they deemed the racial persecution of 1837-8. They would bar from compensation only those actually convicted by the courts or banished from the country. Given a need to meet damages in Lower Canada no less than Upper, the real root of the difficulty lay not so much in the bill to achieve that end as in the nature of the eastern rebellion itself. But in any case, the rebellion accounts had to be closed if a deep-seated sore in the Canadian body politic were ever to be healed.

That was the crux of the *Globe*'s own defence of the Rebellion Losses Bill before a troubled Canada West: that it was necessary to bring concord to Canada, and that simple justice required an act of indemnification for Lower Canada no less than for Upper.[84] Brown himself had no love for the measure as it was drafted, but he feared far worse without it. He was well aware that the rebellion's chief leader, Louis Joseph Papineau, who had now been allowed to return to Canada, was actively striving to promote a new French-Canadian radical and *nationaliste* movement, soon dubbed the *Parti Rouge*, hostile to mere responsible government and friendly to outright republicanism. Failure to meet French Canada's grievance might give him disastrous power. "Depend upon it," Brown wrote afterwards about the Bill, "there was not one of the Upper

Canadian ministry in favour of paying rebels. It is true they did not speak out against it as fiercely as their opponents—but how could they? They would only have flung strength into the hands of Papineau and raised a conflagration which no true friend of the country would have desired to see. Depend upon it, they acted right throughout."[85]

At any rate, whatever the horror with which Tory-Conservatives greeted the indemnification of traitors—and French traitors at that—the Rebellion Losses Bill was introduced by a responsible ministry and passed by a thumping majority, which included a majority of the Canada West members themselves.[86] Yet in response, Tory defenders of British constitutionalism and the forces of order evinced a notable disregard for constitutional processes, and showed an angry readiness to riot. In Toronto, for instance, while Brown was still absent, a vehement Tory mob that included two city aldermen gathered on the night of March 22 to burn effigies of Baldwin and Blake in front of the former's home.[87] Yelling and cursing, they went on to burn another of William Lyon Mackenzie, who had also been permitted to return to Canada, in front of the house where he was staying. They attacked and stoned the residence, and that of Dr. Rolph as well, Mackenzie's associate as leader of the radicals of '37. Then the bold company marched off to recognize the importance of George Brown in the current Reform party, and the influence of the *Globe* in supporting the Rebellion Losses Bill. For half an hour after midnight they howled outside the Browns' home, and battered away at the door. Its strength withstood them; but the bricks they heaved broke through the bolted shutters and smashed windows, before the mob's fire was finally exhausted, and it sullenly withdrew.[88]

Meanwhile in Montreal, though the hated Bill had passed the legislature, the Tories still looked hopefully to the Governor-General to veto or reserve it, after the fashion of his predecessors who had stood by the Crown's true friends and self-appointed guardians of loyalty. Yet Elgin firmly applied the new rules of responsible government. He signed the measure advised by his cabinet and fully endorsed by parliament. Then Tory partisans in the capital exploded into fury. On April 25, when it was known that the Governor-General had accepted the Rebellion Losses Bill, a wave of riot and destruction swept through Montreal; and that night the Parliament Buildings flamed into a wild sky. Once more George Brown missed the savage spectacle. He was back in Toronto now, taking full control of the *Globe*, his work on the Penitentiary Commission concluded. There, however, on May 2, he could witness a milder

Toronto version of the week-long anti-Elgin, anti-Reform and anti-French disorders in Montreal. A noisy, seething multitude gathered in the St. Lawrence Market to burn Elgin in effigy— the standard no-confidence motion of the mob. Alderman Beard presided over the local demonstration, as Tory civic magistrates looked on in an attempt to suggest that the whole city supported the fiery condemnation of the Governor-General.[89] One might think they would have seen enough of blazes: St. James' Cathedral and the old City Hall nearby had both burned down in a mammoth fire of less than a month before.

Brown answered in the best way he could, through the *Globe*, fervently defending Elgin against the "gross violence" and "political knavery" of his foes, drumming up support for addresses of loyalty both in Toronto and throughout Canada West.[90] Above all, he lauded the Governor-General for courageously upholding responsible government, and stressed as hard as he could that the real issues at stake in the turmoil over the Bill were now no less than constitutional rule and colonial self-government themselves.[91] It was an index of the power of his efforts that he was one of three Reformers chosen to present a general address of support to Elgin from the party in Canada West. With W. P. Howland, wealthy Liberal Toronto business man, and Colonel C. T. Baldwin, veteran of the Peninsula Wars and defender of the frontier in the troubles of '37, Brown journeyed to Monklands, the Governor's residence outside Montreal, where the beleaguered Elgin was so affected by their message of confidence that he was moved to tears.[92]

Meanwhile Tory rage was ineffectually wearing itself out. Peace was apparently restored before parliament, now wanly sheltering in Bonsecours Market, was prorogued late in May. Brown himself was soon confident that the time of troubles, of "racial" conflict, was over. "It appears to me," he hazarded optimistically, "that now responsible government is fairly admitted and in practice our *bitter* opposition is past—and with it these periodic political convulsions from which the country has so often suffered."[93] He proved a poor prophet.

6

Violent anger might have passed, but a black bitterness remained with Tory-Conservatives that still threatened to drive them to extremes. It was bad enough that their whole pattern of politics

had been overturned by responsible government, now that the
Governor would no longer heed his loyal champions against
the will of a mere majority, now that half the country was controlled by a hostile French-Canadian block which they saw small
hope of cracking. Worse still, the whole protective commercial
system, within which this strongly mercantile element had
thrived, had been destroyed by Britain's adoption of free trade.
Almost overnight the imperial preferences on colonial grain and
timber had been abolished. Canadian merchants had been flung
out of the cosy warmth of the old colonial system to face the
bleakness of open competition for the British market—and this
in the depths of one of the worst trade depressions Canada had
ever yet encountered.

No doubt the onset of depression had helped Reformers defeat the former Tory regime in 1847, thanks to the ancient
inference that when times are bad, the government is to blame.
Now this same kind of reasoning convinced Tories that the
imperial government's adopting of free trade was itself responsible for Canada's prostration. Britain had both abandoned them
politically and ruined them financially. Smarting over the Rebellion Losses Bill, desperate over the state of commerce, some
of them came up with an answer that confounded all past Tory
tradition: nothing less than annexation to the United States.
But bred as they were to dependence and reliance on the protected market, they could see their sole haven of security behind
the American tariff wall. If this required Canada's political ab-
sorption, it only served Britain right. Scorned loyalists too may
have a fury all their own.

On the whole, the Tories of Canada East succumbed to annexation far more readily than their western comrades. Perhaps
the latter had less bread and butter in their loyalty; and, being
further from the new power of the erstwhile subordinated
French, they felt less need to yield British allegiance in order to
ensure English-speaking supremacy. Canada West Conservatives rather emphasized a return to the principle of tariff protection as the answer to the country's problems. Yet generally
Tories and Conservatives everywhere agreed that something
decisive had to be done. To plan it, the British American League
rapidly took shape in the summer of 1849. Some Reformers
joined the League, themselves distressed over the impact of free
trade. But it was overwhelmingly Tory-Conservative in composition, and in Canada East strongly tinctured with annexationism
besides.[94] Thus the League became an attempt of shattered
Toryism to reconstitute itself on the basis of some wholly new
political programme. And if that programme should be annexa-

tion—then past party conflict in Canada would be dwarfed by that to come.

George Brown watched closely, as League activities mounted in that sultry, feverish, and fever-ridden summer. He had already declared to Baldwin earlier, in a somewhat involved metaphor, "The Tory Party is annihilated, but the atoms of its remains are to the fore, and their very prostration is favourable to their forming new combinations which the fortunes of war may render expedient. They are unscrupulous enough for anything."[95] In every way the League agitation urged him to resistance: as editor of the government organ, charged with combating the party enemy in the realm of public opinion, as a consistent defender of the superiority of British institutions over American republicanism, and as a profound believer in the free-trade doctrines taught by British economic Liberals from Adam Smith to Richard Cobden.

On occasion he left his editorial post to share in some precautionary Reform fence-mending. He spoke at party gatherings at Guelph in June and Brantford in July, and at the former seized the opportunity in replying to the toast, "George Brown Esq., and the Liberal Press of Canada", to make a lengthy defence of Elgin and the cabinet's policies.[96] But on the whole he gave his best efforts to the *Globe* office. There he worked long hours, preparing refutations of the out-of-date fallacies of Tory protectionists on the one hand; telling annexationists, on the other, that the reciprocity negotiations that had been begun with the United States offered the true solution, since the very extension of the noble principle of free trade to Canadian-American commerce would give them the new markets that they sought without the political suicide that they contemplated.

Brown's chief concern, however, was the threat of annexation in the League. The very idea was anathema to him. Tories had "gone demented", he asserted in the *Globe* of June 20, were raving against free trade, responsible government, and French domination, with awful threats of what they, "the Anglo Saxons", would do. He was confident that even so, "a large and respectable portion of Conservatism" would not knowingly support the breaking of the British tie. Yet the "insidious manoeuvres of the League wirepullers" might bring them to it, for "there is but one object in view—annexation". As well he ridiculed League appeals to racial feeling, the fearful Tory outcries against a French minority who asked only to be treated equitably and left in enjoyment of their own ways. After the Toronto branch had met at the local *Dog and Duck* tavern to urge the need of defending English rights against dominant

French power, they were henceforth "the Dog and Duck Anglo-Saxons, gathering in their might".[97] Later, when the Tory Cobourg *Star* was carried away to greet Leaguemen as, "Hearts formed of fire, children of the sun", Brown gained another useful epithet for sunshine Tory loyalists. Now his *Globe* references typically began, "Mr. Gamble, a Child of the Sun . . .".[98]

Still, annexationism seemed steadily advancing in Tory ranks, especially after a party deputation to England to seek the overthrow of the Rebellion Losses Act met with decisive rebuff from the Imperial Government and Parliament. A number of Conservative papers, notably in Montreal, declared openly for annexation, while others, including Toronto's good grey *British Colonist*, hinted darkly at almost inevitable separation from the Empire.[99] This, then, was the ominous background of the grand convention of the British American League that opened in Kingston on July 25, to lay down a future course for Canada.

Yet besides annexationists, Dog-and-Duck racialists, unhappy Orangemen, and simple enemies of the Rebellion Losses Act, the Kingston gathering contained advocates of protection, those who proposed the unconservative-sounding remedy of elective institutions in place of responsible government, and even some prepared to urge a union of all the British North American colonies.[100] And as reports came from its meetings, George Brown was glad to see that annexationism was evidently only strong among the Lower Canadian Tories, who were much in the minority in the whole party. The larger part of the delegates, he was pleased to announce, "were anxious only to make a working political party, ashamed of past violence".[101]

The resolutions finally adopted by the gathering showed him indeed that cooler heads had prevailed among the Children of the Sun. They called merely for retrenchment, a Canadian protective tariff, and a committee to explore the possibility of forming a federal union of the British colonies. Brown was relieved; but scorned "the three small babes of which the League was delivered".[102] No one opposed retrenchment, he asserted; the protection plank was only too typical of "the old fogies of the Conservative party";[103] and while federation might be the best plan, "when the British American colonies become big enough and ugly enough to take care of themselves", it had no reality now.[104]

In later years Conservatives would trace the lineage of Confederation back to the League's resolution to investigate the prospects of federal union. But their long subsequent disinterest in the subject made clear that the resolve of 1849 was little more than a pious wish towards a union that many Canadians of various political shades looked for in the future. For that matter, the *Globe* itself had devoted several long articles in the two years preceding to British American union, federal or otherwise, and had generally concluded that the question had little meaning for the present.[105] In 1849, who could say it was wrong? At any rate, after much annexation puffing, the League had made its harmless declaration, had let off Tory steam—and thereafter rapidly lost its force. By early September, Brown could apparently afford to be lighthearted, when he suggested that, really, the United States might prefer to join Canada were it not for the Tories: "for few men in their senses would choose to be annexed to them".[106]

7

He soon discovered that while the League had proved innocuous, the annexation question was far from closed. Though the Tory-Conservative party had generally evaded the danger, annexationism still lived on amidst disgruntled Lower Canadian Tories and among a sprinkling in Upper Canada. It appealed to radical elements in both sections of the province, moreover: there was yet a possibility that both ends of the political scale might combine against the middle. There were those on the left wing of the Reform party who were already dissatisfied with the achievement of responsible cabinet government, who wished to go well beyond it to establish fully democratic institutions in Canada. And some of these, again, now felt that since the middle-of-the-road Liberal ministers were no more likely to grant fundamental reform than their Tory predecessors, annexation to the United States might offer the shortest and simplest way to complete elective democracy. Still further, the continued economic problem and the persistent unrest among the commercial class in Canada East seemed to give extremist elements good opportunity for pressing forward with their own designs.[107]

In consequence, George Brown had to recognize that annexation was not just a fancy of defeated Toryism. It might also cut deep into his own party. As it finally turned out, while numbers of left-wing Reformers expressed strong impatience with the Lafontaine-Baldwin ministry, few of them, at least in Canada West, were really prepared to go to the extent of annexation.[108] But in the autumn of 1849 it was too early to tell how far that project might appeal to restless Upper Canadian Reformers. Hence Brown soon felt called upon to open a second front in the anti-annexation campaign, directing the *Globe* against his own party's far left as well as against the Tories. This looked all the more gravely necessary in October, by which time annexationism was rising to a new peak.

The *Globe* editor now saw an annexationist newspaper, the *Canadian Independent*, trumpeting the doctrine in Toronto, where, moreover, a major left-wing journal like the Toronto *Examiner* was far from unfriendly to the general idea.[109] He knew that in Montreal an Annexation Association was taking form, its membership not only drawn from commercial Tories but also attracting some advanced Liberals like his own friend, Luther Holton.[110] He knew as well that the *Rouges*, the small but ardent group of young French radicals associated with Papineau, had declared for wholesale democracy and annexation through their own fiery organ, *L'Avenir*.[111] And in Upper Canada it was rumoured that Peter Perry, a strong Reform candidate in the coming by-election in the Third Riding of York, was himself an annexationist.[112] The government leaders were seriously worried. George Brown was worried himself. Baldwin, Hincks, and Brown through the *Globe*, all did their best to bring Perry to disavow annexation.[113] At length the candidate did announce that he would not advocate that measure if elected, although he would still consider it Canada's ultimate destiny.[114] Thus the public turmoil of an annexationist election campaign was avoided at this dangerous moment. Yet the pressures applied by the ministry and its organ did nothing to mollify radical opinion.

In the meantime, while Perry was being brought to order, critical news had reached the *Globe* office. On October 13, the annexationists of Montreal had issued a resounding manifesto calling for union with the United States: a document that soon had over a thousand signatures, most of them city business men and Tories. The issue was fairly joined. Brown furiously propelled himself into it. Amid a furore of press arguments for and against the Annexation Manifesto, the preparation of anti-annexation circulars, and a veritable contest to pile up names on either side, the *Globe* thundered out attacks on the Manifesto —"another piece of Montreal madness"—and rang with calls to sign the Toronto anti-annexation protest.[115] A copy lay available for signature at any hour in its office. It announced a steadily lengthening list of names, and soon could eagerly point out that even in Montreal the anti-annexation signatures far outnumbered those on the other side.[116]

Beyond that, the *Globe* editor seized the Annexation Manifesto and ripped its arguments in all directions. Its black picture of ruin and decay in Canada was "a ridiculous caricature".[117] Its authors saw only the temporary set-backs and wholly ignored the great facts of permanent progress. In any case, the Canadian financial failures so gloomily depicted in the document had far more spectacular counterparts in the American El Dorado sought after by the annexationists. And as for their contention that the province's costly new St. Lawrence canals lay virtually unused, reciprocity and the natural advantages of the St. Lawrence system would soon cram their locks with cargoes. Canada, Brown asserted, could capture the carrying trade of the vast North American interior.[118] His was a declaration of faith in the St. Lawrence commercial system, faith which its merchant masters of Montreal had themselves temporarily forgotten. Yet there was more to his belief in Canada than this.

" 'What but ruin and rapid decay meet the eye!' Do they speak of Canada? Have the men who signed this ever been out of Montreal? Let them come to Upper Canada and we will show them something else than these—we will show them, from one end of the Province to the other, rising villages, elegant cities, magnificent farms, and public works of unrivalled excellence—all the magical product of a few years' labour by a young and poor people. We will take them from district to district, and show them boundless tracts of cultivated land which but yesterday were wilderness. We will show them thousands of families living in comfort and independence who, but yesterday, came from starvation and degradation in Europe. We will show them log huts giving way to frame houses, and they in their turn deserted for comfortable brick and stone dwellings. ... Good roads opening up in all directions, mills, manufactories and stores springing up. . . . Where is the country which can show the progress which these twenty years exhibit in Canada?"[119]

Still further, Brown gave himself to a series of detailed editorials on the political evils of annexation, attacking the faults of republican institutions, the tyranny of universal suffrage, the crying shame of American slavery, in a manner reminiscent of his father's *Fame and Glory of England Vindicated*. "What," he cried, "has republicanism done for freedom?" Virtually nothing, was his answer.[120] So his articles went on, throughout November and into December, driving in point after point to nail down public opinion: to such effect, indeed, that the *Globe* would be given chief credit for checking the spread of annexationism in Upper Canada.[121]

Yet in the later weeks of Brown's campaign the sense of danger seemed to be leaving the *Globe*'s pronouncements. It had gradually grown evident from the far more bulky anti-annexation circulars that annexationists were vocal rather than numerous in the province.[122] On the whole, anti-Americanism and emotional feeling for British ties were still so strong in either party in English-speaking Canada as to make annexation practically impossible. And while French Canadians might not share the rooted British sentiment, the great majority of them were content enough with their new power under responsible government, and alien enough to the United States, to have no desire for revolutionary change. Finally, the repeal of the still restrictive British Navigation Laws and the revival of trade the following year served effectively to wipe out the remnants of annexationism. As for the Montreal business men, their traditional loyalty flowed back more strongly with every rise in the trade curve.

Towards the end of 1849, Brown accordingly could feel that the worst of the annexationist peril had lifted. Yet there was still a threat to the Reform party, thanks to the radicalism that the debate on political fundamentals had stirred to active life. The question of ultimate political allegiance might have been passed by; the demand for immediate political reforms had not. If anything, the threat to party unity grew, as radicals in both sections of Canada began to organize themselves into separate political movements and attacked "the stale doctrine of moderation" which they saw embodied in the Lafontaine-Baldwin ministry.[123] Here then was another task for Brown, the government organist, to meet.

It was a task that pointed to the future. Although the radical upsurge had largely become apparent during the crisis over annexation, it was really a new development that forecast a different party structure in Canada, whereas annexationism itself had mainly come out of the old conflict over responsible government. Essentially, it had been part of the thrashings-about of dying Toryism, whatever left-wing support it had also attracted. Certainly for Brown a phase was ending. Since coming to Canada his chief public interest had been the campaign for responsible government, his chief foes the Tories. But the year 1849, with its Rebellion Losses disorders, the League and the Annexation Manifesto, had really witnessed the hushless death of the old Tory party, and firmly established responsible rule. Now fresh issues and new opponents were emerging for George Brown, most of them far removed from old Toryism. The complex currents rising would cut across the existing Liberal party front and sweep him into different, still more turbulent waters. For the moment only could he sing happily with Charley Corn-cobb of Tyendaga, unofficial poet laureate of Reform:

> *Toryism's sun is set*
> *'Tis down, 'tis gone forever,*
> *Some say that it will start up yet*
> *But will it? Nonsense—Never!*[124]

Cross-Currents in Liberalism

I

Brown was thirty-one in late November, 1849, and by now mature authority was replacing much of the boisterous assertiveness of youth. His long frame had broadened and lost some of its angularity: at six foot two he was massive, straight and strong. The thick red hair was receding slightly; now he affected decent black broadcloth instead of the brass-buttoned pepper-and-salts of earlier years. But his piercing blue eyes were as lively as ever, his features as animated, his laugh as free and hearty. And his energy was still prodigious; so much so that he scarcely understood the meaning of being tired. Everything he did he seemed to do with gusto. He ate enormously, rode strenuously, raced upstairs two steps at a time, and bounded along, coat-tails flapping, when other men walked—perhaps all the while expounding busily to some half-winded companion, who had all he could do to scamper half a pace behind.[1]

This was the man seen by the world at large. There was another, private George Brown, however, the gentle, considerate, much-loved son and brother. Always there were two aspects. The one he presented in public was nothing unless dynamic and masterful, hard-driving to allies, relentless to foes. The other he showed to his family and to those whose friendship reached inside the family walls. Here was charm and kindliness, and an easy simplicity of manner. The first Brown collected fervent followers and bitter enemies alike—but none had more devoted friends than the second. Yet those who knew both Browns knew that they were one: a person of deep but uncomplicated and direct emotions, who poured out his ready energy and combativeness in his working life, then thankfully returned, as often as he could, to a small private world of affection and content. And the thorough-going relaxation and refreshment that he found in this intimate circle of friends and family did much to explain his customary zest for action, and his constantly renewed vitality.[2]

The Browns' new house on Duke Street was the centre of his private world. It stood in a prosperous, brick-terraced row one street north of King, towards the eastern edge of town, but still convenient to the *Globe* office.[3] Six of the family were at home now: George, his parents, his brother Gordon, and two of his sisters. The youngest of the girls, Marianne, had just been married and had moved to Woodstock; for Marianne, the auburn-haired beauty of the family, had fallen in love with a young Queen's graduate, William Ball, who had frequently visited their house while studying theology at Knox. They had married following his ordination, when he became first pastor of Woodstock's new Free Church.[4] But Catherine, with her infectious laughter and quick wit, was still at home, and so was gentle, warm-hearted Isabella. They and their mother in turn fussed over George, poked fun at him, and idolized him. Certainly, though he stayed a bachelor, he was far from a lonely one.

Meanwhile there had been changes down at the *Globe* office. The new weekly edition had been instituted for the country readers in July 1849, and at the same time the regular *Globe* had begun to be issued three days a week, a step largely taken because of the pressure of advertisements.[5] These enlargements soon brought another move for the office, this time to 14 King Street East, close to an old rival, the *British Colonist*.[6] There were other changes coming too. Peter Brown was ready to retire from journalism.[7] Elderly, he was by no means old, and still might spend occasional periods helping with office duties. Besides, he had more than enough to keep him occupied, what with his Free Church interests, the organizing of help for fugitive American slaves in Canada, and soon the new Toronto Anti-Slavery Society, not to mention the reviving agitation over the Upper Canadian clergy reserves. For years yet, his plump, white-haired figure would be well known and highly respected in Toronto: respected even by the High Church Anglican Bishop Strachan, a fellow Scot with much the same indomitable temperament—who once accorded him the crusty tribute, "Peter Brown, you are the greatest Tory in Canada."[8]

When Peter did retire from full-time labours at the *Globe*, his place there was soon taken by his second son. Twenty-two-year-old Gordon had been steadily acquiring training in the varied branches of newspaper work: from apprentice printer to reporter and "Special Correspondent".[9] During the excitement that followed the appearance of the Annexation Manifesto in October, he had been stationed in Montreal in this last capacity, and from there, moreover, had written a lively series of "anti-annexation letters" for Horace Greeley's well-known New

York *Tribune* which gave ample evidence that he too possessed a full share of the family's journalistic talents.[10] Early in 1850, he was named *Globe* sub-editor; and thus began a partnership even more significant than that of Peter and George Brown.[11] For Gordon not two years later took over as managing editor, freeing his brother for a parliamentary career.[12] Thenceforward, while the whole paper continued to reflect George Brown's views and ultimate authority, it was Gordon Brown who ran it day by day. And though George Brown would still be at the printing office as often as political duties permitted, from the time, at least, that he took seat in parliament in 1852, it was Gordon who usually occupied the editorial chair.

The full development of this new partnership, however, was surely not foreseen when Peter Brown retired at the beginning of 1850.[13] At that time George himself was handling most of the editorial work, and would do so for a year and more to come, his decision to enter parliament not yet taken. Moreover, during this period his *Globe* responsibilities were at their full, since his old experienced partner had gone and his young one was not yet wholly qualified. Yet the director of the *Globe* also had another responsibility, that of Prison Inspector, whose duties periodically took him back to Kingston. This appointment dated from the celebrated Penitentiary Commission. The old amateur Board of Inspectors had resigned during that inquiry, when Warden Smith had been removed by the Commissioners, and the government had shortly afterwards named three of the latter—Fergusson, Brown and Bristow—to fill its place until the prison question could be permanently settled.[14] At first, while the Commission had still been sitting, Brown's additional role of Inspector had been no particular burden. But later it required a number of visits to Kingston, and much correspondence, to supervise the management of the penitentiary—especially after he and Bristow were appointed as the first paid government Inspectors in their own right.[15]

Discipline, treatment of prisoners and internal administration could be safely left to the new Warden, but the Board's particular concern lay with the long-unbalanced accounts of the prison. They made successful new contracts for convict labour, built another workshop, and steadily pared away at costs.[16] When the Inspectors reported to the government in March, 1850, they were proud to point out that they had cut nearly £6000 off the average running costs of the old regime.[17] At the same time it was pleasing to observe that the prison punishment rate had been almost halved, that the box had been abolished, and the rawhide

and cat used but thirteen times.[18] (Also, let it be noted, the fiery
Dr. Sampson was getting on famously with Warden Macdonell.)[19]

Brown did not lose interest in broader penal questions; in
fact, he went before the public to speak on them. In Hamilton,
for instance, he lectured on principles of prison discipline, earnestly though somewhat stumblingly,[20] and gave a better address
on that subject before the Toronto Mechanics Institute in April,
1850.[21] This was the city's typical Victorian lyceum, attended for
entertainment and instruction by the best society, no less than
the self-improving workman; all equally ready to be edified by
lectures on penology, the objects and practical advantages of
agricultural organizations, a highly philosophic inquiry labelled,
"Does the Eye or Ear Contribute Most to Man's Happiness?",
or a learned discourse on the Natural History of Man.[22] The last
had been given by a recent Toronto university graduate, Thomas
Henning, and it may have left its mark on Isabella Brown. At
any rate, she subsequently married the knowledgeable Mr.
Henning, while he entered the family firm as secretary-
treasurer of the *Globe*.[23]

Penal affairs remained a significant sideline for George
Brown, but he was also developing another active interest: in
the public protest against American slavery now fast arising in
Canada. He had been reared in Scotland in abhorrence of
slavery, had known the triumphant moment in 1834 when it had
been abolished throughout Britain's dominions. His New York
years had confirmed a strong feeling that the greatest defect in
American democracy was its acceptance of Negro slavery in the
South. And in Canada his feelings were roused still more by the
state of Negro fugitives who had made the perilous journey all
the way to free British territory beyond the Niagara or Detroit
Rivers, only to arrive there destitute and desperately ill-
equipped to survive.[24] To help the escaped slave, he and
his father both joined in the work of the Elgin Association,
founded in 1849, a philanthropic body largely Free Kirk at the
core which sought to establish Negroes on a tract of land which
it purchased in Kent county.[25] The first settlers were placed
there late that year. Others followed steadily, while George
Brown in the *Globe* firmly defended the Elgin Settlement at
Buxton against the prejudices of what fortunately proved to be
an ineffectual minority among white inhabitants of Kent.[26]

Then, in 1850, the passage of a stringent new Fugitive Slave
Law in the United States brought further warm response in
Canada from Negro-sympathizers like George Brown—who

bitterly attacked the measure in his journal. American federal officers were henceforth authorized to secure the capture of escaped slaves within the free states of the North. In consequence, increasing numbers of fearful Negroes began to cross from Northern states to nearby Upper Canada, where they posed a mounting problem of relief. To meet that problem, and to express all possible support for the abolitionist movement in the North, the Anti-Slavery Society of Canada soon came into being. It was centred in Toronto; both George and Peter Brown played enthusiastic parts in it from the beginning.[27] George sat on the Society's executive, along with an aspiring Toronto lawyer two years his junior, Oliver Mowat, formerly of Kingston. Peter was prominent on the speakers' platform at crowded public meetings. Furthermore, Isabella became an officer of the busy Women's Auxiliary, which on occasion looked after 500 cases of relief at once, while her husband, Thomas Henning, held the hard-working job of secretary of the Society.[28] As time went on, however, it was George Brown who particularly made his mark at the public meetings with powerful anti-slavery orations, one of which gained high praise from that most eminent of British Liberals, John Stuart Mill, and further earned the accolade of publication by the august Emancipation Society of Manchester.[29]

Reformation of the prisoner, liberation of the slave—these were strong enthusiasms for George Brown. But first, last, and always, he was a political journalist and a fervent Reform partisan. And from late in 1849 onward into 1850, he grew steadily more concerned with the principal new phenomenon to be noted in Canadian politics: the upsurge of radical opinions among some sections of the Reform party. Indeed, after the annexation crisis of the fall of 1849, he could not help but feel that the most immediate and pressing problem to be dealt with was the rapid rise of an aggressive left-wing faction within Upper Canada, that would soon acquire the inelegant name, Clear Grit. Its members were strongly critical of the Baldwin Liberal leadership: they proclaimed ideas and policies regarded as wrongheaded or even dangerous by the party chieftains. Thus Brown's best efforts now were needed in his government press organ to repel radical onslaughts on the established structure of Reform. The fact was, that the *Globe* editor's thirty-first birthday in November, 1849, had all but coincided with the definite organization of the Clear Grit movement: a movement destined to divide and then remake Upper Canada Liberalism within the decade to come.

2

Though the radicalism he now confronted had blossomed vigorously out of the annexation controversy, its roots went considerably deeper into the past. There had, of course, been sizeable radical elements in the Upper Canada Reform party before the Rebellion of 1837, men who had wanted to introduce the pattern of American elective government as a fundamental answer to political problems, whereas more moderate Reformers had been content to work for the redress of grievances within the structure of the British parliamentary constitution. The Rebellion itself had expressed, then shattered, this earlier radicalism, and sent leaders like William Lyon Mackenzie or John Rolph fleeing into exile and eclipse. Thereafter, their chastened followers had generally backed Baldwin and the main group of Reformers in the contest for British responsible government. But while the Baldwinites had always regarded responsible rule as an end in itself, to the left wing it had remained no more than a means to an end: the way to unlock the door to far more thorough constitutional reform, reform that would destroy every vestige of privilege and outworn aristocracy. As a result, the very triumph of Liberalism in 1848 had invited trouble in the victorious party, as radical hopes began to glow afresh.

On the eve of taking office, Robert Baldwin himself had expressed forebodings regarding "the extravagant expectations of oversanguine friends".[30] And during the Penitentiary Commission George Brown had taken time from the Secretary's duties to warn him of the danger of a rift appearing between the new ministry and at least some of its supporters. "The Reform party is tremendously strong," he had declared, "but no party whatever its strength can withstand heartburning and jealousy in its ranks."[31] By early 1849, moreover, Brown could see plain evidence of a sorry case of heartburn developing among the party Left. They had looked eagerly for the Reform millenium to begin, once black Tory reaction had been conquered. Instead the parliamentary session of 1848 had been quickly dismissed, in order to give the new Lafontaine-Baldwin ministry time to plan its major legislative programme. Impatiently the Left had waited for the much-heralded programme to be set forth when parliament assembled in January of 1849—only to find that, while the mass of government measures looked salutary enough, there was little that could be regarded as basic constitutional reform. Quite evidently, this timorous ministry did not intend to go that far.

In disappointment, radicals began to draw together, pointedly referring to themselves as the "Old Reform Party", with the implication that the ministerial group had been sapped of true reforming zeal by the lotus-land of office. The "Old Reform" resurgence was further stimulated by the amnesty that now permitted one-time rebels and radical leaders to return from exile to their former scenes of glory. That spring William Lyon Mackenzie himself popped up, like an ominous old genie from a jug. His return was only a five-weeks' reconnaissance of Upper Canada; he would not permanently leave his American haven for another year. But his reappearance stirred fervent radical memories, and he began to send increasing correspondence to left-wing newspapers.

Now too his former partner in the old radical leadership, sleek Dr. John Rolph, who had contrived to slip back earlier, was beginning to show new signs of life. "He is bitter, gloomy and revengeful," James Price, the Crown Lands Commissioner, reported darkly to George Brown. "He wants power and can't get it."[32] And the one left-wing member of the ministry, the obstreperous Malcolm Cameron, was growing restive in his comparatively minor post of Assistant Commissioner of Public Works. A simple western timber magnate, Cameron since before the Rebellion had been making a successful political career out of backwoods bluntness—to the extent, on one occasion, of enjoying a wash stripped to the waist in a public bar-room, while on official business with a scandalized Robert Baldwin.[33] "I have no faith in Cameron's prudence—what a minister!" wrote Price to Brown.[34] Already in 1848 Malcolm's failure to co-operate with his colleagues had earned him a stinging rebuke from Baldwin, and the threat of dismissal.[35] He might well become a powerful addition to the Old Reform malcontents.

No small ingredient in their unrest was the resentful feeling that veterans of Reform's heroic early battles for freedom had frequently been pushed aside from favour by mere post-war upstarts—recent arrivals like George Brown, in fact. Brown himself had soon to face this Old Reform resentment in the person of James Lesslie, the tough-fibred owner of the *Examiner*, who had been imprisoned for his radical connections in 1837. The declining *Examiner*, once the dauntless foe of Toryism, had been replaced by the young *Globe* as official party organ: abandoned, it appeared to Lesslie, ungratefully forgotten by the ministers. His brooding bitterness had erupted in a sudden violent quarrel between the two Reform papers early in 1849. The case at issue, the government's dismissal of the medical superintendent at the provincial asylum (another old radical), was really less important than the fact that the *Globe* up-held the ministerial action, while Lesslie was the victim's staunch defender.[36] At once the *Examiner* leaped at Brown's journal, charging freely that it was bound hand and foot to the minis-ters, lived only by their bounty, and had been created because they meant to repudiate "the Old Reform Party" and needed an organ of their own.[37] Of course the *Globe* denied the charges, adding a bit cynically that the last could best be translated, "Gentlemen of the Old Reform Party, take the *Examiner* and drop the *Globe*."[38] The quarrel shortly blew over, as Reformers drew together again to meet the rising Tory outcry over the Rebellion Losses Bill. But while it lasted, several other left-wing papers joined in the attack on the *Globe*;[39] and afterwards the *Examiner*'s hostility stayed very close to the surface. The Old Reform disturbance had only just begun.

Then there was another issue that increasingly engaged left-wing attention: the perennial problem of the Upper Canada clergy reserves, the extensive tracts of public lands that had been set aside at the foundation of that province to create a fund or endowment for the support of a "Protestant clergy". A would-be compromise measure, the imperial Act of 1840, had provided for the various churches of Canada West to share in the glittering reserves endowment which had earlier been the special treasure of the Church of England, defended by the old Tory oligarchy. The settlement of 1840, however, had still left much dissatisfaction behind it: among those who felt that the Anglicans had yet been assigned a disproportionately large share of the clergy reserves fund, those who wanted to see their own church better treated, and those who repudiated the very idea of state endowment for religion. In the last respect, Upper Canada Reformers years before had taken up the cause of secu-larizing the reserves; that is, of transferring their endowment to some wholly secular purpose such as the support of public education.

Nevertheless, the crucial struggle over responsible govern-ment had largely overshadowed the reserves question during the forties, until the Reform victory of 1848 had seemed to open the way for its permanent solution. Furthermore, it was now made known that there was sufficient income accumulated in the reserves fund to distribute it to all the churches promised shares under the Act of 1840; and this had raised the question with new immediacy.[40] The more evangelical Protestant bodies spurned the proffered government silver. The Free Church Synod resolved to forbid its congregations applying for the money, while other denominations seized the opportunity to demand the secularization of the reserves.[41] And by 1849, true to old Reform tradition, radicals had begun to press the cause of secularization once again, denouncing religious endowment as one more aspect of outdated privilege that must be destroyed.

In this spirit, James Lesslie, himself an ardent exponent of religious equality, urged secularization on the Reform meeting which was called in March, 1849, in Toronto to discuss questions of school policy. Lesslie sought to have the meeting petition for the transfer of the reserve funds to public schools, and gained considerable support for his proposal. George Brown was still in Montreal then, but his father was at the gathering. He opposed the petition, contending that the ministers had quite enough on their hands for the time being, and should not be embarrassed by their own supporters thrusting the reserves question upon them as well.[42] After much debate he won his way. Certainly, as leading Free Kirk laymen, both Browns themselves looked earnestly to secularization as the final answer; but they felt sure that the government would take up the clergy reserves in due course, and meanwhile were far more concerned about the strength of the Tory reaction to the Rebellion Losses Bill, which threatened Reform ascendancy and even responsible government itself. Moreover, the next month, the ministry did announce in parliament that it would consider the reserves problem with a view to acting at a later session.[43] This seemed to bear out the Browns' position. In any case, radical importunings on the subject rather declined thereafter; but mainly because of the evident need for party unity in the face of Tory violence.

Yet when the hectic summer of Tory discontent had passed, the radicals' demands rose with greater force: not only for secularization, but for vigorous retrenchment, judicial reform, and the application of the straightforward elective principle throughout the constitution. Responsible cabinet government they dismissed as a costly failure and a cumbrous sham. "Must we," asked Lesslie's *Examiner* testily in September, "abjure a republican simplicity and assume the paraphernalia and ape the pageantry of an aristocratical government?"[44] In its pages Mackenzie's letters from the United States hotly attacked Baldwin's "mongrel administration",[45] while "A liberal of the Old School" added emphatically that the Canada West leader was guilty of nothing less than treason to the Old Reformers for taking into the ministry men of easy political virtue—some of whom had scarcely been with the party five years.[46] The internal party conflict was mounting fast. And now there came the noisy annexation outburst of October.

By and large, most of the Upper Canada radicals did not become active and immediate annexationists.[47] Yet they were quite ready to consider the project for the future, the *Examiner* flatly declaring that failure to secularize would bring on annexation in any case.[48] When ministerial leaders sought strenuously to combat any spread of annexationism within the party, the "ultras" fought back at what they regarded as government dictation and the attempt, notably made by the *Globe*, to cry down fundamental political discussion. That month the whole dispute within Reform found focus in the celebrated by-election campaign in the Third Riding of York, where the locally favoured party candidate, Peter Perry, was a well-known Old Reformer of truly ancient lineage, since he had been a founder of the original Reform group in the legislature of 1824, although out of the Assembly since 1836. It was here that Baldwin, Hincks and Brown all pressed the remarkably close-mouthed Perry to declare himself on the vital topic of annexation.[49] But the most they had achieved by mid-November was the somewhat unsatisfying revelation from the sphinx of Perry's Corners that he would not advocate that measure for the present.[50]

And meanwhile the pressure from the *Globe* and the government leaders had made Perry the rallying-point for all the radical resentments, as left-wing papers lauded his heroic stand against ministerial tyranny over the party.[51] Then on December 4 his Conservative opponent prudently withdrew, thus assuring Peter of an acclamation, but leaving Reformers stewing in their own discord. Thereupon the *Examiner* saw fit to proclaim an outright victory for "the Reform and Progress Party . . . for a long time swallowed up in the present Government party".[52] At the same time, judging the wind favourable, Malcolm Cameron resigned from the ministry.[53] Still further, a group of radicals began meeting in Toronto to plan to extricate the Progress Party from the government maw and to organize its press and parliamentary support.[54] The matter at stake was not really annexation, but the repudiation of existing Liberal leadership and policy. Yet the annexation turmoil had precipitated the final and decisive move.

Brown knew most of the men who gathered in the King Street office of William McDougall, a personable, clever and aggressive, twenty-seven-year-old lawyer who had already tried his hand at journalism with a short-lived agricultural weekly, the *Canada Farmer*.[55] Malcolm Cameron and old Perry met there with McDougall, and James Lesslie too, on occasion.[56] Then there was forthright David Christie, a schoolmate of Brown's Edinburgh High School days, now a prosperous farmer in nearby Wentworth County. And there was Lesslie's "little prodigy", the zealous Charles Lindsey, who was helping to edit the *Examiner* and had worked on McDougall's paper.[57] One other who was soon to join the circle was probably not yet known to Brown. This was young Charles Clarke, spruce, precise, and needle-sharp, at twenty-three already associate editor of the "ultra" Hamilton *Journal and Express*.[58] Brown would come to know him well enough. In fact, almost all this group would play prominent parts in his subsequent political life, some as close friends and allies, others as uncompromising foes.

At present, they were all dangers to Reform unity, men to be closely watched. "Bunkum-talking cormorants," Brown called them, "who met in a certain lawyer's office on King Street and announced their intention to form a party based on 'clear-grit' principles."[59] The term "clear-grit" would stick, though its actual origin was uncertain. Some said it was first used by Christie in conversation with Brown, when he earnestly declared that the new movement wanted no time-servers, no false hearts—"We want only men who are *clear grit*."[60] Others ascribed it to Peter Perry, a country miller by trade, who should know the quality of hard granite that would grind true.[61] At any rate, as widely applied by Brown and others it soon became the accepted title for the radical faction that was now being organized. The *Globe*, indeed, remarked irreverently, "We called the Reformers— the *old* Reformers—clear grits! Awful, ain't it?"[62]

In actuality, the Clear Grits were a combination of Old Reformers and younger Liberal idealists like McDougall, Christie, Lindsey and Clarke, products of an era when democracy and liberty seemed about to triumph all around the world. The former group had chiefly provided an experienced hard core of radicalism and the initial impetus of discontent; the latter would largely furnish intellectual leadership, and a carefully elaborated programme for the days ahead. Among the younger group, too young to have known the earlier days of Upper Canada radicalism, McDougall was the leading spirit: abounding in plans, full of ready argument, although somewhat cold of manner.[63] He was, indeed, a kind of youthful Old Reformer, who recalled one windy December night in 1837, when as a boy on a farm outside Toronto he had been stirred to sudden sympathy for the defeated rebels as he watched the blazing destruction of their headquarters, Montgomery's Tavern, fired by vengeful loyal forces.[64] The others had brought their radicalism with them as emigrants from Britain, ready-moulded in the ardent democratic movements for reform that were sweeping their homeland. Thus the Scot, Christie, and the Englishman, Lindsey: while in his Lincolnshire boyhood Clarke had heard the great O'Connell and John Bright of the Anti-Corn Law League, and been schooled by Thomas Cooper, the Chartist poet.[65] Had he not at fifteen himself drafted a glowing *Address to the Young Men of England*, eloquently beseeching Youth to batter down "the dark and hitherto unfathomable dungeons of ignorance of our modern aristocrats"?[66]

McDougall himself, setting out "to roll the country down to a common-sense democracy",[67] would shortly found the bright and vigorous *North American* as the new Clear Grit organ. The indefatigable Lindsey would assist in its editing while still writing for the *Examiner*, and Christie would give financial aid.[68] As for Clarke, his keen mind and literary skill became second only to McDougall's in clarifying Grit principles for presentation to the public.[69] He would veritably make the People's Charter ring through the Clear Grit platform. And all of them shared the zeal for elective institutions and pure democracy, for secularization and the abolition of religious privilege, that characterized Clear Grittism at its birth.

At the same time this ginger group remained in close connection with the Old Reformers, whose sentiments were much the same as theirs, although less clearly formulated. From the older radicals came Perry and Malcolm Cameron to serve as the first Clear Grit representatives in parliament, shortly to be followed by John Rolph. In fact, Rolph, who had been egging on Old Reformers in his typically devious fashion, was to gain new recognition as the principal Grit leader in the House.[70] Through Charles Lindsey, moreover, the bright young men were linked with Lesslie and the veteran *Examiner*, and with Lesslie's old friend, William Lyon Mackenzie, who became a regular correspondent of that paper.[71] Mackenzie proved too embittered and erratic to stay a member of any group, however radical. But he was a powerful ally in attacking the ministry—not to mention being McDougall's legal client for property claims dating beyond the Rebellion,[72] and Lindsey's future father-in-law besides!

In brief, Clear Grittism was a thorough blend of old and new, of memories running back before 1837 and idealistic hopes unleashed after 1848. It was a blend, as well, of elements derived both from contemporary Upper Canadian society and from across the Atlantic: native North American agrarian democracy, that resented special treatment for clergy lands and wanted cheap, simple government in direct contact with the people, combined with radicalism brought from Britain, which aimed no less at popular democracy and the destruction of inequality in either church or state. Both elements were strong in Canada West, still close to the frontier farming era and filled with recent British immigrants. No wonder that from the end of 1849 Grittism flourished so briskly and spread so rapidly in fertile western soil. No wonder, too, that George Brown found a hard fight on his hands. And this against a movement, ironically, which one day he would come to lead himself.

3

It all went back, Brown said scornfully, to the ministers' refusal to be swayed by a discontented handful in the party. "Because they have not made themselves the tools of a half dozen men arrogating to themselves the title of the old Reformers, we are about to have a 'young Canada party' with the *Examiner* as its organ!"[73] His antagonism, however, to the Grit "young Canada" movement was more than just the official response of the government organist. He distrusted any faction linked with the rebellion and violence of earlier radicalism; he deplored the Clear Grits' preference for American elective institutions over the British responsible government he had battled for so vigorously; and he was deeply suspicious of the annexationist associations of the movement. These were quickly fading, but Brown still feared that they were only being disguised.

In any case, he saw Grittism steadily advancing in Upper Canada during the opening months of 1850. By February, its strong-voiced press not only included Lesslie's and Lindsey's *Examiner*, Clarke's *Journal and Express*, and several papers in the western Peninsula, but the *Mirror*, the Roman Catholic Liberal organ in Toronto, was also deep in Clear Grit notions of elective reform, and McDougall's forthcoming *North American* had been announced. Among the farmers of the western country-side, moreover, Reform unrest still grew: compounded of the rising insistence on a full and final settlement of the reserves, the continued pressure of debts stemming from hard times, and the demand that something positive be done to bring government closer to the people and to lessen the burden of taxes. There was even some die-hard talk still of annexation. A new address to the people on that subject appeared in Toronto in February, while, in the farthest West, the erratic ex-Tory member for Essex, Colonel Prince, was advocating independence. And there was every likelihood that the Clear

Grits would have significant strength when parliament met. They already had two members in the House in Perry and Cameron, the latter a man of cabinet rank; they could probably get old Henry Boulton, who was again a malcontent because the government had turned him down for a judgeship; Prince might act with them, and some back-benchers of radical leanings besides.

In consequence, Brown must have viewed the prospects with anxiety as a new by-election contest loomed that spring. It was a bad time to give the Clear Grits a trial of strength. They stood too good a chance of gaining another parliamentary recruit. A by-election was necessary, however, to confirm John Weten-hall's appointment to the ministry as Malcolm Cameron's successor in the post of Assistant Commissioner of Public Works. Wetenhall, member for Halton, was a loyal government supporter of proved administrative ability, and he had a large following in his own county. Yet it was rumoured that his mental state was not all it should be, that he was subject to strange fits of lethargy and maundering.[74] And the outlook seemed still darker when the *Examiner* called on Caleb Hopkins to oppose him, a former member for Halton who had an Old Reform ancestry nearly as ancient as Peter Perry's, and had small reason besides to love the Baldwin leadership. After all, George Brown himself could well remember going to Halton for Baldwin during the elections of 1844, to ensure that Hopkins would be dropped as the party's candidate in favour of Wetenhall.[75]

Even so, the ministerial choice might still have carried the day, had not Malcolm Cameron seized this opportunity to pay off his score against the government. In mid-February, with loud commotion, he entered the lists as Farmer Hopkins' Clear Grit champion. He began a hot campaign, hammering away chiefly at the ministry's failure to heed his own retrenchment proposals for knocking £15,000 off the expenditure a year—on which issue, Malcolm claimed, he had resigned from office. "A large dose of bunkum," said Brown succinctly.[76] As the *Globe* preferred to explain it, Cameron had sought to push the cabinet into awarding him a larger office by threatening to resign. He had had the Commissionership for Crown Lands in mind, a handy post, thanks to its control of timber limits, for any hard-working lumberman.[77] But, observed the journal deftly: "To his astonishment his resignation was accepted—and his indignation was in proportion to his astonishment. Malcolm was immediately made a martyr, and it was resolved that all his grievances should be represented in the Halton election in the person of Caleb Hopkins. Accordingly, Mr. Cameron posted off to the County, pinned this wretched Caleb to his coat-tails, and told off *ex cathedra* a catalogue of the iniquities of which his late colleagues had been guilty."[78]

It was a palpable hit; still it was hardly sufficient. Black-haired, stocky Cameron, with his bluff and hearty manner, his love of a roaring frontier joke, his bull voice and crushing hand-clasp, was a popular man in the West. With lusty ferocity he blasted poor dazed Wetenhall from one public meeting to the next, while "Uncle" Caleb followed beaming in his wake. Anything the *Globe* could say in those miserable weeks of late February and early March was of little avail. Brown could point out that Wetenhall stood for retrenchment and settlement of the reserves as much as Hopkins. Impatient Reformers preferred to listen to sweeping Clear Grit promises of these measures, freely purveyed by Cameron. The local Tories in Reform-dominated Halton fell in behind Hopkins in the hope of giving the ministry another black eye.[79] Then on election day, March 11, impassably muddy roads kept the loyal Scots vote in the furthest Dumfries districts from coming in. Wetenhall was slaughtered. Charles Clarke had covered the election for the *Journal and Express*. The morning after the polls a gaunt figure wandered into his room, strangely dressed in the guise of Diogenes, carrying a lantern, holding a staff, and asking wild-eyed for an honest man. It was John Wetenhall, his reason finally shattered.[80] "I do not envy either Caleb or Malcolm their feelings," a party friend wrote bitterly to Brown.[81]

Spurred by their triumph, the jubilant Clear Grits held a grand gathering, on March 12, at Markham in Peter Perry's Third York riding, to lay down a complete platform for the faction which the *Globe* now dubbed "the Calebites". With Perry as principal speaker, a cheering crowd adopted a host of resolutions; among other things, demanding the appropriation of the reserves to education, the abolition of the expensive court of Chancery, the extension of the franchise, and the introduction of an elected governor and elected upper house.[82] A week later a second Calebite convention at Brooklin, in Perry's home township of Whitby, tacked on universal suffrage and the election "of all our public functionaries of every grade". "There is no blinking the question," the *Globe* asserted sharply, "the Calebite platform simply proposes to adopt the republican form of government of the United States."[83]

In response, George Brown set out to make a critical investigation into the workings of American elective institutions, from elective heads of government through elected judges to popular pound-keepers. In lengthy *Globe* articles, running over several months, he proved to his emphatic satisfaction that the British system of government, which relied on appointed officials under a ministry responsible to an elected chamber, was more efficient, less corruptible, and gave better expression to the people's will. He contrasted the unwritten British constitution—organic, free to grow and adapt—with the written American—hidebound and lifeless. He denied that wholesale election and universal suffrage democracy gave cheap, good government: they simply invited extravagance and corruption, and the ignorant emotions of mob rule. It was a strenuous and whole-hearted effort, to say the very least.[84]

Then he tackled the other great question central to the Clear Grit agitation in a series on the clergy reserves.[85] As eager as the Calebites to gain a settlement, Brown did not intend them to gain sole credit for proposing secularization. But he upheld the position now being taken by government leaders, that, since the reserves still rested on an imperial statute, the Act of 1840, they could not be disposed of until a measure was obtained from the Imperial Parliament empowering the provincial legislature to deal with them. The Grits declared, however, that the Canadian parliament was quite able to move directly; and that the government claim was mere evasion by ministers who were really reluctant to take up the reserves at all. "I think the administration has sold us on the question of religious equality," Lesslie wrote grimly to Mackenzie, "and if so, they are ruined."[86]

Baldwin, they recalled, was himself an Anglican. It was said that he would not go as far as secularization, and thus wipe out his own church's endowment. But more important was the suspicion that the ministry did not want to move lest it lose its French-Canadian support. As Roman Catholics, the French-speaking Reformers did not approve the principle of separating church and state implicit in secularization; and in any case, tampering thus directly with church-state ties in Canada West might reflect unfavourably on the ties of their own church with the state in Canada East. It might be that Lafontaine, the French-Canadian Reform leader, was willing to see the reserves transferred to the province's control. But what then? Would a ministry whose largest parliamentary following was French Canadian, and Upper Canadian leaders whose success till now had largely depended on the French alliance, proceed with secularization?

The Clear Grits feared not. The spectre of "French domination" of the government came readily to their minds, just as earlier it had to the Tories. Indeed, it rose easily in Canada West (about as easily as fear of "the English" in French Canada)

since the firm-set block of French Canadians in the Assembly
was the fulcrum on which a ministry must turn. "We shall get
no real reforms from the French," Charles Lindsey informed
his fellow Grit, Charles Clarke. "There is some truth in the
story of French domination, depend upon it. What does Hincks
mean by saying that the French do not feel much interest in
settling the reserves? Why that they oppose it, of course."[87]

George Brown, however, maintained his faith in the government's approach to the reserves question. It was the Grits who
were playing false, exploiting a natural Upper Canadian demand for settlement by urging a procedure they knew to be impossible, simply to gain support. And it was unjust to presume
that French Canadians would put obstacles in the way. "If they
do," Brown told *Globe* readers earnestly, "it will be for the first
time, as they have always stood generously by their Upper
Canadian friends."[88] In this wise the editor carried on his contest against the Grits well into the spring, reiterating his confidence in the government on the matter of the reserves, attacking the radicals' programme for constitutional change, emphasizing still the annexationist trend of their "republican" policies
—and finding time as well to skirmish over Calebite retrenchment and judicial reform.

But early in May of 1850 his Clear Grit opponents received
a valuable reinforcement in McDougall's long-heralded *North
American*. Under his able direction, it systematized and forcefully defended the Clear Grit platform as originally laid down
at the "Markham Convention". Even so, the platform would
not receive its full and imposing construction until the following
February, when McDougall and Charles Clarke together put it
all out in the *North American* in eleven major planks and thirteen lighter scantlings ("subjects for immediate legislation");
the whole lucidly explained by Clarke in articles under his well-
known pseudonym, *Reformator*.[89]

From the start the *North American* became the leading Clear
Grit organ; Brown soon found it a more formidable enemy than
its oldest partner, the *Examiner*, had ever been. For one thing,
McDougall proved to be his near-equal as an aggressive journalist—and was certainly at least as pungent in expression, as
witnessed by his variously addressing the *Globe*'s editor as
"political prostitute",[90] "horrible liar",[91] and "mean, quibbling
degraded traitor".[92] For another thing, the young *North American* burned with the clearest Grit idealism, while the creaking
Examiner was somewhat erratic and discursive in its political
arguments. "It commits itself to no certain line of operations,"
McDougall himself complained, "and so is distrusted by all our

leading politicians of the progressive school.''⁹³ Apparently, the *Examiner*'s owner, Lesslie, was more interested in getting his own back at the ministry than in a constructive programme; and his editor, Lindsey, not having full charge, could do little about it. Hence the very decision among Clear Grit leaders to back a dedicated new paper in McDougall's keeping.

The same week as the *North American* appeared, parliament gathered for the session of 1850. As the opening drew near, Brown could only anticipate more trouble for the ministry. Perhaps his diligence on the *Globe* had turned some Reformers away from Grittism and back to Baldwin and Co. Perhaps things could have been worse. Quite probably the radicals would still only be a bothersome nuisance in the House. Nevertheless there they were: two by-elections already to their credit; the *North American* in full cry, closely followed by the *Examiner* and others; and no reason to think that the rising Clear Grit movement yet had reached its peak.

4

Toronto was pleasantly excited in that May of 1850. After ten years, a parliament would sit once more in the unpretentious red-brick legislative buildings on Front Street, left to other, lesser uses ever since the union of the two Canadas had taken the seat of government away to Kingston and then to Montreal. But Montreal's disgrace in 1849 had proved Toronto's gain. The disorders in the former city had brought a decision to move the provincial capital again: first to Toronto, heart of English-speaking Canada, for the rest of the life of the present parliament, next to Quebec, the ancient capital of New France. A permanent home for the perambulating government would be fixed on later—few guessed how difficult that would be. But in the meantime, without looking ahead, Toronto was enjoying its return to eminence. The government offices were in full operation; the old Parliament Buildings had been renovated and restored from their temporary use as the provincial lunatic asylum; and gentlemen were practising their bows for official levees, while mamas and daughters fussed over imported ball dresses for the glittering season ahead.

Brown, no doubt, was as happy as the rest to have parliament in Toronto: if for no other reason than that it greatly simplified the *Globe*'s watch over proceedings. He could go himself to the

reporters' desks in the chamber, when need be, though his parliamentary reporter, George Ure, and his brother Gordon, were
in more regular attendance.[94] He was probably at the opening
on May 14, to hear the Speech from the Throne set forth the
government's programme—only to be dismayed to find that it
contained no mention of the clergy reserves. Although this did
not exclude any action on the question, it was still a serious
omission, plainly indicating a reluctance to proceed in some
government circles. But Brown made the best of it. While regretting the omission in the *Globe*, he praised other projected
measures, and asserted that even if there was some difference of
opinion among ministers over the reserves, this was not sufficient reason to bring on a rupture in the government. The goal
of abolition could as well be obtained through private, non-
ministerial action.[95]

It was with this thought in mind that he had already joined
in founding the Toronto Anti-Clergy Reserves Association the
week before,[96] its aim to organize a mass of public petitions demanding the settlement of the reserves. He now recognized that
at least Lafontaine and the other French-Canadian ministers
were none too ready for secularization. But he still felt that the
government was well worth maintaining, and that concerted
public pressure might bring the French-speaking element to
agree to secularize without dividing the Reformers—above all,
without throwing the game in Canada West to Clear Grit extremists. Accordingly, he was among the varied group of Liberals, ranging from Adam Fergusson to Lesslie and Malcolm
Cameron, who spoke at the first public gathering of the new
Association in Knox Church, and his own speech was a ringing
condemnation of "the cry of vested rights" raised by Tory
defenders of the reserves.[97] The wisdom of his action soon
seemed demonstrated when the infant *North American* tried to
claim the meeting as a Clear Grit triumph. "Wilfully misrep-
resented," exclaimed the *Globe*, decrying McDougall's attempt
to appropriate the anti-reserves movement to the radicals.[98]

Then on June 18, the reserves issue at last came before parliament. Price, the Commissioner for Crown Lands (but in his
personal capacity, and not on behalf of the cabinet), introduced
a string of thirty-one resolutions dealing with the clergy reserves. Essentially, they expressed the widespread dissatisfaction with the existing settlement, and proposed an address to the
imperial authorities requesting a measure that would empower
the provincial parliament to legislate on the problem. The final
disposition of the reserves was left an open question, however,
indicating the ministry's own uncertain state of mind. That was

well illustrated in the full-dress debate which followed. If Price and Hincks were apparently for secularization, Baldwin declared that he put justice to the churches ahead of it, while Lafontaine added that he preferred to see the reserves remain devoted to religious purposes—indeed, the endowments were "sacred".[99]

Nevertheless the resolutions passed over the last-ditch Tory opposition, as did the address to the imperial government founded upon them. Malcolm Cameron had pressed the Grit view in a counter-resolution calling for a provincial bill to repeal the existing reserves provisions, a measure which could then be re-enacted at Westminster. He was decisively defeated, 13 to 56.[100] Yet a closer look at the vote revealed that he had drawn the support of nearly half the Upper Canadian Liberals on this important issue: quite a significant parliamentary beginning for Clear Grittism.

In the *Globe* Brown still made the best of things. Price's resolutions and the address had gone through—a great step forward, he said—"and we sincerely rejoice at the prospect of having every vestige of religious preference swept from the land."[101] Moreover, on the other issues he could see the Clear Grits making much less headway. As expected, Cameron, Perry and Hopkins had won the support of captious Henry Boulton, whose windy oratory on almost every subject regularly drove members to shelter in the bar downstairs. They also frequently gained the co-operation of the *Rouges*, the similar small group of radicals, both French and English, who had emerged in Canada East to press for full democracy and republican institutions, their best-known figure, the aging Louis Joseph Papineau. But on proposals for legal reform and abolition of Chancery, the Clear Grits held only their little core of support. Nor did they do much better on retrenchment or elective reforms. As for independence and annexation, which the *Globe*, at least, had associated with Grit republican leanings, only Cameron among them voted for the first (which gained seven votes in the entire House), and the second was introduced only indirectly, and was readily crushed.[102]

Hence, when the session closed in August, Brown might well afford a sigh of relief. Annexationism was obviously politically dead. Grit radicalism had not proved too severe a threat in parliament—so far, at any rate. And, on the other side, Reform's traditional Tory foes had yet displayed little sign of recovering from their debacle of 1848-9. In fact, under the rather nominal leadership of Sir Allan MacNab—choleric hero, first, of the resistance to the Rebellion of 1837, and, second, of the resistance to the Rebellion Losses Bill—the Tories had remained in-decisive and wracked by their own internal feuds. Any danger to the Reform party still did not lie in this direction.

Yet Brown's relief was overcast by disappointment at the achievements of this first Toronto session, notably less than those of the "great parliament" of 1849. Although a necessary initial step had been taken on the reserves question, it had been effected by parliament at large, not as a government measure, and the differences within the ministry on the future of the re-serves were all too plain to see. While the Clear Grit press, quite undeterred, played up the attractive cause of secularization and the rising cry of "French domination", Brown's own adherence to the government did not change. For the first time, however, his confidence had been shaken. For the first time he began to doubt. And three other dismaying developments of the session darkened the uneasy shadow beginning to play in the back of his mind.

One of these arose out of the government's Common School Bill, introduced by Francis Hincks in June. On the whole this was an admirably designed measure to improve the administra-tion of the public-school system of Canada West. Yet its nine-teenth clause caused trouble: it dealt with separate schools. Since the Union, the scheme of public education had provided that dissentient religious minorities (Protestant in Lower Can-ada; Roman Catholic, most likely, in Upper) might have their own elementary schools and share in the provincial education grants. By now, outside the ordinary "mixed" common schools of Canada West, there were some Anglican and even a few Negro state-aided schools, as well as a number of Roman Catho-lic institutions. But generally separate schools had been regarded in Upper Canada as exceptional safeguards for minority rights, affording "protection from insult", not as a rule in themselves.[103] Their total number was small, and tending to decline.[104] That is, until the Bill of 1850.

On its introduction, it grew evident that High Anglican Tories and Roman Catholic Liberals of Canada West had plan-ned to work together on clause nineteen to force broader pro-visions for the establishment of separate schools. Faced with this threatening combination, Hincks privately agreed to amend the original clause to suit the Roman Catholics without reference to Anglican demands.[105] Henceforth, instead of municipal authorities having a discretionary power to set up a separate school or schools, they would be obliged to do so whenever twelve or more resident heads of families made application in a district where the common-school teacher was not of their faith.

A special safeguard was recast as a general right. By this concession, Hincks, the adroit politician, diddled the Tories, saved the Upper Canada Catholic Liberal vote for the ministry, and perhaps prevented division with the French Reformers, who would naturally sympathize with their co-religionists of the West. Yet the enlargement of the separate-school provision essentially for the Roman Catholics spread concern across Canada West, where many feared that other churches would compete for similar special recognition until the non-denominational public-school system was virtually destroyed.[106]

In particular, the ardent exponents of the separation of church and state were alarmed, and George Brown among them. In the *Globe* he openly disapproved of this yielding to Roman Catholic pressure. "We think the principle thus admitted strikes at the roots of our whole system of national education. It is the entering wedge."[107] Prophetic words. Nor was Brown's apprehension eased by Hincks's explanation in the House that, despite his own preference for the original limitations of clause nineteen, he had accepted amendment in deference to "strong feeling" among his colleagues.[108] Was, then, Clear Grit talk of "French domination" of the ministry so utterly ill-founded? Brown soon let the bill drop in the *Globe* for other matters. But here was a major link in a chain of events that eventually would draw him from the government side.

The next episode might seem a teacup affair, but not when taken with the others. One day in July the *Globe* reporter at the House, George Ure, had the temerity to ask the member for Gaspé, Robert Christie, who was sitting at ease behind him in the public gallery, gaily chatting with some lady friends, to lower his voice because it made it difficult to record Robert Baldwin's speech from the Assembly floor below. Although he was out of his official place, Christie took instant umbrage at this affront to his parliamentary dignity. He raised the matter from his seat the next evening, and his fellow club-members, party differences forgotten, banded together against the press interloper. On motion of Baldwin himself, Ure was called before the House, publicly reprimanded by the Speaker, and ordered to apologize.[109]

But the fourth estate had a dignity just as lofty as the third's. Parliamentary reporters, from the Toronto *British Colonist* to the *North American*, from the *Montreal Gazette* to the Hamilton *Spectator*, met in their turn, and resolved to withdraw from the chamber in protest at this treatment of their *Globe* brother.[110] From the 19th on, the great men of the country were largely left to declaim in a public vacuum—a most distressing state for politicians. Meanwhile the *Globe* resounded with apostrophes to the freedom of the press, the watchdog of the people. It scorned the so-called dignity of the members of parliament: illustrating it, for instance, with an account of a recent outbreak of legislative light-heartedness, when the high Tory MacNab and the low radical Cameron had combined in flicking paper wads at the Conservative member for Carleton—until his move to heave an ink-well had sent Malcolm scuttling on all fours under the table of the Clerk of the House.[111]

The newspaper dispute died naturally when the session ended. But in George Brown, apart from temporary indignation, it left disturbing thoughts. The government had not only failed its chief western journal by playing down, at least, the original incident; its leader, Robert Baldwin himself, had brought the conflict to a head by moving for Ure's official reprimand. What was Brown to think? The truth, in all likelihood, was that the ministers were growing slightly weary of their strong-minded *Globe* supporter, who had been a little critical over the reserves and had openly reproved them on the School Bill. Price might be sympathetic, and a useful channel of communication with the cabinet.[112] But Hincks had no love for him, Lafontaine would hardly approve his Free Church zeal, and Baldwin had earlier found occasion, in his own indirect way, to show young Brown his proper place.[113] Besides, in the past the *Globe* had frequently made clear that its editor supported the Reform ministry as the combination most likely to realize his own principles, but would by no means abandon himself to them. This sort of statement, that he backed them while they were good, may have exhibited the *Globe*'s stout independence of soul and fairly answered Grit charges that it was a mere government tool; yet, often reiterated, it was not calculated to endear George Brown to his party leaders. Nor were his repeated complaints, both in private letters and in print, that government measures were not revealed for public discussion before presentation in the House.[114]

Hence the ministers may not have minded casting an oblique reproof at the owner of the *Globe* through Ure's discomfiture. But their coolness seemed more serious in the next incident, since it concerned a matter dear to Brown's heart, the Penitentiary Commission of 1848-9. And as might be expected, it was John A. Macdonald who raised the subject in the last August days of the session, on behalf of that highly dubious and bedraggled martyr, ex-Warden Smith. The formidably docu-

mented records of Smith's long and harsh maladministration of
the penitentiary Macdonald quite ignored. Instead, in moving
for a special committee of inquiry, he raised the whole dire
catalogue of the Commission's wrongdoing once again: improper procedure, malice, distortion of evidence, and so on. Although his motion was defeated, he left a marked impression
behind him.[115]

When the erstwhile Penitentiary Commissioners had heard
of Macdonald's intended assault, they had sent a joint letter of
defence to the government, trusting it to give their answer.[116]
But the ministers proved strangely silent. Of course, they regretted that Macdonald had brought up the issue, and indicated
for the sake of maintaining confidence in the government that
he should be voted down. Yet essentially they let his charges go
uncontradicted, or left it to lesser party members to deny them.
At this, the *Globe* declared that a stringent investigation of
every action of the Commissioners should be demanded immediately.[117] Brown had no fear of inquiry. Far worse was the
government's semi-silence, almost damning in itself.

Perhaps the ministers had felt that the Penitentiary Commission had pushed too far too fast in condemning the old regime
at Kingston. Certainly at the time they had hung back from
actually suspending Warden Smith, until Chairman Adam
Fergusson had presented them with a *fait accompli*. In any case,
the figure now most thoroughly associated in the public mind
with the work of the Commission—as in Smith's mind and
Macdonald's—was George Brown, the individual who had
drafted its reports, and who still held the post of Penitentiary
Inspector. And once more the government felt no strong desire
to please him. Brown, it may be said, first gained a personal
resentment of Macdonald from his fierce attack of 1850. But
more important at the time was Brown's resentful feeling that
the ministry had gravely let him down.

None of these episodes were sufficient in themselves to turn
him from the government. After the session he continued in its
service, resisting Clear Grit attacks on party unity, writing
Baldwin amicably enough at the close of August for the copy
of a new act "you were good enough to offer me"[118] for publication in the *Globe*. Yet the strains induced between him and
the party leaders in this unsatisfactory parliament of 1850
brought on a state of restlessness that would soon make him
accessible to another powerful current rising in Canada West,
the so-called voluntary movement. It would affect his future,
and that of the Reform party, almost as much as the Clear Grit
revolt that was already so well under way.

5

There was nothing very new about voluntaryism, expressing as it did the desire for the separation of church and state long in evidence in Protestant Canada West and currently displayed in the demand for secularizing the reserves. Yet it was only in 1850 that it began to assume the proportions of a crusade, which in the next four years would loose a veritable holy war in Canadian politics. The name itself derived from the "voluntary principle", which held that churches should rest solely on the conscience and contributions of their members, while the state in turn should know no church connection and grant support to none. In part, voluntaryism stemmed from Britain. There the more evangelical Protestant sects outside the state-established Churches of England or Scotland strongly upheld the voluntary principle, and many immigrants to Canada had carried that conviction with them. In part, voluntaryism was rooted in North America. Canadians of American background—notably Baptists and some Methodists—had often expressed their own traditions of religious independence in opposing state recognition or official privileges for any church.

Moreover, voluntaryism had found ready ground for growth within Upper Canada, where from the start the Church of England had held its privileged position, although the greater part of the Protestant population was non-Anglican. The consequences, of course, had been displayed in protests over the Anglicans' control of the university and many of the schools, their hold on the clergy reserves, and the extra irritant of the forty-four Church of England rectories erected and endowed from the reserves in 1836. Yet in the years before the Rebellion the opponents of Anglican state benefits had frequently been more concerned with securing shares for other churches than with the voluntaryist aim of abolishing state benefits completely. Then in the 1840's the engrossing issue of responsible government had largely stolen the scene. But after 1848, when the problems of church and state gained renewed attention, the pure strain of Protestant voluntaryism became increasingly apparent throughout Canada West.[119]

The University Act of 1849, for instance, had been greeted as a voluntaryist triumph in establishing a provincial university free from church influence or interference. And the reviving popular agitation over the clergy reserves had soon made its prime objective not the more equitable division of the reserves fund among the churches, but the abolition of state endowments altogether. Then the Clear Grits had given effective political expression to voluntaryism by identifying themselves with the cause of secularizing the reserves and abolishing the rectories. In fact, by the middle of 1850, the Grit radical press was fully engaged in preaching the voluntaryist crusade against the entrenched forces of "state churchism": its goal and new Jerusalem, "perfect religious equality", with privileges to none.[120]

If, however, the most immediate "state church" enemy was still the Anglican Tory interest that defended reserves and rectories, the Roman Catholics might also increasingly come in for hostility. The Roman Catholic minority of Upper Canada had usually been on the Reform side in opposing Anglican privilege; but they could hardly embrace the essentially Protestant voluntary principle of church organization, any more than they could endorse the concept of a total separation of church and state: they were, in voluntaryist language, adherents of a "state church". Furthermore, the Catholics were a growing force in Upper Canada by 1850, thanks to the recent large migration of Irish Catholics from their famine-stricken homeland. Increasing numbers brought increasing awareness of their interests as a religious community. Thus their concern for separate schools —though in voluntaryist eyes, tax-supported denominational schools were as much a state-church evil as reserves endowments. The Catholics' success, moreover, in having the School Bill of 1850 amended specially in their favour seemed a dangerous example of sectarian intervention in politics. For the first time, Upper Canadian journals were led to voice antagonism to Roman Catholic claims in the western section, as defenders of the non-sectarian common schools rallied against the threat that public education would be undermined and impoverished.[121] Grit radical journals and voluntaryist religious papers deplored the consequences of the School Bill of 1850 much more strongly than George Brown's *Globe*.[122]

Above all, the fact that Upper Canada had been linked with Catholic French Canada in one united province gave a special weight and significance to Roman Catholic attitudes on "state churchism", once that issue gained new prominence. When Clear Grits were convinced, therefore, that French-Canadian power behind the government was impeding progress in the settlement of the reserves, their press quickly bristled with irate references to "French hacks", "priestism", and "Our Established Church".[123] Upper Canadian rights, declared the *North American* angrily, were in the keeping of Lower Canadian Catholics: "We are bound hand and foot, and lie helpless at the feet of the Catholic Priests of Lower Canada."[124] The language grew corrosive on the Catholic side as well.[125] Voluntaryism *versus* Catholicism: a fierce new storm was blowing up.

There was no question where George Brown stood. By religious training and political conviction he was the foe of every aspect of state churchism. If till now he had not entered actively into the "anti-state-church" protest so far as it referred to Roman Catholicism, it was no doubt because as government organist he had accepted the need of maintaining the link with the French-Canadian Catholic Reformers. Besides, his own dislike for the Clear Grits had led him to regard their voluntaryist professions as not much more than window-dressing for their real republican stock-in-trade. After the disconcerting session of 1850, however, Brown's shaken confidence in the ministry had inclined him more to follow his native voluntaryist bent, with less concern for party unity. And there were disturbing rumours, too, that autumn, of a coming coalition of French Reformers, moderates and Tories, to be formed on the basis of their similar state-church sympathies. He had to discount these rumours in the *Globe*, in October, but added rather dubiously, "we sincerely trust that, so far as the ministerialist party is concerned, no such movement is in any way contemplated."[126] At least he would state his own mind. "Sectarian preferences, whether in the shape of direct endowments or in the modelling of schools or other national systems should be strictly forbidden."[127]

But it was a question far removed from Canada which at last brought Brown's voluntaryism fully into the open, in an outright attack on Roman Catholic state-church tendencies. The so-called Papal Aggression crisis did it: the excited public outburst in England that autumn, that rose in response to a high-flown proclamation by the Papacy of Pius IX. Early in October, Cardinal Wiseman, the newly appointed Roman Catholic Archbishop of Westminster, had made public a recent papal brief creating a full Roman Catholic hierarchy in England with English territorial titles—for the first time since the Protestant Reformation. In sober truth, the Catholic reconquest of Victoria's kingdom was none too imminent. This was merely a reorganization within the Roman Catholic church, expressing the vigorous, newly assertive zeal of the Papacy of Pio Nono. Yet it could hardly have been managed more inauspiciously. The anti-liberal Pope was already regarded in England as the darkest of reactionaries. Now that decidedly Protestant country was shaken by the grand announcement that it was henceforth restored to its regular "orbit" about the Vatican.[128] Did Rome dare to reassert her vanished supremacy over the realm of England? At the theatre, Edmund Kean in *King John* nightly brought the house down as he thundered out the line, "No Italian priest shall tithe or toll in our dominion!"[129]

Perhaps, in the Protestant view, it was a matter of insult rather than injury, but the insult seemed significant enough. When news of the Papal Aggression reached Upper Canada in November, its meaning came in for eager discussion; for that colonial community still vibrated readily to loud sounds from the mother country. The *North American* denounced the intervention of the Pope, "a foreign ruler", in English affairs.[130] The *Examiner* and other voluntaryist journals found in the episode more proof of the evils of state-church pretensions.[131] But the *Globe,* as the government organ, remained relatively silent— until a French-Canadian cabinet minister issued a dangerous challenge to its editor. In Toronto, early that December, the Receiver-General, E. P. Taché, handed George Brown a copy of Cardinal Wiseman's long explanatory address, and somewhat banteringly dared him to publish it. Brown agreed, less gaily, provided it be understood that he would also print his own comments.[132] Half-unrealizing, he thus took a step that would end in making him one of the most revered and most detested men in the whole length of the province.

It was only half-unrealizing, because by now he was fully, fervently, alive to the voluntaryist rallying-call against Catholic state-church power. He saw a newly aggressive, authoritarian Rome reaching out into the public realm in England and elsewhere across the world: the Church opposing the use of national schools in Ireland, demanding extensive school privileges in Canada, allied with despotic governments in combating Liberalism in Austria, Germany and Italy. For him it was a civil matter, the clerical invasion of the political sphere.[133] For his Roman Catholic opponents it was a matter of religion, the defence of the Church's right to its own—and in this basic difference of interpretation lay the source of much tragic future bitterness. But whoever saw more truly, the fact was that the *Globe*'s past few months had only been the brooding quiet before a storm. That December, the storm finally broke.

On the 19th Brown printed "Dr. Wiseman's Manifesto" in nine long columns, then carefully took it up himself in detail. He began with a disavowal. "In offering a few remarks upon Dr. Wiseman's production we have no intention to discuss the tenets of the Roman Catholic Church but merely to look at the question in its secular aspect. As advocates of the voluntary principle we give each man full liberty to worship as his conscience dictates. We would allow each sect to give to its pastors what title it sees fit, but we would have the state recognize no ecclesiastical titles or boundaries whatever. The voluntary principle is the great cure for such dissensions as now agitate Great Britain." So far, this was mild enough. But he had to explain why the papal action in England did trench on public affairs and was not a private matter of religion, as its Roman Catholic defenders asserted. And, paradoxically, by his explanation, Brown opened himself to charges that he was directly attacking the Pope and thus abusing Roman Catholic religion itself.

The trouble was, he said, that the civil and spiritual claims of the Papacy went together: the Pope still claimed perpetual dominion over men and over civil jurisdictions, anathematizing and excommunicating temporal rulers and officials when in the course of their public duties they infringed upon the Church. "By admitting him to exercise the authority which he has now asserted in England, in the eyes of his followers, you admit all his claims." Moreover, there was every evidence that these claims were now being pressed further: in Ireland, for example; in Canada itself. "In our own country—in Upper Canada—do not popery and churchism combine to destroy our national common school system?" He painted a black picture of the baneful effects of papal pretensions and state-church influence on public harmony and happiness, popular freedom and learning: all leading to the conclusion that the dissolution of every tie between church and state provided the only certain cure—and, further, that while this remedy might be slow in coming in Britain, it should at once be applied in Canada.

It was a forthright declaration, made with all the *Globe's* authority behind it. Yet it still might not have been of decisive importance if Brown could only have left things there. That proved impossible, however. Quite naturally, Roman Catholics took him up, chiefly through their organ, the *Mirror*, already roused to religious warfare through clashes with the *Examiner* and *North American*.[134] Inevitably, he replied. Hard words multiplied on either side. By January of 1851 the storm had mounted to a full gale, as Brown proclaimed, "There can be no permanent peace in Canada till every vestige of church dominancy is swept away."[135] The *Mirror* threatened that the *Globe's* course would drive the Roman Catholics from the Upper Canada Reform party; for Catholics, it announced, insisted that their allies should not abuse their religion.[136] The *Globe* rose to this at once: "There is a morbid terror of discussion upon Roman Catholic questions which the leaders of that church have managed to inspire in the minds of politicians of either side. The Roman Catholic hierarchy dare demand in Canada what no other church would dare to solicit. . . . What ho, ye 'Dissenting' Ministers and editors! Come pass under the *Mirror*'s yoke and let the Pope put a plaster on your mouths once and for all!"[137]

Brown had not started it. His Clear Grit foes had first opened the attack on Roman Catholic state-church influence; then Taché had virtually challenged him to join in. The Roman Catholics themselves had made the move in the matter of separate schools, and there was every sign that they meant to go on, under their devoted and uncompromising new Bishop of Toronto, Armand de Charbonnel, a French aristocrat strange to Canada, who sought to save his flock entirely from the Protestant fallacy of non-denominational education: he had already demanded, by virtue of the Act of 1850, that Toronto's two separate schools be increased to seven.[138] None of this removed George Brown's responsibility for the *Globe*'s fateful course at the end of 1850; but it did indicate that responsibility had to be shared. At any rate, he was now irreparably committed to what his enemies would term fanatic anti-Catholicism—but what he considered as the only ultimate road to justice for all faiths and harmony for all citizens: the removal of religion from political entanglements by the way of voluntaryism.

6

Brown fell ill during the height of the anti-papal campaign, for almost the first time in his life.[139] Did this have bearing on the mounting fever of his articles? His mind was deeply troubled, too, about relations with his party. He was by no means blind to the disfavour that the *Globe*'s new course was earning him in ministerial circles.[140] As much he told to a close friend, John Fraser of Prescott, who answered sympathetically, "the ordeal is no small one to sacrifice so much—but what sense would say is folly, faith would see to be true wisdom."[141] Yet during the ordeal he still managed to keep solicitous watch over Fraser's sickly brother, Donald, who had been given minor employment on the *Globe*, sending home long reports on his state of health and plans for its betterment. "You have a warm heart, George, and I feel it all, and most feelingly respond to all," replied Fraser gratefully.[142]

In February of 1851, however, the anti-papal editorials came to an end. The *Globe* apparently was still firmly in the ministerial harness, defending the government's determination to move the capital to Quebec next year against a combined Tory and Clear Grit attack from Upper Canada.[143] But now Brown took another critical decision. The western constituency of Haldimand had fallen vacant through the death of its sitting member: he would run for it himself. This decision probably had no one cause, but was rather the culmination of several developments. By now he could afford to leave the *Globe*. Its finances were sound, and his brother Gordon was qualified to manage it during his absence. By now he had the inclination. After nearly eight years of political journalism and of pushing other men into parliament, after practically winning an election campaign in '47, and being offered several candidacies, why should he not try it for himself? And finally, by now he had a strong impelling motive: to carry voluntaryism into parliament, free from the republican associations of the Clear Grits. In private, he had been urging Upper Canadian ministers to take a firm stand on anti-state-church principles and show their Lower Canadian allies that they would not budge.[144] His arguments had had little success: but they might, indeed, if he could voice them in full parliament. Certainly, his own views came out plainly in the published address that he shortly set before the Reformers of Haldimand: "I am opposed to any connection between church and state. . . . I am in favour of national common school education free from sectarian teaching."[145]

But Haldimand would be no easy nut to crack. It was one western county he was not familiar with, although, of course, his name was widely known there. And while his candidacy had official government sanction (in a somewhat stilted letter from Francis Hincks that said significantly, "If you could be brought forward without dividing the party it would be satisfactory to the ministerialists here"),[146] he would have to run against the imposing figure of William Lyon Mackenzie, who had put himself up as an independent Reform candidate in order to make his return to active politics. Besides, the vehement Mackenzie was not only past master at campaigning; he was certain to attract the Clear Grit dissentients, and perhaps many another Reformer who felt the old magnetism of his name. The elderly warrior had been back in Canada for nearly a year now, and his tortuous struggles to realize money claims from the government had merely increased his enmity towards the ministerial side.[147] Without joining positively with the Grits, Mackenzie was only too glad to work with the anti-government Reformers in Haldimand, and to strike a blow at the Baldwin clique whom he now regarded as virtually his personal enemies.[148]

As for Brown, he soon found himself in the unenviable position of being subject to every criticism levied against the ministry, while receiving practically no aid from the ministry itself. No party leader came forward to lend a hand in his campaign, and to add to his troubles, two other party candidates appeared, residents of the county, each claiming to be government supporters. One of them, Case, the owner of Haldimand plaster workings, had a certain local following: evidently he stood in "the lime-pit interest", decided the *Globe*.[149] The other, Turner, divided the regular county party organization at the very outset of the contest, when he refused to drop his candidacy in Brown's favour even after a solemn arbitration between them had been conducted by township delegates in "Mrs. Campbell's New Brick Building" in Cayuga.[150]

Nevertheless, Brown was in the constituency doing his best from early March onward. He covered Haldimand from end to end, often crossing paths with Mackenzie; and crossing swords too, when they spoke at each other's noisy meetings. It was quickly clear that they were the main rivals; Brown had to spend a good deal of his time refuting Mackenzie's violent accusations against the government's extravagant and reactionary character. "It is a pity to see an old man tell so many downright lies," a friend of Brown's remarked feelingly.[151] The latter himself unhappily reported, "Our disputes have been simply questions of veracity, he asserting some monstrous proposition and I denying it. They say, 'one of us must be an awful liar'."[152]

The nominations that were supposedly a critical trial of strength came on a Saturday, April 5. Mackenzie did not win the test, but then neither did George Brown. It was a wretched day at the county seat of Cayuga, and in the torrential rain only a forlorn three hundred had gathered in the mud about the uncovered platform, where the soggy candidates stood penned.[153] As they were duly proposed, and addressed the audience in turn, it literally melted away in the downpour, until by the time Case had perched himself on the top rail of the hustings to declaim "in true roarer style" only some seventy were left.[154] The clanging of dinner bells from surrounding taverns completed the rout. Few but Case's faithful lingered to hear him —and, as a result, when the show of hands was called for immediately afterwards, he won the majority. He really remained the weakest of the candidates, but the moral effect was only to divide the ministerial Reformers further, chiefly at Brown's expense.

The polls were to open on Monday, April 14. The evening before, at Jarvis, George Brown took time to send his father a final report at the close of a stiff campaign, expressing the cautious judgement that he well might win, but fully alive to the possibility of defeat.[155] "I never fought harder for anything," he wrote, "and never felt more unconcerned as to any great approaching result. . . . I may be defeated, I may be returned by a small majority, and I may possibly sweep the board." He took account of his difficulties, and added bitterly, "Never before has such opposition been brought to bear against any one candidate, and never did candidate in similar circumstances receive *less* support from his party." However, "I have done all that can be done to attain success, and cannot look back with regret . . . my belief is the election is safe—but . . . there is no calculating. . . . I am quite prepared for any result and won't by any means break my heart."

Yet, unknown to him, a new hostile development was under way, one that would destroy his resignation to the possibility of defeat. Roman Catholic forces were at work in Haldimand to turn their co-religionists away from this notorious defamer of their faith. Until now, apparently, Brown had had little awareness that his recent anti-papal articles might rebound against him at the election, presumably expecting that Catholic Reformers would hold to the Liberal ministry and its candidate, as they regularly had done before. Perhaps this was foolish lack of perception; perhaps he did not think that the British Papal Aggression question was an issue in the Haldimand by-election. At any rate, discussions of religious questions had actually played no great part in the campaign. Brown's chief opponent, Mackenzie, was as much a voluntaryist as he was, and their speeches had chiefly reflected the standard Clear Grit attacks on the ministry and the *Globe*'s usual defence of it. State churchism was not an active issue between them.

But Brown was wholly wrong if he thought that Roman Catholics would ignore his anti-papal pronouncements. The Toronto *Mirror* had kept its readers vividly reminded of them during the campaign, and just before the election a fiery handbill was widely circulated, addressed to the Catholic Electors of Haldimand—where dwelled a substantial number of Catholic Irish settlers with strong racial memories. Eloquently it cried, "Will you help to crush the religion of the Holy Catholic Church in this Province? If you will, vote for GEORGE BROWN. Are you willing to prostrate yourselves like cowardly slaves or beasts of burden before the avowed enemy of your country, your religion and your God? If you are, vote for GEORGE BROWN. Would you bring shame and disgrace upon the memory of the martyred dead whose kindred dust now sleeps in the graveyards of green Erin? If so, vote for

GEORGE BROWN. You will not, you cannot, you shall not be guilty of such a crime before God and men; you will think on the gibbets, the triangles, the tortures, the hangings of the past; you will reflect on the struggles of the present; you will look forward to the dangers, the hopes, the triumphs of the future; and then you will go to the polls and vote AGAINST GEORGE BROWN!"[156]

"I think we have the Catholicks," an agent had gleefully written to Mackenzie.[157] Whether or not the Catholic Irish would think on gibbets and tortures, doubt and discord had been flung into Brown's camp at the crucial moment. As the polls opened, Catholic supporters of the government hung back or voted against him. Mackenzie piled up an early lead, and in those days of open, long-drawn-out polling this was often of decisive psychological influence. At the end of two clamorous days the old radical was securely in; and George Brown was nowhere. His defeat probably owed quite as much to Clear Grit feeling and Mackenzie's prestige as it did to the Roman Catholic vote. Nevertheless, when he thought upon results, he saw the last factor as the vital one that had turned the scales against him: and his jubilant enemies took the same stand. The outcome in Haldimand thus seemed simply to demonstrate the compelling power of Catholic sectarian influence in politics. Nor would Brown forget it. His first election failure delayed his entrance to parliament only for a matter of months. But the lesson that he drew from this defeat was almost as important in his career as any of his subsequent victories at the polls.

7

There was not much resignation left now in Brown. When hostile papers from the *Mirror* to the Grit *Journal and Express* taunted the *Globe* with having ensured its editor's defeat through the anti-papal editorials, he swiftly retorted in its pages: "If the day has really come when men are to be debarred from going into Parliament on the Reform interest unless their religious sentiments are agreeable to the rulers of the Roman Catholic Church, the scene that has just been enacted may not have been without its advantages. If Reform Candidates are to be tested by adherence to their sectarian views by Roman Catholic electors then the Protestant section of the party should be apprised of it."[158] He denied that he was inciting Protestants to a religious war. He continued to condemn the "miserable sectarianism", the feuds and outrages of the Orange Order.[159] "We defy anyone to show a line advocating mere sectarian principles or measures in the *Globe* . . . this is the whole sum of our offending—because we asked that the Roman Catholic Church should be placed on precisely the same footing as other churches."[160] Yet his paper's return to hot religious controversy with the *Mirror* in late April and May, after silence on the topic since February, showed very plainly the anger that had been aroused by the Roman Catholic action in Haldimand. They had acted as a divisive sect; they would be treated as one. "If we stand alone, we will speak out!"[161]

Nor was this anger the only bitter fruit of the by-election. Almost as strong was Brown's indignant feeling, already expressed in his letter on election eve, that the ministry had wholly failed its follower, letting him incur the weight of Mackenzie's charges against the government, but doing nothing in return to bring ministerialists into line behind him. He must have shared the thought voiced by the Guelph *Advertiser*: "If Mr. Brown had stood as an independent member, not as a ministerial candidate, he would have had a much better chance of success."[162] The path of independence was beckoning. Indeed, Brown was quite obviously moving down it, for the *Globe*'s renewed and even wider attack on Catholic state churchism was certainly no part of government policy for the party organ.[163]

The parliamentary session that began on May 20, 1851, soon carried him still further. The Speech from the Throne, he found, gave no indication that the ministry was willing to discuss plans for the final abolition of the clergy reserves. There was only a bare acknowledgement of an imperial dispatch which stated that the question of the necessary enabling legislation would be put before the Parliament at Westminster. Eight days later, a government announcement that the reserves would not be brought up at all this session merely seemed to prove that the Reform administration had bowed to state-church influence, centred in the solid core of its Lower Canadian Catholic support. A still worse sign were "ecclesiastical corporations" bills, measures granting corporate legal powers to Roman Catholic or Anglican religious bodies and securing them unlimited rights of holding property. Alarmingly enough, these were endorsed by western Liberal ministers like Hincks, as well as by French-speaking members of the cabinet. No exponent of voluntaryism could lightly agree that the state should thus underwrite the building of new ecclesiastical endowments, held in perpetuity.

Nevertheless, it was the other current running strong in Up-

per Canada, Clear Grittism, which was responsible for the ultimate crisis in Brown's relations with the government. The Grits
in the House now had the vengeful aid of the new member for
Haldimand, William Lyon Mackenzie, and it seemed that the
last fourteen years in the political wilderness had hardly weak-
ened his aggressive powers, as he went avidly war-whooping
after Baldwin and his colleagues. The Clear Grits readily
backed Mackenzie, when on June 26 he moved, seconded by
Caleb Hopkins, for the abolition of the Upper Canada Court
of Chancery. Because of its costs and professional complexity,
Chancery had been a leading target in the Grit campaign for
low-priced justice, easily available to the poor but honest liti-
gant. Yet it was also the apple of lawyer Baldwin's eye, having
been reformed by him but two years earlier. He could scarcely
avoid regarding Mackenzie's motion as a direct attack upon
himself.

It was defeated, but only thanks to Lower Canadian votes.
There was actually an Upper Canadian majority in favour of the
motion.[164] Mackenzie had had a satisfying measure of revenge;
the Grits were overjoyed at the evidence of new-found
strength; and the sensitive Robert Baldwin brooded, deeming
this an outright denial of Upper Canadian confidence in his
leadership. On the night of June 30, he rose in parliament to
reveal a momentous decision: he would resign that leadership
forthwith, and plan to retire from the cabinet.

There was perhaps no need for the western leader to take the
rebuff over Chancery as a decisive defeat. Though the Clear
Grits had certainly made headway into Reform ranks, they had
gained their sectional majority only with the support of the
Tories, and by detaching some government followers on this
issue alone. Yet Baldwin had needed only this blow, worn and
unwell as he was, and deeply disheartened by the divisive movements in Liberalism.[165] His partner Lafontaine felt much the
same: he was plagued by *Rouge* radicalism in Canada East and,
as he said, sick of "the group of chisellers at present in the
House".[166] Not long afterwards he announced his own decision
to retire at the end of the session. Both the captains of bygone
battles for responsible government were out of sympathy with
the growing extremism in politics. They had done their work,
and were ready enough to leave sorely troubled Reform to
other hands. With them passed the Great Ministry of 1848: a
gloomy, discouraged end to brilliant achievement.

Liberalism was in crisis. So was George Brown. Despite all
differences, he had kept a high respect for Robert Baldwin,
granting his honest adherence to the most basic Reform principles, whatever his state-church inclinations might have been in

the particular matter of religious endowments. But Francis Hincks, who was Baldwin's chosen successor as western party leader, had an old and dubious reputation for putting expediency ahead of principles. Brown considered that Hincks had done so in the School Act of 1850, yielding to Roman Catholic sectarian schools for the sake of temporary party advantage. Moreover, on assuming Baldwin's mantle in the House on June 30, the new leader had spoken ominously of the need for western Reformers to come to terms with the state-church views of Lower Canada in order to preserve the common party front.[167] Then too, there were unhappy memories of personal friction; the old Brown-Hincks rivalry as editors of the *Globe* and *Pilot*: Hincks's accusation in 1845 that Brown was conspiring to steal his Oxford seat; and Brown's unthankful work in 1847 in helping to elect Hincks to that seat, during the latter's absence from the country.

Baldwin's guiding hand was gone, while Price, the firmest voluntaryist in the ministry and Brown's chief contact there, would himself retire at the close of the session. Hincks was left in full control—Hincks who took occasion in his inaugural speech as leader to condemn the *Globe* for criticizing ministerial support of ecclesiastical corporations, and who darkly warned that "new combinations" might be formed to carry on the government if Reform unity was not maintained.[168] To Brown at breaking-point, this was simply throwing down the gauntlet. In his next *Globe*, on July 3, he grimly picked it up.

"When in the middle of the fourth session of a Reform parliament, we still find ourselves without any intelligence from England on the Reserves question—when we find sectarian grants so long denounced actually increased . . . and dangerous measures for the acquisition of property by ecclesiastical corporations not repealed but increased—and when we find our friendly cautions on these exciting subjects treated with resentment and threats—we can no longer be silent." It was argued that anti-state-church forces were in the minority in Canada as a whole, that if Reform leaders adopted a fully voluntaryist policy the party would go down to defeat before "new combinations". But even were this so, Reform should make a bold and honest stand against state-church evils. The *Globe*, Brown said with hard significance, was at once prepared to take up that position—though "ten years opposition stared us in the face".[169] And bridges were soon burned, when he added strongly that the government's present drift left "but one course for the opponents of priestcraft and state churchism—energetic, united, unyielding opposition."[170]

He had broken with the party leaders; the *Globe* quickly

abandoned the last traces of organship: the turmoil of voluntaryism had swept them too far for any easy return. In fact,
the whole western Reform party was plainly in turmoil, dis-
rupted by the dual forces of voluntaryism and Clear Grit radicalism. But what blame had Brown himself to bear for this
sorry state of disunity? He had fought it strenuously in regard
to Grittism, and had been coldly repaid by leaders he had defended. He had not begun the assault on the exponents of state
churchism, and for nearly two years had repudiated the rising
Upper Canadian cry against French domination. Yet it would
be absurd to deny him his own share of blame: his attacks on
Roman Catholicism that had turned first English- and then
French-speaking Catholics against him, further to embitter the
internal party quarrels. He might honestly believe that he had
only attacked the unwarranted political claims and not the doctrines of Catholicism. But it was hard to separate Roman Catholic civil interests from spiritual tenets—he had said as much
himself.[171] And the ardour of his own Free Kirk beliefs, plus
the habitual sting of the *Globe*'s tongue, had only aggravated
the angry Catholic reaction to his stand.

Equally, however, it would be absurd to place the onus on
Brown for bringing religious antagonism and sectarian strife
into a sweetly harmonious Canadian political life. If Roman
Catholics were going to act as a religious faction in politics to
demand more separate-school privileges—deserved or not—
they would invoke a similar kind of opposition. It was a positive
challenge when their *Mirror* flatly declared, "The ministry that
would introduce a measure to repeal the nineteenth clause of the
present School Bill could not live twenty-four hours after."
Should the French Canadians' dislike of secularization influence
government policy on the reserves, then they would have to
face the charge that Lower Canadians were blocking the settlement of an Upper Canadian question. If they should also use
their power to push bills for ecclesiastical corporations, they
would as surely invite western voluntaryist resistance. The rise
of sectarian strife in Canada had far bigger causes than the
person of George Brown.

But he would move with it, come to the fore because of it,
and end by shaping a new western Reform party under his
leadership. First, however, Liberalism would have to go down
in cross-currents before it could be remade. And first George
Brown would have to start again, outside the party organization,
in the independent political role to which the last two years had
led him.

Independent Member

I

The well-worn penitentiary question came up again, just as Brown was moving to the final breach with the ministry. On June 24, 1851, two days before Mackenzie made his telling attack on Chancery, the insistent John A. Macdonald revived the issue by once more calling for a committee of inquiry into the Report of the Commission of 1849. Once more his demand was rejected by ministerial forces less concerned to defend the Commission than the government which had accepted its findings. Yet in the four-hour debate on the topic Macdonald again concentrated his attack on the chief author of the Report, accusing the ministers of "cowardly fear of George Brown who had so completely bullied them": an unlikely charge, considering the tension between the parties involved, although its truth perhaps was less important than the calculated aggravating effect on either side. And Macdonald, still implacably blind to the black record of his protégé, ex-Warden Smith, magnified his old accusations against the man he regarded as Smith's prime persecutor.[1]

Brown had no adequate defender in the House, but he could reply in the *Globe*. He did so in a vehement, meticulously detailed rejoinder to Macdonald's free-swinging assault.[2] His enemies, from Clear Grits to the Conservative Macdonald, might try to discount the weight of his denials. Yet their proof lay in the voluminous mass of Commission documents, and it was from this basis that he spoke with such conviction. Again the penitentiary question passed by, in the excitement over the far bigger issue of the moment, the break-up and reconstruction of the Liberal government. Undoubtedly, however, Macdonald's violent charges rankled with Brown, and undoubtedly the former remained unsatisfied, still storing up his grievances. Five years hence the Commission records would be finally examined—but only after a fierce explosion between these two antagonists.

The penitentiary encore was not the only distraction for
George Brown during the mounting ministerial crisis. A few
weeks later he was involved in a sportive little riot, chiefly worth
attention because it was quite typical of Tory direct-action politics in Toronto of the day. The Toronto Anti-Clergy Reserves
Association had planned a meeting for the evening of July 8,
in the city's proud new auditorium, St. Lawrence Hall, en-
nobled with white Corinthian pillars, after the Temple of
Jupiter Stator, crowned with an open cupola containing a massive one-ton bell, and gleaming within with fresh paint and a
highly emblematical ceiling.[3] Both George and Peter Brown
were among the group on the platform that night, waiting their
turn to address the assembly, when a gang of Orange Tory
toughs planted in the hall began to howl down the speakers.
Then they rushed the platform, shoving the others aside to shout
their own amendments. They took over completely, until Chairman Adam Fergusson managed to call a hasty adjournment.
The meeting broke up in utter confusion, leaving one, St.
Crispin, "the Orange shoemaker", standing at the front of the
platform wholly carried away on a picturesque flight of oaths
and oratory, while an Anglican minister tried desperately to
cram a hat over his mouth.[4]

The adjourned meeting met again in St. Lawrence Hall on
July 23, jamming the gallery and the eight hundred seats on
the floor below. But by the merest chance the Tories had called
an anti-Anti-Reserves meeting of their own nearby, outside the
City Hall, where, after burning speeches, the audience were
told that they could whip the Association bunch and advised to
go home. Who could be blamed for the bellowing march on
St. Lawrence Hall that followed? This time, however, the
defenders were better prepared; they held the barred inner
doors as the mob surged against them. Checked, the attackers
swirled around the building, and began hurling stones through
its high windows, while Brown and the other speakers had to
shout above shattering glass and the shrieks of the ladies in the
beleaguered audience. They all had to sit from 10:30 to midnight, while the clamorous siege continued, and a messenger
slipped through to the Garrison for troops. Finally a company
of the 71st came pounding up to disperse the mob—proving
among other things that the Garrison at least still had the function of defending Toronto against itself.[5]

However rousing the episode, it could nevertheless only
briefly turn attention from the all-important question of the
reconstruction of the government. This, in particular, involved
strengthening support behind Hincks in Canada West, where

the Clear Grits had so cut into ministerial ranks, and where George Brown's defection had made it necessary to find a new press organ. Actually, since Lafontaine was still formally at the head of the ministry, and was apparently prepared to stay there until the end of the session, Hincks could not yet undertake to offer definite posts in a new cabinet.[6] But the question of reconstruction was no less real for that, especially as a general election would follow this final session of the old parliament returned in 1847. Accordingly, meetings of Reform politicos, secret closetings with the new western party leader, "informed" predictions and contradictory rumours, kept the Toronto capital twittering with excited gossip throughout the height of the summer. Hincks planned to coalesce with MacNab and the Tories to head off the radicals? Wrong—he would bring in the Grits to keep the Tories out, and had promised Brown a cabinet seat to win back the *Globe*. Was it true the French and Tories would join together in a common state-church front? No, the mass of Upper Canadians would combine to check French power —they would for certain.[7]

Throughout the flurry of rumour the *Globe* maintained an anxious watching brief. For all its separation from the government, it still hoped that new western ministers might stand on anti-state-church principles.[8] In that event, it promised still to give outside support, and urged Upper Canada Liberals not to put union with French Canadians ahead of their own desires for reform. "If unity with the French is to come first and the voluntary principle after it—then we say we are quite satisfied that the reserves three years from now will be divided among the sects, and we will have sectarian education, sectarian grants and sectarian corporations to the heart's content of the veriest priest in the country."[9] The only honest course, the paper held, was to put Upper Canadian views on church and state squarely to the French Reformers. If they could not accept the West's adherence to these opinions, then the alliance should be broken, and the Upper Canada Reform party come out for "practical voluntaryism". "All we ask is that the French Canadians will not help our enemies against us on our vital questions. It is no question of coercing them—it is they who coerce us."[10]

As for an offer of cabinet office, Brown had not received it and Hincks would scarcely be inclined to make it, even if the *Globe* editor would ever have served under him, or have been accepted by the French Canadians. In fact, the ministerial negotiations had begun with efforts to find another journal to replace the *Globe* as official mouthpiece in Canada West—while the latter tartly expressed "our perfect good will towards the plan of establishing a new organ. For ourselves, we have had enough of it."[11] This organ would have to be established in the chief western centre, Toronto. But no one stood ready to launch a new paper, and hence the choice was necessarily limited to the other city Reform sheets, the *Examiner*, *Mirror* and *North American*. The *Mirror* was not prepared to leave its distinctly Roman Catholic basis; and though Lindsey, the *Examiner*'s editor, was willing to talk terms, its owner, Lesslie, was himself too engrained a voluntaryist to have anything to do with a ministry that showed leanings to state churchism.[12] That left only McDougall's *North American*, which from the start had been so hot against the government. Yet the ministry's need was urgent, and in that need, aspiring William McDougall perceived the very opportunity for a Clear Grit triumph. He coolly informed Lindsey, for transmission to Hincks, that the price of the *North American*'s support would be nothing less than Grit representation in the cabinet.[13] The need indeed was urgent. His price was accepted.

"The government have knocked under—struck their colours," McDougall crowed to Charles Clarke on July 25. Malcolm Cameron and John Rolph, two seasoned radicals, were to enter the cabinet—"these being the men I have insisted should be accepted."[14] The new ministry, said the Clear Grit kingmaker, would go forward with "all reasonable progressive measures", though "the Platform as a whole of course must be laid aside".[15] Evidently high Grit ideals were coming down, now that practical benefits lay ahead. And in seeking more help on the *North American* from Clarke, who yet had to eke out his income from journalism by working in a drug store, McDougall promised rosily, "If we can get to the top of the heap we can perhaps do for you something more congenial than standing behind a counter."[16]

McDougall and David Christie worked out the details of a confidential bargain; the other leading Grits endorsed it.[17] Before the end of July, therefore, the basis for a Clear Grit-Hincksite coalition had been laid. The definite formulation of the new ministry still had to wait on Lafontaine's retirement two months hence; but early in August the news of the underlying contract leaked out. "Francis Hincks has gone over teetotally to the Clear Grits," Brown announced incisively in the *Globe* of August 7, "entered into unreserved alliance with that amiable family! The whole thing is funny—exceedingly funny —but it may work, notwithstanding. We have no fear from the ultraism of the Clear Grits in office, and have no doubt that the *North American* speaks for its party when it avows its willingness to postpone the half—aye, or the very whole of the budget—'for the sake of Union'. Her Majesty's Government *must* be carried on, and your Clear Grit in office will be a very different animal."[18] In fact, Brown added, if radicals would only hold true to their anti-state-church principles on the ministerial side of the House, the *Globe* would not condemn the union. But he seriously doubted that they would do so. The ministerialists would not likely turn Grit: thus the ultras must virtually have yielded up their doctrines for a share of power.[19]

Of course, the *North American* angrily denied the slander.[20] Yet events soon proved that the radicals had perforce abandoned most of their demands for elective democracy, administrative purity and the destruction of religious privilege when they joined with the ministerial forces they had previously denounced as reactionary, corrupt and Catholic-dominated. Perhaps the *Globe* had not been wrong in ascribing the Clear Grit revolt largely to an envious yearning for office. This was only part of the story, particularly in the case of younger Grit hopefuls like McDougall, and the radical following in the country. But it surely helped to explain Rolph's and Cameron's ready flip into the ministry—especially when the latter accepted the post of President of the Council, an office he had warmly attacked as useless, during his earlier selfless zeal for retrenchment.[21] At any rate, the Old Reform politicians now seemed to find little difficulty in combining with their former foes.

As for McDougall himself, he plainly did not feel that he had abandoned his ideals in proposing coalition. He and others like him viewed the presence of Rolph and Cameron in the cabinet as surety for Clear Grit Reforms: if some of them had to be put by, more could still be gained in office than outside. Events again would show, however, that the Grit representatives in the cabinet were sadly outnumbered, and broken reeds to begin with. McDougall's apparent triumph of 1851 would do little to realize the radicals' aims in their next three years of sharing power. The fact is that McDougall's whole career revealed a dangerous inclination to grasp too eagerly at office, less from ambition for himself than for his particular cause of the moment; and in the long run this tendency to make expedient compromises would do both the man and his cause far more harm than good.

On the other side, Hincks found even less difficulty than the Clear Grits in reaching an expedient compromise. No doubt, the French Canadians would have to be won over to an alliance with fire-eyed radicals, "les socialistes", and brought to accept secularization of the reserves as a government policy—one clear

gain on which the Grits insisted. But Hincks himself was quite
in favour of secularization, if politically feasible, and Lafontaine's retirement would remove the main centre of French
resistance in the ministry.[22] Apart from this, as a highly "practical" politician Hincks's first concern was government strength,
not problems of principle. His favourite, oft-repeated argument
was that if the Liberal party did not hold together (in short,
did not say the same thing whatever it might be) the Tories
would return to power.[23] Besides, by this time he was thoroughly
caught up in the railway fever that had begun to sweep Canada
in 1851. He was eager to call truce to internal party differences
in order to get on with the real business of developing the country, and, above all, with the construction of a great main line
from one end of the province to the other—the costly project
that would become the Grand Trunk Railway of Canada.

Indeed, as parliament drew to a close in August, railway projects were competing more and more effectively for public interest with questions of church and state. For the time being,
the matter of ministerial reconstruction seemed almost in abeyance, especially when Hincks brought up and passed his measure
for a "Main Trunk Line" in the last days of the session, providing for rail connection from Quebec to the western border,
as part of the greater intercolonial scheme to link the British
American provinces from the Atlantic coast to the heart of the
continent. Brown himself approved the purpose of the bill—
"We are clearly in favour of building the road from Quebec to
the St. Clair at all hazards."[24] Still, he felt that a dying parliament should not have taken on the great new measure, and that
it should have been left to a reconstructed ministry to introduce.[25]

At all events, the basis had been found for a reorganization
of the Liberal ministry. The present interregnum could not long
continue, and already election talk was in the air. The old parliament passed away quietly on August 30. The *Globe* noted
that of its last old guard of twenty-four hanging on for "midnight legislation", six were attending to business under the chairman, nine engaged in conversation and by-play, four reading,
two sleeping, and two humming "Auld Lang Syne".[26] And
George Brown's paper itself prepared for new business with a
forthright election platform.

NO RESERVES!
NO RECTORIES!
NO SECTARIAN SCHOOLS!
NO SECTARIAN MONEY GRANTS!
NO ECCLESIASTICAL CORPORATIONS!
NO RELIGIOUS PREFERENCES WHATEVER![27]

2

Railways were still in the limelight that autumn. In mid-September the *Globe* editor went himself to report on the "Great Boston Railway Celebration", that brought together the President of the United States and the Governor-General of Canada to expatiate on the miracle of railways, heaven-sent progenitors of wealth and industry and of brotherhood among the nations. The occasion was the opening of the Grand Junction Railroad, which carried the line between Albany and Boston down into the mast forest of the Atlantic docks, thereby linking—so the motto of the day claimed—"Liverpool, Boston, and the Canadas".[28] The link was a bit tenuous, and smacked of high optimism and low press-agentry. But the claim itself, the fervid oratory, the gathering of North America's notables—including Francis Hincks and Sir Allan MacNab from Canada—all signalized the glowing enthusiasm of the young railway era that would transform the face and very structure of the British North American provinces within the next two decades.

Not a month later, Toronto had its own railway celebration to mark the breaking of the ground for the Ontario, Simcoe and Huron, usually called "the Northern", the first line out of the city. It would run some ninety miles to Collingwood on Georgian Bay, and give Toronto a short rail route to the lumber, mines and commerce of the Upper Lakes, as well as closer connections with the hinterland of prosperous farming settlements which lay northward from the town. Brown must have been in the bubbling crowd on Front Street by the Parliament Buildings, that brisk October afternoon, to hear the Governor-General again perform on railways, while Mr. Palmer took his daguerreotypes, and Lady Elgin daintily lifted the first sod to place it in the handsome carved oak wheelbarrow held out by Toronto's Mayor Bowes—dressed himself for working on the railroad in cocked hat, sword, knee breeches, silk stockings and silver-buckled shoes.[29]

Other railways, too, were under way in the humming province of Canada, stimulated by renewed good times, which they in turn were blowing into a full boom. The St. Lawrence and Atlantic was thrusting down from Montreal towards Portland and the seaboard, to give the province the all-important winter outlet denied it by the long freeze-up of the St. Lawrence River. There were schemes for lines from Montreal to Kingston, and Kingston to Toronto, that soon would be incorporated into the bigger Grand Trunk project, crossing the province from end to end. And beyond Toronto, the Great Western was being surveyed for over two hundred miles, from Windsor at the south-western tip of Upper Canada's Peninsula to the Niagara River: its aim, to provide the most direct connection between the interior of the continent and the eastern American railroads serving the great port of New York.

The Great Western that tapped the broad Peninsula would be linked as well to Hamilton, and soon afterwards to Toronto. In fact, this latter city would become the centre of a widespread railway web, radiating northward, and to east and west. With its commerce already booming, and plans afoot to enlarge it further by providing better marketing facilities as well as the latest means of transport, Toronto now was fairly embarked on a vigorous endeavour to organize and direct the life of the whole western section of the province. And just as his city's influence would steadily expand throughout the western regions, so would that of George Brown and the *Globe*. It was early yet to tell; but the man and his journal were to become veritable symbols of Toronto's rise to dominate the West in this fast-growing boom of the railway-building fifties.

Furthermore, the mounting boom brought Brown himself to invest in western development, like many another speculative Toronto business man of the time. With funds earned from his city newspaper enterprise he now bought wild lands in the Peninsula, in the south-western county of Kent, along the projected route of the new Great Western Railroad.[30] If the line went through as anticipated, his forest tract seemed certain to become valuable property for settlement. This, however, was more than mere land speculation. Brown was a city man by origin, experience and livelihood; yet there was in him a deep chord of feeling, perhaps ancestral feeling, for the world of the country-side and the life of the farmer. The health of Canada, he recognized, depended fundamentally on the well-being of agriculture. As his knowledge of the farming West had grown, the *Globe* had shown increasing interest in agrarian concerns: nor was this unconnected with the spreading rural circulation of the *Weekly Globe*. And the western Peninsula was the area that attracted Brown above all. Here the farmer's self-reliant energy was even yet transforming ancient wilderness into productive fields. His own purchase of land would link him with that vital process, give him some share of his own in the vigorous growth of the free western country-side.

Accordingly, by the early autumn of 1851, he had acquired nearly eight hundred acres of Crown land in Kent's northernmost township of Zone, that bordered on Lambton County:

fairly level but well drained land, its loam and sandy soil covered with superb stands of hardwoods—oak and curly maple, hickory and cherry.[31] He made his initial purchase while his friend Price was still Crown Lands Commissioner, which may have helped him to obtain his selection; but he gradually added to his holdings by buying neighbouring tracts from private owners.[32] He had close on 4000 acres when the Great Western rails went through along the line expected. A way-station, Bothwell, was established on his estate. Farmers came in, cleared fields pushed back the forests. His settlement of Bothwell became a thriving reality.[33]

This achievement, however, took several years to realize. And in September, 1851, while Brown was just beginning his investment in western lands, his venture gained another more immediate significance. He was asked to run for Kent as an independent Reform candidate in the coming general election.[34] Should he do so, his property would give him a valuable local interest in the county, and help counteract the widespread rural prejudice against "outside" candidates which had been one factor in his defeat in the Haldimand by-election. Besides, Brown already knew Kent, and had known it since the mid-1840's, when he had first built up a following for his old *Western Globe* in the far Peninsula. There were good friends as well in neighbouring Lambton County, then combined with Kent for purposes of parliamentary representation. In fact, the initial suggestion that he should stand for Kent came in a letter of September 11 from Port Sarnia, Lambton's county seat.[35]

The letter was from young Alexander Mackenzie, a keen voluntaryist Liberal, a former Scottish stone-mason who was now flourishing as a building contractor in the rising little port on the St. Clair. Brown knew Mackenzie and his elder brother, Hope (a Sarnia shipbuilder), as members of a fraternal band of stout Reformers active in municipal and Lambton county politics.[36] They were close followers of the *Globe*; he stayed among them on visits to the district. There was a similar group of friends in Kent itself, prominent among them Archibald McKellar, the reeve of Chatham, who like Brown had warmly supported the work of the Elgin Association in settling Negro fugitives at Buxton in Kent.[37] These were the men, the two Mackenzies and McKellar, who were largely behind the proposal that the *Globe* editor should try for parliament again. They would, moreover, become his lasting political associates— particularly the diligent, devoted and single-minded Alexander Mackenzie, Brown's chief parliamentary lieutenant in later years, and his successor as a Liberal leader.

Kent seemed to offer good prospects, as Brown debated the suggestion that he run. Reform sentiment was strong in the riding, particularly in Lambton, and much of it was hostile to the existing ministry. No doubt this expressed western rural resentment against governments that seemed to do little for the ordinary people of the country-side but tax them, and yet let fat clergy reserves endowments exist: the sort of feeling that hitherto had helped to send Clear Grits to parliament. That well-known Grit, Malcolm Cameron, was himself from Sarnia, and had represented Kent for years. But now the Clear Grit radicals had gone over to the ministry, while Cameron (perhaps wisely) was not intending to try for his old seat again. Hence it followed that the anti-ministerial spirit, which in Haldimand had worked against Brown as a government candidate, in Kent might well work for him if he ran there as an independent Reformer. All in all, the county looked promising for a voluntaryist, anti-government Liberal of George Brown's character and standing.

Still, he by no means leaped at this new chance to enter active politics. He was of two minds now about the whole idea. He had, he said, "been long enough behind the scenes to lose all sublime ideas of parliamentary life".[38] He really wondered whether journalism and parliamentary duties could be satisfactorily combined for long, or whether he might not do better service to his political opinions as full-time editor of the *Globe*.[39] Undoubtedly, too, the Haldimand election had been an unhappy experience, and Brown was a sensitive loser. "It takes all one's patriotism to think without quailing of a second contest," he uneasily replied to Mackenzie's letter, "and three months' annual residence at Quebec for four years—leaving business to take care of itself."[40] The feelings that in earlier years had made him resist the suggestion of running for parliament returned again, inevitably strengthened by his disappointment in Haldimand.

On the other hand, he was quick to assure Mackenzie, "there is no constituency I would feel so gratified to represent, were I in parliament, as Kent."[41] And he knew now that he could safely leave the *Globe* in his brother Gordon's hands during any absence. (Gordon, incidentally, had just capped his full journalistic training with a three-months' visit to England to report the wonders of the Great Exhibition of 1851, held in that apotheosis of the greenhouse, London's giant new Crystal Palace.)[42] Above all, the same deep concern for voluntaryism which had done so much to make George Brown run in Haldimand that spring was no less compelling in the autumn. It had, if anything, been heightened by his open breach with a ministry which he considered had sold out completely to state churchism. Someone must be there in parliament to take a stand for true Reform. Someone had to give a lead to the voluntaryists of Upper Canada, left with scarcely a voice in politics since the defection of the Grits. The obvious choice was the *Globe* editor, the chief Liberal critic of the new government combination. As Brown himself expressed it to Mackenzie, a nomination in Kent "would be a loud testimony in favour of the cause in which I am enlisted . . . of making the voluntary principle in all its length and breadth the great issue at the coming election. . . . I fear I would not have the courage to resist such an offer were there a likelihood of success."[43]

Thus he intimated that his name might be put forward in Kent: hesitantly, and not with any great ambition for a parliamentary career. He was ambitious enough in other ways— to succeed in journalism beyond all rival, to gain and hold authority over public opinion. But he did not go eagerly into political life; he faced it soberly, as a duty to his principles. If there was ambition here, it was less for himself than for the convictions that he held. True, once he had taken the plunge, the surge of his assertive energy and self-confidence would sweep him onward to the front ranks of parliamentary combat. Yet he would never be fully at home in politics. He was impatient always to win and have done—which led his adversary, John A. Macdonald, to remark on one occasion, with some truth, that he could beat George Brown because Brown could not see beyond a temporary and immediate political advantage.[44]

At any rate, Brown's friends put up his name when the Reformers of the United Counties of Kent and Lambton met in nominating convention at Dresden, on September 26. Archibald McKellar sat as chairman of the gathering; Hope Mackenzie was its secretary.[45] An anti-ministerial majority quickly swept aside the government candidate, Arthur Rankin, and resolved to call on George Brown. Hope Mackenzie jubilantly sent the convention's formal requisition to him.

Brown was pleased, quite naturally; yet still he hesitated, asserting that he might serve better "firing away in the *Globe*", telling Alexander Mackenzie that he still "wished to escape" if there were any alternative.[46] In mid-October he went down to Kent and Lambton to investigate the situation for himself. Though he found the picture hopeful, he still delayed replying to the convention requisition until he had full and frank assessments from McKellar and Mackenzie.[47] Kent itself, he knew, had a sizeable Roman Catholic vote, though Lambton was strongly voluntaryist. Then there were Tory-Anglicans to contend against, and entrenched local ministerialists; not to mention the power of government patronage behind Rankin, together with the hostile influence of Malcolm Cameron, still a name to be reckoned with in the West.

"I hope you are not too confident of success," he warned Alexander Mackenzie. "There will be great opposition against me, and unless Lambton goes almost unanimously for me, it will be all up."[48] But his energies had been aroused; his determination was hardening. "Depend upon it," he told the Mackenzies, "when I do come out, I will not let the grass grow under my feet. My defeat would be made a regular party affair and every engine put into use to effect it. Can you stand all this? Stand by one poor editor against the whole force of Romanists, prelatists, ministerialists, Clear Grits, and Arthur Rankin's thousand pounds? You are 'regular bricks' if you can put your faces to it. Look at it fairly—and if you say so, I am with you."[49] They said so. Brown replied decisively, "*I will run for Kent and Lambton*. Put plenty of work on me. I can speak six or eight hours a day easily."[50]

In such a fashion did this Toronto Liberal, this urban journalist, link his political destinies with Kent and the world of the western farmer—the agrarian Canadian West that he would represent in parliament for some sixteen years, uniting it under his leadership, focusing it on Toronto, until he had built a political force as powerful as that of French Canada in the United Province. It was a world that was already in process of rapid change. Not far removed from the raw frontier in some areas, and still thickly forested in others, it had in older settled districts turned increasingly from simple subsistence farming to much more complex commercial agriculture, and this on a sizeable scale. Well-knit towns and villages were emerging from haphazard, straggling hamlets. In these centres, steam-driven mills were adding their insistent pounding to the slow creaking of the water-wheel. Local roads, still, were often all but impassable; but macadamized main highways were linking up large districts, bringing their inhabitants into closer contact, shaping a common awareness of western interest. Above all, the railway era that was imminent would vastly speed the whole tempo of change. It would help to bind the West into one articulate, self-conscious community—a community aggressive yet uncertain, ardently independent of spirit, but somehow searching for direction and effective leadership.

The people of the West still commonly dressed in homespun, lived largely on salt meat and coarse breads, and drank native whiskey as a cheap, wholesome table beverage. But store clothes, more varied diet—and the temperance movement—were just around the corner. So, too, was the reign of George Brown, the uncrowned king of the Western country.

3

Meanwhile the reconstructed government had finally made its appearance. Under some pressure from Hincks, Lafontaine had resigned at the end of September.[51] His most distinguished follower, A. N. Morin, Speaker of the House in the late parliament, succeeded him as eastern leader of the Reform ministry, while Hincks, of course, held first place in the western section. Yet more weeks of negotiation were required before the cabinet posts were fully sorted out. Hincks brought Morin and his friends to agree that Clear Grit tigers would become tame tabbies in office, and Cameron and Rolph moved in placidly enough to the posts of President of the Council and Commissioner of Crown Lands. Difficulties arose elsewhere. Hincks himself held on to the office of Inspector-General, which well suited his prime interests in financial and railway matters. But he wanted a loyal supporter in the important legal post of Attorney-General and so chose W. B. Richards who had law as well as loyalty—while another pressing claimant, John Sandfield Macdonald, had only the former.[52]

The imperious, clever but conceited Sandfield considered he had every right to move on from the office of Solicitor-General, which he had held in the ministry since 1849, to that of Attorney-General. He was undoubtedly a man of standing: a capable minister and lawyer, the chief Reform figure in the eastern or St. Lawrence River region of Upper Canada. He had also been the principal emissary for the government in the negotiations with McDougall that had brought the Clear Grits into coalition.[53] Yet he had perhaps been chosen to conduct those negotiations because he was more than a little sympathetic with some of the Grits: assuredly Hincks did not trust him too far.[54] Hence his demand by very right to the Attorney-Generalship was refused. The sensitive Macdonald ego was left sadly bruised. He never quite got over the notion that he was disinherited by the Hincks-Morin ministry—or rather as he put it sourly, "let go to pasture like an old horse".[55]

At length the completed cabinet was sworn in on October 28. The *Globe* greeted it with no great surprise: indeed, the real sensation in Toronto of that week was the visit of Jenny Lind, and her two glorious concerts in St. Lawrence Hall.[56] In any case, for weeks before, the journal had been dissecting the expected Grit-Hincksite union of opposites, conceived in trickery and negotiated with falsehood; and before that had published a fat series of open letters from George Brown to Francis Hincks,[57] attacking the latter's leadership and rehearsing Brown's reasons for turning against the government (which, moreover, now proceeded to replace him as a Penitentiary Inspector).[58] All this supplied excellent campaign material for the elections that were soon expected. Shortly after the new government had been announced, the writs at last were issued for election, and mid-November saw the campaign in clamorous full swing.

Brown put out his own formal election address in the *Globe* of November 15. It was a clear-cut exposition of his governing beliefs and principles: "I am in favour of the total separation of Church and State, and think that the Reformers should make this principle, in all its consequences, the foundation of their political structure, and stand or fall by it as a party. . . . I believe that pure religion will prosper far better if left dependent on the voluntary contributions of the Christian people than when pampered by the State. . . . I am the earnest advocate of national education. The cry of 'Godless education' which has been raised against our excellent national system is most hollow. How can it be 'Godless' to give man the means of perusing the Bible? How 'Godless' to raise his intelligence and develop faculties which had otherwise lain dormant? Have we not enough of sectarian hatred now that we must parcel out the very children into Methodist boys, Presbyterian boys and Roman Catholic boys? Is our Christianity really such that, consistently with its principles, the youths of two sects cannot learn to read and write on the same bench?"

Turning from the arguments of voluntaryism, he went on to support representation on the basis of population, extension of the suffrage, reciprocal free trade with the United States and the other British American colonies, and—showing he was well aware of the need for material development—the trunk-line railway across Canada, together with the fullest improvement of the provincial canal system. Then, for an effective close, he nudged the good Kent voter in his local patriotism: "Although not a resident, I possess a valuable property in the County and am deeply interested in its advancement."

His manifesto issued, Brown left for Kent and Lambton. Within two weeks he had held some twenty meetings arranged

by Archibald McKellar and Alexander Mackenzie, despite the
usual bone-wrenching roads, the unrelenting, icy winds, and the
six- to eight-hour speaking he had contracted for. Sometimes he
could find lodging in hotels, at others in mere bush cabins. In
after years, McKellar liked to recall with shouts of laughter the
night that the two of them were invited to shelter in a one-room
cabin, where a highly embarrassed Brown had to undress in full
view of the family females and dive wildly for bed in his shirt
and underwear.[59] Yet every sort of pain was necessary, since
formidable efforts were being made against him. As might be
expected, Roman Catholic forces were marshalled in opposition.
A deputation came down to Kent from Toronto and reissued the
Haldimand circular to Catholic electors, while Bishop Charbonnel himself arrived for a two-weeks' stay at the peak of the
campaign.[60]

Furthermore, Malcolm Cameron himself took a hand. No
doubt the Grit paladin remembered his successful intervention
in the Halton by-election of 1850, when he had virtually taken
over Caleb Hopkins' campaign against John Wetenhall as a
radical foe of the ministry. Now, though he had changed sides,
he meant to do the same for Rankin, the ministerial candidate
in Kent. Confidently he wrote to his friends in his old constituency, promising George Brown "a coon hunt on the Wab-
ash". "Stir up the electors," he urged. "Drive him home!" And
to his Irish allies, "Let everyone that hates a traitor come, and
we will sing *fagh a ballach* to him" (Clear the Way—a battle
cry of the Catholic "White Boys" in Ireland).[61]

Then, all anticipation, Malcolm came down like a wolf on the
fold, while the *North American* solemnly warned Brown that
"one was after him, mightier than he, whose shoe latchets he
was unworthy to unloose".[62] But the duels that followed did not
work out quite as expected. Black-browed "Coon" Cameron
stormed and thundered; towering Brown out-thundered him.
Malcolm grew witty over his opponent's repudiation of the party
unity he had so long defended. George cuttingly alluded to
the Grits' sudden conversion to Reform union when they had
done their utmost to destroy it—a spiritual transformation
brought about by Hincks's "good offices". They fought seven
and a half hours at Donelly's, five and a half in Plympton, and
seven hours at the Port Sarnia meeting.[63] By this time a reeling
Cameron was ready to give up. It was said that he privately
admitted to Alexander Mackenzie that Brown was going in,
and it was useless to oppose him.[64] In any event, "the Coon"
quietly backed out in mid-course, leaving poor Rankin unde-
fended. In some degree John Wetenhall had been avenged.

Polling day was December 12. It was quickly evident that Brown indeed was going in. By the close of excited but fairly orderly voting, he held a clear lead both over Rankin and the Tory candidate.[65] The official declaration of his election came later, according to custom, at the Chatham courthouse on the 20th. It was a bright day of triumph for the Brownite independents, who had overcome both regular parties, and their man himself was plainly in high fettle. "Men of Kent and Lambton," he proclaimed to a jubilant crowd, "I congratulate you most heartily on the victory you have achieved! Since the result of the poll was ascertained people have been congratulating *me* on the event—but I have felt that the laurels of victory were to you, not to me. Never had candidate less right to plume himself on his personal influence in any political contest; the battle has pre-eminently been one of principle, and the victory is a triumph of principle—not the man."[66]

Amid cries of approval, he described the imposing hostile forces that had been overcome, even noting in passing the influence of the local agent of powerful timber interests, one Berryman by name. But Mr. Berryman was present in the audience and began to heckle vigorously. Brown in mellow mood forgave him: he would yet live to vote for George Brown. "No, I won't!" yelled Berryman angrily.

"Yes you will—now don't commit yourself prematurely. I appeal to the audience if so good-looking a gentleman could possibly be so hard-hearted."

"I am not good-looking—I am *not* good-looking!" stuttered Berryman in hot confusion.

"Oh yes you are," soothed Brown, to rising laughter. "Don't deny it—you *know* you are."[67]

In the meantime the elections elsewhere had produced little apparent change. By January of 1852, the Hincks-Morin ministry had gained a majority in both sections of the Union of about the same size as that held by the former Baldwin-Lafontaine government: although in Canada West, the Clear Grit faction now comprised about as many members on the government side as did the Hincksite moderate group. "Uncle Caleb" Hopkins and old Henry Boulton had retired from parliament, and Peter Perry from this world altogether; but younger Grits had more than taken their place, among them David Christie, the new member for Wentworth. It seemed that many western radical voters had been effectively swayed by McDougall's energetic arguments that the coalition represented the triumph, not the surrender, of Clear Grittism.[68] No doubt as well, John Rolph's pontifical utterances to that effect—his name still carried great weight with the party rank and file—had persuaded many discontented Upper Canadians that the answer to their troubles lay in the accession of advanced and devoted Reformers to the ministry. Only in Kent and Haldimand, where William Lyon Mackenzie had retained his seat, had Reform independents been elected; and Brown and Mackenzie were still as much opposed to one another as they were to Francis Hincks.

At the same time the Tory opposition had altered somewhat in quality, if not in size, for some of the most thorough-paced Tories had been replaced by milder Conservatives. "Compact Toryism is dead and gone," noted the *Globe* hopefully.[69] There was besides an obvious desire in both parties to push on with practical matters, railways especially. All this augured well for the Hincksite coalition, which was really based on covering over the disruptive issues in the ranks of Reform. But it was only a matter of time before they would reappear, and before growing numbers of western Liberals would recognize the fruitlessness of the "new combination". The strength of the ministry, the apparent renewed order in the party, was merely temporary—and not much more than illusory. Nothing at all had been settled. So the independent member for Kent would make plain when he came to his first parliament in 1852, to undertake the tasks of breaking up an empty alliance and winning all "true" (voluntaryist) Reformers from an unprincipled government.

4

Parliament would not meet until August of 1852. In the months before there was somewhat of a lull in political excitement. Railways again held the centre of the stage, and for much of the time Premier Hincks was out of the country, in the Maritime Provinces and then in England, conducting lengthy negotiations for the grand intercolonial and trans-provincial projects, the lines from Quebec to Halifax and from Quebec to the western Canadian border. This, in fact, was still the happy time of railway projecting, when almost everyone was in favour of building everywhere—confident of golden returns from trunk routes and branches from Smith's Corners to Jones's Mills alike, little reckoning on the monumental cost of railways in an underpopulated, raw new land like Canada. Undoubtedly the enthusiasm worked to minimize party strife; on all sides Sir Allan Mac-

Nab's presumed remark, "My politics now are railroads", was quoted with sage approval as the very essence of modern statesmanship.

That ancient Compact warrior was well ensconced aboard the prosperity special as president of the Great Western Railway. Tory-Conservatives and Hincksite Reformers, ex-annexationists like A. T. Galt, French moderates like G. E. Cartier, were crossing party lines with real or imaginary iron rails. Clear Grit David Christie and pure independent William Lyon Mackenzie would work together for the Buffalo, Brantford and Goderich across the western Peninsula.[70] And the *Globe* was urging a third railway from Toronto, via Whitby, north-east to Peterborough, in addition to the routes projected to the west and north.[71] Later Brown himself even put forward a tentative offer to build a line through Whitby, as agent for a Toronto group of contractors.[72]

But the railway honeymoon could only obscure for the moment the underlying strains in the political structure of Canada. They would, as a result, stand out all the more sharply when parliament met again. The divisive church-and-state issues remained unsettled. In this respect, the period of deceptive calm had even produced several more trouble-making developments. In Britain, in February, Russell's Whig administration that had promised an act to transfer control of the clergy reserves to Canada had been replaced by Derby's Tory regime, firmly opposed to tampering with existing arrangements. The result would be new voluntaryist pressure from Upper Canada for a Canadian act of secularization, with a clause suspending it until the imperial authorities had transferred the power over the reserves. Anything else, it was argued, would weaken the impact of the colonial demand on Britain—and, moreover, prove the bad faith of the Hincksite ministry.

In contradistinction to this impending voluntaryist demand, another separate-school offensive was shaping up. The *Mirror* had made the Catholic position quite clear: "There is no use beating about the bush; Catholics are determined to have their separate schools even at the cost of breaking up the Reform party."[73] Early in 1852, the determined Bishop Charbonnel issued plain warning to Egerton Ryerson (still Chief Superintendent of Education for Canada West) that Roman Catholics would no longer be satisfied with non-denominational schools with religious safeguards, and the safety-valve right to separate schools as "protection from insult". "Mixed schools," the Bishop sweepingly declared, were "the ruin of religion and a persecution for the Church." Here was a positive expression of the militant new Catholic zeal spreading under a revitalized

Papacy. "We must have and we will have full management of our schools."[4] Here, too, was the portent of new sectarian education bills—and stiff work ahead for George Brown.

The ecclesiastical corporation question was quite as threatening. There would be a rising flood of measures in the new parliament incorporating French-Canadian Catholic hospitals, convents, and cathedrals. All were anathema to the voluntaryist of Canada West; but they also expressed the strong Roman Catholic devotion of French Canadians who could be no less stirred by the spectacle of an aroused Papacy, and the resurgent spirit of ultramontanism. The eager rallying about the faith that was Catholic Europe's reaction to the anti-clerical and anti-religious revolutionaries of 1848, could find warm response in French Canada, a pre-eminently loyal province of the Church. Hostile to the merely secular state, anxious to uphold the Church's sphere of authority in this world—socially conservative while religiously aggressive—this spirit in French Catholic Canada was the very antithesis of western Liberal voluntaryism. Diametrically opposed forces would further rack apart the uneasy union of two peoples.

There would, besides, be other points of conflict. Upper Canadians had begun to demand reform in the system of parliamentary representation, in an attempt to overcome "French domination" of the union. Their demand would grow steadily louder. Among Clear Grits, moreover, there was still a rooted yearning for elective institutions; and at least as far as an elected Upper Chamber was concerned, it was shared now in quite a variety of political quarters. Even the happy harmony on railways would break down, once Hincks had returned from England in June, with an agreement in his pocket to build a trunk-line. All in all, by the time parliament came together in Quebec, to which the capital had now been moved as planned, there was no reason to expect anything but a very stormy session. So George Brown must have felt as he journeyed eastward to parliament in mid-August. Certainly he was ready for a stand-up fight.

He arrived in time for the opening on the 19th, and found the old French capital practically *en fête*. That morning the narrow streets were astir with townfolk thronging up to the austere grey stone legislative buildings that stood high on the towering rock of Quebec, commanding a magnificent prospect of the ship-filled harbour, the pastoral Ile d'Orléans, and the broad, silvery sweep of the St. Lawrence. The city that had long held sway over Canada ruled once more. Not even dull skies and a heavy shower of rain at noon could depress the crowd outside the former Lower Canadian Parliament Buildings, chattily comment-

ing on the members as they collected, and waiting sociably for
the Governor-General to arrive.[75]

At two o'clock a flourish of trumpets and cannon booming
from the ramparts announced the coming of Lord Elgin in the
state carriage, surrounded by the scarlet, blue and gold of his
military escort.[76] The vice-regal party swept solemnly into the
richly furnished Legislative Council Chamber. Black Rod sum-
moned the Assembly members, knocking three times at the
closed door of the chamber of the people's representatives, to be
admitted only by their will. The ancient but vital ceremonies
of English parliamentary freedom were carried through in the
living heart of New France: a blending that yet might promise
well for the two peoples of a divided Canada.

When the assembly got down to work, Brown might gaze
about him and measure this small but potent society of eighty-
four members—forty-two from each section—a society he had
often viewed from the sidelines but never before known in his
own right. He sat in a handsome oval chamber, hung with por-
traits and lined with rows of walnut desks, divided by a central
gangway that ran the length of the oval up to the dais and the
massively carved Speaker's chair.[77] Here the newly elected
Speaker was enthroned: John Sandfield Macdonald, not fully
mollified by the ministerial support that had ensured him the
honour, but vain of the post, his sweeping black gown and tri-
corne hat, and the white kid gloves that he wore with a great
carnelian ring over one gloved finger—which made his magis-
terial gestures all the more impressive.[78] To Sandfield's left
were the opposition forces, a motley of twenty-odd Tory-Conservatives, a few eastern radicals or *Rouges*, and a fringe of
western independent members. Across the gangway, and on the
Speaker's right, the ministerial ranks were deployed. Some fifty
strong, they comprised the largely French Lower Canadian
phalanx and the Hincksite Upper Canadian moderates, together
with their Clear Grit allies: all fronted by the great men of the
cabinet.[79]

There sat wiry Francis Hincks, sharp-featured but for his
wide and mobile mouth, always feverishly busy at his desk
drafting statements, scribbling notes to his staff officers, or holding whispered conferences. As a speaker, he was rapid to the
point of stammering, yet effective enough with his razor tongue
and acid phrase. He was affable in disposition and clear-headed
in his generalship, but vehement and unscrupulous as well—
"the Hyena" to his enemies. Nearby were his Grit colleagues:
burly Malcolm Cameron, as irrepressible as ever, and the cor-
pulent dignity of John Rolph, with his handsome head and

hooded eyes, his ingratiating voice and air of chill finesse. Then there was Attorney-General West, Richards, and the Lower Canadian ministers led by the sensitive and conscientious Morin: among them, Chauveau, a noted *littérateur*, and Drummond, the Attorney-General East, who was properly silver-tongued in his native Irish tradition, yet a bit inclined to pomposity besides. Still other ministers there were, like Taché and John Ross; but they sat in "another place", the Legislative Council.

On the other side of the House, as Brown looked from his seat at the far end of the chamber, he saw oppositionists as varied as the gallant and gouty Tory hero of 1837, Sir Allan MacNab, and the irascible prime rebel of those days, William Lyon Mackenzie, hoary-headed now, a little deaf, and inclined to fits of elderly drowsiness between his slashing outbursts. Then there was Louis Joseph Papineau, also nearing the close of an eloquent career, who opposed the government as a *Rouge* republican and anti-clerical, while Joseph Cauchon did so as an ultramontane conservative: the two were at either end of the scale of French-Canadian nationalism. As for the rather undistinguished pack of Tory-Conservatives, John A. Macdonald was obviously rising well above the rest, widely regarded as heir-presumptive to MacNab if not as actual leader already. Long-nosed and loose-limbed, he was genial in manner yet stinging in debate; seemingly offhand to the point of negligence, but devastatingly perceptive when he cared to be. He was an apparent trifler whom George Brown might never understand: any more than he could appreciate Brown's own uncomplicated directness.

The opposition forces had anything but unity. Brown stood ranged in arms against the ministry with blades as ill accorded as Macdonald's springy scimitar, MacNab's rusting claymore and Mackenzie's antique scalping-knife. Any one of them might suddenly slash at his own head; nor would he fail to return the compliment. Essentially he would have to work alone. He was fully prepared to do so, and determined to take the plunge into parliamentary debate at once. Any preliminary period of waiting to become accustomed would only make it harder: "It's just like 'ducking'," he observed.[80] He therefore took the earliest chance to speak in the opening debate, on the address in reply to the Speech from the Throne, which traditionally afforded opportunity for wholesale criticism of the nature and policy of the government. And so it was that on August 27 George Brown rose in a full and expectant House, no stranger to his reputation, to make his initial parliamentary address.

As usual, he started mildly enough; almost diffidently, as he expressed a fear that the cabinet had not received due justice, and offered to yield the floor if a minister wished to speak. Morin, however, ironically begged him to proceed, and very soon the new member began to warm to his subject.[81] His normally level and softly Scottish voice rose in compelling force, broadened in accent. His tall broad-shouldered frame seemed to loom over the whole assembly, as he vividly portrayed the history of the Reform party since the time of the contest against Metcalfe—a history he was more than qualified to present.

He paid tribute to the worthy services of Hincks and Morin in the party's long struggle for responsible government; and then, little by little, point by point, revealed how they and their adherents had fallen from the high ideals and bright hopes of progress that had inspired Liberalism in its earlier days. He traced the consequent rise of a rebellious Reform faction, the Clear Grits—who, however, "saw everything with distorted vision and denounced without measure".[82] He described the failure of the government to deal with Upper Canadian problems, and the tightening of the French-Canadian brake on ministerial advance. The House followed him closely. He had few gestures but an emphatic beating of his forearm, no elegant phrases or debating tricks. But the deep and vibrant voice held power, commanding power, product of his abounding vitality, indomitable conviction, and massive marshalling of facts. This was no mere appeal to the emotions. The strong response he roused, whether of anger or approval, came basically from the relentless hammering home of closely reasoned arguments, complex without losing cogency, long-drawn-out but always fluent and lucid.

Then he came to the present coalition, recounting in sharply documented detail how the Grits had negotiated to enter office with the eastern and western factions they had so utterly condemned, how Hincks had flatly denied in parliament that any such negotiations were under way—this just before the *North American* and *Examiner* had publicized their successful outcome! Indisputably, he declared, *someone* must have swallowed their beliefs. Had Hincks accepted elective institutions? What had happened to Grit anti-French, anti-state-church professions? Had the Lower Canadians yielded to western voluntaryism? It all led back to his main charge, that the leaders of the party had betrayed the heart of everything that Liberalism had striven for so ardently. For the essence of the British responsible system was that men took office or resigned it according to the political success or failure of the principles they upheld. "If a public man can hold one set of principles out of office and another in office, responsible government is a farce!"[83]

Ministerialists were squirming in their seats, oppositionists urging him on, while Hincks grew pale with suppressed anger. Thus he continued for two punishing hours—and by the end had clearly demonstrated that here was a new parliamentary master, one who would not for long stand unsupported. There might be more theatrical or amusing performers; but few would stay away henceforth when George Brown spoke. His speech, in fact, was an overnight sensation. The Tory *Patriot* exultantly reported that his "withering exposure" had rendered Francis Hincks "as amiable as a famished wolf",[84] while the Quebec correspondent of the Toronto *Colonist* dashed off, "He has succeeded in making himself the common topic of conversation in this city today."[85] Back in Kent his loyal followers were in transports of delight. And from this moment forward men across the West began to watch for Brown's utterances in the House as regularly as they had turned to the *Globe* for his editorials, increasingly approving his stand for Upper Canadian rights in the face of a powerful but time-serving government. From his very first speech, the parliamentary champion of Upper Canada was in the making.

5

As a matter of fact, he made himself so effective as to earn the most flattering attention from the government side—caustic rejoinders from Hincks, much thrashing about from Cameron, and Rolph's silkiest denials that the Grits had at all departed from their doctrines. The ministerial press took him up at length. As the editor of the new Port Sarnia *Shield* observed, "Some of the government organs cannot seemingly write an article without having Mr. Brown for the text."[86] Alexander Mackenzie was that editor, and the secretary still of Brown's constituency committee. The two men were in constant and increasingly friendly communication, Brown claiming membership as a "Heelander" in the Mackenzie clan that was keeping its "blood warm on the banks of the St. Clair". "I am half a Mackenzie man myself," he announced gaily, "and I feel my full right to be as proud as Lucifer."[87] And later, "Do shoal down petitions about the Reserves, Rectories, Sectarian Schools, Maine Law and Sabbath desecration. The more the merrier. You will see me abused in the papers, of course, like a pickpocket, but don't pronounce against me till you hear me out. I know you won't. Write often, and speak plain."[88]

The "Maine Law", incidentally, was a proposed prohibition measure, designed after that currently enforced in the State of Maine. Although not a teetotaller himself, Brown did hold to temperance, and had come to feel that the alcoholic excesses in Canada—where whiskey almost literally flowed like water— could only be met by official prohibition. Certainly he had at least some reason for alarm; for, as he noted in parliament, a province of less than two million people then contained the truly staggering total of 931 whiskey shops, 58 steamboat bars, 3430 taverns, 130 breweries, and 135 distilleries.[89] Later he dropped the Maine Law, because he came to feel that the amount of public opposition to it would make it impracticable to enforce.[90] But at this time his support of prohibition only strengthened him in western quarters, chiefly rural, where a zealous movement was now under way against the hard-drinking habits inherited from the backwoods. Similarly with his efforts for a measure restricting Sunday labour: sabbatarianism was a powerful force in the righteous West. In York County, around Toronto, for example, stern by-laws had been enacted just the year before, prohibiting inhabitants from hunting, fishing, or swearing at their cows on the Sabbath.[91] George Brown, accordingly, was only making his mark as a true exponent of Upper Canadian opinion.

He did so in a more material way when Hincks proposed a scheme for differential duties and tolls favouring the movement of trade by the Canadian St. Lawrence route over the American Erie Canal. Brown opposed the plan, both as a free-trader in ideals and an Upper Canadian in interest. He believed in the natural advantages of the vast St. Lawrence system, but did not want to see them "artificially" supported by a pattern of preferential charges. As the *Globe* put it, "It is free competition with other routes which alone will produce the desired end of bringing freight to its lowest possible rates."[92] Inland Upper Canada, in short, wanted a free choice of access to the sea and to foreign goods; the present scheme sought "to force us to resume our vassalage of Montreal", to the detriment both of the western farmer and the western merchant.[93] Here Brown was plainly standing as the champion of his section of the province, its agriculture and growing commercial interests alike; the West would not fail to take note of it.

It was the same when the clergy reserves came up again in September, and Hincks introduced a new set of resolutions for transmission to Britain, warning of dire consequences arising in imperial relations from the Derby regime's refusal to proceed with the transfer of the control of the reserves to Canada. Brown attacked the resolutions as a sham and empty threat—that hid, moreover, the government's failure still to pronounce for secularization. If they really wanted to impress the British authorities, let them pass a suspended secularization bill, to remain in abeyance till an imperial transfer was effected. "Let the voice of the people of Canada be heard plainly and respectfully, and there will be no serious opposition from Great Britain."[94] Significantly enough, one prominent Clear Grit here expressed his agreement. Charles Clarke had removed to Elora, a village in Wellington County in the very heart of the Peninsula, and taken over the aptly-titled Elora *Backwoodsman*. In this journal he supported a suspended secularization measure, adding that if the Hincks-Rolph ministry could not carry it, "it is not a whit stronger than the Baldwin-Lafontaine cabinet on this question, and the people of Canada will derive no more benefit from it."[95] Already the disillusionment was setting in that would turn the western Grit adherents increasingly away from the coalition ministry, and towards George Brown.

He was also defining his parliamentary position on other questions of long-lasting importance. For example, in mid-October he stood out against the proposal to turn the appointed Legislative Council into an elected body. The Elective Legislative Council Bill was naturally supported by the Clear Grit members as an instalment of the elective institutions they advocated; but many others backed it for quite a different reason: as a more effective bulwark against radicalism, one not open to the charge that the present nominated upper chamber represented no one but its own members. French ministerialists, in particular, looked to a reconstituted Council to resist demands from western radicals, while many Tory-Conservatives hoped that a fairly high property franchise would give their party control there and counterbalance Reform power in the Assembly. But Brown argued that two elected chambers would upset the working of British responsible government. A cabinet could not be responsible to two different sets of elected representatives, especially if they should be dominated by two opposed party majorities.[96]

An elective second chamber, he asserted, belonged to the American system of government, where powers were divided between president and two houses of Congress, and not to the British where power was unified in a cabinet resting on a parliamentary majority.[97] Moreover, the upper house in the British system was not intended to be a separate political force but only a court of review, usefully modifying legislation. He put it simply as a choice of British or American institutions—and fought vigorously for the former, in company with other staunch believers in a parliamentary constitution like John A. Macdonald. The Elective Legislative Council was staved off, though Brown would later have to combat it again.

Shortly afterwards, the engrossing railway question came to the fore, when debate was opened on the bill to incorporate the Grand Trunk Railway of Canada. This represented a decided revision of Hincks's "Main Trunk" project, put through the previous session. The earlier scheme had first provided for the building of a line across the province as a public enterprise, dependent on the imperially guaranteed loans that were looked for to finance a whole great intercolonial railway system, extending from Halifax in Nova Scotia to the western borders of Upper Canada. But the negotiations held in London in the spring of 1852, between the British government and the provinces of Nova Scotia, New Brunswick and Canada, had broken down, and no imperial guarantee was forthcoming for the funds required. As a result, the intercolonial railway proper, the section from Halifax to Quebec, had to be set aside: for more than ten years, as it turned out.

Hincks, however, was still eager to go ahead with the line across the Canadian province. His very political future had demanded that he should not leave England without at least an arrangement for the much-heralded trans-provincial route. And there he had been approached by William Jackson, member of the great Peto and Brassey firm of railway contractors, who were earnestly seeking new employment for their costly capital equipment. Jackson's impressive offers to give Canada a "first-class English road" quite conquered the provincial premier.[98] He came back to Canada carrying an ill-considered agreement with Jackson for the construction of a privately owned and operated Grand Trunk. It proved to be one of the most expensive bad bargains in Canada's chequered railway history.

Strong opposition could be expected to the Grand Trunk Bill that sought to implement Hincks's agreement with Jackson, especially as Canadian promoters already held charters to build over sections to be traversed by the proposed railway. Outcries arose that Canadians could do the job themselves, more cheaply, and without the introduction of a company essentially under outside control. This was George Brown's own opinion when the bill came under debate. He fully agreed that a trunk line should be constructed; but saw no reason to turn it over whole-sale to British contractors and promoters, since in any case Canadian provincial and municipal credit would inevitably be thoroughly involved in paying for it. In parliament he likened

Hincks to the rash young business man who, declining his
friends' offers of help, rushes to open up shop with capital
borrowed at exorbitant rates of interest. What advantage had
Jackson over other contractors? Why should Canadian companies have their charters revoked in favour of a monopoly?
And why should English stockholders draw dividends from
Grand Trunk traffic—that is, from the people of Canada—when
the high costs of the Jackson line essentially would fall on the
Canadians themselves?[99]

The whole scheme, he contended, granted a "European scale
of profits" to the contractors.[100] It was extravagant; it was
ridiculous. He fought it long and hard, in company with John
A. Macdonald; but the government majority, the golden eminence of the Jackson firm, and the glowing talk of riches to come,
finally overwhelmed all opposition. Yet once again Brown's
decided stand against the original Grand Trunk measure would
be remembered afterwards, when, long before completion, the
railway was floundering in a dismal swamp of debt. The fact
was that from the start the line was borne down by the pressing
weight of the financial charges against it—which now included
buying in the Canadian promoters as well. Hence public aid
had to be extended to save the huge project: time and time
again. And hence the Grand Trunk became dependent on the
Canadian government, which, in turn, was in too far to let it fail.
There arose a dangerous and demoralizing connection between
the Railway Company and public affairs, as Grand Trunk influence, jobs, contracts, sustained the ruling politicians, while
the ministry sponsored new railway drafts on the provincial
treasury—and men who shared as government directors of the
Company in framing its requests then met as members of the
cabinet to consider granting them. Mounting debt, waste and
venality were the bitter fruit of the measure George Brown had
unsuccessfully opposed.

Other railway bills followed. Parliament, however, had
hardly had time to reach the explosive issues of church and state
when on November 11 it adjourned until February 14, because
of the alarming ravages of cholera in Quebec.[101] That still re-
current menace of the seaport town had even carried off one
Lower Canadian member, poor James Terrill, and the rest were
not at all displeased to leave for home. But Brown had been back
in Toronto for only a few weeks, going over *Globe* business with
his brother Gordon, when he set off again two hundred miles
further westward to Kent and Lambton, to attend a festive
round of meetings in celebration of his work in the session thus
far.

Approaching Port Sarnia in a mild and snow-free early December, he was met ten miles from town by a gala procession, and escorted in over the new plank road, seated in a shining four-horse carriage and preceded by a full brass band, all blowing fiercely, hired for the occasion from Port Huron just across the river on the American side. Behind the carriage, with banners fluttering, came a long train of vehicles of every description, while cheering horsemen careered about them. It was all very stimulating, and Alexander Mackenzie, sitting grandly with Brown as they bowled along, must have been proud of the welcome that his committee had organized.[102]

The member talked vigorously across his constituency for a week and more, then dashed off another hundred miles to a big anti-state-church meeting at Guelph. Christmas and New Year's —the latter more important to a true Scot—were spent in Toronto with his family; but early in 1853 he was away again to other parts of the Peninsula, for gatherings at Woodstock, Ayr, Galt and Glenmorris. At the last-named, he took on his former schoolmate and present Grit opponent, David Christie, in a free-for-all debate. It was now a bright, hard-frozen January, and the roads into Glenmorris were filled with lines of jingling sleighs under a brilliant winter sun, as the countryfolk poured in to witness this battle of Edinburgh giants.[103] Afterwards all agreed that George Brown had had the best of a ringing combat, for Christie, who claimed still to be a thorough voluntaryist, found it hard to explain the company he kept with state-church forces on the ministerial side of the House—where Brown unkindly designated him as "the last rose of summer left blooming alone".[104]

Then in early February the independent member set out from Toronto for Quebec once more, a four-hundred-mile journey that was no easy progress in winter in this pre-railway age. It was true that the traveller could take a circuitous route via Niagara to the American side, in order to take advantage of railroads in operation in New York State that would carry him by stages close to Montreal, and all for $20.[105] Moreover, the sleigh route beyond that city to Quebec was well organized, with small but comfortable sleighs admirably handled by polite French-Canadian drivers, and taverns that were models of cleanliness and kindness unknown at Toronto (as the *Globe* was quite willing to point out).[106] Yet it was still a lengthy and arduous trip, at times through streaming blizzards when the horses plunged off the track, and unbridged fords offered at least the danger of overturning on jutting ice-floes. Small wonder, then, that only about thirty other members arrived with

Brown in time for the reopening of the session in "this most frigid of cities".[107]

Despite the winter rigours, he had in the three-month adjournment travelled at least fifteen hundred miles to spread his views among the population of the West. It was this sort of effort, no less than his parliamentary labours to uphold Upper Canadian interests, which was making him so powerful a figure in the western countryside—the man called "Geordie Broon", "Big George".[108] In the House he still might stand alone against an apparently overwhelming mass of opponents; but that was no measure of his rising political strength. And now, back in Quebec, in March of 1853, he was preparing to take up another cause that would add increasingly to his following. This was representation by population: the demand that parliamentary seats no longer be divided equally between the two sections of the union, but re-apportioned to give a larger number to the now more populous Canada West. In time, it would shake the United Province to the foundations.

6

The idea of representation by population did not begin with Brown, either as divine revelation or original sin. During the 1840's Lower Canadians had felt a right to greater representation for their section of the union, when as the older community it was still the more heavily populated; and in 1849 French-Canadian *Rouges* had introduced a first abortive measure for representation according to population into parliament.[109] But in general, during that decade, the common struggle over responsible government had preoccupied both sections of Canada; it was really only with the fifties that they were free to turn their thoughts to the question of representation. In any case, by this time, the considerable growth in population since the union seemed to make necessary some redistribution of parliamentary constituencies. Then the decennial census of 1851-2 established the anticipated fact that Upper Canada had gained far more than Lower from the total increase: indeed, the western section now had passed the eastern in population. The comparative figures stood at 952,000 to 890,000, and the West gave every indication of steadily lengthening its lead, largely because of the much higher proportion of immigrants who had been attracted to fertile, empty western lands.[110]

In consequence, representation by population won increasing attention in Upper Canada. It seemed a reasonable enough basis for reform, when some members now represented 15,000 people and others 60,000. Clear Grit radicals had already raised it in the sessions of 1850 and '51 (this in their ardent pre-ministerial days) as a measure of obvious democratic justice.[111] Conservatives also took it up; demanding an increase in parliamentary seats in the hope of offsetting the French-Canadian power that did so much to keep their opponents in office.[112] Accordingly, when George Brown included representation by population in his Kent election platform of late 1851, he was only joining a procession that at one time or another, and for their own purposes, included men as far apart as Louis Joseph Papineau, Malcolm Cameron, and John A. Macdonald.

Yet by now the church-and-state disputes were straining relations between the largely Protestant West and the predominantly Catholic East, and giving a highly charged significance to a proposal for representative reform that would strengthen the one section in politics at the expense of the other. Undoubtedly the popularity of the idea mounted in the West because of resentment of French-Canadian influences in government. Undoubtedly, too, French Canadians did exercise an influence in politics beyond their actual numbers; for while the English-speaking majority of the whole union was effectively divided by party and religious loyalties, the French-speaking element was far more closely held together by a united Roman Catholic faith and the defensive traditions of a once-conquered people. And so the compact strength of the main French-Canadian block in the Assembly played a leading part in the calculation of government majorities: with a corresponding effect on the shaping of ministerial policies.

Accordingly, George Brown, like many another western voluntaryist, saw representation by population particularly as an answer to the French Catholic influence that had led Liberal governments to support, and even to foster, the baneful force of state churchism in upholding state religious endowments, separate schools and ecclesiastical corporations. "What has French Canadianism been denied?" he wrote at the end of 1852. "Nothing. It bars all it dislikes—it extorts all it demands—and it grows insolent over its victories."[113] More seats for Upper Canada, however, would indisputably reduce the weight of the French vote in parliament. Then ministers need not bow so readily to the East, the Reform party would be strengthened against the promptings of Roman Catholic opinion, and Upper Canadian institutions might be saved from state-church inroads.

It was a sectional and a sectarian view. Yet there was evident good reason for its attractiveness in the West.

There was no denying the critical strength of French Canada in union politics, nor the increase in state-church legislation. There was no denying that French strength, thrown behind the western Roman Catholic minority, could force the pace on separate schools. In fact, French Catholic votes would be largely instrumental in fashioning a dual school system for Upper Canada which it would scarcely have enacted for itself. Whether or not the system could be justified on grounds of wisdom, equity, or expediency, the Upper Canadian majority would certainly not regard its own coercion with content. And when westerners recalled that the commanding eastern power was entrenched in the union by the scheme of equal division of seats —that ascendant Canada East actually contained fewer voters than Canada West, and the disproportion between them was steadily growing greater—then their cry of "rep by pop" gained ever more indignant force.

Of course that cry expressed sectional and sectarian antipathies. Yet they were first of all inherent in the very nature of the union of two different Canadas. Conceivably, too, "rep by pop" might not be a full or final solution to the problems of that union, threatening as it did to replace eastern ascendancy with western, Catholic aggression with Protestant—which thereby earned it the decided hostility of French Canada. Still, the existing situation held no solution either: and to those who recognized that fact, representation by population seemed an eminently logical and straightforward answer. So it appeared to the direct mind of George Brown. Furthermore, the ministry had now agreed that the representation in parliament should be enlarged, though still equally apportioned, and that within each of the two sections seats should be redistributed to suit the population changes. Morin had introduced a bill to that effect in the fall of 1852.[114] Why, then, not apply the same principle of redistribution according to population to the province as a whole? A union was a union. Why should there be a line of cleavage down the middle?

Brown seized the chance to make this point when Morin's Representation Bill came up in the committee of the whole, early in March of 1853. Bluntly he announced, "I cannot understand why we are asked to pass a bill for future years giving one portion of our population larger representation than another, just because they live in a different part of the country."[115] Then to put himself plainly on the record, though without expecting to win approval for his proposal, he moved a resolu-

tion calling for representation by population—"without regard
to any separating line between Upper Canada and Lower".[116] The
two sections should be treated as one.

It was defeated, of course, 57 to 15. The bill went through
without it.[117] Yet in this amendment of March 9, 1853, George
Brown had placed before the legislature the first clear-cut formulation of the idea of representation by population "without
regard to a separating line". It was also the first to be introduced
in parliament since the revealing census, and the first of a long
series of similar resolutions. Clear Grits, now that they were
allied with French ministerialists, might claim that they had
only advocated the principle as a means of redistributing seats
within the existing two-part structure of the union.[118] Conservatives might also drop it as too abstract a notion—and perilously
democratic as well—once they had undertaken their own wooing
of the French Canadians.[119] Brown, however, had made plain
the essential aim of representation by population: neither local
redistribution of seats, nor universal suffrage; but basically the
removal of the barrier of separate sectional membership in parliament, so that all Canada could be represented on the same
basis.

This was the kind of definite proposition to which discontented westerners could rally. It also revealed that Brown
viewed representation by population as a positive means of
reconstructing the union of the Canadas. Opponents would
charge that he was blundering ahead to smash it. His answer
was that he believed in a Canadian union, and sought to make
it real by obliterating the rigid sectional division in politics that
had produced dual party structures and premierships, double
cabinets and administrative departments. Some might contend
that this was a specious claim: that the effect of his proposal
would only be an angrier division of French and English in
Canada. He could at least reply that the present scheme had not
produced their happy concord. Instead, it had only put a pre-
mium on their differences.

Furthermore, Brown did believe that Canada was one, and
should be treated so, proclaiming that, "The two provinces are
indissolubly bound together".[120] "What affects one must affect
the other," he affirmed, and vigorously repudiated "this doctrine
of a representative having one conscience and principle of action
for one part of the country and another for a different part".[121]
Sectionalist he was, despite this, with little patience for the
equally sectional views of men in "a different part" of the country. Yet he also had a fundamental feeling for union, which in
time would bring him to admit the need of granting special con-

stitutional safeguards to the French Canadians, so that they could accept a definite majority of English-speaking members in parliament. And ultimately this feeling would lead him to the concept of a federal union in itself, which was surely not the course of a mere parochial politician. Men of the latter sort preferred to advocate the division of the United Province as the quick solution for Upper Canada's problems; but Brown held out against this over-simple answer.[122] In fact, his continuing adherence to representation by population as a constitutional remedy, as opposed to the separation of the Canadas, showed the truth in his contention that his basic aim was effective union, and much more than sectional agitation leading to disruption.

Was he wrong in his remedy, honestly wrong, but sadly wrong-headed as well? The fierce sectional struggle that grew up over "rep by pop" might seem to prove as much. Yet Upper Canada increasingly felt grievances to be met, if Lower Canada felt rights to be protected. The existing union could not answer both claims: and eggs must be broken to make omelettes. At long length, the outcome was the recasting of that union in the broader, federal form of 1867, together with the final recognition in the federal parliament of the principle of representation by population. Brown had much to do with both these very positive results. Now in 1853, he had taken a first step that would lead to the destination of Confederation. If he had not originated "rep by pop", he had decisively identified himself with it and given it force—with imposing consequences for the whole course of Canada's development.

7

"When I get rich on politics," he wrote, "perhaps I will be able to pay some one to assist me. Meantime I do public business first, my private affairs second, and as much correspondence afterwards as I can overtake."[123] Ruefully he reported to Mackenzie, "a pile of letters unanswered big enough to stuff a reasonably sized sofa".[124] But there was so much to be done. There were constituency affairs and local appointments, on which he held, "I go dead for getting every office for Reformers—especially *Brownies*. But we must not forget the public interest. Where a man is decidedly better for the office even the Brownies should go to the wall."[125] There were long reports to be sent to leading constituents like Archibald Young of Port Sarnia,[126] *Globe* business to be dealt with, and requests that he investigate various Crown land titles or the activities of western road companies. Allan Macdonell of Toronto was engaging his interest in the opening of lands on Lake Superior;[127] Edward Chaplin, prominent Montreal merchant, wanted information on the prospects of securing reciprocity with the United States: British, American and Canadian authorities had been probing the subject at least since 1849. Hincks, said Chaplin, was "decidedly neglecting the interests of the mercantile community— give him a dig on this account."[128] And at the same time, in this spring of 1853, church and state questions were coming to dominate parliament again. They demanded Brown's close attention in the House, once he had made his initial bid there for representation by population.

There was Hincks's new University Bill, for instance, which seemed further woeful evidence of ministerial backsliding from the Liberal stand on a completely secular University of Toronto taken in Baldwin's Act of 1849. The new bill would reduce the provincial university to little more than an examining body, transferring its teaching functions to a state-maintained University College, and permitting church colleges to affiliate with the University and share in any surplus income.[129] Brown strenuously opposed the destruction of the grand design for a single public institution of higher learning, wealthy enough to attract the brightest talents to its staff. The result, he forecast, would be "a multitude of small sectarian colleges, with chairs clubbed together and filled with inferior men, the youth educated as sectarians, and sent abroad with all the prejudices of narrow education".[130] A one-sided view perhaps: but the long series of amendments which he moved that April, although defeated, marked him as a leading defender of the concept of a central university against equally one-sided local and sectarian onslaughts. Moreover, in these efforts he had the assistance of A. J. Fergusson, member for Waterloo, son of his old friend Adam Fergusson; and with this one supporter began the formation of a "Brownite tail" in parliament.

More bitter, however, than the struggle over the University were those over separate schools and ecclesiastical corporations, since these last two church-state issues set Protestants against Catholics and Upper Canadians against Lower in a way that the university question did not. The government brought in another School Bill which went much further in erecting a dual educational system in Upper Canada, because it effectively gave Roman Catholics a separate financial structure for their schools, directed by their own incorporated boards of trustees.[131] This measure had been in the offing for some time. The year before, Morin had promised the Archbishop of Quebec that he and his colleagues meant to achieve the same educational privileges for Roman Catholics in Canada West as those held by Protestants in Canada East:[132] a just-sounding formula of parity, except that the two situations were not the same. While the common schools of the West were secular and non-denominational in character, those of the eastern section were Roman Catholic in their teaching and connection. This had left education on a distinctly religious basis in Canada East, and had thus necessitated separate institutions for its Protestant minority.

At any rate, the government had drafted a School Bill for Upper Canada in the fall of 1852. It did not come up for debate in its final form until the spring of 1853, but when it did, produced a mass of petitions on either side. Those from Canada West were nearly unanimous in seeking the abolition of separate schools; it was notable that the only petitions demanding them for the West came from Canada East.[133] In parliament Brown and William Lyon Mackenzie moved for their total destruction, and Hincks snappishly credited the former with "producing a very pretty little agitation" on the subject.[134] It was of no avail, however. Every amendment was defeated, and the bill itself passed by the weight of Lower Canadian votes. For only ten Upper Canadian members supported the ministers on the final vote, against seventeen opposed.[135]

It was defeat again for the member of Kent, yet not without compensation. He had obviously led in expressing the sentiments of a large segment of western opinion, both in the House and the country, and he had made very plain the power of the East over the West in the matter of schools policy. The Clear Grits, furthermore, were rendered restive and embarrassed in their adherence to the ministry. They stayed away, or voted unhappily for the measure with protestations of the need for party unity—all too conscious that George Brown was upholding the very position which Grittism had taken in its bold, brave days before joining with the ministerial coalition.

The conflict over ecclesiastical corporations made these things even clearer. Bill after bill was put through, incorporating Lower Canadian Catholic monasteries, religious societies, colleges, hospitals and charitable foundations. They were on the whole joint products of French Canadian influence behind the government, the demands of a vigorous Catholic piety, and the natural expectations of a homogeneous Catholic community that did not regard social, educational and welfare institutions as

mainly secular concerns, as did the divided Protestants of Upper
Canada, but took for granted that its one Church would play a
dominant role in these fields. Nevertheless the corporation
measures were further miserable embarrassment to the discon-
solate Grits, while the government itself grew weary of their
number, and introduced a general bill to cover the chartering of
religious, educational and charitable bodies.[136]

To the Upper Canadian voluntaryist, who objected to the
very principle of the state authorizing and empowering religious
organizations beyond granting them the bare protection of their
funds at law, this general bill was almost the worst step that
could be taken. It gave such a free hand that it virtually invited
the multiplication of permanent and near-autonomous church
corporations. Brown moved into a strenuous attack. Year by
year, he indignantly protested, parliamentary tables had groaned
under the weight of measures chartering churches, nunneries,
missionary societies, Hôtel Dieus, Frères Chrétiens, and the
Jesuits. Now all barriers would be swept away! Priestcraft,
mortmain, would cover the land; the young would be lost to
sectarianism, even though "the mission of the clergy is to preach
the Gospel not teach the alphabet".[137] Protestants like Brown
would raise soulless atheists, charged angry French Canadians.
Formal Catholic training cloaked infidelity, he hotly retorted—
and the House broke into an uproar.[138] Again two zealously
different religious outlooks could not come within miles of one
another.

And again the bill passed the House, by virtue of Lower
Canada and the dragooning of the Upper Canadian Grits: who
sat, like David Christie, in silent horror of what they were doing.
Out of pure expediency, to do down the government, John A.
Macdonald had swung the Conservatives behind Brown's attempt to block the measure.[139] When it had passed, Macdonald
at least enjoyed himself by exploiting the Clear Grits' discomfiture in a breezy, sparkling speech, declaring that they could
never face their constituents again, lest—with reference to
Christie's encounter with Brown—they be "Glenmorrissed in
Upper Canada". With his usual perception, he added smoothly
that the Grit gentry had been most ungrateful to desert "the
honourable member for Kent, *their natural leader*".[140]

There were similar loud clashes over the Three Rivers Cathedral Bill and the Ste. Hyacinthe Cathedral Bill. As to the first,
Brown had the satisfaction of laying before parliament two
petitions against it signed by some 160 French-speaking inhabitants of Three Rivers—proving that Lower Canadians themselves were not always behind every new measure of ecclesiasti-

cal incorporation.[141] As to the second, he saw it thrown out in the Legislative Council, after some diligent spadework on his part. He characteristically reported to Alexander Mackenzie, "I lobbied the Old Ladies for a week before they came up to scratch like trumps."[142] Yet all the while tension was mounting in the country, as the sectional and religious conflict went on in parliament, and as the "factious member for Kent"[143] played a leading part throughout. And then, the sudden intrusion of a complete stranger into Canadian affairs touched off an explosion —notably to affect George Brown.

The stranger was the imposing, fervid and theatrical Father Alessandro Gavazzi. He was an Italian patriot and ex-military chaplain of '48, who had broken with Rome when it set its face against Italy's Liberals in that revolution: a renegade monk or an evangelical crusader, depending on where one's own face was set.[144] Now he was engaged on a North American mission of preaching the evils of Popery; and when he swept northward into Canada, late in May, he came as a burning brand of passionate conviction, who aroused vehement response from Protestant and Roman Catholic alike. In Toronto his lectures at St. Lawrence Hall were a public sensation, as he poured scorn on the "blindness" of the popish system, and dramatically thundered, "No peace with Rome!"[145] But then, with this sort of record behind him, he boldly, or foolishly, moved on to the heart of thoroughly Catholic French Canada, to the capital city of Quebec, which was already deeply stirred by the excited religious disputations that were going on almost daily in its legislative halls.

It was on the electric evening of June 6 that Gavazzi addressed an audience in Quebec's Free Presbyterian Church on St. Ursule Street. Not long after 9:30, as the tall, black-frocked figure was blasting away at Cardinal Wiseman's activities in England, someone yelled—"That's a lie!"—and, as if at a signal, a shower of stones crashed through the windows. A mob burst headlong into the chapel and poured down the aisle, intent on dragging Gavazzi down from the pulpit. He defended himself manfully, both with fists and a stool, but was finally tumbled fifteen feet into a struggling mass of friends and foes below; from there his supporters managed to rescue him before he incurred serious injury. Others of the audience were less fortunate, for the whole church was now a chaos of battering fists, sticks, howls, and the shrieks of women. Nor was violence checked till troops arrived about ten o'clock to scatter the mob.[146] Disturbances had not ended, however. A strongly Irish crowd of several hundred re-formed, and marched off fiercely to the

Parliament Buildings to seek the politician whom more than anyone else they identified with anti-Catholicism. They massed about the doors. "Brown, Brown," they roared, "We'll treat you like Gavazzi!"[147] But he was not there. He had not yet come in for a late night session. Frustrated, the throng at last dispersed. It was an anti-climax; but the Gavazzi troubles had still to reach their peak.

The next day in parliament Drummond, the Attorney-General East, deplored the outbreak, explaining somewhat lamely that although he had asked for adequate police protection around the chapel the magistrate in charge had been too ill to act.[148] Brown tried to speak, but was ruled out of order. Drummond, however, did advise the proprietor of the Russell Hotel, where Gavazzi was staying, to post armed men at the windows with instructions to shoot if necessary. That day, in fact, Russell's was in a state of siege; and when the inflammatory Italian left for Montreal by boat in the evening, guards lined the streets leading to the docks.[149] On June 9 he spoke at Zion Church in Montreal. It was there that the disastrous climax came.[150]

Another ugly riot broke out, a spatter of shots was exchanged between Protestant and Catholic participants, and troops, this time ready to hand, were hastily ordered in. Someone gave a detachment orders to fire—who, it was never settled—and a volley struck into the dispersing Protestant congregation. Nine were killed, one died later, over a dozen were wounded.[151] Those responsible for the tragedy of military confusion were never effectively prosecuted. But far from shocking Montreal into order, for days afterwards anti-Protestant bands continued to attack evangelical churches and molest their ministers. This without restraint from either civic or provincial authorities, as the most turbulent Roman Catholic elements worked off their spleen and the more moderate, apparently, let them do so.[152]

Of course, in Upper Canada, the disorders produced almost as strong a reaction. There was a wave of furious indignation, wild talk about St. Bartholomew's Eve and Protestant martyrdom. For better or worse, it served to enhance the stature of George Brown. The very fact that he had been chief villain, next to Gavazzi, in Catholic Quebec made him a hero in the Protestant West. His refusal to be overawed by the disturbances at the capital, where he ploughed straight on in attacking the power of priestcraft embodied in religious corporations, brought him vigorous approval from angry Upper Canadians. He was the one man in parliament, they warmly agreed, who stood unbowed by Lower Canadian Catholic violence, who upheld the principle of religious freedom before a spineless ministry that even condoned the suppression of liberty by lawlessness. Harassed Lower Canadian Protestants, too, were ready to endorse the judgement.[153] Parliament finally adjourned a few days later, still in the bitter, strained aftermath of the Gavazzi riots. They had left Brown a far more influential figure than he had been when the session began.

But there was more reason than that. The anger over Gavazzi would fade; Brown's eminence would not. The long session of 1852-3 in itself had made the difference. When it opened, he was a highly prominent political journalist, but an unknown parliamentary quantity. At its close, he was one of the leading men in the Assembly. He was still very much an independent member: if there was a Brownite faction in parliament, it consisted so far of himself and Fergusson, with William Lyon Mackenzie as co-belligerent rather than ally on most church-state questions. Yet, despite his lack of big battalions in parliament, Brown's commanding presence and his fighting prowess, and the growing awareness of the popular support which he and the *Globe* were gaining by championing the rights of Upper Canada, forced every member of the House to weigh him heavily.

He had the potentialities of leadership. Another election, a shift in party alignments, might bring him parliamentary supporters enough. And there was increasing talk that the present structure of parties no longer fitted the real divisions in politics: the *Globe*, indeed, had been saying as much at least since December of 1851, when it had urged the French Canadians and Tories to combine on grounds of their common state-church principles.[154] Now the existing Liberal party looked finally to be foundering on the rocks of sectarian and sectional disagreement. Ahead there seemed to be the opportunity for a new Reform organization, shorn of state-church influences and standing squarely on the doctrine of representation by population. Party reconstruction—without doubt, that was now the dominant interest of the very independent member for Kent.

Party Upheaval

I

The close of the long parliamentary session in June of 1853 did not greatly lower the pitch of political excitement, but at least it gave Brown some time to devote to the *Globe*. In July he went down to New York on business, and paid a visit as well to the recently opened Crystal Palace, America's version of the great London Exhibition.[1] His main purpose, however, was to buy a new rapid-action rotary press from A. B. Taylor and Company, which would allow the *Globe* to expand from thrice-weekly to daily publication.[2] The age of the daily was now opening for Toronto journalism. It was the result of fast-growing newspaper readership; the result, in turn, of prosperity and progress in Upper Canada and the steady improvement of communications. More frequent postal service and lower rates, better roads, and increasingly the construction of railways, were all enabling the press to reach an ever-wider audience. The changes in particular favoured the growth of the bigger journals in major urban centres, and notably permitted the Toronto press to extend a metropolitan dominance over opinion outward across the West. It followed naturally that George Brown would see in these developments the opportunity to enlarge his own powerful newspaper.

Furthermore, the Toronto *Leader*, now the *Globe*'s chief competitor, had already launched a daily that July.[3] The *Leader* had been founded the year before by James Beaty, a prosperous leather merchant in the city, and largely expressed the views of the Hincksite section of the ministerial combination. Thus it met a need for press support decidedly felt by Hincks and his Upper Canadian friends, since the old *Examiner* had continued to be erratic, and even critical of government state-church policies, while McDougall's *North American* had remained closely identified with the Clear Grit wing of the party. The *Leader* had quickly risen to prominence, thanks to helpful government patronage and the expert editing of Charles Lindsey, late of the

Examiner—one former Grit idealist who had now fully committed himself to Hincks and "moderation".

The swift advance of this well favoured government organ was demonstrated by its beginning a daily edition but a year after foundation; and the competition from a powerful Liberal rival must have spurred Brown to publish daily also. In any case, however, the continued growth in the *Globe*'s circulation and the auspicious set of the times would surely have brought him to that course. The Northern had sent the first train out of Toronto in May; the Grand Trunk was a definite promise; the Great Western was laying down a mile of track a day, paying munificent boom-time wages of a dollar daily; and Toronto itself was already a city of 35,000 that supported fourteen newspaper enterprises, secular and religious.[4] The *Globe*, with a circulation of 6000, was doing ten times the business of its first year.[5] This was the moment for expansion. Everything pointed to it.

But it took time to make provision for the change. Not only was a new press needed from New York, but a bigger steam-engine from Kingston to drive it, a fresh font of type from Buffalo, larger paper contracts with the *Globe*'s regular supplier, John Taylor's "spacious mills on the Don", and, finally, more staff and roomier premises for the enlarged enterprise.[6] Quarters were found in the Commercial Bank building—on the site of the present thirty-two-floor Bank of Commerce. Here, at 22 King Street West, George Brown took over half of a three-storey brick edifice, together with a long extension for the presses behind.[7] At last, on October 1, the first issue of the *Daily Globe* appeared. It was well received. Within three months, Brown could claim that total circulation had jumped by more than 2000, while the daily edition (the weekly was continued for the more remote country districts) was outselling all other papers in the city.[8] Extensive and expensive improvement was evidently being satisfactorily rewarded.

The new *Globe* premises faced north on King Street, and one reached them through a narrow stone arcade that ran in an unconvincing Italianate fashion along the front of the plain Commercial Bank building.[9] On the ground floor was the business office, the composing-room above, and on the top floor, the cluttered editorial precincts.[10] Here, after his return from parliament, George Brown might usually be found; that is, unless he was off on a trip to Kent and Lambton or holding forth on some Reform occasion elsewhere. Whether he was away or not, his brother Gordon was on hand to manage the office, to supervise the staff and draw up the editorial page. But when George was in attendance there were regular conferences between the brothers, first thing every morning, to plan the programme for the day. Afterwards Gordon Brown would summon the reporters in, to make known the decisions they had reached. Since both men were strong-minded and hot-tempered, policies were often decided to sounds of battle emanating from George's office.[11] And when a strained and tight-lipped Gordon called in the staff to issue their instructions, they knew that the long-limbed figure sprawled out in his chair, cooling off, was still very much the final master of the *Globe*.

Nevertheless the partnership was highly successful. Arguments, once over, were forgotten; each man knew the other's qualities intimately, and thoroughly relied on them. George Brown, a youthful-seeming thirty-five, appreciated his brother's editorial talents, and the fact that in smooth, efficient daily supervision of a newspaper, he was probably the superior of the two.[12] Gordon Brown, at twenty-six, no less looked to George's energetic direction of the whole enterprise; for business decisions as well as the broadest lines of editorial policy remained the latter's overriding responsibility.[13] Furthermore, the partnership was as flexible as it was close. When the elder Brown was in Toronto, he could, without displacing Gordon, join in writing editorials, in reading and revising proof, and, in particular, in checking with utmost care and a thick lead pencil all the lengthy reports of speeches he had given.[14] At the same time the proprietor had the satisfaction of knowing that he could practically leave the *Globe* for months on end without it showing any sign of flagging or of changing direction, thanks to the skill and understanding of its regular managing editor.

In some ways the younger Brown was a slighter, smaller version of his massive brother. There was the family resemblance in features and colouring, the same Scots flavour in speech, the quick response, the same strong doctrines warmly held. But the sensitive meticulous Gordon was far more the man of thought, not action.[15] Unless aroused, he was quiet and retiring, while George was exuberant and forthgoing. His erudition went deeper: he had possibly inherited more of their father's taste for learning. George, it is true, was versed in political economy and constitutional history, and all the British periodicals and parliamentary papers he could lay his hands on.[16] Yet Gordon had an interest in philosophy and literature which his brother largely lacked.[17] Perhaps as a result the former's full-dress editorials had something of the quality of essays, well constructed and considered. On the other hand, George's flowing productions might often have been as well delivered verbally, in parliament or on the hustings. Both men wrote forcibly enough, but while George slashed, Gordon stung; and while the former overpowered with heavy emphasis and masses of factual references, the latter reached for literary effect and compelling turns of phrase.[18] Still, in either case, the strong impact on the public mind was much the same, since they both expressed virtually identical opinions. To the ordinary reader, the *Globe* under both Browns always spoke with one voice.

It was Gordon, however, who provided the executive capacity now needed to manage the staff and the complex operations of a large daily newspaper, whereas his brother had really only conducted the *Globe* during the comparatively simple, almost personal journalism of an earlier day. Certainly in later years, the paper's continued success would be attributed in no small degree to the abilities of its managing editor. In fact, Robert Sellar, a prominent journalist who began his own long career on the *Globe* under Gordon Brown, would remember him as "the best newspaperman Canada has yet known".[19] By comparison, the elder brother was both less and more: less as a clear-headed editor and orderly administrator; more as a man of vision, enterprise, and, of course, as a sweeping force in politics. But whatever comparisons might be drawn, it was George Brown's supreme good fortune to have Gordon as his able and devoted chief minister to maintain the *Globe* empire which was still the necessary foundation of his advancing power in the land. A journalist-politician could not have been better served.

2

He and Gordon had good reason to debate on *Globe* policies that autumn, as from the summer of 1853 the crumbling of the existing party structure grew plain for all to see. On one side Tory-Conservatives were racked with arguments between those who would come to terms with French Canadians to regain power and those who kept alive the Tory anti-French tradition. The latter had been markedly strengthened by the angry re-action to the Gavazzi riots, and the *Globe* in an outburst of articles on "Protestant Union" did its best to urge Conservatives and Orangemen to enter an alliance against domineering Catholic power.[20] The Orange Order, that bulwark of Conservatism, itself divided, one group of lodges supporting a pro-French policy, the other advocating a common front with western voluntaryist Reform.[21] And when a party oracle like the *Montreal Gazette* could come out in August for a new programme remarkably like George Brown's—including representation by population and no sectarian privileges—Conservatism was obviously in a state of some disorder.[22]

But Reform was in still worse a state. The mass of French-speaking Liberals, alarmed for Roman Catholic rights, had grown increasingly conservative in outlook, as they stood embattled to defend their religion and their culture. They warily eyed their western Clear Grit allies, their very opposites in radicalism and voluntaryism, while the unhappy Grits chafed at the frustration of their own cherished designs for fundamental reform. As the *Globe* remarked, how could this ill-assorted union of "advanced Reformers and French Conservatives" endure?[23]

Caught in the middle of the Liberal combination, the Hincksite moderates had little aim left beyond keeping office, to carry on with the Grand Trunk and sponsor further railway business. Harassing from the western flank were the Brownite Independent Reformers. Out on the eastern flank were the group of *Rouges*, broadly divided from the main or *Bleu* block of French Canadians by their democratic ideology and predominantly anti-clerical attitude. The condition of the Reform party was approaching the chaotic. Hence the *Globe*'s appeal across present party lines for Protestant Union constituted an unpleasant threat to those who still hoped to sustain the existing ministry.

The Hincksite *Leader*, for one, reacted strongly. Accusing the *Globe* of pandering to religious prejudice, it produced the rather unlikely story that Gordon Brown had visited its editor, Lindsey, and confided to him that "the Protestant cry was a capital one with which to humbug the public"[24]—unlikely, first, because if it were true, the *Leader* editor would have been about the last to hear it; and, second, because the cynical comment hardly accorded with the character of the Browns, much less with the blind bigotry and wild fanaticism regularly attributed to them by their foes (including the *Leader*). The Browns in any case reprinted the tale, for what it was worth, but took seriously only the charge that they were pressing an assault that would break up Liberalism for the sake of an intolerant Protestant supremacy. The aim, they replied, was not Protestant supremacy but the equality of all churches before the law, Protestant and Catholic alike; and far from this constituting an assault, it was wholly a defence against continued Roman Catholic encroachment.[25]

As for the danger to party unity, they had long ceased to

worry about that. Hincks's "bogey" that the Tories would return to power if Liberal union failed meant simply nothing: "In ten years no government has done so much to please the old Tories as the present administration."[26] Why stay with a set of ministers who had become "mere oysters sticking to a rock"?[27] Nor were they alarmed by the prospect of a period in opposition, if the existing Reform front collapsed. No party could remain in power forever. But one grown old in office, they averred, could be rejuvenated by a stay in opposition.[28]

Yet, quite without the Browns' assistance, a new development dealt heavily with the troubled ministerial combination. At a time when effective leadership above all was necessary, if the discordant elements were somehow to be kept together, Hincks became involved in a blatant financial scandal. That September, a suit in Chancery brought by the City of Toronto against its Mayor began to uncover an episode best left hidden in the enterprising life of Francis Hincks. In his capacity of Finance Minister he had co-operated with Mayor Bowes in carrying through the refunding of Toronto's civic debt: "co-operated", it now grew evident, to the extent of splitting a £10,000 profit on the deal. They had silently bought up the city's old depreciated Northern Railway debentures for £40,000—then turned them in for shiny new bonds worth £50,000, according to the terms of the very bill that they had worked to pass.[29] And this neat but nasty "£10,000 job" was only one of several scandals which now began to come home to the Liberal leader. The truth was that he had used his privileged position and undoubted financial talent altogether too generously in his own behalf.

In a reckless era of railway promotion and heavy Grand Trunk spending, corruption might come easily enough to men in public life. Yet the spectacle of the Crown's first minister fattening himself in such lavish fashion was too much even for the robust stomachs of the day. The *Globe* was naturally outraged. But further, William McDougall, the veritable architect of the Hincksite-Clear Grit coalition, was at last utterly dismayed. Bitterly he told his friend, Charles Clarke, "God knows I have been willing to say nothing of many things that have displeased me for the sake of great things—but this is too much."[30] Hincks had to be rejected as leader, "openly and boldly".[31] Christie might replace him. Yet McDougall made a left-handed acknowledgement of George Brown's rising stature in western Reform when he added, "We can work our cards so as to get support of the Brown rank and file at the polls while repudiating him as a leader."[32]

On September 22, the *North American* did come out with a

denunciation of Hincks—which only added to Reform disorder. The Clear Grits now had little confidence left in their own ministerial leaders, Rolph and Cameron, two lost souls in the cabinet. It was Brown who had voiced the real Grit sentiments in parliament on French Catholic domination, voluntaryism and representation by population. Yet the principal Clear Grit idealists, men like McDougall, Clarke and Christie—and many still of the back-bench and up-country adherents—could not forget Brown's fierce attacks on the radical movement ever since its start. Moreover, in so far as they still looked for elective reforms, they regarded him as almost reactionary in his defence of the existing parliamentary system. It would, accordingly, require the final disruption of the Reform party before they could bring themselves to join forces with him.

Nothing, however, altered the steady drift to party break-up during the fall and winter of 1853-4, as fresh scandals were disclosed concerning Hincks, as talk of new party groupings continued on all sides, and as the *Globe* and George Brown kept up their demands for a clean sheet and a fresh start. The latter went on tour again. East of Toronto he addressed meetings at points along the lake front. The banquet given to him by Reformers at Cobourg called forth a most interesting reaction from an old adversary, the Tory Cobourg *Star*: "Had it been given on grounds of his services to Protestantism, it would have brought forth every Orangeman in the country."[33] Conservatives might disagree with him on the clergy reserves—"but if the reserves must be secularized, every Conservative in Canada would join Brown in his crusade against Roman Catholic endowments."[34]

West of Toronto, he swept from Oxford through to Kent, speaking on invitation from Conservatives as well as Liberals; and at Wardsville was preceded to the village square by an enormous flag, hand-worked by the ladies, which displayed on one side, "Hail Advocate of Civil and Religious Liberty!" and on the other, "Honour the Defender of Constitutional Rights!"[35] (It had to be enormous.) Returning to Guelph for a meeting in Christmas week, he ran into some disturbance when a brisk three-sided scrap broke out between Brownites, Catholic Irish, and followers of pugnacious William Lyon Mackenzie, who turned up in person to dispute with him.[36] But by the beginning of the new year he was back at the *Globe* office to work away at recasting the outworn party system.

For some two years now he had been bluntly advocating, and no less predicting, the union of the main body of the French, the *Bleus*, with the outright die-hard Tories. Those who shared

George Brown in his later thirties
(*E. J. Palmer, Toronto, Canada West*)

Peter and Marianne Brown
(Courtesy Miss Bessie Ball, Woodstock, Ontario)

Church Street, Toronto, and St. Andrew's Church
(*Ontario Archives*)

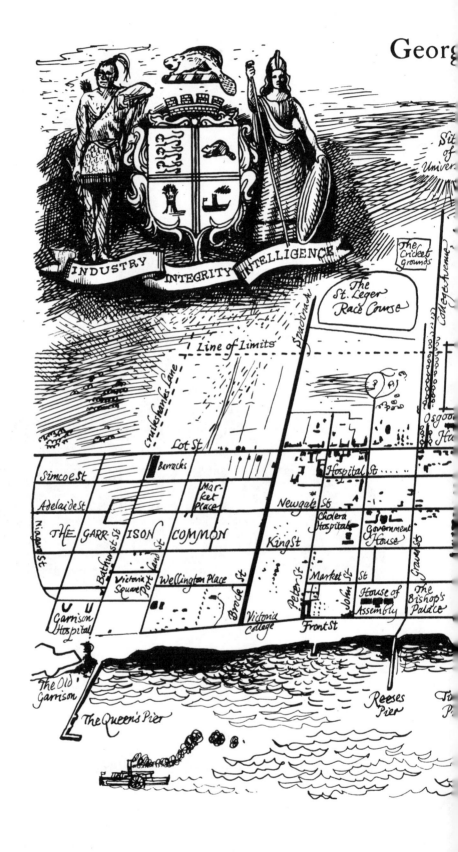

INDUSTRY INTEGRITY INTELLIGENCE

Sit
of
Univer...

The Cricket grounds

The St. Leger Race Course

College Avenue

Line of Limits

Spadivach

Cruikshanks Lane

Lot St.

Barracks

Hospital St....

Osgoo...
Hu...

Simcoe St.

Adelaide St.

Niagara St.

THE GARR ISON COMMON

Bathurst St.

John St.

Market Place

Newgate St.

Cholera Hospital

Government House

King St.

Graves St.

Victoria Square

Wellington Place

Brock St.

Peter St.

Market St. St.

John St.

House of Assembly

The Bishop's Palace

Garrison Hospital

Victoria College

Front St.

The Old Garrison

The Queen's Pier

Reeses Pier

Ti...
P...

rown's Toronto 1843

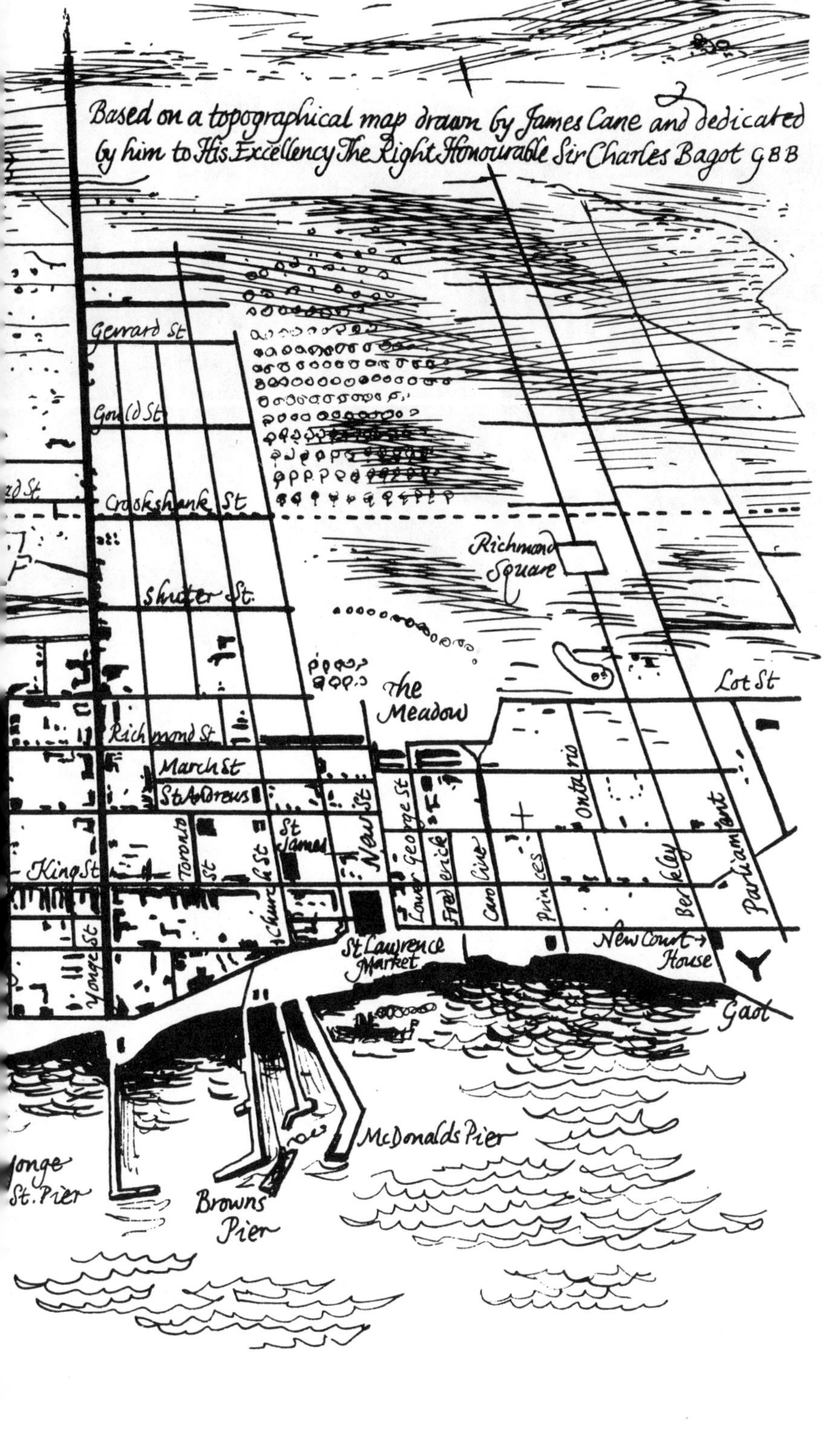

Based on a topographical map drawn by James Cane and dedicated by him to His Excellency The Right Honourable Sir Charles Bagot GBB

Gerrard St

Gould St

Crookshank St

3rd St

Richmond Square

Shuter St

the Meadow

Lot St

Richmond St

March St

St Andrews

Toronto St

Church St

St James

New St

George St

Lower

Frederick

Caroline

Princes

Ontario

Berkeley

Parliament

King St

Yonge St

St Lawrence Market

New Court House

Gaol

McDonalds Pier

Browns Pier

Yonge St. Pier

Looking West on King Street, Toronto, in the forties
(*Ontario Archives*)

London, Canada West, in 1848
(*Ontario Archives*)

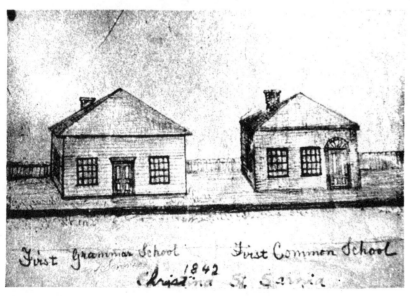

The Public Schools of Upper Canada, Sarnia
(*Ontario Archives*)

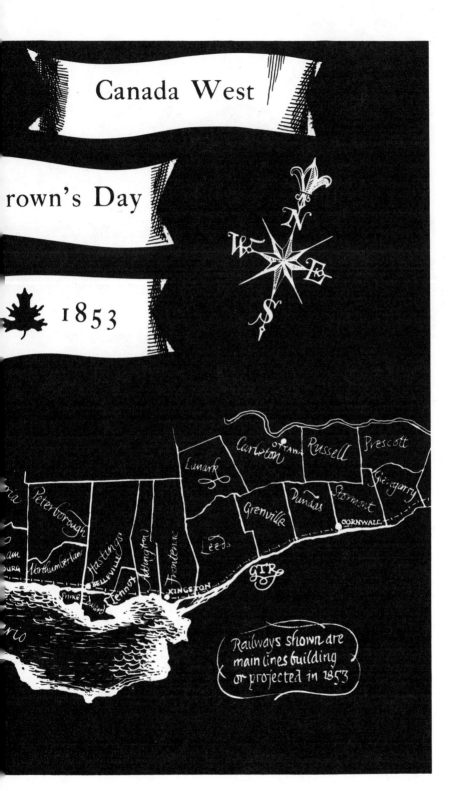

Canada West

rown's Day

1853

Railways shown are
main lines building
or projected in 1853

John Sandfield Macdonald
(Ontario Archives)

Antoine Aimé Dorion
(*Ontario Archives*)

St. Lawrence Hall in the 1850's
(*Ontario Archives*)

state-church principles, those who mistrusted progress, obviously belonged together; and their conjunction would lift a dead
weight from the Reform movement. Yet he only required the
more reactionary elements of the two parties to combine: "Liberal Frenchmen, liberal Conservatives, liberal Reformers, will
all rally under one banner and find no differences sufficient to
divide them".[37] Brown's own object, in short, was a broad new
Reform party spanning the middle ground in politics: certainly
upholding British constitutional principles; but just as certainly
maintaining the voluntary principle inherent in his view of
Liberalism.

He clearly did not envisage a solely English-speaking or
western sectional combination. The French-Canadian *Rouges* of
the East could well come in. They had from the start opposed
clerical influence in the politics of Lower Canada: their anti-
clericalism was a minor French-Canadian strain that rose quite
naturally in a community where the major chords expressed
devotion to Roman Catholic authority. And while *Rouges* definitely endorsed the separation of church and state, their initial
republican and democratic doctrines were being satisfactorily
played down in parliament, as they concentrated on more immediate causes such as the abolition of the old seigneurial tenure in
the East. Their original leader, Papineau, had proved little
more effective than Mackenzie in his return to politics; they
were drifting from his most extreme ideals. Furthermore, they
had allies among the small but by no means insignificant English-
speaking Reform element in Lower Canada. The *Globe*, indeed,
had testified to the existence of a "truly liberal party" among
both peoples of the eastern section "which in a few years will
have great weight in the community".[38]

Nevertheless it was true that Brown's chief and immediate
interest lay in the reconstruction of the Reform party in Upper
Canada. He saw good prospects here of winning over substantial
numbers of Conservatives, considering how divided they were
about their future course, and considering that on his autumn
swing throughout the country-side Conservatives no less than
Liberals had expressed strong resentment of Catholic power in
politics.[39] The only real issue still standing between the western
parties seemed to be that of the clergy reserves. When they had
finally been disposed of, parties could combine anew. Granted
that hidebound old Tories would seek out the Catholic conservatism of the French *Bleus*; the mass of British, Protestant adherents of the Conservative party would surely never do so. "We
believe," the *Globe* had confidently declared, "that they would
prefer to support a liberal progressive government."[40]

But what if these Conservatives looked not to a progressive "Protestant party" to support, but rather to the "railway party" represented by Hincks and his faction? The possibility considerably exercised George Brown in the early months of 1854, as his journal protested its belief that "the honourable members of the Conservative party" would never join with the corrupt Hincks.[41] Nevertheless he had to recognize that there was a project other than his own afoot to form a broad-based new political combination. It would be weighted on the right, rather than the left, and would combine Tories and Conservatives with both Hincksite moderates and *Bleus*. The influential Ogle Gowan, Grand Master of the Orange Order, was pushing it in the pages of his organ, the Toronto *Patriot*.[42] Both Hincksites and Conservatives were eying it with interest.

Such a combination would leave the western Grits and Brownites very much alone, and would drastically cut into Brown's own scheme for building up a powerful new Reform alliance. It was a thoroughly ominous alternative. He could only hope, and contend against it in the *Globe*, as winter passed into spring—to bring the approach of another parliamentary session, and the chance to see party reconstruction carried into actual effect.

3

A strange repetition of disaster forced the postponement of the session of 1854. On February 1, fire gutted the old legislative buildings at Quebec, and then on May 3 destroyed the convent that was being remodelled to house parliament. The *Globe*'s remark that at least Hincks might be glad of some delay promptly brought the Toronto *Mirror* and Kingston *Herald* down on it for making horrid insinuations; whereupon the paper solemnly replied, "We do not believe that Mr. Hincks set fire to the Houses of Parliament; in fact, we are convinced that he did not. There—if that is not a handsome admission from an opponent, we do not know what is."[43]

Other news of moment was the outbreak of the Crimean War with Russia, received in Canada, in mid-April, with loyal effusions of British patriotism. Yet the province's attention soon returned to its own affairs, in the expectation that the coming session should in any event settle two issues of long standing: the Upper Canada clergy reserves and the ancient encumbrance of seigneurial dues in Lower Canada. The latter was as much of interest to the East as the former to the West. Brown himself had spoken in the previous session for the abolition of seigneurialism, as a proper step in Liberal progress.[44] As for the reserves, over a year before, the Aberdeen Whig-Peelite ministry that had replaced Derby's Tory regime in Britain had expressed willingness to transfer their control to Canada. The long-desired imperial act of transfer had even finally been passed, before the preceding session of the Canadian legislature had closed, although too late for the House then to move upon it. Now, at long last, the way was clear to settle the reserves. Could Hincks and the ministry possibly fail to act on them?

Expectation reached its peak when the postponed parliament at last opened in temporary quarters at Quebec on June 13. The Assembly was housed in the city's Music Hall, a handsome chamber whose one unlikely drawback was poor acoustics.[45] George Brown had not arrived when Lord Elgin came down to deliver the Speech from the Throne, driving under wooden arches hung with drooping, fading evergreens. (There had been more delay, and the decorations had been up some time.)[46] But he was in his place as the debate on the address in reply to the speech began on June 16. And it promised to be a lively occasion, since the ministerial programme as revealed in the throne speech had turned out to be nothing but a short list of non-controversial measures—no legislation at all on clergy reserves or on seigneurial tenure.

The ministry blandly explained that, as the Representation Act of 1853 (increasing the members from each section from 42 to 65) would go into effect at the next election, it was not proper to legislate on fundamental questions before obtaining a new verdict of the people.[47] This did not go down too well, because the same ministers the previous session had earnestly insisted, hand on heart, that enacting a provision to alter the representative system would in no way limit the authority of the existing House.[48] It seemed far more likely that Hincks, faced with discord in his own party and with his own leadership in disrepute, did not dare to proceed on major issues, but felt that if he postponed the struggle and avoided possible defeat in parliament he might yet manage to survive.

Yet members had come girded for action, prepared to settle old aggravated issues one way or another; and here they were practically being told that they were incompetent to do so. Their resentment poured into the debate, until it built up like an angry sea, breaking furiously over the ministers' heads. John A. Macdonald for the Conservatives made an especially vehement at-

tack on the government's "most rampant corruption". "Their
only tie," he cried, "is common plunder!"[49] Every ministerial
sin of commission and omission was canvassed, while government supporters hurled back recriminations. But more important, the failure to act both on the reserves and seigneuries invited Upper and Lower Canadian critics to combine in censuring
the ministry, while in the government ranks *Bleus* were af-
fronted and the Clear Grits had now had more than their fill
of putting up with Hincks in the hope that he would ultimately
secularize.

Brown saw the opportunity, and proceeded to exploit it in
his own speech on the address. Conciliatory to the ordinary
ministerial Reformers, he focused sharply on the defects of the
leaders themselves. He could readily believe, he said forgiv-
ingly, that government supporters had many times voted against
their own principles and professions from a misplaced confidence
in the administration, trusting it to carry out its promises on one
or two main questions.[50] Now they could plainly see a mere
unprincipled clinging to office in its true light. Let them deal
out retribution!

Retribution followed swiftly. That same day, June 20,
amendments to the address deploring ministerial inaction on
the seigneuries and reserves were introduced by J. E. Cauchon
and L. V. Sicotte, two French Canadians in opposition, the first
a right-wing independent and the second a *Rouge*.[51] From Upper Canada they were strongly backed by Brown and John
Langton—a very independent Conservative—while Joseph
Hartman, a Clear Grit, even moved a sub-amendment specifically regretting the lack of a secularization bill.[52] This last
proved too specific for all the varied anti-government forces to
support; but they joined behind the more indefinite censures
proposed by Cauchon and Sicotte. Both passed, 42 to 29, as
many of the *Bleus* and most of the Grits voted with the opposition.[53] In fact, in this double defeat the Hincks-Morin ministry
had held but five ministerialist votes from Upper Canada, beyond those of the western cabinet members themselves.[54]

The next day the beaten government held secret conclave,
while the House stood adjourned and wondered. Would Hincks
resign, or seek a dissolution and a new election? They found
out when they met again on June 22—in sudden, startling
fashion. In response to a question from the Conservative leader,
MacNab, Hincks coolly announced that parliament would be
prorogued at once, with a view to dissolution. At once? The
Governor-General was already on his way to dismiss the legislature: they could hear cannon outside saluting his approach.

There was numbed silence as Black Rod was admitted to
summon the members before the Governor in the Council
chamber. Then the dazed House burst forth in uproar at this
carefully timed coup. Conservatives howled their protests,
baulked of a hoped-for invitation to form a cabinet. John A.
Macdonald, almost beside himself, stood raving at the ministry;
George Brown was roaring about unconstitutionality at the same
time; while William Lyon Mackenzie, like a tiny ancient fury,
bounded up and down in a shrill frenzy of reproach.[55]

It was all to no avail. The Speaker rose, the ministerialists
trooped out, and violent anger ebbed to seething impotence.
Not that Speaker Sandfield Macdonald rose willingly, however: he was far too conscious of his own and the Assembly's
dignity to submit quietly to these proceedings. In the Council
chamber he read Lord Elgin a veritable lecture asserting that
the government's conduct alone had prevented the faithful
Commons from carrying out their proper legislative functions.[56]
It briefly made him a minor constitutional hero, but changed
nothing. The "Cromwellian Prorogation"—as the *Globe*
termed it—moved to irrevocable completion.[57]

Dissolution quickly followed, and writs were issued for a
general election. But the government's manoeuvre had not
erased the mark of its defeat. Moreover, before leaving Quebec,
George Brown held a significant meeting with a group of western Liberals. They included the ex-Speaker, John Sandfield
Macdonald, whose early coolness to the Hincks ministry had
now become strong antagonism, A. J. Fergusson, already
Brown's close ally, and several of his former Clear Grit enemies,
including Joseph Hartman and David Christie. According to
the *Globe* report, the meeting fully recognized the "utter faith-
lessness" of the Hincks government and made a compact to
oppose it at all costs.[58] Here was at least a beginning to the reconstruction of Reform.

Back in Toronto, Brown busied himself with his own election
preparations. His former seat, combining Kent and Lambton,
had now been split in two under the scheme of enlarged representation, and by early July he had been offered a candidacy
for both counties. He felt reasonably sure of Lambton, perhaps
having in mind staunch friends there, including his efficient
local agent, Alexander Mackenzie. Kent was more divided and
uncertain, unless another good friend, Archibald McKellar,
would come forward. Brown had told Mackenzie, "I think
Archy McKellar could carry Kent. If he don't run, I fear Tories
will carry the county, unless I do—and I might have a tight
squeeze."[59] But happily McKellar would stand; and Brown

put up for Lambton, not at all displeased to learn that his old rival, Malcolm Cameron, would be his ministerial opponent there. Meanwhile Mackenzie was sending him confident assessments of Brownite strength in the constituency: "Brooke, you recollect was all Tory, but now they are all *protestant*, and the reeve, who is a Tory, informs me that they will go George Brown on that score very thoroughly."[60]

Cameron, however, could still wield considerable local influence, as an old inhabitant of Sarnia and the owner of large sawmills there. Yet despite this influence—and despite lures of government contracts for barrel staves, promises of post offices, generous tavern entertainments, and chartered steamboats to bring shock troops of lumbermen from the woods up-lake—he could not overcome Brown's organization, nor shake his popularity with the determined voluntaryists of Lambton.[61] The two contenders held another strenuous, perspiring round of debates, while the temperature soared into the nineties. But when the polls closed on July 25, Brown was in with a firm majority, and Cameron was out of parliament for the first time since 1836.

Meanwhile, Gordon at the *Globe* was campaigning for the defeat of the government in the elections generally. That was the first objective, the prerequisite to Reform reconstruction; the second, to elect candidates who would support secularization. The two fitted together, since it was Hincks's failure to abolish state-church endowments which had especially to be punished, while the disposal of the reserves would remove a barrier to the reconstitution of parties. Hence the *Globe*, in the prevailing state of party flux, proved willing even to back Conservatives running against ministerialists, in ridings where there was no Independent Reform candidate and where the Conservative was ready to support secularization. For the fact was that a number of Conservative candidates, seeing the handwriting on the wall, did go on the hustings advocating the very measure that their party had so long opposed.

Of course, the ministerial press made much of the *Globe*'s conversion to Toryism. Had it not actually declared that it would support John A. Macdonald if he ran in Renfrew against Hincks?[62] "It is not the Tories that we dread now," came the answer, "but the traitors in our own ranks."[63] It would be far more serious to see Hincks win than to add one more state-church Tory to a declining faction in parliament. Once again the *Globe* was gravely underestimating Macdonald; but there was no conversion here: only a necessary choice of evils in the campaign to overcome false Reform leadership.

By early August, election results were nearly complete. In Canada East the opposition Liberals had been strengthened. The *Rouges* had advanced in quality as well as quantity, for they now included men like the urbane Antoine Aimé Dorion, the best mind in the movement, a brilliant debater equally effective in French or English, and his brother, impetuous Eric Dorion, "l'enfant terrible", an editor of the *Rouge* organ, *L'Avenir*. Associated with *Rouges*, moreover, were a number of English-speaking eastern Liberals; notable among them, Alexander Galt and Luther Holton, partners in railway enterprises as well as political allies, and the latter an old Montreal acquaintance of George Brown. In Canada West the Independent Reformers had similarly made gains. True, two of Brown's close companions had failed to gain seats, McKellar in Kent and Notman in Middlesex; but a number of ardent new voluntaryist members had won election. And on the balance, it seemed that a combination of anti-government Reformers, disgusted ministerialists and secularizing Conservatives, would have the power finally to overthrow the Hincks cabinet.

Nevertheless the outcome remained anything but certain. It would depend on the course of events when parliament met. As the *Globe* remarked, "Never before were party bonds so relaxed, at no previous moment were Upper Canada politicians so free to act independently."[64] If anything, the election had tended to weaken both the Tory and Clear Grit extremes, and to indicate that power would lie with some new central combination. Would it be the one Brown had in mind? At any rate, if Hincks was tottering, MacNab, Macdonald and the Conservatives had not done more than hold their own. Secularizationists had invaded their ranks, internal quarrels still were rife, and Macdonald himself was disgusted with the party's failure to make gains.[65] Hence Brown could give strong answer to the charge that he had been playing into Tory hands: there was no out-and-out Conservative majority in Upper Canada, but rather a majority of members ready to secularize the reserves.[66] The auspices seemed good for pulling down the old ministry and establishing the reign of Liberal voluntaryism.

Yet he was aware that Conservatism still might block the way, if its supporters would not fall in with his own party design for the future. Even while endorsing Conservative candidates during the election, the *Globe* had not ignored that other dark possibility, that a Conservative-Hincksite-*Bleu* coalition might emerge afterwards.[67] The journal and its owner simply had to trust that a majority of Conservative hearts would prove pure, Protestant, and progressive. The party rank and file would surely

not accept a reactionary combination engineered by their leaders.
"Will they support corruption for a consideration? We cannot
believe it."[68] He and the *Globe* would go forward in that faith
until the new parliament could provide a definite answer.

4

In any case, whatever happened, Brown's first and fundamental
interest was the reconstruction of Reform—not union with
Conservatives. He hoped for their accession, yes, but on Liberal
voluntaryist terms. He sought to realize a set of principles and
policies, not merely to promote another office-holding coalition,
nor to win power for himself. His aims came through with
clarity in a confidential letter he sent off to John Sandfield Macdonald, member for Glengarry, composed late one August night
when the elections were over and the problem now was how to
prepare for parliament.[69] He wrote to Sandfield as an old associate, ever since the days twelve years before when the Cornwall
lawyer had served as a local agent for the newly founded
British Chronicle. He wrote to him as a Reformer of considerable stature and much parliamentary experience, a former minister in the Baldwin government, the valiant Speaker of the last
House. And he wrote to Sandfield, a firm foe of Hincks, to urge
him to take command of the Reform array which he, George
Brown, was striving so earnestly to assemble.

"My dear Macdonald," he began, "I congratulate you most
heartily on the result of the elections. Moreover, your 'tail' will,
I imagine, be much longer in this Parliament than it was in the
last. From what I have heard, there is no doubt of it. Many of
the Independent Reformers look to you as a leader, and if you
take your stand firmly and wisely—and without delay—the
game is in your hand."

He moved on to a ticklish point: Macdonald had a pride at
least as great as his own, and was decidedly more sensitive. "You
will have seen the *Leader* endeavours to make bad blood between us by ranging you among my followers; I have not
noticed the thing in the *Globe* for two reasons—first, it would
be attracting additional attention, and second, because I could
not do so without defining my true position, which would be
inexpedient at the moment to do publicly. To you, however,
I mean to speak plainly. Our long friendship entitles you to it—
and your conduct to me in the Speaker's chair and our compact
at the breaking up of the house also demand it."

Now came the essence of the matter. "I tell you frankly, then, that far from having any ambition to be the head of the party— *I would not take office under any circumstance were it offered to me.* All I desire is the success of the principles to which I have attached myself, and if you can form a government pledged to separation of church and state—representation by population— and non-sectarian schools—I will not only aid you in doing so but will support your government with all my heart and vigour."

He offered practical advice on tactics. An immediate understanding should be reached among Independent Reformers. If they went into parliament unprepared to act in concert, Hincks might still manage to keep the bulk of the party overawed. But if Sandfield had previously ascertained that he could form a better government, nothing could hold support behind Hincks as leader. As for the Speakership, he assumed that Sandfield would again be put up for that post as soon as the new parliament convened—"in approbation of your closing speech". Returning him to the chair would be the opening blow at the ministry. But it need not prevent his relinquishing it to take the Attorney-Generalship and form a government, in the event of Hincks's resignation. He should, moreover, go down to Quebec ahead of time to see "Sicotte, Young, Dorion and other Lower Canadians you expect to act with". For, Brown added, "It is clear that the natural allies of the Reformers of Upper Canada are the *Rouges* (so called)."

Thus the long midnight screed, setting forth Brown's battle plan. That Sandfield's reply is not preserved does not detract from its significance; but he most likely read it with interest and approval. He would have been the first to concede that J. S. Macdonald was the rightful successor to Hincks as Liberal leader. And he had nursed resentment at being excluded from the Attorney-Generalship ever since the formation of the Hincks-Morin ministry in 1851, when he had predicted darkly, "I will show whoever may be in power what *one* man can do."[70] He and George Brown now went travelling through the West, towards the end of August, 1854, to gather support for Sandfield's candidacy as Speaker. An anxious Hincks asked his own agent in Oxford, Shenston, to report as soon as possible what success they were having. "I believe they went together," he wrote uneasily.[71]

A few days later it was time to leave for Quebec and the Fifth Parliament of the Union, to open on Tuesday, September 5. Groups of Reform members were on hand by Saturday the 2nd, however, busily caucussing and canvassing to secure the election of their favoured candidates as Speaker. At a time when the whole party was in such an unstable condition, a victory by one faction or another in this initial test of strength might play a critical part in shaping a controlling majority in the House. The ministerial Liberals in caucus chose George Etienne Cartier, a prominent *Bleu*, and a hard-headed Montreal lawyer who was widely acceptable to Hincksites and "railwaymen", since he had played an active part in floating both the St. Lawrence and Atlantic and the Grand Trunk: the latter company had made him its solicitor for Canada East. The western Independent Reformers were meanwhile pushing Sandfield Macdonald, though the eastern *Rouges* preferred Louis Sicotte. A deadlock in their joint caucus was averted when a steering committee that included Brown and Holton suggested that the first task was to combine to defeat Cartier.[72] After that, the best man might be left to win. He might well turn out to be Sandfield: for Brown knew that his own candidate had even drawn a minority of votes in the ministerial caucus itself, before Cartier had been chosen there.[73]

The House opened, Cartier was duly proposed—then duly beaten. The count was close, 59 to 62, and it took seventeen Conservative votes added to those of the anti-government Reformers to turn the trick.[74] Still this plainly demonstrated that the elections had not strengthened the ministry: it had failed to obtain a majority. Sicotte's name came up next. As the members voted it seemed evident that he too would be beaten, whereupon Reform would surely rally behind Sandfield Macdonald. But suddenly Hincks called out, "Put me among the Yeas!" At this the body of his supporters fell in to vote for Sicotte, who now won handily—76 to 41.[75] Macdonald had been circumvented. Hincks had not saved his own position, but in falling he had toppled Sandfield also, and had the bitter satisfaction of defeating a far closer personal enemy than Sicotte. Still further, he had upset George Brown's calculations at the very outset.

Two days later the government was again defeated, over a disputed Lower Canadian election, and Francis Hincks took the occasion to resign. It was merely the occasion, not the reason for his going. His case was hopeless, and he knew it. The resignation of the cabinet took place on Friday morning, September 8. Thereupon the Governor-General called on Sir Allan MacNab as official leader of the opposition to form a government. Brown, watching closely, could hardly have been surprised. The *Globe* itself took the news calmly. Even the announcement that Mac-Nab was consulting with Morin and his Lower Canadian colleagues in the late ministry caused no great concern, for that was quite in keeping with the expectation that Tories and *Bleus* would join forces. Let them hive off together. Confidently the paper prophesied, "A thoroughly Liberal administration must soon be formed to satisfy the desires of the country."[76]

Two days passed. Then on September 11 came an alarming report, the worst possible news. MacNab had certainly succeeded in forming a coalition: not only with the French, but also with the Upper Canadian Hincksites! It was that sweeping coalition so much to be dreaded. It went beyond a union of right-wing elements to bring in centre groups as well, and wreck Brown's own scheme for a comprehensive left-and-centre party. In the new MacNab-Morin cabinet that was now announced to a wondering public, the Lower Canadian ministers were to remain unchanged. The Upper Canadian section would consist of three Conservatives, MacNab, John A. Macdonald and William Cayley, and two Hincksite Liberals, John Ross and Robert Spence. Premier MacNab had agreed to carry out the secularizing of the reserves—the very desecration he as a Tory had resisted tooth and nail. Ex-leader Hincks had negotiated for the admission of two of his friends to the cabinet—accepting with great equanimity the horror he had warned his followers against for three years, the accession of Conservatives to power. And John A. Macdonald, the real talent in the ministry, had found no difficulty himself in taking seat with men he had but recently denounced as utterly, hopelessly, sunk in corruption. Said the *Globe*, in the black realization of defeat, "Of all the abortions it could enter the mind of men to conceive—it is the greatest."[77] Strong words, and strongly meant.

Yet this Liberal-Conservative coalition controlled an overwhelming majority in parliament. And it would live: live to become gradually a party in its own right, while the remnants of Liberalism left in opposition became, still more gradually, a rival party grouping. The old Reform party had divided, collapsed, and disappeared. Conservatism had modified old Tory principles to enter a new and highly significant relationship with French Canada. The Canadian party structure had unquestionably been altered; but not according to George Brown's specifications. Why had he failed?

In the first place, he had been out-manoeuvred. So fluid was the party situation when the session began that, had Sandfield Macdonald won the speakership, the moral victory for the Independent Reformers might have shaped a very different realignment of forces. But Hincks had effectively destroyed that possibility, then had welcomed overtures for an alliance from

MacNab. In the second place, Brown had been over-sanguine—an inherent failing. In his own enthusiasm for voluntaryism he had counted on a similar spirit to swing Protestant Conservative support against French Catholic influence. But as the passionate religious conflict of 1853 faded into memory, the mass of Conservatives were more affected by the plain political fact that gaining power in Canada meant reaching terms with the main French-Canadian block. Brown did not ignore that fact himself; but his way was to meet it head-on, with a massive formation which would bring the French themselves to terms—terms such as representation by population. It did not work: the bulk of Conservatives and English-speaking moderate Liberals were still ready to accept the union as it stood. Upper Canadian grievances would have to rise still further before there was a definite western majority ready to back Brown's programme of forcing the sectional problems of the United Province to a clear-cut issue.

In the third place, finally, Brown had failed to give due weight to one important element in the political situation. Looking to the issues of church and state to determine lines in politics, he had not sufficiently considered the power of railway interests to influence party combinations in that era of rapid growth and ready government spending. The sectional and sectarian conflict and the politics of railways were both potent forces; and if a "doctrinaire" like Brown overstressed the first, "practical" politicians like Hincks and his successors rested too much upon the second. Neither could really be ignored.

In Brown's own incomplete assessment, he had tended to regard the Conservative party too largely as the instrument of an out-dated and crumbling Tory state-church clique, and thus readily available for carving up and re-apportioning. Yet the party by this time had been making a notable adjustment to the times. "Develop the country" could be sound Conservative as well as popular doctrine; party leader MacNab had summed up his politics now as railways; and Montreal Toryism in particular could welcome the Grand Trunk as the railway reconstruction of its old St. Lawrence empire of the waterways. Similarly, the conservative-minded French-Canadians — whom Brown had viewed solely as the defenders of an unchanging society and culture—were reaching their own accommodation with the railway era. Their hostility to the alien powers of commerce and capitalism had lessened markedly: French Canada had its own railway projects; the businesslike Cartiers had replaced the stately Papineaus in political ascendancy. And generally, *Bleus* and Tory-Conservatives could find much in common, in material terms, with the Hincksite Liberals who had virtually led Canada into the railway age, and tied the provincial government to the Grand Trunk. In short, if Brown had not been blind to the possibility of a Hincksite-Conservative-*Bleu* coalition, he had greatly underestimated its likelihood. For he had not properly weighed the railway factor in his own political calculations.

That factor would be evident enough under the new Liberal-Conservative ministry, where the President of the Grand Trunk, John Ross, still held a cabinet seat, and "railwaymen" gathered eagerly at government doors. At times, moreover, Grand Trunk spending and railway influence under the new Coalition would make the brave days of Francis Hincks (now a modest ministerial supporter) look almost primitive by comparison. But still more obvious for the present was the fact that George Brown had been flatly defeated in his own efforts to recast the party structure. His enemies were jubilant; although the *Globe* did the best it could with the Coalition's lack of principle, and scoffed at its supposedly Liberal membership—"a corrupt schemer like John Ross, an india-rubber jumper like Robert Spence".[78] Nevertheless, with scarcely a pause or backward glance, Brown went on working to remake the Reform party, to build anew on the fragments left outside the Coalition of 1854. It would simply take more time than he had anticipated. He did not mean to fail again.

5

On September 11, the day the Liberal-Conservative Coalition was announced, thirty-eight members from both sections—fourteen from Lower Canada, twenty-four from Upper—met and issued a statement condemning the deplorable ministerial alliance.[79] This comparative handful comprised the initial opposition to the new government, and it was diverse indeed. From Lower Canada there were *Rouges* like A. A. Dorion, the Montreal associates, Holton and Galt, and some French-speaking Liberals of less certain colour, shading to disgruntled *Bleu*. From Upper Canada there were Clear Grit radicals like Hartman and Rolph, who had either crossed the floor during the brief June session or when the Coalition had been formed. There were Independent Reformers linked with Brown, and others from eastern Upper Canadian ridings who rather looked to Sandfield Macdonald. Then there were a few "loose fish", who might yet be lured to the government side, if the bait were right. And there were one or two thorough-going independents like William Lyon Mackenzie.

This was the dubious material from which a new Liberal party would have to be constructed: or rather, two associated parties, for at present the eastern and western opposition forces were co-belligerents rather than allies. They were two loose sectional groups, considerably at variance, the *Rouges* expressing a left-wing French-Canadian *nationalisme* of their own. They would each have to go some distance to consolidate themselves, and to work out measures of effective collaboration. No doubt, the governing Coalition contained almost as much diversity. Yet it rested on a broad acceptance of a central, "liberal-conservative" position that overrode sectional differences. It also had the useful cement of government patronage to seal up any cracks, and could command a certain habitual loyalty to its own side in politics—the inside. Government spending to keep constituencies content, close connection with powerful Grand Trunk interests, might do a lot to strengthen a very mixed ministerial alliance.

In any case, if George Brown wanted to rebuild Liberalism in his own section of Canada, he would first have to aim at closing the rifts in the existing Upper Canadian opposition, and at restoring unity among the remaining adherents of Reform across the western country-side. He now sat on the front opposition benches in the House (at least he had risen this far in the world) along with Sandfield Macdonald, Rolph, and Mackenzie. But all these men were there by virtue of their personal prominence: they did not really control the scanty ranks behind them. John Rolph had somewhat redeemed himself by voting against the Hincks ministry to bring it down; but he was now an aging, played-out politician, not trusted by the Clear Grits themselves.[80] Mackenzie was in a hopeless minority of one. Brown had only some four or five close followers, and there was still a gulf between him and the Grits. As for Sandfield Macdonald, he could conceivably have pulled the factions together, as the least objectionable to them all. He tended to regard himself, moreover, as of somewhat superior status; and perhaps was suffered to do so in recognition of his previous distinctions, and in the hope that he might actually develop into an effective leader.

Unfortunately, he did not. He proved instead that he lacked sufficient ability to meet the difficult situation. He was at best a good second-rater, when first-class talent was needed. Moody and mercurial, Sandfield easily became discouraged, and since he consistently over-estimated himself, his wounded pride led him to brood and put the blame on others. Besides, he had never been physically strong, and now ill-health began to reduce his activities in parliament.[81] Even further, he was a Roman Catholic: rather a nominal one, it is true, who opposed separate schools and priestly influence, and did not mind receiving chatty diatribes from his Cornwall business partner (a Presbyterian Scot) on the latest machinations of the local Catholic clergy.[82] Still, Sandfield was a Catholic in a largely voluntaryist contingent, and his position must have been affected thereby. At any rate, he failed to hold the dominant role in the western opposition. Almost by default, it fell increasingly to Brown. He was already well established as an outstanding parliamentary critic; now he took a leading part in attacking the Coalition.

There was a pause, however, as parliament was briefly adjourned at the end of September, once the new administration had ridden through the debate on the address: "ploughed" might be a better description, since the vote was 70 to 33.[83] The House had also expressed its approval of the Reciprocity Treaty on September 22; but that long-sought agreement, negotiated with the United States during Hincks's time, by now caused little stir. Even back in June, when the Treaty had been finally signed in Washington, an early advocate of reciprocity like the *Globe* had taken the news quite calmly, remarking that while that measure would bring some of the blessings of free trade, its passage "some years ago" would have been of more benefit to Canada than to the country in its present highly prosperous condition.[84]

On October 10 the government met the House again with its own programme ready to present. The two most important items in it were a bill for the secularization of the clergy reserves and one for the abolition of seigneurial tenure—twin measures which the Coalition had accepted as essential. The Attorney-General West, John A. Macdonald, introduced the Clergy Reserves Bill himself, while charges of desertion of principle flew not only from the opposition but from a furious Tory rearguard still struggling to save the church endowments. Macdonald explained, however, the regrettable necessity of yielding to the inevitable. This might be unimpeachable statesmanship, and deft politics as well, to enact the enemy's measure when it could no longer be resisted. But the Reform opposition was not disposed to see much statesmanship in Macdonald's neat reversal on a position which they through ten years' effort had worked to make untenable.

Nevertheless the western Liberal opposition were ready to

approve Macdonald's Bill in outline, because it would at last dispose of the clergy reserves, even though it provided for the reserves funds to go to the municipalities rather than to public education. In this respect, William McDougall, who was still a power in Clear Grit circles, admitted confidentially to William Lyon Mackenzie that, "it will be good policy for the Reform opposition to accept the Bill as it stands if they can't amend it. They ought not to give this rascally Coalition the credit of any measure that is even passable, and the people have been bamboozled so long, and by Reformers too, that they are ready to take almost anything that can be called 'secularization'."[85]

Brown for his part also sought to make the most of the Bill, whoever was putting it through. He noted points of criticism, however, flaws which should be remedied when the proper time came. And as the legislative process ground on, through October and November, he raised his detailed objections in debate. The chief of these concerned the provisions in the Bill whereby the clergy of the various churches then receiving stipends from the reserves could continue to receive them to protect their life-interest. These payments might either be made annually to individuals, or they might be lumped together for each denomination as a whole and invested as a capital sum, which would then provide a yearly return as income for its clergy.

Brown had no objection to the principle of safeguarding the vested rights of present encumbents, but he did condemn the proposal to give churches the right to commute their clergy's claims upon the reserves into permanent capital funds. This would merely set up ecclesiastical endowments in another form. Commutation would alter a temporary church claim on public money into a perpetual interest. He moved a series of recommendations against it: in fact, he took the lead among the opposition in discussions over the Bill, and managed to place some qualifications on the right of commutation.[86] But the voluntary principle had not been fully realized. When the Bill passed its final reading in late November, the *Globe* averred, "We rejoice in the fact of secularization but mourn over the conditions with which it has been accompanied."[87] None the less it added, with a bow in the right direction, "The exertion of the voluntaries have, however, been successful, chiefly because their views recommended themselves to an acute and liberal-minded people, as the Canadians undoubtedly are."[88]

Secularization had finally been won, whether in spite of or because of the party upheaval; both, perhaps. Next came the Seigneurial Bill, which was Lower Canada's *quid pro quo* for supporting the reserves measure. Again Brown approved its general purpose while contesting specific provisions: notably that which would lay the cost of compensating seigneurs for loss of dues upon the whole provincial revenue, rather than on Lower Canadian income alone. Yet he did back A. A. Dorion and the *Rouges*, in telling Drummond, who had introduced the Bill, that the country wanted final and compulsory settlement of seigneurial rights rather than some drawn-out, permissive process.[89] Brown, in fact, was beginning to co-operate in the House with the fluent, graceful Dorion, who by sheer intellectual ability was gaining much the same pre-eminence in the eastern Liberal opposition as he himself was in the western. They co-operated to such a degree, in fact, that some voluntaryists even Browner than Brown were soon complaining about his and Sandfield Macdonald's association with "Dorion of Montreal" and his unsuitably French faction.[90]

Of more immediate significance was the way in which Brown and his former Clear Grit foes were obviously moving closer together. When they had first faced the Coalition side by side, there had been little more than a chilly truce between them. But it grew less chilly as they found themselves echoing one another's voluntaryist opinions during the vigorous debate on the Reserves Bill. Brown gained Grit votes for his amendments; and his views and William McDougall's on the commutation "dodge" were plainly much the same.[91] In consequence, some interesting olive branches now were cautiously extended by the principal press organs on both the Brownite and the Clear Grit sides. Past differences were not to be forgotten; but present common interests deserved equal recognition.

The *Globe* delicately observed that it no longer saw any reason to complain against the Clear Grits. "If in some things we differed and perhaps do differ still, no one will deny that we approach nearer than any other two sections of Canadian politicians."[92] The Grits' fault had been that, "either for the sake of office or from an unfounded hope that they might secure the passage of Reform measures, they had supported the late government". Now that they acknowledged their error by denouncing Hincks and all his works, "we have no hesitation in, at all events, co-operating with them". Then came a bolder statement: "Should time prove that the union can be lasting, we shall heartily rejoice at harmony so auspicious for the Reform cause."[93]

McDougall's *North American* made much the same approach. It was not remarkable, it asserted, that *Globe*, *North American* and *Examiner*, George Brown and John Rolph, should all "row in the same boat".[94] They were of the same party, shared the same objectives. The journal glanced back to Brown's stand against the Hincksite-Clear Grit alliance formed in 1851. His opposition to that partnership had then seemed wrong, and his efforts to embarrass it at birth still appeared so. However— "We freely admit that we do not view his opposition in the same light now. He knew Mr. Hincks better than we did; he knew the duplicity and power of the priest party in Lower Canada and its hostility to our principles better than anyone of those who aided in the combinations of 1851."[95] Here was a thorough-going admission from editor McDougall, the chief agent behind the combination in question. He followed by holding out his own hand. "When the ship of the constitution is in danger of sinking, every one who pulls with us shall be welcomed as a friend."[96]

Parliament rose for a winter recess on December 18. Brown went back to Toronto after three and a half wearing months that had witnessed the final ruin of the old Liberal party. Yet before this same period had ended, the first tentative steps had been taken towards Reform reconstruction: reconstruction now to be based essentially on an alliance between George Brown and the Clear Grits. That alliance would still need time for realization. There was a whole chasm of bitterness between its partners to be closed. But by the end of 1854 one could see the process was beginning.

6

Obviously, a junction of Brownite and Clear Grit forces would greatly aid the cause of Reform recovery. They were the two strongest elements in the western opposition. Since Sandfield Macdonald had failed to assume effective command, his own strength was virtually restricted to two or three personal followers from his own Upper St. Lawrence region, a little Liberal enclave at the eastern end of Upper Canada. The Grits and Brownites, however, held seats scattered across the bulk of Upper Canada, from the Lake Ontario shore westward. And they did have much in common: their views on church and state, western rights, and French Catholic domination. If they could forget past antipathies, and perhaps set aside differences on elective *versus* parliamentary institutions, they yet might shape a strong new power to combat the ruling Coalition.

Furthermore, they could complement one another. The Grits had numbers to supply. They were by far the largest western opposition faction and were strongly rooted in the rural democracy of the Upper Canadian farming population. Yet their leaders in the House, Rolph and Cameron, had failed them, and radical journalist-pundits like McDougall and Charles Clarke had proved better at drafting programmes than at pushing them to success. On the other hand, George Brown could provide forceful leadership, and a flourishing press enterprise with unsurpassed power to influence public opinion. He and the *Globe* could offer precisely what Grittism lacked.

Certainly the main Grit newspapers were at a low ebb by the beginning of 1855. For months previous, William McDougall had been ready to sell his *North American*—still the principal Clear Grit organ—discouraged both by the failure of his political designs and by his constant financial difficulties.[97] McDougall was a gifted journalist, undoubtedly, but he could no longer make his weekly pay in the new age of dailies. James Lesslie's old radical *Examiner* was facing the same sort of problem. In fact, he proposed to merge the *Examiner* with both the *North American* and William Lyon Mackenzie's *Message*—a rather eccentric sheet, begun in 1853, that appeared whenever its proprietor found sufficient cash. As Lesslie said, only large journals with sizeable staffs could survive nowadays in the metropolitan press, or manage to compete outside Toronto with the many local papers that had sprung up.[98]

His suggested merger of the radical press failed, however. Mackenzie was not interested; McDougall wanted to sell out completely.[99] And George Brown, now back in Toronto, was eager enough to buy. In mid-February, 1855, he purchased the *North American*, debts, subscription lists and all.[100] The *Examiner* held out till August; then it too was absorbed into the *Globe*.[101] While Mackenzie carried on, in his own highly individual way, his small journal had not the importance of the two chief Grit organs. Their fusion with the *Globe* meant that in the press, at least, a substantial measure of Reform unity had been gained. Indeed, McDougall in his final *North American* issued a strong plea for union: "There is no *cause* for division, no excuse for separate cliques or factions."[102] Suiting actions to words, he entered the *Globe* office as a major addition to its editorial staff. As a result, it became possible for Gordon Brown himself to leave the office for considerable periods, and during the next few years he made trips to Britain, and for an interval even edited the Quebec *Gazette*.[103]

By now Charles Clarke, another influential Grit journalist,

had also given up his own Elora *Backwoodsman*; though from
his home in the heart of the western peninsula the "Elora wire-
puller" maintained close touch with a wide circle of Clear Grit
politicians, editors, and party workers. Gordon Brown approached him on behalf of the *Globe*, amiably suggesting that he
become political correspondent for the area.[104] But Clarke was
not as ready to come over as McDougall. He and a considerable
Grit element in the West remained cool to George Brown,
chiefly because they clung still to the old demand for elective
institutions, which the latter continued to repudiate. Hence,
whatever Brown's gains in absorbing the chief Clear Grit journals,
he was still far from effecting a binding alliance with the
whole mass of Grittism.

Meanwhile, by the end of February, Brown had returned
to parliament at Quebec. There had been significant changes
since it last sat. For one thing, a new Governor-General presided at the reopening, Sir Edmund Head, the former governor of New Brunswick. The *Globe* had greeted his appointment
fairly agreeably; he was a capable and strong-minded Peelite
Conservative, it noted, but would not likely use his influence to
favour the Conservative side under responsible government in
Canada.[105] For another thing, the Lower Canadian section of
the cabinet had been altered. Morin and two colleagues had retired, Taché in the Legislative Council assuming the eastern
leadership; and one of the new ministers was the vigorous, ebul-
lient Cartier. Short, stocky, and sharp-witted, his hair *en brosse*
and bristling, he was a mass of aggressive energy no less formidable than George Brown.

The latter had come to Quebec plentifully armed with petitions for the amendment of the commutation clause in the
Clergy Reserves Act. His efforts at revision failed, however:
the Coalition ministry considered the question closed. Similarly,
he failed in his opposition to their Elective Legislative Council
Bill, although when it came before the existing Upper House
that body obligingly threw it out. He failed still further in
another rep by pop motion, which he and Hartman tacked to
the elective council measure while it was under debate. Yet he
carried twenty Upper Canada opposition votes with him, and
that in itself was good augury of growing Reform agreement.[106]
In any case, no other outcome could be expected while the
Coalition held so overwhelming a majority. Thus parliament
moved across the spring, with no surprising developments. But
late in May, when the session had only days to run before the
prorogation, the ministry suddenly pushed forward a new
separate-schools bill. It was surprise enough.

The Lower Canadian government leader, Taché, had first introduced this Upper Canada School Bill in the Council on May 12. Few members of the Assembly had expected that so critical a subject could be covered in debate and carried into legislation in the short space remaining to the session. In fact, by the time the Bill came up for discussion in the Lower House many Upper Canadian members had already left on the long way home, believing their most serious tasks to be completed.[107] The contents of this measure proved serious in themselves. In response to steady pressure from Charbonnel and other Roman Catholic bishops, it would enable any ten persons to establish a separate school and thereby have a claim on public funds.[108] But the manner in which it was handled seemed far more serious. Canada West, the section to be affected, had known nothing about it: in fact, the government's own Superintendent of Education, Egerton Ryerson, had been kept completely and astonishingly in the dark.[109] It was introduced at the last moment in the Assembly, when Lower Canadians were clearly left in control—for the Conservatives and Hincksites from the West might scarcely approve the Taché Bill themselves. And it was pressed forward in all haste by its sponsor, John A. Macdonald, who introduced it on May 22 and moved the second reading for the next day.[110]

Here were the earmarks of conspiracy, not to mention thoroughgoing Lower Canadian influence. Brown tackled Macdonald almost incredulously when he brought the measure in. Did he really mean to press so vexed a question when half the western members had gone home? That was the intention, came the plain reply.[111] Brown fought it strenuously, every inch of the way. He even won a number of modifications by the third reading; but the ministry proceeded undeterred. He made a final urgent appeal: "Only twenty-five or thirty Upper Canadian members are now here, and I ask if it is fair that such a bill should be passed and go into operation before the people of Upper Canada know anything about it? I appeal to the honourable members from Lower Canada, to their own sense of justice and fair play, whether such a thing should be done. I have spoken longer than might be desirable at this period of the session, but I can only say that I have spoken my honest feelings, and I have spoken them the more strongly because there are so few here from Upper Canada—to speak for those who are so grossly to be wronged!"[112]

But eastern votes carried the measure past all vociferous opposition. In fact, these same votes carried it against an actual majority of those western members who were still present.[113]

Lower Canadians had passed a bill of major, of crucial, importance to Upper Canada, against that section's own expressed
desire. Never had the fact of Lower Canadian domination, of
French Catholic power, seemed more obvious. Things were no
better: they were worse under the Coalition and the shift in
parties. Never before had the existing provincial union looked
so unsatisfactory to aggrieved Upper Canadians. In response,
demands that the existing union of the Canadas be altered rose
with redoubled force across the West. And George Brown's
principle of representation by population gained strong new
cogency from the lesson of the Taché Act of 1855.

7

Rep by pop was not the only solution talked of in the angry
West that summer. Many preferred a simple cutting of the
Gordian knot—separation of the Canadas, dissolution of the
union. It was so obvious an answer that at one time or another a
variety of discontented groups had urged it, from Tories to
Clear Grits. The original Grit radicals, for instance, had not
infrequently argued that elective institutions and pure government could only be secured when Upper Canada was herself
again, free from the Lower Canadian influence that sustained
a selfish and lethargic clique in power.[114] Of course, this opinion
had not been much in evidence during the Grits' period of sharing power themselves. But an inveterate old radical like William
Lyon Mackenzie had kept up a demand for repeal of the
union.[115] Possibly he unconsciously longed for the smaller
Upper Canadian stage that he had once dominated.

Brown himself had always stood out against dissolution. Even
after he went into opposition in 1851, and attacked French
power over government, his own newspaper had ardently com-
bated any thought of dissolving the union. That way was
defeat, subsiding into a petty parish existence. His own answer
was the very opposite: a closer union based on representation by
population. For reasons of defence and trade, the natural unity
of the Canadas provided by the great St. Lawrence system—the
continental destiny that lay before all Canadians—the United
Province had to be maintained: "We will rather seek to extend
our boundaries than contract them."[116] Brown looked, in fact, to
a future British North American state that might span the continent. And to that end, "to be a great state, we must continue

our alliance with Lower Canada, and even extend our borders further to the east".[117] Separation was merely "the advice of the coward".[118]

This was the long view, however, and dissolution might look a good deal more attractive in the short run, especially to disconcerted Grits who now in 1855 revived their earlier interest in that proposal. Their local western papers took it up, the *Examiner*, too, in its dying days; while Grit politicians made speeches to their constituents urging the repeal of the Act of Union.[119] As petitions for repeal were organized, it seemed apparent that the agrarian democracy of the West did not share Brown's feelings for the union. The Upper Canada farmer might well see little value in it. Separate, he argued, and escape the baneful power of "Frenchmen" in distant Lower Canada: western wheat would still go out to market, through New York or Montreal, through one province or two.

But Brown, the city journalist and Toronto business man, looked at things differently. He gave far more weight to the commercial implications of the union, recognizing that it was an economic if not a political success, that the two Canadas together had built an immensely valuable trade and transport system, and that dissolution could seriously upset not only Upper Canada's commerce but ultimately its agricultural prosperity as well. The inland West needed the freest possible access to the outside world, that its products might reach world markets readily, and its imports come in cheaply. It required the use of the St. Lawrence route unhampered by separate provincial jurisdictions, such as had existed in the old days of two divided Canadas. The American Erie Canal offered an alternative pathway to the ocean; and the West's ability to use either route could help to keep the freight rates down. If, however, the unity of the St. Lawrence were lost, then Upper Canada might be left to face trade barriers on both routes, and with little it could do about it. As the *Globe* expressed it bluntly, dissolution of the union would place the West "at the mercy of Brother Jonathan and Jean Baptiste".[120]

Accordingly, in the summer of 1855, Brown and the *Globe* launched a strong campaign to bring home to Upper Canadians, (and more specifically, to Clear Grit farmers) the broader values of the provincial union. The *Globe* hammered away at dissolution, admitting good reason for its popularity but stressing the harm that it might do. At the same time it argued eloquently for representation by population as the just and effective remedy for Upper Canada's wrongs, a cure that would none the less maintain the union and its merits. Was this a mere sectionalist campaign, harping on a narrow and disruptive principle? At any rate, it served to combat a far more thoroughgoing sectionalism in Upper Canada, and presented rep by pop as the very means of preventing the disruption of the United Province.

George Brown went forth to speak once more. At the village of Brampton, on a warm and drizzling July evening, he attended a banquet for some two hundred picked Reformers; held in a capacious tent.[121] The number was not large, compared to open public meetings; but it was a significant gathering that brought together both Clear Grit and Brownite M.P.'s, together with newspaper editors and leading Peel County party men. It must have been sticky and oppressive under that damp canvas in the humid weather, and the lengthy round of speeches could not have lightened the oppression. Joseph Hartman and other Grits addressed the audience to urge dissolution as a Reform policy. William McDougall even mildly endorsed it.[122] Then Brown rose to offer representation by population instead.

His very presence could send an expectant ripple through an audience: the tall, broad-shouldered frame, the tawny red hair, the handsome, large, expressive features and strong jaw; the clear blue eyes that dilated and grew luminous as he spoke. He began, as usual, almost haltingly, as he admitted that his own policy for Upper Canada would not be achieved overnight.[123] The first need was for the people to pledge their parliamentary representatives to representation by population, and then to keep them to it by rewarding or punishing them at elections. A united Upper Canada Reform party, he said more boldly, could carry rep by pop. There were Lower Canadians in parliament, both French and English, who would accept that principle if Upper Canada only showed itself determined: their votes added to a solid Reform block from the West would produce the necessary majority. The real obstacle, he emphasized, was not Lower Canada, but those Hincksite Liberals who had divided and betrayed the party by joining the Coalition. They must be brought to reason, or else be driven from parliament by a united Upper Canada's insistence on representation by population. It could be done, and would be done—if the people and the party would simply stand by that demand!

His deep voice rose in vibrant power, as enthusiasm mounted through the audience. "I cannot think it would be statesmanlike, because Upper Canada representatives of the hour are traitors to their cause, to yield up the solid advantages obtained by the present union of the two Canadas. I could fancy if a dissolution were accomplished today, that ten years hence we would look back with astonishment at the utter imbecility of

1,300,000 Anglo-Saxons in Upper Canada and 300,000 in Lower Canada, frightened by some 700,000 Frenchmen into surrendering forever the noble St. Lawrence and all the fertile land it traverses. . . . " He paused as cheers burst forth. "For one, Sir, I will never be a party to such a transaction—until every other remedy has failed!"[124]

He carried the meeting. Even the advocates of dissolution admitted it. And somehow this seemed to be a turning-point. Following Brown's speech in the tent at Brampton, Reform papers widely praised the doctrine he had advocated there. Said the *Globe* exultantly, "The Reform party of Upper Canada has unmistakenly accepted Representation by Population as its foremost measure."[125] Undoubtedly there was keen response all across Upper Canada. The *London Free Press* noted "many valid reasons" against dissolution;[126] the Prescott *Telegraph* observed, "we are decidedly in favour of the *Globe*'s theory";[127] and the Galt *Reformer* predicted, "Let Upper Canadians only prove true to themselves and it will be impossible to resist a demand so just and equitable."[128] The Kingston *Commercial Advertiser* emphatically declared, "Representation by Population has become the rallying cry of the Reformers of Upper Canada."[129] The *Globe* added a gleeful final comment. It remarked that all Conservative and HinckSite papers were avoiding rep by pop "as if it were a pestilence raging in their town".[130]

By September some of the excitement had waned, but Brown had plainly gained a major success. He had largely won the Grits from dissolution to his own policy. He had, in fact, largely diverted the flood of western feeling over the Taché Act to representation by population, and impounded it as power behind his own demand. He had besides given Reform a vital rallying cry, a simple, direct, but meaningful slogan on which to unite and act. "Rep by pop"! It would ring through Canada in future, to recruit that massive Reform array which Brown had long been striving to assemble, attracting moderates and even some Conservatives to its side. And for the present, through representation by population, he had found a policy on which Grits and Brownites could effectively join forces, putting by their conflicts over elective institutions at least until it could be realized. With the summer of 1855, Reform reconstruction had taken a long leap forward.

In a real sense, Brown at last was making clear headway on that problem of recasting parties which had dominated his thinking for more than two years. Would the party he now was building be very different from that which he had projected before the Liberal-Conservative Coalition had emerged to upset his plans? Not as different as one might think. It would still be voluntaryist, and uphold those principles he had expressed to Sandfield Macdonald just before the Coalition was formed. It would even be moderate in its basic character, although his approach now lay to Clear Grit radicals and not Conservatives to join with him. For despite Brown's fervent views on sectarian and sectional questions, his fundamental political ideas remained cast in the moderate, Whiggish mould of mid-Victorian British Liberalism. He would not yield those ideas, and move toward Clear Grit radical doctrines: the Grits would come to him. Not without reluctance and hostility on the part of deep-dyed believers in elective institutions and sweeping change—but they would come to him.

As a result, when the Brownite Reform party finally took shape, it would express the outlook of middle-of-the-road Victorian Liberalism far more than radical, agrarian democracy. In short, the new Liberal formation which George Brown would organize at last out of party upheaval would be much the same as he had always intended it to be.

The Press.

Rebuilding Western Reform

I

Sixty or seventy workmen were banging away at old Government House in the early autumn of 1855, completing alterations before the Governor-General arrived to take up official residence in Toronto.[1] The seat of government was being shifted from Quebec, in that clumsy alternation of the capital which was itself an indication of the deep sectional division in the union. The Upper Canada Parliament Buildings were again being renovated: University of Toronto students had not improved them during a temporary occupancy, and the medical dissecting rooms in one wing had left strange smells and a pile of bones behind.[2] The government departments had been housed already, some down town in the Albany Chambers, some—the Executive Council among them—in the redecorated old Toronto General Hospital that stood well out on King Street and close to Government House.[3] And at the last-named, elegant marble chimney-pieces had been installed throughout and a fashionable verandah strung across the façade, while the whole rather bleak exterior had been brightened with fresh stucco.[4] Sir Edmund Walker Head would have a mansion befitting his vice-regal dignity.

Early in October, the Governor-General and his western ministers advanced on an expectant Upper Canada to tour the western section before settling down to duty in the new capital. The round of visits, loyal addresses and gracious replies went off very well, except for one unwary statement by the Governor at Hamilton on October 15. There, in paying appropriate compliments to the rapid progress of the West, Sir Edmund had in part ascribed it to "the superiority of the race from which most of you have sprung".[5] At any rate, that passage was in the report which Gordon Brown took down at Hamilton and duly relayed to the *Globe*, from where other papers copied it.[6] The remark itself was no more charged with meaning than the usual profundities of after-dinner oratory; but it was far from

wise in a sectionally divided province. Lower Canadian journals
fell on it at once as an ominous sign of anti-French feeling in
high places; Upper Canadians, in return, saw it as expressing
the Governor-General's just sympathy with the interests of
English-speaking Canada.[7] There was a brief outburst of excitement, all rather embarrassing to the Olympian detachment of
the Queen's representative.

It was urged in his defence that he had been misquoted, that
Gordon Brown had jumbled his remarks; or even worse, that
George Brown had "cooked" the report back at the *Globe* office.[8]
Head himself, however, privately admitted to having uttered
"some incautious words" at Hamilton, and a few days later at
Toronto strove to explain them away.[9] The incident passed off,
yet impressions remained that would not be easily erased. Head's
statement would be dragged up repeatedly thereafter in the heat
of sectional conflict; so would the charge that the *Globe* had
been responsible for "the lie".[10] Head was a man of decisive
character, of definite likes and dislikes. From the moment of
entering the West he felt no cause to love George Brown—the
man regarded as responsible for any utterance in the *Globe*.

It was quite possible, however, that Brown was not even in
Toronto when Gordon first brought back the Hamilton report.
That autumn he was finding time at last to spend on his holdings in Zone township, Kent County. The investment he had
been making in western lands since 1851 was now developing
into a sizeable business enterprise. The railway had done it:
the Great Western had passed along his property as the rails
went down between London and Windsor. In the spring of
1854, he had accordingly contracted with the Railway Company
to furnish cordwood from his forests for the ungainly wood-
devouring locomotives of the day.[11] He put a hundred axemen
to work to clear the heavy timber, and each cord they cut and
stacked brought $1.75 from the line.[12] Early in 1855 the Com-
pany agreed to establish a regular station on his estate, where
engines were already halting with the four impatient whistle
blasts that signified "wood up".[13] He would provide the land
for the station site, build sawmills there, and lay out a village
nearby: there was hardwood far too good to burn, and spreading
stump fields to invite farmers, now that transportation would be
available. And so the little way-station of Bothwell came into
being, where the Great Western cars came clattering and sway-
ing out of the forest, and ground to a screeching stop.

A few cabins sprang up to do business with the passengers at
the station. There was a tavern there soon, the little log-built
"Sebastopol", proudly named in honour of the capture of the

great Russian fortress in the Crimea that September.[14] Town
lots were surveyed in ragged fields, roughly stumped and
ploughed, for Brown's village of Bothwell that was beginning
to take shape. He was busy with a hundred projects—a steam
sawmill, a cabinet factory, a door, sash and shingle plant, a
grist-mill, a foundry and a machine shop.[15] Besides town lots,
farms were to be sold in a 3500-acre tract around Bothwell.[16]
But several hundred acres were reserved as a farm of his own,
where he might realize his own blithe vision of the rural life.
He was cutting roads, northward to the Lambton County line,
southward to the London-Chatham highway.[17] Then there were
the cordwood-cutting operations to look after, the stumping
and ploughing, a potashery that converted the slash to a saleable
product.[18] He paid his working force with his personal notes,
that freely circulated as currency in this western domain.[19] For
Bothwell, like Canada, was growing on credit, confidence and
hope.

The "Laird of Bothwell" (the name came naturally enough)[20]
saw his own fortunes and those of Canada inextricably tied up
with railway progress. He was whole-heartedly behind it, both
as an interested investor and as a Toronto citizen who recognized
that his city's destinies depended on the steady improvement
of its rail communications. Previously the urgency of church-
and-state questions might have made him give railways a sec-
ondary position in his own political pronouncements. But this
by no means indicated any hostility to their development. If
he had attacked the Grand Trunk scheme, the biggest of them
all, he and the *Globe* had repeatedly made clear that it was the
extravagant promotion and political entanglements behind the
Grand Trunk which they opposed, not the construction of the
great line itself. Hence in the preceding session Brown had voted
aid to the Grand Trunk—which went on soaking up money like
a sponge—declaring that the work must assuredly be carried
forward.[21] The *Globe* had added that though the original financial agreement for the road had been "pregnant with evil", Mr.
Brown now considered it his duty to help it to completion;
though always with watchful qualifications.[22]

Their enthusiasm was quite unqualified, however, when it
came to the Great Western. "A brilliant success," acclaimed
the *Globe* ecstatically in September, 1855: "It is not only one
of the most profitable railways in the world—it is one of the
best managed."[23] No less admirable was the Hamilton-Toronto
extension which would link the capital with the Great Western,
when it opened in December. And Toronto's Northern Railway
to Georgian Bay was quite as warmly endorsed. Long before,

the *Globe* declared, the builder of Yonge Street, Governor Simcoe, had visualized his road as a highway from Toronto to the Upper Lakes and the vast territories beyond. Now the Northern would realize Simcoe's splendid concept, as the wealth of the western half of the continent came pouring down its rails to a mighty Toronto entrepôt.[24] It was a splendid concept in itself—and faith in railways was the root of it.

Railways and Toronto were, in fact, thoroughly entwined in the pages of Brown's journal. In the closing months of 1855, when the confidence of boom-times was soaring, the *Globe* eagerly outlined the process whereby Toronto's commercial sway would spread out along the rail routes. The Northern, the Grand Trunk east and west of the city, were to do their part. But the opening of the line to Hamilton would place Toronto in a position to replace that town as the chief wholesale centre for the rich Peninsula, because of the capital's wider railway links and greater business facilities.[25] And Toronto should push still other lines to gain mastery of the entire trade of Upper Canada. The *Globe*, in short, was voicing the aspirations of its fast-growing native city to organize the economic life of the West about it: just as George Brown, the Toronto leader, was seeking to organize the West politically behind his own party programme.

December saw the peak of fervour over the great new means of transport, as Toronto buzzed with preparations for a lavish Railway Festival. Ostensibly it would celebrate the opening of the Toronto and Hamilton, but it was really a public jubilee for the railway god himself. George Brown was named a member of the Festival Committee of prominent citizens, organized in the Mayor's Room on December 3.[26] Straightway they made plans for a gathering of 5000 people, to be held in the capacious new Northern Railway workshop, which would be transformed for the occasion into a ballroom four times the size of St. Lawrence Hall. They issued invitations far and wide across Canada and the United States. The Governor-General was asked; the mayors or representatives of Chicago, Boston, Detroit and Rochester.[27] Cartier and MacNab, among others, were requested to represent Canadian railway interests outside Toronto. In fact, about the only leading railway politician not invited was Francis Hincks, and he had left Canada in November to find a milder climate as imperial governor of Barbados. "As for the expense," the *Globe* said loftily, "we imagine if the people of Toronto think fit to spend twenty thousand pounds instead of ten thousand dollars for an entertainment, it is nobody's business. Toronto is too large a place in the estimation of its own citizens to permit them to do anything in a shabby or mean manner."[28]

By the great day, December 20, all was ready in the exuberant city.[29] The guests had been pouring in for two days by special trains. Stores on the main streets had been decorated. The Northern freight house, where a banquet for two thousand would be served, had been festooned with banners, while the walls of the workshop-ballroom shone with gas jets that spelled out such appropriate terms as "Welcome" and "Reciprocity", together with the initials of Victoria and Albert, Napoleon and Eugenie—and those of railways serving Toronto. The fixed machinery and three lines of track within the workshop had been hidden under richly carpeted wooden platforms or disguised as settees. A fountain in the centre spurted seven streams of water into a pool where bobbed an assortment of stuffed ducks. And overhead bright flags, glistening chandeliers and shimmering gaslight stars completed an effect that was truly indescribable. The *Globe*'s proud judgement could hardly be contested. "They will undoubtedly be the most magnificent entertainments ever given in Canada."[30]

The banquet was a shining feast of optimism and cordiality. The innumerable speeches, the repeated prophecies of endless railway progress, were each applauded with unabated enthusiasm, while political foes congratulated each other back and forth in a rosy aura of goodwill and champagne. "My good friend, Mr. Brown," beamed Cartier—"and I call him my friend, although a political opponent. . . . "[31] And, "seeing Mr. Cartier present", Brown was no less genial in paying tribute to the city of Montreal, to which "we are indebted for the commencement of this great effort to construct railways in Canada".[32] Toronto, he said, with generous candour, had by no means played the part that Montreal had done. Then turning to MacNab, he poured more praise upon him and the people of Hamilton for their work in building the Great Western, which so deserved Toronto's thanks.[33]

Next he swung to future prospects: the opening of the great land that lay far to the north-west, above the Lakes, to be tapped through Toronto's own Northern Railway. "We look upon this northern country as peculiarly our own," he announced with emphasis, as Toronto cheers resounded to the roof.[34] He happily endorsed other railway projects under way or talked of: then came the greatest project of them all. "And there is another road which a great many of us yet hope to see undertaken, and that is a road from Toronto to the Pacific." Was this hope illusory, he asked? Five years before it might have seemed quite as illusory that Toronto would have rail connections as far as the Mississippi. Yet that was an accomplished fact tonight. "We have been placed," he cried, "in communication with markets that we never knew of before—and if there is a country or a city that have reason to be gratified that railways are brought into operation, it is Canada and the City of Toronto!"[35]

The banquet adjourned, the ball began at eight o'clock, and by eleven the workshop-ballroom held a full five thousand. They danced to the lively music of the Rifles Band, gaily promenaded about the fountain with the ducks, the sensation of the evening, and freely sampled the buffet supper and plentiful champagne. The ball went on in a whirl of bobbing crinolines and flying coat-tails; they danced till five in the morning under the multi-coloured gas-jets.[36] And when it was over, and the carriages trotted off to houses and hotels, there was happy, tired agreement that it had been a wholly elegant and sumptuous occasion, truly in keeping with Toronto's stature as a modern metropolis. Next day the grateful guests departed from the city, just before the winter's snows came down. The Great Railway Festival passed into memory, as the *Globe* wished all satisfied Torontonians a heartfelt Merry Christmas.

2

But with the new year, 1856, renewed religious discord quickly drowned the happy notes of railway harmony. Bishop Charbonnel let loose a thundering pastoral, declaring that Roman Catholic electors in Canada who did not use their votes on behalf of separate schools were guilty of mortal sin, and that confessors were no less guilty who granted absolution to parents, electors and legislators who supported mixed schools.[37] "If this does not establish Separate Schools," the *Globe* said sourly, "nothing else would."[38] Then came the shock of the Corrigan murder trial at Quebec, where seven Irish Roman Catholics stood accused of brutally beating Edward Corrigan, a Protestant Irishman, to death. The evidence seemed plain enough, and the dying victim had identified his chief assailant. Yet at the end, according to the press reports, the French-Canadian judge presiding at the trial had given a charge to the jury that virtually invited acquittal, whereupon the jury of Irish and French Catholics had returned a verdict of not guilty.[39] News of this unexpected verdict reached Upper Canada on February 18, just after Sir Edmund Head had driven in a closed sleigh to open parliament in frost-bound Toronto. The House got down to business in a nasty mood, as Upper Canadian members spoke angrily of the gross failure of justice in Lower Canada, and the necessity of investigating Judge Duval's alarming charge.

There were other signs of discord in the legislature, within the ruling Liberal-Conservative Coalition itself. The Upper Canadian half of the Coalition was decidedly in trouble. On one side, ministerial Liberals were dismayed by evidence of continued eastern domination such as the Taché Act, and swayed by George Brown's progress in reconstituting Reform. On the other, the Tory right wing of the Conservatives were still resentful over the destruction of state-church privileges, and distrustful too of the alliance with the French Canadians. John Hillyard Cameron was emerging as the right-wing champion, a highly successful Toronto lawyer who was also a rising power in the Orange Order. Wealthy, eloquent, experienced in politics and thoroughly ambitious, Cameron posed a serious threat to the MacNab-Taché Coalition as the potential leader of a resurgent and intransigent Toryism.

And while both ministerial flanks were thus beset in Upper Canada there was trouble at headquarters as well. Ross and Spence, the two Hincksite Liberals in the cabinet, were urging that the government be reconstructed: that it could not hold its Liberal following unless it were freed of Tory dead weight, notably embodied in the premier and Conservative leader himself, that stout but gouty knight, old Sir Allan MacNab.[40] It was a thinly veiled secret, moreover, that the chief Conservative magnates were almost as dissatisfied as their Hincksite colleagues with MacNab's leadership, which seemed to have little purpose beyond that of blissfully enjoying the long-awaited fruits of office. Just before the new year the *Globe* had surmised that the growing agitation in ministerial papers regarding government shortcomings was calculated "to aid Mr. John A. Macdonald in the war he has been waging within the walls of the cabinet against Sir Allan MacNab".[41]

MacNab was doomed, said Brown cheerily, but could not cry out. He was cast for the Desdemona of the cabinet, while Macdonald played the jealous Moor to Spence's Iago.[42] Othello-Macdonald may not have appreciated the casting. At any rate, he felt it necessary to deny "the absurd grounds of suspicion that we want to get rid of MacNab".[43] But the feeling was widespread. Macdonald was "the coming man", to more than the *Globe*. Certainly Ogle Gowan, Grand Orangeman, could recall to John Alexander that while still in opposition at Quebec he, Macdonald, had privately declared that he was to be real leader of the party—though he had publicly denied it when Gowan had published the report in his *Patriot*.[44]

The conflicts in the Coalition, the strains among its leaders, were obvious points for attack in the House, as the debate on the address unrolled. The government replied with similar attempts to exploit divisions on the opposition side. Hence a session that began in any case with harsh feelings over the Taché Act and the Corrigan affair rapidly degenerated into exchanges of more heat than brilliance, that came to little more than, "you're another". When, accordingly, Sandfield Macdonald denounced the hopeless disunity of the government leaders, Sydney Smith, Hincksite member for Northumberland, sharply rejoined that the honourable gentleman should look to his own side of the House, where he "was now only an ex-leader", and where the member from Lambton, George Brown, "was always sitting quietly in his seat, looking on, pulling the wires over the *oi polloi*—a mixture of Clear Grits, disunionists and annexationists".[45] And when oppositionists deplored the clash of viewpoints on the ministerial side—Tory anti-French feelings and Hincksite disdain of "fossil Toryism"—government supporters sneered at groups so different as western Reformers and eastern *Rouges*, pretending to have common interests. Cartier, indeed, could brusquely warn Holton and Dorion that they would be hunted out of Montreal for supporting "the nauseous political banner of the member for Lambton".[46]

It grew steadily more obvious that George Brown was the prime target for the best government sharp-shooters. The attention was flattering, but dangerous in its aim to spread distrust and dissension in Reform ranks by presenting a Brown avid for power. When the member for Lambton rose in turn to speak, he vigorously repudiated the trouble-making charge that he had usurped the leadership of the opposition. There was no such post, he said emphatically; there could not be until the Reform factions were reunited.[47] At the present, Liberalism had been rent in pieces, and it was difficult for any one man to speak for all the varied elements left outside the Coalition. He readily admitted differences among the opposition: it was still in healthier condition than the ill-assorted ministerial medley that had simply swallowed up its principles. Then he turned to his own position.

"So far as I am concerned"—and Brown was weighing his words—"in entering upon the course which I have followed since I first took my seat in this House, I resolved to regard myself as a 'government impossibility' [He was quoting the ministerial press]. I have never, Sir, concealed from myself that the position I have felt it my duty to take upon this floor, and the bold tone of speech which I have felt called upon to adopt as a Protestant Upper Canadian, must so alienate me from the gentlemen of Lower Canada as to forbid, for the present at least, those ambitious aspirations so freely attributed to me." His voice rang with conviction as he continued, "If I can succeed in obtaining the formation of a Government pledged to carry out those principles which I value so highly, I will have accomplished the end for which I entered parliament—and will retire to private life, well rewarded."[48] It was a plain statement of purpose, a pronouncement on his role in politics to be substantiated by his whole career.

John A. Macdonald followed, however, to renew the accusations that Brown hungered after power, to claim that his honourable friend had been ready enough himself to seek a coalition of parties in 1854. The assault went on. Indeed, by the time the debate wound to an irascible conclusion on Thursday night, February 26, five cabinet members and still more government supporters had virtually made George Brown their text. One diligent member counted that he had been mentioned no less than 372 times upon the floor.[49] Now it was late. The House was tired out, with tempers worn dangerously thin by the veritable slanging match on either side. And as the last clause of the address was put to the vote Brown finally got the chance to speak again. "I have waited patiently until all the gentlemen opposite have got through with their attacks," he said, tense with strained emotion, "and would now with leave of the House say a few words in reply."[50]

He meant particularly to meet the charge made by Macdonald and his colleague Spence that he had been willing enough himself to look for an alliance with the Conservatives back in 1854. But their professions then, he argued, had been very different, and close to his own opinions.[51] He had not changed since—the Conservatives had. And point by point, item by item, he proceeded vehemently to demonstrate how remarkably they had altered their views, and notably, Macdonald, since the Coalition had come into being. Spence got even harder treatment: that avowed moderate, who now piously abhorred all extremist doctrines, had once subscribed to a Clear Grit radical platform that included rep by pop and no separate schools, when he had been nominated in Halton in 1851.[52] Brown was running hot after his quarries now. They grew just as hot. "It's not true—not true," shouted both Spence and Macdonald, breaking in repeatedly. Spence, in fact, hurled back a furious denial of his every connection with the wild radical platform. At this, Grit David Christie thrust an oar in: he himself had been at the Halton nominating convention in '51—he knew that Spence had endorsed its platform to gain the nomination—and (with a flourish) he could produce this letter from a delegate to prove it![53]

There was uproar; and, in its midst, John A. Macdonald, whose usual easy composure had been rasped away, completely lost control of his strong temper. He streamed out a fierce volley of abuse; then, only seeming to recover, as the Speaker urgently called him to order, and the House watched open-mouthed, began a violent tirade against all the iniquities of George Brown. Swiftly, savagely, Macdonald swung to an old and cherished grievance, the Penitentiary question. Here was the issue he had unsuccessfully raised in three previous sessions of parliament, in an attempt to gain justice, as he saw it, for Henry Smith, the disreputable ex-Warden of the Penitentiary, and no less in an effort to punish the man he above all held responsible for Smith's wrongs: the former Secretary of the Penitentiary Commission, George Brown.

Brown might keep alive old angry memories. Macdonald showed the same capacity. He poured his long-stored-up resentment into the most slashing, sweeping, and personal accusations, that went well beyond those he had made in earlier years against the Penitentiary Commissioners in general. Brown, he swore passionately, had falsely recorded evidence—had altered written testimony after it had been agreed upon and signed—had suborned convicts to commit perjury—had even obtained pardons for murderers who would give false evidence. He repeated his charges twice, and with biting emphasis declared that he could prove every word of them.[54]

The members sat aghast as Macdonald's outburst ended. Brown rose, pale and shivering with rage but still grimly clutching at his own control. There was not a vestige of truth in the Attorney-General's remarks. ("Liar!" yelled Macdonald.) He had taken down his words, would hold him responsible for proving them. He would move a committee of investigation tomorrow.[55] That was all. That was all he dared permit himself to say. The House immediately broke up, tremulous with excitement, almost awed. Somehow they sensed that two towering rivals, the two men who had obviously emerged as the principal figures on opposing sides in parliament, had opened an unbridgeable gulf between them. They were not now divided merely by the battle-front of politics. There was something more here—a personal conflict of high pride and strong temperament, a veritable clan feud of the Macdonald and Mackenzie.

Next morning, in a taut, uncomfortable Assembly, Brown moved his committee to inquire into the charges expressed in Macdonald's words. "If a fifth of them were true, they should have sent me to the Penitentiary—not only banish me from this House, but stamp me with infamy for the rest of my life." And this, he asserted, eight years after the original Commission; during much of which time, "I had been on terms of personal friendship with the Attorney General".[56] Replied Macdonald dourly, "I brought these charges before. I offered to prove them then, and I can prove them now."[57] The House moved on to other things; of far less moment for the future course of politics.

3

The Corrigan case came up a few days later, when John Hillyard Cameron sought to launch an inquiry into the acquittal of the defendants by moving for the production of Judge Duval's charge to the jury. His motion clearly challenged the MacNab-Taché Coalition government, dependent as it was on an alliance of French- and English-speaking forces. It was, no doubt, an attempt by Tory malcontents to draw the Conservative party from entanglements with Liberals and French Canadians, with the thought quite possibly in mind that Cameron, not Macdonald, might come to inherit the party leadership. Yet it also expressed widespread Upper Canadian resentment over the Corrigan case, and thus Brown and the western Reformers could readily give their support. In fact, the great bulk of the western members backed Cameron's motion in the face of government opposition. It was carried on March 10, 48 to 44, and there were but two negative votes from Canada West, apart from the ministers themselves.[58]

The Coalition had been decidedly defeated. Would it resign? True, the thumping reverse in Upper Canada alone need not bring its fall. While there had long been talk about the "double majority principle"—that a government should be required to hold a majority in each section of the union, lest either of them be oppressed—it had never been accepted as a binding constitutional rule. Yet the sectional defeat was a serious embarrassment: and beyond that, the ministry had been beaten in the

House as a whole. Macdonald accordingly announced that Cameron's motion must be rescinded or the government would resign. It was not rescinded—and the government did not resign. But instead it met a direct vote of confidence, which took the issue away from the heated Corrigan question.[59] Its adherents returned; the cabinet was saved; and simply advised the Governor-General not to comply with the motion requesting production of the judge's charge. Still, if the regime had endured, its troubles were patently obvious.

It put forward an Elective Legislative Council Bill, which finally carried—despite George Brown's continued opposition—creating an enlarged Upper House in which, however, the existing appointed Councillors would keep their seats. It raised the tariff, in order to gain revenue to support another instalment of aid to the faltering Grand Trunk—three million pounds; the public debt was soaring. Duties on manufactured goods now reached the level of 20%, which the *Globe* deplored as a step backward to the old fallacy of protectionism.[60] But chiefly the government remained preoccupied behind the scenes with the question of its reconstruction. Indeed, the struggle there was sharp enough to precipitate the resignation of John Ross, the leading Hincksite, from the cabinet in April. Manoeuvres and counter-manoeuvres continued. So did the rumours and denials: that Macdonald had finally taken over the Conservative leadership, that Cameron would replace him—even that Brown and MacNab were closeted in an attempt to combine both ends against the middle.[61]

Meanwhile the Committee to investigate Macdonald's charges against Brown was sitting almost daily. Seven backbench members had been named to it: two Conservatives, two Hincksites, a *Bleu*, and two opposition Liberals—which weighted it on the ministerial side.[62] That had to be expected; it was not a court of law but a parliamentary inquiry, and the predominant side in the House naturally gained the larger membership. Yet as Macdonald and Brown presented their cases before it, the political bias of its members became increasingly apparent. Above all, it grew apparent from the record of proceedings, wherein Brown steadily built up a well-substantiated case which at length virtually changed Macdonald from the accuser into the defendant. The majority of the Committee, however, gave Macdonald every benefit of doubt. They minimized Brown's points as far as they could, and, when it came to any objections, regularly carried votes to sustain the former's pleas and to overrule those of the latter. This itself might seem a biased judgement. But an examination of the copious minutes of the Committee makes any other hardly possible.[63]

The first blow to Macdonald's case came March 17, the seventh day of the Committee's sittings. The Attorney-General and his counsel, Philip Vankoughnet, had brought in various civil servants to verify the general assumption that the original body of evidence taken by the Penitentiary Commission had been destroyed in the burning of the old legislative buildings at Quebec. That established, it would have been necessary to proceed on the basis of the Commission's printed Report alone, which contained a digest and selection of the original evidence, and only necessary for Macdonald to produce witnesses to swear that the final record had been falsified; that is, that it did not agree with their memory of the actual testimony which had been transcribed and signed before the Commissioners some eight years earlier. But on March 17, Vankoughnet, in rounding out the question, asked George Brown as a mere matter of form if he himself knew anything of the fate of the manuscript records, before the strenuous feat of recollection should be set under way.

"The original books containing the evidence are in my possession"—thus came the cool but staggering answer—"and have never left it for a single hour."[64] He had kept them; kept them ever since they had been returned to him, after the Penitentiary Report had been laid before parliament; and he now stood ready to produce them in three large handwritten volumes of royal-sized pages. He would, he said, have been a fool to have submitted them before, out of the safe-keeping of the Committee. Now let hostile witnesses make their claims—and let them then be tested against the first-hand record!

This striking disclosure considerably changed the plan of attack. Instead of arguing from witnesses that the Commission records had been falsely kept, Macdonald and Vankoughnet decided to call very few, and to concentrate chiefly on showing that passages of evidence had been wrongly transcribed from the manuscript books into the final report. They vigorously contended that this would prove the charge of falsification. Brown and his counsel, Miles O'Reilly, protested as vigorously that the real record was the handwritten original; that clerical errors could creep into the copying, done by other hands in any case; and that, while there might admittedly be errors in judgement in the condensing of some passages of evidence (they did not claim infallibility) this scarcely constituted deliberate falsification.[65] The Committee majority disposed of the problem. They voted to accept Macdonald's view.[66]

He now proceeded to build his case chiefly on some seven or eight instances taken from the whole long Penitentiary Report, most of them illustrating fairly minor peculations of ex-Warden Smith. From these Macdonald sought to prove malicious distortion or suppression of evidence. And this, it was held, would then indict the whole Report—and George Brown as Commission Secretary and chief author—with perverting the record. To aid in his effort, Macdonald did call on a few witnesses; though only two were of the hundred or more who had actually testified before the Commission of 1848-9. As might be expected, one was the former Warden, old Henry Smith himself, whose petitions had originally launched Macdonald on his course. Smith's son, Henry Junior, now sat as Solicitor-General in the government, while the father himself was securely ensconced in the Grand Trunk office in Montreal. The other witness was James Hopkirk, the former Inspector at the Penitentiary who had been so closely implicated with Smith in general maladministration. And he was brought up from his own snug new harbour as Collector of the Customs at Kingston.

It did not do much good. Smith, under Brown's knife-edged cross-examination, admitted that he could not point out any passage of evidence that had been recorded falsely; admitted that every piece of testimony at the inquiry had been read over, and if necessary amended until he, the Warden, was satisfied; admitted that a prisoner whose pardon Brown was supposed to have secured was actually recommended for it by himself. And when Smith did seize on an omission, at least, in the recording of the evidence, he had it demonstrated to him that this particular piece of the record was not in Brown's handwriting at all, but in that of Commissioner Thomas, another of Macdonald's own witnesses! About all Macdonald got out of it, as he now began to fight an increasingly defensive action, was Smith's unhappy agreement that it was he who had assured the Attorney-General that charges could be substantiated against George Brown.[67]

As for Hopkirk, here Macdonald did a little better. Although the ex-Inspector had to deny any personal knowledge of the truth of the charges, when Brown cross-questioned him, he did succeed in throwing out suggestions that the former Secretary had intimidated or suborned witnesses and made misrepresentations to them. Unfortunately the effect was somewhat spoiled at the very end, when an over-eager Hopkirk gave as a notable example of Brown's "suborning" the fact that two guards who had been dismissed by Warden Smith, and who had given evidence against him, had been "immediately restored" by the Commission Secretary as an object lesson to the prison staff that it paid to testify the right way. "Are you quite sure?" urged

Brown earnestly. Hopkirk had no doubt of it: "Quite sure,"—
Brown had controlled the entire affair. "Now Sir, please look
at the records of the Commissioners."[68] The records were produced. They revealed the fact that the sinister Secretary had not
even been in Canada at the time of the dismissal and reinstatement of the guards. For weeks before and after, he had been
in the United States touring penal institutions there. "I may
have been mistaken in some particulars," offered Hopkirk
lamely.[69]

The inquiry had dragged on into May, when parliament
became the focus of new conflict and excitement. The ministry
was again in trouble; a crisis had arisen over the seat-of-government question—one of the thorniest problems in all the spiny
thickets of Canadian politics. The provincial capital could not go
on shuttling back and forth forever. Yet any attempt to fix on
a permanent home not only called forth sectional rivalries, but
also those of Montreal as opposed to Quebec, Kingston *versus*
Toronto, and so on. A motion in favour of Quebec was actually
carried; but it was not a ministerial measure, since the government could not unite on the question, and all members of the
House had voted as individuals: the voting majority was merely
a chance combination of contending groups. Its verdict was soon
challenged. On May 14, when George Brown moved that it was
inexpedient to appropriate money for permanent buildings at
Quebec, as the government now proposed, the *Rouges*, Papin
and Holton, added amendments that made the issue a direct test
of confidence in the ministry.[70] It was a good test too, for there
was a feeling that the ministry had evaded the unpleasant task
of sponsoring a capital, then taken advantage of a *fait accompli*.

The debate that followed was long and keenly contended,
but when it ended on May 20, after an unbroken, thirty-hour
marathon sitting, the ministry won the vote, 70 to 47.[71] Yet
again it was beaten in Upper Canada, where many of its supporters definitely turned against it on the seat-of-government
issue. Here it lost by six votes, far less than on the Corrigan
question.[72] This time, however, the western ministers evidently
took the blow much more seriously. Macdonald, Cayley, Spence
and Morrison—the moderate Liberal who had replaced Ross—
all resigned, leaving only the premier, poor old MacNab,
rattling emptily in office. Reluctantly he resigned himself. The
captain had to abandon ship because all his crew had dived
overboard.

Three days later the unabashed crew climbed back aboard—
first lieutenant Macdonald now commanding—with Vankoughnet as an additional Conservative to replace MacNab, left bob-

bing hopelessly in the Coalition's wake. Otherwise the reconstructed government was just the same, although the Lower
Canadian leader took precedence in what was officially the Taché-
Macdonald regime. Without doubt, the quick change had saved
the Coalition, by thwarting the right-wing Tories and strengthening those Conservatives with whom the Hincksite Reformers
were willing to work. Yet the internal conflicts which had been
settled by John A. Macdonald taking full control of the western
government forces had been resolved by a somewhat dubious
manoeuvre.

The restored Upper Canadian ministers carefully explained
that the obvious want of support for the western section of the
late government had made the reconstruction necessary. They
did not, they claimed, approve of the double majority system
as an abstract rule, but in practice one section of the province
could not long be governed against its will.[73] Accordingly they
had departed the cabinet, and entered a more acceptable one.
All very well: if it were more acceptable. But the new reconstruction, on meeting the test of want of confidence moved by
Dorion and Brown, squeaked through by only four votes in all
—and in Upper Canada was beaten by fifteen![74]

Macdonald and his colleagues had resigned, on May 21,
when the government had a majority of 23 in the whole House,
but was in a minority of six in the western section alone. They
did not resign, on May 30, when the government held a general
majority of four but was *fifteen* short in the West. It all showed
how circumstances could alter cases. It left the starkly plain
impression that the real purpose had been the dumping of
MacNab. Macdonald, however, boldly defied the charge.[75]
The argument now was that simple, classic one: the Queen's
government must be carried on. The cabinet remained; the
issue was closed.

4

By this time the parliamentary Committee on Macdonald's
charges was also approaching its final, decisive vote. Brown's
own witnesses had been called in May, among them two other
members of the Penitentiary Commission, William Bristow and
Chairman Adam Fergusson. They had strongly repudiated the
charges, and in any event, affirmed the responsibility of all the
Commissioners for the proceedings of 1848-9; including the

selecting of evidence for the final Report, which had been chosen after general discussion and with unanimous consent. Moreover, Macdonald's own Commissioner-witness, Sheriff Thomas, expressed his disbelief in the accusations; and when the Attorney-General claimed that Brown had not substantiated the brutality of punishments under Warden Smith, declared that he himself had "the best reason to know that the flogging was excessive".[76] For Thomas had drawn up the statistics from the prison's Punishment Book!

All in all, Macdonald was left with a large proportion of his contentions effectively refuted, the remainder resting on the unsupported word of Smith and Hopkirk, and as flatly denied by Brown's own witnesses. Not a very strong position. Accordingly, in his closing address the Attorney-General laid great stress on the fact that he had brought these charges before, that he had believed the gentlemen (Smith and Hopkirk) who had made them originally, and that he still held these two to be "worthy men". But he added, "I do not wish to say that Mr. Brown was guilty of the charges contained in the petitions I presented to parliament, and which I repeated on the authority of those petitions. All I want to show is that I had authority to say from the statements made to me by the petitioner and other credible persons that it was so. God knows no man has regretted more bitterly than I do the language that I used which has led to this investigation in a moment of irritation."[77]

No doubt that was true: Macdonald had surely regretted the violence of his outburst. But that admission did not clear George Brown of charges of criminal conduct. No doubt, moreover, Macdonald had believed those who had told him of Brown's misdeeds. Yet establishing his own sincerity in bringing accusations did not exonerate George Brown, nor change the fact that the charges were personal, specific, and far beyond those earlier put to parliament. In fact, Macdonald still made every effort to implicate Brown: so that the verdict at least should be a true Scots one of "not proven".

And that, indeed, was the finding of the Committee on June 5, together with a mild rebuke to Macdonald.[78] Again the issue was decided on political lines. The two opposition members on the Committee backed a resolution entirely denying each charge against Brown. One of the Hincksite members, moreover, even put forward a compromise motion declaring that while the Attorney-General had acted under the conviction of truth, his charges had completely failed to be established. But the ministerial majority carried a statement of solemn inanity, which noted that though there was some evidence of falsification in the

Penitentiary Report, the Committee held no opinion as to how
far George Brown might be personally responsible; that in any
case two convicts who had been witnesses against the Warden
had been recommended for pardon by the Commission through
its Secretary; and that it was regrettable that the Attorney-
General had reiterated in the heat of debate the charges which
he had previously made in parliament.

This resolution, adopted as the Committee's report, meant
practically nothing as a settlement of the question. If there had
been falsification, had Brown committed it as charged, or had he
not? If he had acted for the Commission in transmitting recommendations for pardons to the government (a secretary, after
all, writes letters) did this mean that he was guilty of suborning
witnesses? And if he were guilty, then why should Macdonald
be rebuked? And why rebuked in any case for repeating charges
"in the heat of debate", if he had already put them before parliament? It was no wonder that Brown was left dissatisfied—to
say the least.

The evidence of falsification had been dubious, picayune, and
offset by massive testimony against it. The two convicts whose
pardons were still allowed to cast a shadow over him had been
released long after the Penitentiary inquiry, one of them three
years later. And when he had produced official records showing
that both pardons had been applied for by petitions from outside
groups, and that there were strong reasons for clemency in either
case, Macdonald had simply suggested that the outside applications had been put-up jobs. This when one petition was the
product of twelve Lower Canadian Catholic priests, and the
other signed by the then-Mayor of Montreal, John Moir
Ferres, who sat as the Conservative Chairman of this very
Committee! Obviously, either the majority of the Committee
members nourished an astonishing faith in Brown's powers of
subversion, or else they were prepared to vote as good politics
dictated. At all events, the insinuation that Brown had paid two
convicts with pardons for committing perjury stood in the Committee's final report.

He still hoped to get fairer treatment from the House at
large. But during June, Macdonald and Ferres repeatedly
pushed off any action on the report, despite opposition attempts
to force it to consideration. Parliament was prorogued on July
1, and thanks to the delaying tactics the Committee's findings
were never received in the Assembly, nor entered in its journals.

The work of the inquiry was plainly being consigned to the
safekeeping of oblivion. But if Macdonald wished to forget it,
Brown could not. The former might have exhausted his

emotions on the subject, and perhaps counted it as one more political engagement that could have gone better, or indeed far worse. A frustrated, seething Brown, however, felt that the stain of unjust and impossible charges had been left upon him— charges that could have meant criminal action had they been definitely upheld. To a man of his high spirit and keen sense of personal honour, it was gnawing bitterness to be left thus. And Macdonald was responsible. Brown could never regard him merely as another political rival while these accusations stood between them. Many might sympathize: some feel that he was right.

5

Apart from the matter of Macdonald's charges, things were going well for Brown that summer. The troubles of the Coalition in the long and brawling session of 1856 had sent more members across to his side of the House. Though some returned when the Taché-Macdonald cabinet showed its determination to survive, the Liberal opposition kept several new adherents. In fact, the Hincksite Liberal faction behind the ministry was clearly dwindling, while the western Reformers grew stronger on the opposition benches. Brown's efforts to give direction and unity to his party were meeting more success. In May, he saw his prime measure, representation by population, gain a majority of Upper Canadian votes, though defeated, of course, in the Assembly as a whole.[79] Even the most hard-bitten western radicals were displaying a degree of willingness to commit themselves to George Brown's policies. One, indeed, told William Lyon Mackenzie quite simply, "An administration with Mr. Brown at the head would be an improvement—therefore let us have it."[80]

Similarly in June: while his motion to abolish separate-school laws inevitably was lost, he drew so many Upper Canadian votes (including thirteen ostensibly pledged to separate schools) that a severe check was given to Catholic hopes of further expansion.[81] Furthermore, the government grew fearful of the strength of Upper Canadian antagonism, and would not sponsor further Roman Catholic demands.[82] To a large extent the schools question thus lost its prominence in active politics for several years to come.

Brown's private affairs were prospering still more brightly.

On his Bothwell property, a thriving village was arising, one
that had 450 inhabitants by the end of the year.[83] A general
store was opened; four more taverns joined the "Sebastopol" to
minister to the passing railway trade; and two steam sawmills,
the cabinet factory, the grist-mill, foundry and machine shop,
now provided thriving local industries.[84] At the same time his
newspaper enterprise was expanding almost as rapidly. The
Globe's circulation had reached 18,000, and the daily edition
was twice the size of that first issued in 1853.[85] He had to install
a big new double-cylinder press to keep pace with the demand.[86]

To some extent, undoubtedly, Brown's own advancing fortunes merely reflected the radiant good times that still spread
across the province and especially Upper Canada. Only the
benefits of the railway-spending spree were being felt thus far;
the costs of extravagant overbuilding were yet to be made
known. And if the close of the conflict in the Crimea in January
had spelled the end of a booming wartime grain market, the
increasing trade with the United States under the Reciprocity
Treaty promised to offset any very serious loss.

The Canadian West was confident, and nowhere more so than
in its capital, Toronto; where a whole crop of expensive new
buildings expressed the opulence and self-assurance of the aspiring metropolis. Among them were the stately, classical
Mechanics Institute and Music Hall; the new General Hospital,
up-to-the-minute even in its "modified Old English" architecture; and, most notable, the magnificent new hotel, the Rossin
House—five storeys of white pressed brick and dressed Ohio
freestone, containing fifteen ground-floor shops with plate-glass
windows, more than two hundred richly furnished chambers, a
great reception hall, tea-room, billiard room, ladies' parlour
and gentlemen's baths.[87] It filled the need for first-class accommodation in a place like Toronto, said the *Globe* with satisfaction.[88] It was worthy of a city of over 50,000, which in a decade
had trebled its population with the expansion of the West.

And Toronto's eyes were turning to new prospects of expansion, far to the north and west: to the immense, empty wilderness of British territory above the Lakes, where the Hudson's
Bay Company held all the lands that drained into the great
Bay by virtue of its Charter of 1670, and controlled the regions
beyond, as far as the Arctic and Pacific, by licence from the imperial government. Half a continent was in the tenuous keeping
of an old, unchanging fur-trade monopoly; and on the whole
wide sweep of north-western plains there was but one tiny
settlement, at the junction of the Red and Assiniboine Rivers,
huddled near the Company's Fort Garry. Yet by this time the

existing Canadian West was filling up: it was only the year before, 1855, that the *Globe* had reported the auctioning of the last block of wild land in the lake-hemmed western Peninsula. There was, it said, still much room for intensive development on the lands of Canada West—but new frontiers of settlement must lie elsewhere, beyond the rugged, forbidding shores of the Upper Lakes. The article was aptly titled: "New Lands to Conquer".[89]

At the same time Toronto had the instrument in hand to begin the penetration north and westward, its Northern Railway. City business men had built the line as the shortest passage from the Lower to the Upper Lakes at Georgian Bay. From the Georgian Bay port of Collingwood, a line of steamers could cross Lakes Huron and Superior to reach the far North West. The *Globe* had written glowingly in 1855 of the "Great Northern Route" that could bring an ever-growing flood of western traffic down to enrich Toronto.[90] George Brown had spoken in the same terms at the Railway Celebration in December of that year.[91] For both shared the hopes emerging in their home city, in the bright mid-fifties, that a huge western empire of trade and settlement might be made tributary to the rising metropolis of Canada West. And in the summer of 1856, as a group of Toronto business men took active steps to open communications with the North West, Brown and his journal began a powerful campaign to awaken Canadians to the value and potentialities of the great Hudson's Bay territories.

Of course George Brown had been interested in the North West long before that moment. Its magnitude, its promise, had caught his imagination ever since Robert Baldwin Sullivan had given an eloquent address on the vast western land at the Toronto Mechanics Institute, in 1847, and he had taken all of it for publication in the *Globe*.[92] The next year, too, his attention had been roused by reports from England of a petition received from the inhabitants of the Red River settlement protesting against alleged Hudson's Bay misgovernment and exploitation of the Indians of the North West.[93] Thereafter he had watched the activities of various critics of Company rule with sympathetic interest: Alexander Isbister, for instance, a native of the Red River living in England, who had pressed the petition from its inhabitants on the Colonial Office; William Kennedy, Isbister's uncle, for thirteen years a clerk of the Company; and John McLean, another former Hudson's Bay man and celebrated explorer, who in 1849 had published his highly critical *Notes of a Twenty-Five Years' Service in the Hudson's Bay Territory* and caused considerable discussion. Brown was also in touch with a friend of Kennedy's in Toronto, Allan Macdonell, a firm believer in the value of the western country who sought a charter for a railway from Lake Superior to the Pacific.[94]

So it was that late in 1850 Brown had published in the *Globe* a lengthy protest of his own against Hudson's Bay rule—"It is unpardonable that civilization should be excluded from half a continent on at best a doubtful right of ownership"—and had gone on to urge an inquiry into the legal validity of the Bay Company's charter.[95] The same day, incidentally, he was seen in Armour's bookshop in Toronto asking for any works available on the Hudson's Bay Company and hotly defending the truth of Kennedy's allegations against the Bay.[96] He then had written to John McLean at his home in Guelph to enlist his aid in backing up the protests at the Red River. McLean had cordially agreed, and sent suitable remarks for publication in the *Globe*.[97] He had also informed its editor that, "The limits of Upper Canada ought to extend to the Rocky Mountains on the West", and proposed that the Reform party take up the issue as "a national, a Canadian question".[98]

But there the effort had lapsed for the time being, as shortly afterward Brown had become involved in the all-engrossing controversy over Papal aggression and "Dr. Wiseman's Manifesto". He subsequently raised the question of the future of the North West in his maiden speech in parliament in 1851, and briefly in the sessions of 1854 and 1856, while the *Globe* published an article or two. In general, however, there were too many other pressing matters before him. McLean evidently realized as much, for once in 1853 he wrote that he had explained to Isbister in England that he was sure that Mr. Brown had not forgotten the Hudson's Bay question, but was too fully engaged against an overwhelmingly powerful ministry to bring it up—"until you had breached the enemy's defences more. (Pray, is it so? Do you expect a surrender soon?)"[99] At any rate, it was not until Toronto interests undertook definitely to move north-westward in the summer of 1856 that Brown launched his intensive agitation in the *Globe*.

It really started with an editorial of August 1, announcing that, since there was no longer any doubt of the success of the route to the West via Collingwood and the Upper Lakes, a company would be formed in Toronto to build steamers for the trade. It was only natural that Northern Railway men—Mr. Brunel, the Superintendent, Messrs. Worts and Cumberland, two of the Directors—were particularly concerned with the venture. But, the *Globe* emphasized, "there is no question that the merchants and other residents of Toronto are deeply interested in everything which will develop the resources of the North West route."[100]

Meetings were held to organize the company, attended by the Toronto Conservative M.P.'s, Vankoughnet and J. B. Robinson—and, interestingly enough, by J. Gordon Brown of the *Globe*: for in the cause of Toronto enterprise, party lines could be forgotten.[101] On August 12, the North Western Steamboat Company was founded. Gordon Brown was named a member of the committee engaged in raising its stock subscriptions. With his brother's full support, he set himself to the task, holding promotion meetings all the way to Collingwood.[102]

Meanwhile George Brown guided the *Globe* into the mounting campaign on the North West. Eloquent editorials urged Toronto to seek its destiny there. Though the city, the *Globe* said, might congratulate itself on rapid growth so far, its own hinterland was limited to the good lands of Canada West, whereas places like Buffalo, Cleveland and Chicago drew on the whole rich trade of the American prairies. Would Toronto be satisfied to be "the entrepot of a district"?[103] Would it share in the commerce of the great central plains or be capital of the County of York? The wide British North West could be Toronto's own: this was no barren, frozen land as ignorance had it, but a fertile and well-watered region, rich in natural resources. And the city's position would enable it to reap the rewards of north-western settlement and development—rewards from transport, manufacturing for western farmers, the tapping of minerals, and commercial services. Others would gain control of the country if she did not. "Toronto cannot afford to neglect her interests when all is progress about her."[104]

From this appeal specifically to Toronto's metropolitan ambitions, Brown moved on to rouse Canadians generally to press for the opening of the North West, at present stagnating under a fur-trading company indifferent or even hostile to progress. That same month of August, the first of a long series of letters signed "Huron" were published in the *Globe*.[105] They ran until November, and caused much stir by their vigorous attack on the Bay Company's trade monopoly, their advocacy of a new Canadian North West Company to capture western commerce, and their prophecy that "fifty million of people would inhabit that immense territory which the Hudson Bay Company now claim and control."[106] There were other articles as well, declaring the Bay Charter to be illegal and invalid, and warning that if the North West were not opened to Canada it might be lost to the United States as Oregon had been lost, since the Americans in Minnesota were already organizing communications of their own that linked the Red River area southward to St. Paul.

Doubtless in this concentrated effort George Brown made good use of the talents of William McDougall on the *Globe* staff. From the start of his *North American*, McDougall had advocated the acquisition of the North West, and now he could express his ardent enthusiasm in the *Globe*. Some, indeed, might think that McDougall wrote the "Huron" letters; but that correspondent explicitly denied that he was either fur-trader or lawyer, which seemed to eliminate John McLean as well as McDougall as author.[107] "Huron", however, did assert that he was a Canadian, who sought "Canada for the Canadians"—and not for some two hundred Bay Company shareholders in London.[108] He believed, as Brown believed, that the North West should by right be part of Canada. That demand was the natural culmination of the *Globe*'s campaign.

Early in December, Toronto's Board of Trade held a significant meeting, presided over by W. P. Howland, a prominent Brownite Liberal sympathizer, who with his brother controlled extensive milling, lumbering, and wholesale produce interests. With engrossed attention the meeting heard speeches on the North West from Allan Macdonell, who claimed to be one of the first to bring the "Hudson Bay question" before the public, and from Captain William Kennedy, who had been born and brought up in the territories, and been recommended to command an expedition to their farthest reaches, searching for Sir John Franklin.[109] Kennedy praised the "Huron" letters in the *Globe*, described the North West's wealth, and the desire of the Red River Settlement to escape Hudson's Bay jurisdiction. And at the end, the Board earnestly adopted a petition to the provincial legislature, requesting an investigation of the Hudson's Bay Company's title to the North West.[110]

George Brown seized eagerly on this important step forward. A new spate of *Globe* articles now appeared on the "Great North West": they advocated its incorporation in Canada. Boldly they assumed the prior right of the Canadians to the West, as heirs to the ancient claims of New France. The question, simply, was how best to take over "the vast and fertile territory which is our birthright—and which no power on earth can prevent us occupying".[111] By the end of 1856, a new plank had been added to the Brownite platform, to join non-sectarian education and the voluntary principle, representation by population and the elimination of a dividing line between the Canadas: the annexation of the Hudson's Bay territories.[112] Brown had commited his journal and himself to a grand new effort. It was nothing less than the expansion of Canada across the great interior plains, and ultimately to the Pacific. No cause he had thus far taken up might have more consequence than this.

A variety of forces had shaped his weighty commitment. Incipient nationalism was one. From the earliest days of the

Globe, Brown had written of the Canadian nation of the future; no paltry province, but a continental realm, to which would belong—by a wholly Canadian version of manifest destiny— the immense British western territories of plains, mountains and Pacific slopes. In resisting dissolution, moreover, he had repeatedly argued that Canada should not break up its present union but go forward to build a broader state. Assuredly he also had in mind that his own solution to the union's troubles, representation by population, would be well-nigh irresistible if all or part of the Hudson's Bay territories were annexed to Canada and largely settled from Canada West—thus wholly overbalancing the East. Then there was his recognition that Canada West was filling up, in need of new lands to settle; together with his belief that the Hudson's Bay "furocracy" would never develop their holdings and neglected the interests of settlers already at the Red River. Finally, and very much in evidence, there was his close identification with the expansionist spirit of Toronto, displayed in his direct appeals to the aspirations of its business men.

Yet the annexation of the North West could appeal quite as strongly to the far larger agrarian community of Upper Canada. Land-seeking farmers, Clear Grit radicals, could readily agree with George Brown, the *Globe*, and Toronto that the North West should be won. The demand spread rapidly through most of the Upper Canada Reform press. And George Brown could make good use of this common sectional interest in his endeavours to reorganize the forces of western Liberalism. In fact, the time to achieve reorganization seemed finally at hand. Under his lead, a united western party was about to take clear shape.

6

On December 15, a printed circular went out from the *Globe* office to all the opposition members and principal Reform journalists of Canada West. It invited their signature to a call for a grand party convention, to be held in Toronto on January 8, 1857, and to be attended by six prominent Liberals from each Upper Canadian constituency. The names of Gordon Brown and William McDougall were appended, as "joint secretaries of the local committee".[113] The document itself elaborately proclaimed the reasons for calling a convention.

"An urgent necessity now exists for an efficient political movement to oppose the reckless administration of public affairs under which Canada now suffers. Sustained in office mainly by the Representatives of one section of the Province, the Government systematically pursues a sectional policy humiliating to the inhabitants of Western Canada and most injurious to the moral and material interest of the whole country. The expenses of the State have vastly accumulated—the public debt is enormously increased—equality of representation is denied—our noble National School system is assailed—the Provincial revenues are appropriated to local and sectional objects—the most easterly city of Eastern Canada is formally selected as the permanent seat of government—and principles of Legislation are resorted to in every emergency ruinous to public credit and demoralizing to our public men."[114]

"For various causes unnecessary to recapitulate here" (the circular continued diplomatically) "the Liberals of Upper Canada have for some time past been disunited; but these causes are now in great measure removed, and it is thought that no serious obstacle now stands in the way of a thoroughly efficient organization for practical ends." Consequently, an attempt would be made to construct a definite party union or Reform Association, based on a well-understood set of principles and policies. Nine were given; among them, representation by population, no sectarian grants, national education, impartial and free from sectarianism, free trade, curbs on public extravagance, and "the incorporation of the Hudson's Bay territories as Canadian soil". In short, the party would be grounded on the *Globe*'s platform. Then came the peroration: "If you approve of these principles and measures, if you are prepared to stamp them on your political banner, and unseduced by the temptations of office, to struggle with a single eye for their accomplishment, we respectfully invite you to join us on the 8th, and aid us with your advice and influence in uniting all earnest men in the good cause."[115]

The invitation was well received across the West. The desire for harmony was running high among Reformers. Swept by enthusiasm for rep by pop and North West annexation, former Hincksites could forget George Brown's attacks, and inveterate Clear Grit radicals drop their suspicions that he was a mere conservative at heart. Had not Brown gone to a political banquet in Elora, in November, and there been warmly introduced by Charles Clarke, that epitome of Grittism?[116] The mood of hopeful cordiality was still strong as Liberal delegates began to gather in Toronto in early January, in no way chilled by the bitter cold that brought accidents or delays on the railways into town.

By noon on the 8th, 150 Reformers of varied shades, some of whom had not sat together for years, had packed the undistinguished public hall on Temperance Street.[117] They sat behind closed doors in private deliberation, while the ministerial press, suspicious of the whole convention novelty, denounced the conclave as the "Temperance Street Conspiracy".[118] In the amiable, encouraging bustle, there were thorough-paced Brownites like Archibald McKellar of Kent, A. J. Fergusson, Brown's earliest parliamentary ally, and John McMurrich, another prominent Toronto business Liberal, who opened the proceedings. There were seasoned Clear Grits as well, like John Rolph, Joseph Hartman, David Christie and Charles Clarke. And among the moderate, ex-Hincksite Liberals present there was the clever and convivial Michael Foley, who had made a name for himself since entering parliament in 1854, although his ready wit tended to grow blurred from all too much conviviality. Venerable Adam Fergusson Senior was in the chair; Gordon Brown and McDougall were the secretaries. But obviously, the guiding spirit throughout the day was George Brown. He spoke on the main issues, and kept the discussion moving forward whenever it threatened to bog down in old differences. Before the meeting closed in much goodwill, at about eleven in the evening, he saw his own political platform—the platform of the *Globe* and of the circular—enthusiastically adopted, North West and all, as the programme of a reconstituted Reform party.[119]

Two incidents, however, suggested that rifts still might lie beneath the surface of new-won unity. The first arose when Foley objected to a portion of a resolution which called for the gradual assimilation of the local institutions of Canada East and West, on the grounds that this would offend Lower Canadians, keep them separated from the western Liberals and so prevent the success of Reform principles.[120] Brown was on his feet immediately, to point out that Hincks had tried the conciliation of Lower Canada once before, with disastrous consequences to Liberalism; and that the one real way to achieve the success of Reform principles was for the West to stand firm upon them, particularly on representation by population.[121] There was tension for some moments, as Foley resented what he called "the delicately put imputation" that he was backsliding, and insisted on a division.[122] He got only a handful of votes: Brown's position was too much in accord with the widespread western feeling that the Lower Canadians had ruled because they were a close-knit, unyielding group—and needed some of their own medicine. Following the vote, however, there were renewed expressions of good feeling on either side, and

Foley professed to be glad of the little storm that had cleared the air.[123] Harmony was soon restored. Yet there loomed the possibility that the moderate wing of the reunited Reformers might some time come to feel as Foley did, and weaken the party front through willingness to soften principle in order to conciliate.

On the other side, the issue of elective institutions, which still lay between the Clear Grits and George Brown, threatened to come up when an Oshawa journalist, Abraham Farewell, tried to move the establishment of vote by ballot.[124] This might sound innocuous enough, but it was then a Grit radical plank, and it could have opened the way for all the rest of their platform of constitutional reforms. Again George Brown was quickly on his feet, to urge that there was wide disagreement on that device among Reformers—he himself opposed it—and that, as it was not now a practical or pressing issue, it should not be allowed to divide the party.[125] He had his way, after a brief discussion. But once again it showed the possibilities of dissension, this time on the hard left of the new Reform front.

Nevertheless, that front was established with overwhelming approval for each principle adopted. Furthermore, a party organization termed the Reform Alliance was set up, to give it definite structure from headquarters down to the farthest backwoods township.[126] There would be a Central Committee in Toronto, County Committees in each parliamentary constituency, and Township Committees below them. Secretaries of the subordinate committees would be *ex officio* members of the committee above them, thus providing links between the various levels. And at the top would stand an executive subcommittee comprised of fifteen members of the Central Committee: final control would lie here. The Convention wound up its affairs by voting the Toronto delegates present members of this Central Committee.[127] Thus they left the direction of the new Reform Alliance to a group in Toronto made up chiefly of George Brown and his associates: business and professional men like Howland and McMurrich, Gordon Brown or McDougall, or the successful lawyer and Toronto alderman, Oliver Mowat, Q.C.

The fact was that this Brownite Liberal party—for so it might be called—had effectively combined urban Toronto leadership with western agrarian support. It was another sign of Toronto's growing ability to dominate the western section of the union, to organize and direct its political activities as well as its economic life. True, not all the elements of Upper Canadian Liberalism had participated in the Toronto Convention. Few delegates had come from the Ottawa valley, none from the eastern St. Lawrence counties where Sandfield Macdonald ruled his own little group of Liberals.[128] Sandfield had indeed been conspicuously absent: he did not intend to play second fiddle in a symphony scored and directed by George Brown. Moreover, the eastern-most districts of Upper Canada were more closely tied to Montreal than Toronto, and did not share the sectional sentiments of the greater part of the West with the same degree of intensity. None the less, by far the larger and more populous portion of Canada West had been represented at Toronto, with many delegates drawn from areas east of the city as far as Prescott, as well as from the entire western Peninsula. Even if a fringe of Upper Canada Liberals held themselves aloof from the new Reform Alliance, it was still broad based and widely supported across the West in general.

Western Liberalism had been recast in a formidable sectional movement. Focused on the expanding metropolis of the West, the Brownite Liberal party expressed aims common to Toronto business men and Upper Canada farmers alike; to resist the domination of the East, political and economic, and to extend the western realm into an immense new area. Toronto merchants, then the city's dominant business group, could also join with farmers in rejecting tariff schemes that might benefit Lower Canadian interests but hamper the free movement of western goods to and from the outside world. Thus the Reform Alliance endorsed the principle of free trade.[129] Again Toronto business and the agricultural West could come together to oppose the Grand Trunk Railway; as a mighty instrument of eastern domination sustained by the alliance of Catholic French Canadians with Montreal finance. For if western farmers chiefly blamed Grand Trunk influence for the public extravagance that steadily increased their taxes, Toronto interests, competing ever more widely with the older metropolitan centre, were no less aware of the Grand Trunk's power to tap off trade to Montreal. Westerners, then, might well approve of western railways, but combine against the eastern railway giant.

In truth, the reorganized western Liberal party found no great difficulty in linking Toronto urban leadership with rural numbers. But it was George Brown, above all, who had been the agent principally responsible for shaping the powerful sectional combination. Closely identified with Toronto, but with followers all across the West—a city man in background, yet fully at home in the rural scene—he had by his own and the *Globe*'s persuasive efforts remade the Upper Canada Reform party. He would not be formally named its leader until the next year. But he was already what his own abilities and the *Globe*'s strong voice had made him: the unrivalled chieftain of an embattled West.

Leader — and Premier

I

There was no doubt of the enthusiasm and good fellowship that was sweeping western Liberalism. "The Reform Alliance is a decided success—I never saw a greater party unanimity," announced William McDougall happily. "Let us begin a new movement," he urged Charles Clarke, "and forget all past dissensions."[1] Clarke reciprocated with a letter to Brown praising McDougall's qualities;[2] Brown cordially referred it to McDougall at the *Globe* office;[3] while an attentive Alexander Mackenzie hopefully advised his namesake, William Lyon Mackenzie, that, "now it seems to be quite possible to make our principles and party the dominant power in the state, if you and other Reformers fall in heartily with us."[4] Brown went up to Lambton immediately after the convention in Toronto, to spread the word in his own constituency. There were a host of Reform meetings in other constituencies, besides, as the local committees were organized down to the township level. The new mechanism began to function, to consolidate party reunion and ensure support for the programme—all with a purposeful eye to the next general election.

The session of parliament, however, which opened towards the end of February, 1857, did not in itself supply an important test for the young Reform Alliance. The balance of forces in the existing House was already established, and not likely to alter to any appreciable extent. The real opportunity would come with fresh elections, when a united Liberal party might sweep the West and produce a very different kind of parliament. Nevertheless, the session did consider several of the issues which would no doubt be significant when elections finally arrived.

For one thing, the North West came up at the very beginning. The imperial authorities had decided that the whole question of the Hudson's Bay Company's position in the western territories would be examined by a Select Committee of the House of Commons, and the Canadian government had announced that

Chief Justice Draper would go to England to represent Canada's interest at the grand inquiry. But the Chief Justice's instructions were somewhat cloudy. The former Conservative premier was to stand four-square on Canada's rights (unspecified) and fearlessly to seek nothing less than information.[5] The fact was that the provincial cabinet had been pushed on to make some gesture by the imperial move, on the one hand, and the Canadian agitation on the other; but as yet it really had no policy on North West expansion. After all, it was finding the existing Canadian union quite enough to manage.

Brown fervently attacked the government's vagueness and hesitation in his own opening speech on the Address. They were, he argued, throwing away the ideal opportunity to press for the acquisition of the North West.[6] But his glowing discourse on the value of the territories was to little avail; nor did a committee of the Assembly on which he sat thereafter achieve much more than the gathering of information on the western country.[7] Meanwhile, however, Gordon Brown had taken more direct action. Along with Howland, McMurrich and William Mc-Master (another wealthy Toronto business Liberal) he had put up funds to send an expedition westward under the persuasive Captain Kennedy, on a venture that combined commerce and exploration.[8] Accordingly, Kennedy's party set out to trace the most practicable communications route between the head of the lakes and the Red River, while both the Browns and the *Globe* waited eagerly for his findings.

Then in March, the shop-worn seat-of-government question came up in parliament again. The cabinet had now been seized with the splendid idea of transferring the whole problem to Queen Victoria: humbly, loyally—and with much relief. Let Her Majesty select the capital: her decision would surely be impartial. Moreover, any criticism might well be deemed disloyal, and an unpleasant load would be cleared off ministerial shoulders. But George Brown, for one, strenuously objected that this was nothing less than the abdication of responsible government.[9] The decision would simply be made by Downing Street officialdom, since the Queen acted only on advice. He was not far from wrong: Governor-General Head was soon busy sending forward arguments to the Colonial Secretary, Labouchere, in favour of his own choice, the centrally-located town of Ottawa.[10] Still, a formal reference to the Queen would at least put off the vexing question; a bare House majority was found to pass the resolution requesting royal intervention.

April brought new excitement with another bill to aid the Grand Trunk—"the annual thunderbolt", announced the

Globe.[11] Sixteen million dollars of public funds were wanted this time, to save the blighted "private" enterprise once more. By now, in any event, the golden gleam of railways was becoming rather tarnished in the public eye, as the speculative building boom produced its mounting bill of failures, fraud, and jobbery between railway contractors and politicians. "Corruption committees" were seeking action on these matters across the province, and George Brown was receiving earnest confidential legal advice from his friend, Oliver Mowat, on measures to check the grave public evil.[12]

Brown, accordingly, managed to obtain a committee to investigate the whole subject of Grand Trunk's finances. His searching efforts turned up an incredible tangle of waste, confusion and venality.[13] He produced explosions as well. Two leading eastern business Liberals, Galt and Holton, had been important Grand Trunk contractors; they were rigorously examined before his committee. Tempers were rubbed, and grew heated, as Brown drove on inexorably with the railway question. Accusations began to fly in both directions, until a furious Holton charged his chief inquisitor with trying to read him out of the Liberal party.[14] Galt, too, was left bitterly resentful; but Brown's breach with Holton seemed the more significant. He had known him for years. He had lost a valuable personal contact with Lower Canadian Liberalism.

Then Brown's relations with Dorion grew strained as well, when the western champion opposed a plan to build the Grand Trunk eastward from Levis to Rivière du Loup, denouncing it as one more piece of typical blundering extravagance, although the *Rouge* leader supported this further extension of the line across his own section of the union.[15] The whole wrangle over the railway (which left ministerialists beaming) made all too clear the damaging consequences of Brown's own exacting, uncompromising temperament. Yet it also showed the difficulty of holding two sectional Liberal parties in a common working relationship. It was a difficulty which George Brown would still somehow have to meet. But so far, that sectionally-minded leader was hardly prepared to consider the problem.

He was busy enough, at any rate, after parliament closed in June. Gordon had journeyed off to England on behalf of the Northwestern Steamboat Company, and until the autumn the direct management of the *Globe* fell on the elder brother again.[16] In August he could announce in its columns the results of the grand imperial inquest on the West, the findings of the Select Committee of the House of Commons. It had not seen fit to question the validity of the Hudson's Bay title to the North

West, though it had recommended that fertile districts such as
the Red River and Saskatchewan valleys might be acquired by
Canada once that province could open communications and
maintain government therein.[17] To Brown this was thoroughly
unsatisfactory, and largely the result of the Canadian government's not making a firm case in London. "The country which
is ours now by legal right, we may have possession of by giving
security to maintain roads and establish civilized institutions—
and meantime it is to remain in the hands of monopolists who
have never opened a road or done one act for the material or
moral elevation of the people of the Territory!"[18] The agitation for the annexation of the North West would have to continue: in the first place, to commit the Canadian government
itself.

But soon other more immediate concerns began to force themselves upon him. As autumn approached, it grew evident that
the great Canadian boom was running increasingly into danger.
Two of its essential attributes, railway-building and wheat production, were facing serious trouble. By now the constant railway expansion had been stretched to the snapping-point. The
failure of the smaller lines threatened bankruptcy for local
municipalities that had heavily invested in them. Too late the
Globe sounded warnings against the reckless misuse of municipal credit. At the same time, moreover, it had to report the
destructive inroads of the weevil, midge and fly into what had
promised to be a bumper grain crop.[19] The Minister of Agriculture, poor Vankoughnet ("Vanweevil" to the *Globe*) could
only fuss helplessly. And as western farmers and merchants,
both far over-extended in anticipation of the harvest, were
looking urgently for new money to borrow, the financial panic
of 1857 broke on the London and New York money markets.
Canada reeled under financial collapses and bankruptcy. By
mid-October a deepening depression engulfed the province that
had stood so lately at the full peak of prosperity.

Brown did not go untouched himself, and his Bothwell
enterprise was hit particularly hard. Land sales there dwindled,
instalment payments also: it was a struggle to keep his ventures
afloat at all. Yet the gravest blow that struck him now was not
financial but closely personal—the tragic death of a beloved
sister, Catherine, in a railroad disaster on the Albany line near
Syracuse. Ironically enough, Catherine had just recovered from
serious illness, and was taking her father, old Peter Brown, on
a long-promised visit to see his eldest daughter, Jane, and her
husband in New York. They were en route near Syracuse, on
the stormy night of October 15, when a rain-sodden railway

embankment had suddenly collapsed, plunging the train in wild wreck twenty feet downward into a flooding creek. Peter Brown had been pulled out only bruised and shaken. Catherine had been drowned.[20] She had been the last of the sisters still unmarried and at home—as keen-minded and energetic as George, yet always with a warm and winning gentleness. He had felt especially close to her, for they had been companions since childhood, with less than two years' difference in their age. Her death was a numbing loss.

So much so, that for weeks on end he could do or think of little, although politics now were moving into a critical new stage. It was growing evident that the government was preparing for an election in the near future. Parliament's term would expire in the following summer, in any case, and since there was not much likelihood that the economic gloom would lift by then, the ministry's best course seemed to be to get the elections over with as soon as possible. Moreover, a sudden dissolution might catch their opponents unprepared. The Coalition government was reshaped once more. Taché retired; Macdonald became first minister, with Cartier as his chief eastern colleague. Then on November 25, the Macdonald-Cartier cabinet made known that elections would be held almost at once. And Brown, willy-nilly, found himself thrust into the midst of campaign preparations. The time of testing had arrived for the Reform Alliance.

2

"I have no heart for politics or anything else," he told the faithful Alexander Mackenzie dejectedly, "but like a dog in the traces of his cart must drag on."[21] He had even thought of retiring at the end of the current parliament. But now he knew that he could not, not when his cause would surely suffer. Reform recovery faced too sharp a challenge in the sudden election. From the *Globe* office he sent a call to action throughout the network of the Alliance. "Parliament will be dissolved forthwith and the elections pushed on with hot haste. Not a moment is to be lost in getting out Reform candidates in all the constituencies. One hour of exertion *now* is worth a week's toil a fortnight hence."[22] The *Globe* began to announce the approved candidates, as mouth-piece for the Central Committee. Its proprietor, in all but name the western party leader—though no one still officially held that position—prepared to give his services in any doubtful riding where his voice could aid the Liberal nominee. And he replied formally to a requisition calling on him to stand again for Lambton, apologizing for his late neglect of political concerns, the result of "severe domestic affliction".[23] He would run for that constituency, he asserted, if its county committee strongly desired him as a candidate.

Yet Brown was really none too eager to make Lambton his seat in another parliament. It was a large constituency, well populated by this time, and it produced more private business for its member to conduct than many other western ridings. There were frequent private bills to undertake; county appointments and municipal concerns to look after, of course; and always transactions for important constituents that had to be carried forward at the seat of government. From the start Brown had found these Lambton affairs a heavy charge on his time. Now that he would obviously have to devote himself far more to party matters as a whole, he thought of seeking a less demanding constituency to represent. He had already intimated as much on his visit to Lambton in the preceding January.[24] Now, while stressing his readiness still to offer for the county if urgently requested, he openly advised the Lambton committee—and more privately and fully its secretary, Alexander Mackenzie—to find a local candidate in his stead.[25]

Here the name of his old opponent Malcolm Cameron came up once more. It was plain that Cameron was still a formidable figure in the county, at any rate with George Brown out of the way. Perhaps he could be won to the cause of Reform reunion. In all the haste of these elections, as Brown frankly admitted to Mackenzie, there was a problem of finding a sufficient number of able candidates to run in all the Upper Canadian constituencies.[26] He held no brief against his former rival in Lambton: "If Cameron were only repentant and thoroughly covenanted to go for the points [of the Alliance] and against the ministry —it would be no loss to let him in."[27] Consequently, prompted by the sitting member's willingness to step down in Cameron's favour, a delegation approached the veteran Sarnia politician. They found him eager to return to public life and apparently ready to endorse the platform of the Reform Alliance.[28] Brown turned his attention elsewhere.

He had received several offers of other nominations. Among them, that from North Oxford seemed the best to take. This would be a smaller, less exacting constituency, and above all a secure one, which would leave him time for the Reform campaign in general. Besides, Oxford had really been the seat of

his very first election success, when he had worked to carry it
in 1847 for the absent Francis Hincks. The Scots of Zorra in
that county were as heartily willing to support George Brown
as they had been ten years before. He went up to the riding
early in December to make his acceptance and launch his own
campaign. Meanwhile, however, developments were taking
place in Toronto which could hardly be ignored.

There, quite unexpectedly, a requisition had been put in circulation urging George Brown to stand for one of the city's
two seats. The signatures appended were mounting daily: 973
on December 4, 1301 on the 5th, 1716 by the 10th—including
several hundred Orangemen.[29] It was a signal phenomenon in
Toronto, where city politics had long been dominated by entrenched Tory-Conservative forces, effectively sustained by the
shock troops of the Orange Order. But the powerful sectional
currents were undermining the allegiance of many Toronto
Conservatives and Orangemen, as they looked askance at party
leaders who had so fully committed themselves to French
Canada, as they remembered the Corrigan case and the Taché
Act with sharp resentment, and as they heeded Brown's call to
unite the West behind the justified response, the demand for
representation by population.

Then, too, the city's Liberals were stronger than ever, and
notably well represented in its influential business community.
Furthermore, the emphatic appeal of Brown and his journal to
the metropolitan ambitions of Toronto reached beyond party
differences among its citizens. All in all, he stood a good chance
now of carrying a Toronto election. And since he had rebuilt
his party as a western block directed from the city, he would
plainly crown that achievement if he could sit in parliament
for the capital itself. Aroused by the exciting prospect, all signs
of lethargy left him. His old enthusiasm and energy came
sweeping back, as he resolved to try for Toronto as well as for
North Oxford. Gordon and McDougall could carry on the latter campaign for him.[30] He would concentrate his whole effort
on the city.

His strongest rival in the coming contest was John Beverley
Robinson, Toronto's mayor, son of the ablest member of the
old Family Compact, the elder (Sir) John Beverley. Robinson
Jr. had ability of his own, as well as bearing a name powerful
in the Tory Toronto tradition. Brown, however, would not
necessarily have to defeat him to be elected: at this time the
rule still held that the two top candidates at the city's polls
would each gain one of Toronto's pair of seats. But he would
need to overcome two other candidates in a several-sided con-

test, W. H. Boulton and John G. Bowes. The latter, the ex-mayor of Toronto discredited in the old Ten Thousand Pound Job, might not prove too hard to beat, but the former, also an ex-mayor, and Tory member for Toronto from 1844 to 1854, would be a much stiffer proposition. Brown had to anticipate a difficult and probably tumultuous election of the noisiest city type.

It was tumultuous: from the very first open meeting before the City Hall, when the rival candidates strove vainly to make themselves heard above groans and catcalls from varied sections of the audience, right up to the election itself, when pitched battles raged around the polls and clods of mud and half-bricks considerably thickened the air. The Brownites, however, stood undaunted throughout, howling out their man's campaign song "The People's Champion", sung to the tune of *The Arethusa*—as follows:

> *When Popish rage killed Corrigan,*
> *They thought they could inquiry ban,*
> *Alas! They did not know their man!*
> *Hurrah for our brave defender!*
> *With single front, like hero old,*
> *Their hosts he braved—their crimes he told.*
> *Full soon they paled, like cravens quailed;*
> *They knew that though he seemed alone,*
> *The whole of the land and he were one!*
> *Hurrah for our brave defender!*[31]

To be sure, there was some tendency among those Orangemen who had turned to Brown to chant as well, "Let Derry Walls your motto be, With Brown you're safe, with Brown you're free!"[32] In short, it was as the Protestant champion that they largely gave him their support. Tough old Captain Bob Moody, a veteran Lake Ontario "salt", even seconded Brown's official nomination with the rousing cry "Come up to the polls like men and Protestants!"[33] But Brown himself explicitly declared that he did not want his stand put in such a light, reiterating, as many times before, that he sought not to fight a religious battle of Protestant against Catholic but to take religious influences out of politics—"that the law shall know no man's religion".[34] Whatever his views on that subject, however, his advocacy of rep by pop, the common schools, and North West annexation were widely and eagerly applauded. He set them forth in mass meetings in St. Lawrence Hall and Temperance Hall, at smaller gatherings in each city ward, in taverns or hotels, and at rowdy assemblages in the market square. All this in bleak rainy weather, while he laboured under a bad cold, and when John Beverley Robinson and friends often dropped by to add as much confusion as they could.

At length the voting began on Monday morning, December 21, while the *Globe* scattered through its columns, "Vote Without Being Sent For! Vote When You Finish Reading This Line! GO TO THE POLLS AT ONCE." The appeal was strident; yet it was not just a matter of urging apathetic voters away from warm firesides, but of exhorting them to the battle-ground of the polls, where, quite conceivably, they could have their heads broken or at the very least their coats ripped up and their hats pushed in. Bands of dockside toughs, sometimes five hundred strong, were roaming the streets, seizing and forcibly holding critical polling stations for Boulton or Robinson voters.[35] A handful of police could do little; the raiders had to be driven off by quickly mobilized Brownite forces. But Canadians of the day clearly merited the parliamentary franchise, for somehow they still voted. And when the conflict and the polls finally closed in a driving snow-storm, it was apparent that George Brown was in. Not only that—he had topped the polls, with Robinson his second.[36] An excited, cheering crowd tramped through the slush on King Street to the brightly lit *Globe* office, field headquarters in the struggle.[37] There the People's Champion gratefully met them at the steps, while the telegraph chattered the news across Canada that the western Liberal leader had conquered in his own home city.

Elsewhere throughout the West the elections were going wonderfully well. North Oxford, too, returned Brown with a thumping majority, while his old friend, Archibald McKellar, won in Kent. His Toronto associates, Howland and Mowat, carried ridings near the city; and this Toronto leadership element in the Reform parliamentary contingent was further to be strengthened when William McDougall was subsequently elected for North Oxford, which Brown relinquished in his favour. Only in Lambton had his close friends received a setback. There, rising doubts of Malcolm Cameron's real willingness to work with the reorganized Reform party had finally brought out Alexander Mackenzie's brother, Hope, to run against him. But Cameron, the old hand, the "Coon", had beaten his inexperienced opponent.

Nevertheless, this failure could not cloud the dazzling victory that was evident by early January of 1858. No less than three of the five western cabinet ministers had gone down before Reformers—Cayley, Spence and Morrison. The Conservatives

had suffered seriously, and the Hincksite ministerial Liberals
had been reduced to a pathetic handful. In consequence, Premier
John A. Macdonald's coalition forces were now in a decided
minority in the Upper Canada half of parliament. The election
had been virtually a personal defeat for him, just as it had been
a personal triumph for George Brown. For while the onset of
bad times had no doubt worked against the government, the
Reform Alliance had worked still more effectively. It had func-
tioned successfully in meeting an election called on short notice.
The programme that it had adopted had both united Liberal
efforts and gained widespread popular support in an Upper
Canada roused to the shortcomings of the existing state of union,
and the failure of the government in any way to deal with them.
And the Reform Alliance had been largely Brown's achievement. Its policies were essentially his own. Its success was his
success, all across the West.

It was true, unfortunately, that in the East the opposition
had done far less well. There *Rouge* Liberalism had lost ground
before the Catholic Conservatism of the *Bleus*; and before a
counter-surge of eastern sectional opinion that, as expressed in
Quebec's prominent *Le Canadien*, had urged all true French
Canadians to unite against "la radicalisme Brownite"—against
the terrorism and wild doctrines of George Brown and the
monstrous fanaticism of the Clear Grits.[38] Yet Dorion's hardy
little band of survivors had at least been joined by a brilliant
new recruit, Thomas D'Arcy McGee, a strong Liberal but no
anti-clerical; indeed, a staunch Irish Roman Catholic. He had
been a Young Ireland rebel-sympathizer in his own land, then
made his way to publish Irish Catholic journals in the United
States. But turning from republican extremes, he had moved up
to Canada and become a loyally British editor in Montreal.

Furthermore, although the government's preponderant
strength in Lower Canada still gave it a majority in the union
as a whole, its support in the East was uncertain at the edges,
and there were particular dubious quantities like Cauchon, who
had been in and out of the ministry, and Sicotte, who was still
in, but might shift once again. Still further, a number of Lower
Canadian elections were being protested on grounds of fraud.
Quite a group of eastern ministerialists thus might be unseated
—for, as it turned out, there had been frauds aplenty. In the
three Quebec constituencies, for instance, it was discovered that,
along with five thousand other improbable voters, Julius Caesar,
George Washington and Judas Iscariot had each exercised their
franchise.[39]

Hence it did seem possible that effective collaboration be-

tween western and eastern Liberals might do enough to alter
the balance and bring the government down. In any case, there
was every need to establish closer connections between the two
Reform bodies, if the victory under George Brown in Upper
Canada were to be exploited to the full. But Brown was a sectional leader. Could he be more, without weakening his own
Upper Canadian purposes, and without alienating forces that
had backed him, essentially, in a plain demand for justice for
the West? Here was a ticklish problem in leadership, not easily
to be solved by one of his political character and personal inclinations. Previously he might almost have ignored the question, when the immediate and pressing need was the reorganization of Reform within his own half of Canada. But the very
success of his efforts there, his very triumph in the election of
1857-8, had now brought him up against a problem which must
ultimately decide whether he was simply a powerful sectional
politician, or had some claim to wider statesmanship as well.

3

He had turned thirty-nine now. His face seemed more lantern-
jawed, his long, straight nose more prominent; his hair-line
was hovering in that uncertain region between a high forehead
and undisputed baldness. Yet the impression he still gave was
one of enthusiasm and activity more youthful than his years.
It was heightened, if anything, by the contrast between his
portentous black-clad frame and animated features—the broad,
mobile mouth and quick-flashing eyes—set off as they were by
the close-trimmed red side-whiskers he had cultivated. Certainly, whenever he spoke in public he continued to radiate im-
ulsive energy and invincible self-confidence.[40] Nevertheless,
even this energy had found its limits, and his assurance was by
no means as complete as the world at large might judge.

The fact was that the apparently robust, exuberant Brown
of public life could so over-exert himself that private moods of
disheartening fatigue resulted, moments when he felt drained
of strength and without power of decision. His impulsiveness
could carry him too far. He counted too heavily on resources
that had once indeed seemed limitless. Midway through his
first parliament in fact, when strenuous efforts had made him a
leading member of the House in but one session he had experienced the sudden onset of mental and physical exhaustion.

It had soon passed, but at the time he had felt himself "sick in body and sick in mind". "I don't know how it is," he had told a friend in Sarnia gloomily, "but I cannot stand hard work as once I could. . . . I sometimes wonder if I am getting old before my time."[41]

There was really no great reason for that concern: his strength continued to be remarkable enough. Yet he would keep up activities both in public and private life sufficient for about two other men. He managed at once to direct the western Reform party, sustain the largest newspaper in British North America, actively participate in the anti-slavery movement and various philanthropic endeavours, and as well look after sizeable business interests that ranged from farming, lumbering and manufacturing enterprises at Bothwell to the sale of valuable lands he had also acquired in North Wentworth.[42] The very range of these activities may have made him less effective as a politician. That much, indeed, seemed evident when it came down to constituency affairs, the weight of which had led him to give up the Lambton seat, because its local business used up too much of his scarcest commodity: time. To him, looking after county matters, handling private concerns for constituents—even answering their letters—were laborious tasks which he tried dutifully, but not always effectively, to complete.[43]

From the start he complained of this burden to Alexander Mackenzie. A member's life, he lamented, was the "hardest kind of work night and day",[44] and, again, "I cannot get through all my business and might as well confess it."[45] Yet here, quite possibly, he revealed a political short-coming that was not entirely the result of having too many commitments. His chief rival, Macdonald, was always happy to serve a constituent or an adherent generally, real or potential; and his attitude came not only from shrewd consideration of sound politics but also from an affable willingness to please. Brown, on the other hand, might try to be of service, yet often found small pleasure in the effort, especially when "obliging" private interests might be connected with the log-rolling and jobbery of contemporary political life. Even with his close friends he was usually far behind in correspondence, and often apologizing abjectly for neglecting them. He had a "special pocket", he said, in which he carried the most pressing letters for immediate response, but he was forever emptying them into a vast box of unanswered correspondence on his desk—then reclassifying them into his pocket again, with utmost resolution, but still without reply.[46]

Sometimes he wondered whether he should really be in parliament at all. He was never wholly at ease there. A powerful speech, a strenuous party battle, might bring him a surge of exaltation. But in quieter moments, and above all in his periods of depression and self-doubt, he might think seriously of limiting his political activities to the *Globe* again. Moreover, he was quite conscious that being a journalist had its drawbacks for a parliamentary career.[47] Of course it had its advantages too: the power of the *Globe* was the very foundation of his political strength. Yet he realized that, as the *Globe*'s proprietor, every utterance of his paper was attributed to him personally, and that his freedom of manoeuvre was circumscribed by the authoritative public pronouncements of its columns.[48] The uncompromising thunder of *Globe* editorials, a strong point in his journalism, was a weak point in his politics whenever the need arose to win new friends or negotiate agreements with allies.

This did not mean that Brown would have wished for liberty to trade on principles, in the decent obscurity of politicians who did not stand in the floodlight of the *Globe*. The point was, rather, that he thought essentially as his paper wrote—with blunt forthrightness. It was politics which he found restraining, not journalism. That, however, still left the problem of whether he could combine the two professions with complete success. In point of fact, he did not. He remained the journalist in politics, the forceful wielder of words and mass opinions, not the skilled master of men and tactics. And it followed that he always regarded politics as a job to be done and finished, to gain some definite end; not as a craft to be practised, or even a life itself.

Yet now, early in 1858, Brown had to consider that the job might never be finished, that Upper Canadian Reformers might not, despite their election victory, achieve their purposes without effective co-operation from Reformers of Lower Canada. He had always recognized that even when Reform had won the West, at least a minimum of eastern support would still have to be secured, in order to carry the Brownite programme through parliament.[49] Realizing the need was one thing; reaching a satisfactory agreement with eastern Liberals was another: an enterprise demanding skill and patience in negotiations, every readiness to conciliate, and a good deal of freedom to make compromises. The very qualities most in demand were George Brown's chief weaknesses. Furthermore, while the *Rouges* of Lower Canada might stand opposed to Coalition misrule and excessive clerical influence in politics, they were, after all, French-speaking Roman Catholics in the great majority. Brownite diatribes against French Catholic power did not invite their hearty sympathy, and Brownite appeals to purely western aspirations left them cool. Still further, the working arrangements Brown had built up with the *Rouges* in parliament since 1854 had largely broken down during 1857, what with his own concentration on the reorganization of Reform in the West, and his open clash with eastern sectional interests over matters pertaining to the Grand Trunk.

Nevertheless, the general elections had only made more plain the need for eastern and western Reformers to find some common basis of action, if the Coalition government were ever to be overthrown: something beyond the superficial compromise of the Coalition forces to maintain a shaky *status quo* in the deeply troubled union. Liberals of the East were coming to acknowledge the inevitability of change in the structure of that union, as Canada West's lead in population lengthened steadily, and as westerners bitterly complained that five Upper Canadian voters only counted for as much as four Lower Canadians. But few, if any, Lower Canadian members of parliament could agree to support representation by population or other wholly Upper Canadian demands without the assurance that the rights and vital interests of their own section would be safeguarded.

Here the *Rouges* had pointed to a possible solution, when Dorion in the session of 1856 had suggested a federation of the two Canadas as an alternative to rep by pop.[50] A union on a federal basis might answer Upper Canada's protests against eastern domination by giving it a separate provincial government to deal with its own concerns. In like manner, a federal system could protect Lower Canada's special interests from domination by the more populous West—which could then be allowed the majority of members in a new federal legislature charged with such matters as were common to both sections. Though Dorion's proposal was presented as little more than a passing thought in 1856, it might yet take root and grow. And another prospect was being talked of in the press, a federation which would reach beyond the Canadas to bring in all the British colonies in America.[51] It arose not merely in response to Canadian difficulties: it bespoke that vague but enduring dream of British North Americans that some day another great union might span the continent north of the territories of the United States.

As for Brown, his thoughts were firmly fixed on representation by population. He did not ignore the possibility of other solutions, but he regarded them as complex and remote when an immediate remedy was needed, and when his own seemed straightforward and incontrovertibly just. He foresaw a movement for dissolution of the union if representation by population were not soon realized.[52] He hoped to bring Lower Canadian allies to accept his measure as logical and inescapable—in order to make an avowed union a true union. In any case, whatever the final answer might be, the first requisite was for the western Reform leader to open discussion with the *Rouges*. And whether or not he was well suited to that task, George Brown began to make the effort almost before the election clamour had all died away.

By mid-January he and his Toronto associates were earnestly considering how best to approach "our friends in Lower Canada".[53] The obvious direct approach to Dorion and his French-Canadian followers seemed inadvisable to begin with, since, as Brown asserted, "Dorion and his friends have so frequently repudiated our policy".[54] But John Simpson of Bowmanville was in town, and Brown consulted him: he was an elected Liberal member of the Legislative Council, and a prominent Upper Canadian banker with useful connections in Montreal and the East as well as with Toronto and the West. Simpson replied that Henry Starnes, an English-speaking eastern member and brother-in-law of Louis Sicotte, would shortly be visiting him in Bowmanville. He would sound him out on the matter of obtaining Lower Canadian support for rep by pop.[55] It was a roundabout way of opening communications eastward, but that in itself indicated how wide the sectional rift had become.

The approach became more direct once Starnes had talked with Simpson. Conveniently too, Brown came down in their direction to speak at an election victory dinner held in Belleville on January 21.[56] They met him at the Bowmanville station afterwards, on his way back home, and accompanied him for part of the journey along the Grand Trunk, engaged in frank and not unpromising discussion. As Brown subsequently recorded the conversation, Starnes had declared "that he and his friends (Sicotte, etc. I suppose) were prepared to go the full anti-state Church ticket—and that they admitted rep by pop must come and were prepared to concede it—but how to do that and be returned for Lower Canadian constituencies they could not see. I endeavoured to put the measure in the most favourable light, and declared that so long as we had the principle fully admitted and adopted we were ready to hear reasons as to any of the details."[57] The talk went no further than that. Certainly no definite alliance nor projected Reform government were mentioned. Yet here was the germ of possible East-West understanding.

The Conservative *Montreal Gazette* got wind of the discussion and generously expanded it to a proposal for a full-blown opposition alliance. Brown was quietly amused, and pleased to hear that "it has done me some good in Lower Canada, as people begin to hope that I am not so savage as I was supposed to be."[58] And by this time he had re-established contacts with Luther Holton as well, a more significant figure in the East than Starnes. The two men quickly buried their angry recriminations of the session of '57 and returned quite readily to their old basis of friendship. They had always had much in common: their rooted belief in the free-trade doctrines of orthodox economic liberalism, their interest in financial questions, and their strong evangelical Protestant background. Holton himself came up to Toronto; and after their talks together, Brown could tell him with cordial satisfaction, "Your arrival here ended all difficulties as to communicating with the Rouges."[59]

Holton shortly returned to Montreal, and there, towards the end of January, Brown sent him a long, illuminating letter, clearly setting out the stage he had now reached in thinking of the problem of the union.[60] "No honest man," he wrote decidedly, "can desire that we should remain as we are. Yet what other way out of our difficulties can be suggested but a genuine legislative union with rep by pop—a federal union—or dissolution? I am sure that a dissolution cry would be as ruinous to any party as (in my opinion) it would be wrong. A federal union, it appears to me, cannot be entertained for Canada alone but when agitated must include all British America. *We* will be past caring for politics when that venture is finally achieved.

"I can hardly conceive of a federal union for Canada alone," he continued. "What powers would be given to the state legislatures and what to the federal? Would you abolish county councils? And yet if you did not, what would the local parliaments have to control? Would Montreal like to be put under the generous rule of the Quebec politicians? Our friends here are prepared to consider dispassionately any scheme which may emanate from your party in Lower Canada. Their plan is for rep by pop and a fair trial of the union in its integrity. Failing that, they are prepared to go in for dissolution, I believe—but if you can suggest a federal or any other scheme that could be worked, it will have our most anxious examination."

He urged Holton, moreover, to "sketch a plan of federation such as our friends below could agree to and could carry". Did Holton send him such a plan? No record remains. Yet what does remain is the fact that Brown stood willing either to examine the possibility of federation as a solution or to "hear reason" from Lower Canada on the actual application of representation by population. It was a step towards enlarging his political horizons that, in the fullness of time, might lead him from the confines of sectional opinion towards a broader statesmanship.

At any rate, Brown had succeeded in renewing relations with the *Rouges*. His contact widened. For instance, Joseph Doutre, one of the most prominent exponents of Liberalism in French Canada, earnestly discussed with him "a platform upon which homogeneity can be given to the actual opposition, and I hope, the future government".[61] Doutre expressed approval of "almost everything" in Brown's views except his stand on the separate-school issue, which, he urged, would have to be modified in order to defeat the "Jesuit Party" in Lower Canada.[62] In response, the *Globe* came out in early February endorsing Doutre's platform as presented to a *Rouge* gathering in Beauharnois.[63] It called for rep by pop, Montreal as the seat of government, and national education *in the future*. Even on schools, apparently, Brown was preparing to seek a settlement that could win a measure of Lower Canadian acceptance. It was true that the schools issue had not been seriously agitated of late, either by Catholics or Protestants. Perhaps some accommodation could yet be reached upon this dangerous topic.

And so this journalist-partisan of the West—with all his limitations as a politician—was moving on from purely sectional campaigning to the wider problem of reaching terms with the East. He had not moved very far. He still had far to go. Yet the very effort indicated that he was not all heedless dogmatism and blind over-confidence as his enemies would charge. In any case, the opening session of the new legislature was almost on him. He would have to meet it in the hope that the still uncertain link of understanding between western and eastern Reformers could be shaped more strongly in parliament itself.

4

Meanwhile, John A. Macdonald had also been busy making new political arrangements. His were the more conclusive; still, they had to be, since he faced the necessity of replacing three defeated western cabinet ministers before parliament should meet. He also sought to repair his badly shaken position as western government leader by the tried expedient of detaching prominent Reformers from the opposition. For where would the Liberal-Conservative "coalition" be in Upper Canada if there were virtually no Liberals left in it? Accordingly, Macdonald won back Sydney Smith, awarding him the Postmaster-Generalship; Smith was an ex-Hincksite who had supported the Coalition until eighteen months before. He even approached Sandfield Macdonald with the offer of three cabinet places for himself and two followers.[64] But while Sandfield briefly entertained the alluring idea, he soon found out that only one of his little band of eastern Upper Canadian Reformers would follow him across the House.[65] In fact, his own brother, Donald Macdonald, the member for Glengarry, wrote to Brown to deny most indignantly that he would accompany Sandfield on such a journey; and Sandfield, rather grumpily, stayed put.[66] "He has assuredly put his foot in it," remarked Brown, with possibly a touch of relish.[67]

The efforts to rebuild the western section of the government continued for some anxious weeks in Toronto, while the premier pressed a policy of silence on Charles Lindsey, editor of the ministerial *Leader*, lest Brown's "area-sneaks hanging round the Rossin House" should find out all too much about his difficulties.[68] Finally, Macdonald had to rely on bringing John Ross, the Hincksite president of the Grand Trunk, back into the cabinet, and on securing another seat somewhere in the Assembly for Cayley, his defeated Conservative Inspector-General. Towards the end of February, Cayley had been provided for, while Ross, fortunately, held an appointed seat in the Legislative Council. The completed government could now face parliament, due to open on the 25th. But it did so all too conscious of its weakness in the West. Meanwhile Brown had called a caucus of the whole opposition on the 23rd, to make arrangements for the opening battles of the session.[69] He was, in short, now acting and being regarded as the leader of a reunited opposition, a revitalized and highly confident opposition, eager for the attack and anticipating victory ahead.

In the new House the ministers were on the defensive from the start, as they struggled over the Address, and had to fight a succession of disputed election cases. Brown's own speech on the Address centred, of course, on a demand for representation by population, as he contended that the elections had clearly proved that the people of Upper Canada recognized a crisis had been reached in Canadian affairs, and that the union had to be recast. He charged as well that the ministers had no policy, no measures to meet the equally great commercial crisis; he deplored their failure to act effectively on the Hudson's Bay territory; and he warned that Upper Canada's grievances must be settled lest the only alternative to the existing state of affairs be a dissolution of the union. There were, he said, two sets of laws, local institutions, habits and prejudices in Canada—and the whole trend of legislation and public policy was further to divide the two parts of the province. The greatest mistake of the union had been to confirm these sectional differences at the outset; but instead of seeking to harmonize them, successive governments had steadily made them wider. His own answer was the principle of common representation. Yet he appealed to the House whether in advocating representation by population he had not always pledged that he was ready to meet Lower Canadian members fairly, and accept any proposal from them for the removal of sectional ills. Some said dissolution, some rep by pop, some federation of the two Canadas, or of all the British American provinces—he was convinced Upper Canada would take one of these, rather than continue the existing system of public demoralization.[70]

When the vote finally came on the Address the government was maintained by its Lower Canadian support, although the Upper Canadian count went quite decidedly against it.[71] If Brown's opening bid for rep by pop had failed, Reform prospects for the session still looked bright. The government had equally failed to attract any significant new strength. The chief editorial writer of the Conservative Toronto *Colonist*, George Sheppard, reported frankly to a political foe, but personal friend, Charles Clarke, that he did not believe the ministry could last—even though "they are buying up all the loose fish".[72] And following a short recess, from late March to early April, the searching debate on remedies for the ills of the union went forward, since no one could deny the critical strength of sectional feelings, while various elements in the House each had their favourite solution to propound. Thus the grand canvassing of the constitution continued, as spring passed into summer; not without heated outbursts, as when the Provincial Secretary, Loranger, was alleged to have exclaimed of Lower Canada, "Nous avons l'avantage. Profitons-en!"[73]

The double-majority principle was examined long and earnestly. First raised in the 1840's, it was advocated by many French Canadians; and John Sandfield Macdonald notably endorsed it as a means of making the existing union work without doing injustice to either half of the province. The sad truth about the double majority, however, was that it required precisely what governments had not been able to achieve, namely, to keep a majority in each section. Furthermore, it was opposed by Brown and his followers as enshrining the very dualism they sought to escape, while Macdonald and his cohorts stood by the existing union and the single majority as the true embodiment of British parliamentary practice. Then William Lyon Mackenzie brought up his pet motion for the dissolution of the union, but got nowhere; while Malcolm Cameron went back to one of his early loves and on his own introduced a bill for representation by population. It was thrown out—though the ministerial majority that did so contained only nine Upper Canadian votes.[74] Still, these were all old straw. An interesting new note came with the resolutions for federation put forward by Alexander Galt, who had left his former opposition allies and now sat as an independent.

Galt was separated now from any hot partisan group, and was in any case a member of that Lower Canadian English minority which lay, so to speak, between the main sectional contenders. He was well placed to offer a solution that recognized both the wrongs to be rectified for the West and the rights to be protected for the East. Yet he went further than a federal union for the Canadas alone. He also called for the incorporation of the North West Territories, and union with the other British colonies, all on the federal principle, all in one general confederation of British North America.[75] Here was the essential scheme of Confederation, introduced for the first time into the Canadian parliament.

At that time, however, such a project still seemed largely visionary, and the House gave it far less attention than was paid to the double majority or to representation by population. When Galt's resolutions were introduced, Brown, in fact, sought to move an amendment to take the vote on rep by pop first. He did not want to interfere with the discussion of federation, he declared, but, "before I can vote on a proposition for a federal union I must know whether representation by population will or will not be granted."[76] He suggested an agreement on both sides of the House for a full-dress debate on representation by population, double majority, and federation, the three great competing solutions for the problems of the union. To this Galt assented, but John A. Macdonald announced that the government could not guarantee that the time would be available,[77] while Cartier urged Galt to continue now, since he knew that many Lower Canadians who would never accept representation by population would consider federation if Upper Canada should in future have a decidedly large excess of population.[78] As for Dorion, he saw merit in a federation of the Canadas, and even in representation by population with proper safeguards, but deemed a federal union of British North America madness—at least for a century's time.[79] Thus Galt's resolutions were commented on, and fairly quickly laid aside. Yet it might become significant that men of different parties with very different answers for the question of union saw future possibilities in some application of the federal principle.

It was past midsummer before the constitutional debates at length wore themselves out, without reaching any conclusion in a too-divided House. Another theme of almost equal interest had emerged meanwhile, however: that of the state of the public finances, which appeared to be in pretty parlous condition under Inspector-General Cayley and the Macdonald-Cartier administration. They were scarcely wholly to blame, not in that doldrum summer of 1858, year of the rust, the weevil, and stagnant markets. Revenue had dried up with trade: there was a serious deficit to be dealt with when Cayley introduced the budget in June. Yet Brown, the opposition's chief financial critic, could also accuse the minister of concealing still more deficit. Two-fifths of the previous year's revenue had been obtained by borrowing, moreover, and the monumental growth in the public debt could plainly not be attributed merely to bad times since the fall of 1857. The deficit was really the consequence of expensive (Brown would say wildly extravagant) policies of development, of railway building, and above all, the Grand Trunk. Two "railwaymen" regimes, first that of Hincks, then the Liberal-Conservative Coalition, had added $25 million to a provincial debt that had stood at less than $28 million before 1852. They had nearly doubled it in six years; the Coalition had added more than $11 million in the last three years alone.[80]

Granted that the over-confidence and speculation of boom times had been responsible for much of the increase; granted that railways did not come cheaply, and that the Grand Trunk, disastrous as it was, could hardly be abandoned: the fact remained that a small colonial community in the depths of depression and facing a double load of debt might not unreasonably inquire of the government whether all this burden had been strictly necessary—and what it intended to do about it. That, certainly, was George Brown's position, particularly when he had sought on so many previous occasions to expose the waste and corruption of bland "developmental" railway politics. Now as a member of the Committee on Public Accounts, he raked Cayley and his figures relentlessly. He charged the minister with carrying through ruinous sales of public debentures in England, with omitting payments from the public accounts and inserting those not made.[81] He revealed an extra deficit of some $3,400,000 on the 1857 accounts, shown by the reports of the Provincial Auditor himself.[82] And generally in accusing Cayley of ineptness, favouritism and deception, he left the stark impression that the ministry was bankrupting the country. In any case, the country's need of revenue was such that Cayley took the inevitable course: he raised the tariff. It probably was inevitable, because however much Brown and the *Globe* might point out waste and urge retrenchment, not enough saving could have been effected to meet the already crushing debt burden in a time of falling revenue. Yet to good Cobdenite free-trade Liberals like the Reform leader and his journal, it was absurd to raise customs duties higher when trade pre-eminently had to be encouraged; and worse than that, it could represent a return to the false doctrine of protectionism.

The tariff had already been raised in 1856 to a level of 15% on imported manufactures, thanks largely to an earlier need of money for the Grand Trunk. But the increase in the tariff of 1858 to 20% on many items was the first with an avowed purpose of giving protection to home manufactures as well as that of collecting more revenue.[83] To be sure, it could be described as "incidental protection", incidental to the primary need of obtaining a larger income. None the less the height of the new duties could mean that Canada was passing from a revenue to a protective tariff; and the protection provided was real enough for newly developing home industry, whether it was excused as incidental or not. Moreover, this development could definitely be related to a powerful agitation for protection directed by the "Association for the Promotion of Canadian Industry", which had been launched at a meeting in St. Lawrence Hall, Toronto, back in April.[84] The leading force behind it was an old friend, Isaac Buchanan, now an ardent advocate of railways, paper currency, and high tariffs, all combined.

The Association signalized the rise of a new interest in Canada, and markedly in Toronto: domestic industry—which in time would drastically affect the pattern of politics in Canada West. For the present, however, it was chiefly regarded by the *Globe* as exemplifying "the old demand, so often exposed and refused" for bounties and state aid to enterprise, a demand which the modern age of free-trade enlightenment could never again admit.[85] It was thus a positive indication of a return to the dark ages, when the government gave a sympathetic reception to a delegation from Buchanan and company, who even submitted a complete new model tariff for consideration.[86]

Nevertheless, the Cayley tariff that resulted seemed on the whole a jumble without principle, its only real aim to grab more money so that ministers could continue to ensure their places by the lavish expenditure of public funds.[87] To the *Globe*, its protectionist increases turned out to be mere "sops".[88] That was Brown's attitude in parliament as well: he chiefly attacked the tariff as manifesting waste, bad management and empty expediency.[89] Again the government passed it through by the weight of Lower Canadian support. But the powerful criticisms of a programme of higher taxes in depression times spread uneasy discontent even in ministerial ranks—a feeling soon to be revealed in government defeat.

Before that occurred, the harsh quarrels over fiscal matters brought on a sudden new explosion, which only redounded to Brown's credit. On the night of June 25, the House was still sitting in consideration of the estimates. Feelings were high, for the government accused the opposition of obstructing the voting of supplies, while the opposition charged that the government was trying to escape further investigations. Threats of violence had been voiced on either side.[90] Then, in an angry House, Powell, the member for Carleton, sprang up heatedly to bring an old and garbled charge against George Brown: that he and his father were public defaulters, who had embezzled municipal funds in Scotland and run off to America to evade the law.[91] It was a very old charge—raised, for example, back in the early *North American,* though McDougall had publicly retracted it years ago.[92] It had been brought up in newspapers and election campaigns since, but never introduced into parliament before.[93] Now as Powell violently pressed the accusation, the House cooled rapidly, and there were cries of protest from either side. Brown, however, begged him to go on to the end, so that once and for all he could reply.[94] Then he rose in a stilled Assembly— and it was a painful task to undertake for a man of his temperament. Yet, though he was plainly under much emotion, he managed to give a matter-of-fact and dignified response.

Quietly he made clear the actual circumstances of his father's financial loss in Scotland, noted that the money had been made good by guarantors, and that Peter Brown had struggled to repay them and also meet his business obligations. He explained that he himself had been a boy of seventeen at the time, and not involved, except that he too had striven to help his father meet the claims against his name. They had gone on doing so in Canada, and thus had had to live a carefully frugal life: for while it was possible in this new country to own large properties on paper, it was no easy thing to realize cash from them. But last year it had seemed that they would finally be able to settle all accounts. They had even planned a return to Scotland to settle them in person—when the bad times that had struck the province had made it all impossible. Nevertheless they would keep on till every obligation was cleared, and he had placed Peter Brown's debts as the first charge on his own estate. He made a simple, moving tribute to his father—"I think I could appeal even to his political opponents to say if there is a citizen of Toronto more thoroughly respected and esteemed." And he closed with deep emphasis and obvious affection: "No son feels prouder of his father than I do today."[95]

His statement was received on both sides of the House with respect and no little admiration; the episode had only added to Brown's personal stature. The next day the press commented most favourably. Even the Conservative *Colonist* reported "marked expressions of sympathy from members irrespective of party" and asserted that Brown had "put on record a complete vindication".[96] This, however, brought the wrath of the party leaders down upon the chief Conservative organ of the ministry, for what its editor, Sheppard, called "the crowning sin" of admitting Brown to be right in anything.[97] As he related it, John A. Macdonald, "full of passion, wrote an insolent letter" demanding a retraction.[98] Sheppard and his colleagues refused. Aroused in any case by the ministry's failure to achieve anything beyond keeping in office, the *Colonist* came out the next day with a startling editorial, "Whither are we Drifting?" Expressing sharp unrest, it read in part: "A season of extreme financial difficulty is yet before us, and how do the ministry propose to pilot the vessel of state through the rocks? By what policies are we to be governed, by what principles are we to be guided? Popular endurance is rapidly approaching exhaustion. Trade and industry are paralysed, and the whole machinery of government is running rapidly to wreck. Is it a decree of destiny that Mr. Macdonald shall be the everlasting Prime Minister of Canada? We must face issues. Worse can happen than a ministerial defeat."[99]

The tide was plainly running strong against the government when the leading Upper Canadian Conservative journal moved on to outright revolt: the ministers had hastily to found the Toronto *Atlas* to replace the *Colonist* as official organ.[100] And the tide revealed itself in parliament two weeks later, when on July 23 the government was actually beaten on a proposal to institute tonnage dues on the St. Lawrence River. It was a fairly minor matter; there was only a majority of two against the ministry.[101] Yet it expressed some of the distrust of their financial policies, particularly their adding to the costs of trade. The ministers sought to make light of the incident, Cayley noting that only £17,500 were involved. It was merely "an accidental majority", added Macdonald airily.[102] Brown took them up at once, emphasizing the steady decline in the ministerial following. "For their recklessness and folly that majority has gradu-

ally dwindled down to thirty—twenty-five—twenty—fifteen—
ten—eight—and now to a majority of two in the whole house
against them. And yet there they sit, scarcely conscious of this
defeat, exclaiming it is only a matter of £17,500!"[103]

Exaggeration or not, the ministry had no reason to regard
their situation easily. There had been an Upper Canadian
majority against them almost solidly throughout the session:
never had the Coalition ruled the West so steadily against its
will. Their support in the whole House undoubtedly had dwindled: a week before the tonnage dues came up, they had held
only a ten-vote margin in a want-of-confidence motion put by
Sandfield Macdonald and Skeffington Connor, an old associate
of Brown's.[104] Perhaps even more foreboding was the evident
improvement in Brown's relations with the eastern Liberals.
He had not only worked effectively with Dorion in the Assembly; he had made close contact with the able new Liberal
member for Montreal West, Thomas D'Arcy McGee.[105]

McGee, besides his quick wit, warm good humour, and
friendly "Paddy" grin, had displayed admirable and powerful
debating skill. On his maiden speech the *Globe* hailed him as
"undoubtedly the most finished orator in the House".[106] Moreover, he was ready to support representation by population; and
he saw the chief enemy of Roman Catholicism in the Orange
Order, which of course was largely allied with the government
forces. On the other hand, he spoke firmly and well for separate
schools. The *Globe* had to grant his remarks on this theme, "the
best address from that point of view ever presented to the
House".[107] And Brown, while just as firmly opposed to them,
was obviously not stressing the attack on separate schools, nor
emphasizing anti-Catholic arguments. He was, perhaps, still
trying to chart the ground on which he could meet frankly and
fully with Liberals from the East. As it was, a veritable alliance
was emerging between Brown and McGee, which many Catholics as well as voluntaryists deplored. As many others hailed it
as a most promising development: though for the ministry, it
could only have been one of the most unpromising developments of a thoroughly unpleasant session.

Brown really needed more time, had he known it; still more
time to explore the areas of contact with the East: time to thrash
out and determine policies that might ensure a definite degree of
Lower Canadian support. But as ever he was impatient, over-
eager; concentrating on the obvious gains being made against
the government during the session, not sufficiently concerned
with what the next steps should be. He had pushed them hard;
he might push them over: and that seemed to be enough. The

triumph of his demands would surely follow. But if time was running out for the retreating government, it was also running short for the leader of the opposition. The pattern rising through the session of 1858 was coming to its climax. It would reach it, late in July, on the seat-of-government question. Just ahead lay victory—then sharp frustration for a still inadequately prepared George Brown.

5

Back in January the Queen's choice in the seat-of-government sweepstake had been announced: Ottawa had won the prize. It might turn out a good choice in time, and a reasonable compromise between contending sections and rival centres; but for the moment it went far towards pleasing no one. Supporters of Toronto, Kingston, Montreal and Quebec could all agree that Ottawa, lately Bytown, was still a back-country lumber village, a shanty town chiefly noted for wild brawls among its lumbermen-inhabitants, and completely lacking in the history, dignity and importance befitting a national capital. Further than that, there was the question of how the Queen could have made the choice at all. She could only act on advice, which surely must have ultimately come from Canada. For knowledge of that distant country was limited in England to the degree that the august London *Times* could make Montreal its own selection as the capital, on the firm ground that Montreal was in Upper Canada.[108] Had not the Canadian cabinet, then, evaded its responsibility, and let the capital be chosen by a backdoor method that had given the Canadian people no voice? It was certain that the seat-of-government question would come up in no friendly fashion during the session of 1858. When it did, a shaky government would be in even greater trouble.

Dorion, in fact, introduced resolutions on the seat of government just before the ministry's defeat on the matter of the tonnage dues. They asserted that the choice of Ottawa was not acceptable, and that Montreal should be the permanent seat. The government treated this as a want-of-confidence motion, while George Brown proclaimed "the real issue tonight is Bytown or no Bytown".[109] Though the ministry was sustained, they notably lost nine French-Canadian supporters.[110] And then a few days later, on July 28, the matter was raised again, in the discussion of an address to the Queen on the subject of the capital. Joseph Piché, a *Rouge*, moved in amendment that Ottawa ought not to be the permanent seat—and all the anti-Ottawa feelings combined. Despite John A. Macdonald's indignant cry that this was an insult to Her Majesty and a disgrace to the House, a number of *Bleu* members trooped to join the opposition in the vote: Piché's amendment passed, 64 to 50.[111] Amidst jubilant opposition cheers, George Brown called upon those who had voted for the motion to mark their sense of its significance by voting the adjournment. Macdonald declared that he would treat this as a test of confidence. The eastern ministerial members who had thus expressed their protest now came back, and the adjournment was lost, 50 to 61.[112] The government had survived; yet it had had a very bad evening, the worst of a whole series, and there was no sign of any improvement ahead.

When the House finally rose in weariness at two in the morning, Macdonald, Cartier and their ministers gathered in an anxious meeting to discuss what should be done.[113] Certainly they were still in office; but they had only won the adjournment by eleven votes, three members who had voted non-confidence in the government before had been absent that evening, and there were nine cases of election fraud still hanging over their heads.[114] And this after a succession of near shaves that had grown much worse. The finances were in bad condition; it was now clear the harvest was a failure; the chief western Conservative organ had deserted them, raising public outcry against a policy of drift. The constitutional problem was pressing, and they could no longer bury it under a coalition with no solution of its own. Something fairly drastic would have to be done, if their position were somehow to be saved.

Perhaps the best way would be to resign the position outright, to give up office: the opposition forces would never be able to form an effective government, and would simply prove their incapacity to rule. Then the old ministry could triumphantly return, as all who had deserted it came tumbling back, chastened by the awful threat of George Brown on the government benches. Adopting this bold but astute strategy, the cabinet decided to resign over the seat-of-government question. It was also excellent tactics: it took the argument off constitutional problems, higher taxes and financial failure, and placed it safely on an ancient, abstract issue—loyalty. The Queen had been insulted, her judgment impugned. The ministry could go out still undefeated, but on a high note of moral censure. It would pass its own want-of-confidence motion in an unmanageable Assembly, that needed to be brought to heel.

Early the next morning the Macdonald-Cartier government resigned. When the House met at ten, John A. Macdonald rose to announce that fact, and to assert with vigour that the "act of discourtesy and rudeness" and positive illegality committed by the Assembly had left the cabinet with no other course but to withdraw.[115] That done, an agitated House adjourned to await the appointment of new ministers. Macdonald and company had little to do but to sit back and watch the predictable course of events. George Brown would obviously be sent for, as the recognized leader of the opposition. The play now was up to him.

He was sent for. Shortly after the adjournment, a note came from Governor-General Head offering the senior member for Toronto the leadership of a new administration. The brief and formal message said little more beyond requesting an acceptance in writing, if Brown should so decide.[116] Undoubtedly elated, though hardly surprised, he set off buoyantly down King Street for Government House, to wait as formally on His Excellency and request time to consult his friends.[117] Should he form a government, could he form a government? These were the questions to be decided within the next two days, days of close deliberation and negotiation with Upper Canadian followers and Lower Canadian allies. That afternoon he called a meeting of the western opposition members at his home on Church Street, and they gave him their enthusiastic and unanimous support.[118] That evening he opened discussions with Dorion, as the leader of the Lower Canadian opposition.[119] These, however, promised to take far longer to conclude, when so much still had to be done to reach an accord between the divergent interests, policies, and outlooks of the two sectional Reform groupings.

Perhaps, in view of the opposition's weakness in the East, he should not have gone on further. The Macdonald-Cartier government had not really lost a vote of confidence. A Brown-Dorion cabinet might therefore simply meet defeat in a hostile Assembly. Nevertheless, Brown's own inclinations could only have been to continue, to damn all possible torpedoes and drive full steam ahead. Single-minded as he was, he saw the goal nearly within reach, the success of his cause—and how could he refuse to grasp at it? Yet if he were single-minded, he was not simple-minded. He knew there were dangers if he acceded to Head's offer—and dangers no less real if he rejected it. He had tried for years to bring down the Liberal-Conservative Coalition. Could he now stand back when they had brought themselves down? If he did, he well might blast the party he

had so laboriously reconstructed in Upper Canada, shatter a
Reform union still not hardened in the mould. He had made
himself the champion of militant Upper Canada. What would
happen to the crusade for justice if he now tamely backed away
from the seat of power, because the perils were great? A refusal
on his part to try to form a government could wholly destroy
the West's confidence in him as a leader. Of course it would
have been far better if a chance at office had come up with Reform better situated in both sections to meet it. But the chance
was upon him now, and the only thing he could see to do was
take it. Should he fail, it might be easy for party enemies to
jeer at him. Should he not try, it seemed certain that party
friends would do so.

Besides, the conversations that night with an intense and
hopeful Dorion appeared to give good reason to believe that a
Reform cabinet might successfully be formed.[120] The negotiations went on all the next day, Friday, July 30, with Brown only
calling briefly on Head by appointment to say that he would
give his final answer Saturday morning.[121] Piece by piece, the
ministry was fitted together in the dog-day heat of late July.
Its Upper Canadian section, and easier half to build, would
consist of George Brown as Inspector-General, Sandfield Macdonald as Attorney-General West (yes, Sandfield would come
in), Oliver Mowat as Provincial Secretary, Michael Foley,
Postmaster-General, and James Morris as Speaker of the Legislative Council. It was a wide-based representation of western
Reform, though with no ultra-Grit radicals included. Mowat
was a new man; but had already made clear his ability in the
House, and was plainly strong in the Brownite tradition. Foley
was the ablest of the moderate, ex-Hincksite Liberals who had
turned against the Coalition; and with all his faults, Sandfield
was a leading Reformer of long standing. James Morris, too,
was a well-known Reformer from the eastern district; though
unlike Sandfield, he had been in close and confidential communication with Brown during the recent elections.[122] There
was also Skeffington Connor outside the cabinet in the post of
Solicitor-General West: a prominent Toronto barrister and lec-
turer at the University who in Baldwin's time had put up money
to help found the *Globe*, and had worked with Brown on the
Reform Association of 1844.

As for the eastern and more difficult part of the government,
that too had been successfully constructed. Dorion stood at its
head, of course, as Commissioner of Crown Lands. Then there
was Luther Holton for Public Works, J. E. Thibaudeau as
President of the Council, Francois Lemieux as Receiver-

General, L. T. Drummond as Attorney-General East, and finally, Charles Laberge as Solicitor-General East. This was also a broadly representative group of eastern Liberal opinion, ranging from French and English *Rouges* like Dorion and Holton to Drummond, a former member of the Hincks-Morin government. Considering the relative weakness of the eastern opposition, moreover, it was a strong and able body. Yet it might have done better in attracting support had it spread its net still wider: there was one serious omission: Joseph Cauchon, now one of the most potent critics of the Coalition.

Brown had wanted him decidedly. "His force would have been everything for us," he said later, "and his influence with the hierarchy and the pungency of his pen would have placed us in an entirely different position in the Quebec district."[123] The matter of the Quebec district was of some importance. Lower Canadian members tended to look either to a Montreal or a Quebec centre of influence; there was at least as much rivalry within Canada East between these two large cities as between Toronto and other communities in the West. To be strong in Lower Canada, therefore, a government had to be well based in both the Montreal and Quebec districts. Montreal was well looked after in the prominent person of Dorion, while the *Rouges* were fairly firmly rooted in its general area. But they needed someone comparable for Quebec, someone who might obtain significant support among more uncertain French-Canadian followers of the Coalition: who were by no means so invincibly devoted to it as the Macdonald-Cartier press sought to declare. They had won over Lemieux, former member of the MacNab-Taché and Taché-Macdonald ministries, who sat for Lévis, and in the Quebec area they also had Thibaudeau. Still, the leading eastern ministers, Dorion and Holton, were identified with Montreal, and their cabinet colleagues, Laberge and Drummond, also held seats in the Montreal region. Nor were the Quebec representatives the equal of Cauchon in ability and stature.

Dorion fully agreed with Brown as to the service that Cauchon could render the ministry, but also felt that the hostility of his friends to such an accession would be "quite insuperable".[124] The *Rouges* too well remembered Cauchon's past as a rampant Conservative; he might now have broken with the ministry and be in opposition, but the memory of his pungent sarcasm and the fiery invective he had heaped upon them still rankled. And so he had inevitably been set aside. Brown went to Cauchon and frankly explained the position. He reported, however, that "he was awfully cut up about not getting in".[125]

Thus to begin with, the Brown-Dorion government could not make the most of material available in Lower Canada, where it most needed strength.

Nevertheless, it was striking that a government had been achieved at all, considering the bitter background of sectional and sectarian conflicts—a government, moreover, which contained so many prominent, capable and powerful Liberal members. There was even a majority of Roman Catholics—this in a cabinet led by George Brown. Of course, in Lower Canada, as might be expected, all except Holton were Catholic. On the other hand, in Upper Canada, Sandfield Macdonald was hardly an ardent son of the Church, while Michael Foley, who also opposed separate schools, represented a continuance of the former Catholic-Irish association with Reform which had never wholly disappeared. Still, the fact that so many Roman Catholics could join with George Brown, and he with them, in one government, showed that he could not have been quite as intransigent, as impossibly anti-Catholic, as his enemies so often urged.

The fact was, that the differing interests—Catholic and Protestant, Upper Canadian and Lower Canadian—had been willing to seek a basis of agreement. And they had found one that permitted them to join in a ministry dedicated to settling the great problems of the union. There had not been time to work out policies in detail, but the meetings between Brown and Dorion had thrashed out essential terms of understanding. On that basis the government had successfully been constructed. At Brown's home on Church Street, and in Dorion's room in the Rossin House, the two leaders had fully and frankly deliberated their points of difference: the large, earnest Scotsman, arguing hard but amicably; the courtly, compact *Canadien*, weighing every word.[126] Brown had said that representation by population must be met. Dorion had admitted it; but insisted that French-Canadian institutions be protected by constitutional checks, and Brown had agreed. They discussed the mode of such protection: whether by a written constitution, or a Canadian Bill of Rights guaranteed by an imperial statute, or by a federal union. There was not the time to settle finally on one or another; and these again were matters that properly required weeks, not hours, of negotiation, had the time been there. At any rate, there should be representation by population along with constitutional guarantees for French Canada: that was the all-important step forward.

Similarly with regard to education: Brown stood for a fully national system, while Dorion required protection for Roman

Catholic interests. They agreed to investigate Ireland's national schools (possibly at McGee's suggestion), in an attempt to establish a single state educational system with modifications to meet religious needs: this to be effected by means of a government bill on which their cabinet should stand or fall.[127] Once more a great deal of work would have to be done here to discover whether a feasible compromise could be attained; but still this ministry stood ready to make the effort and face up to the consequences. So it was with the seat of government. It was not to be passed off on the Colonial Office, but tackled directly by a ministerial bill. Again the cabinet might not survive the effort—and again it might, since Brown's own position was that the permanent capital should not be chosen until the inherent sectional division of the union had been settled, and he then was ready to accept Montreal as the answer.[128]

So, too, with seigneurial tenure, still a vexed question in Lower Canada. The ministry was prepared to seek a final settlement to the seigneurial claims, with protection this time for Upper Canada, whose rights and revenues would need to be safeguarded. It was, in short, the most general kind of governmental compact, vague and incomplete. Yet it was quite enough to justify the initial formation of a cabinet, and to let it meet the House. Thereupon, it might look for an adjournment to enable it to mature and define its policies, just as other ministries had done before. This much was certain: a great deal had already been accomplished by Brown and Dorion in composing a surprisingly strong ministry with a broad programme, in the short space between Thursday and Saturday mornings.

6

Now on Saturday morning, July 31, Brown could give a definite answer to Governor-General Head. Once more he set out eagerly down King Street, through the dusty summer heat to Government House, bearing a formal acceptance: "Mr. Brown has the honour to inform His Excellency the Governor-General that he accepts the duty proposed to him in His Excellency's communication of 29th instant and undertakes the formation of a new administration."[129] There was a stiff interview between two men who did not like each other, and who each held a very definite idea of his own importance—the ceremonious but insistent Brown, whose journal had increasingly criticized the

Governor for showing too much partisan attachment to his late Coalition ministers; the polite but punctilious Head, who regarded Brown as a trouble-making demagogue more than a political leader who deserved authority.

And in the interview, in obviously no friendly fashion to his prospective chief minister, Head sought to make clear that he would promise nothing for the future. Indeed, what he said amounted to a chill warning that he would not guarantee to dissolve parliament, if the new ministry were defeated in the Assembly, to enable Brown to appeal to the people in fresh elections.[130] This was of vital significance. The whole survival of the Reform regime might turn on dissolving to fight a general election, since it was so probable that the Brown-Dorion administration would face an opposed majority in the existing House. Yet at this Saturday meeting, Brown seemingly did not pay much regard to Head's monotorial cautions. No doubt, with his usual impetuosity, he was thinking only of pushing on, all too conscious of his success thus far. In any event, he had not yet completed final arrangements for his government, nor handed in its members' names. He well could feel that when Head saw them he would have to recognize that this was a ministry that deserved every consideration. Perhaps, too, he was nettled by the Governor's unamiable lecture: George Brown would have no man talk down to him, least of all an ex-Oxford don.

It might seem evident enough that Head had not the faintest intention of being helpful; but Brown's direct, incautious mind was full only of the immediate next step: complete the ministry, and talk of later questions afterwards. And so he left Head, disregarding any danger sign because of his own characteristic limitations, while His Excellency, dwelling within limitations of his own, was conscious only that he had done his duty and made his position plain. Yet he did not see that his warning actually was meaningless. He had not refused a dissolution, but merely to pledge it in advance—which Brown should not have asked, and, in fact, had not.[131] Head had really said no more than the patently obvious: that he would, or would not, grant dissolution as the case arose. To a man like Brown, this was virtually a challenge to go ahead and find out.

The near-premier plunged back into his round of cabinet conversations. Thus Saturday passed away, and Sunday, August 1, also. By now reports that he had been able to form a government were spreading, and there were incredulous flutterings in the ranks of the Coalition, which had so persistently written him off as a "governmental impossibility".[132] The ex-ministers, it was said, looked "very blue".[133] They had not fully expected this. Brown should have collapsed at the first hurdle, and proved his utter incapacity to gain support from any but a die-hard group of Grits. The House would meet tomorrow. The Coalitionists began to rally against more trouble than they had anticipated. That Sunday, the Grand Trunk ran a special train to bring back to town Macdonald-Cartier supporters who had scattered eastward for a long, easy week-end.[134] And that same night Brown received a special communication from the Governor-General which showed Head's own awareness of the crisis that was impending when the Assembly should meet.

Brown had learned that Dorion had been taken ill—not seriously, as it happened—and had gone to visit him in his bedroom at the Rossin House. It was a sultry summer night, full of the distant rumblings of thunder. At ten o'clock, there was a knock at the door. The Governor-General's aide stood there with a message. It was a detailed, written memorandum with an ominous ring about it that this time could hardly be ignored.[135] It substantially repeated what Head had said to Brown the day before regarding a dissolution. Then it went on to discuss the possibility of merely proroguing the present parliament for several months; but hedged this with so many stipulations as to the legislation which His Excellency thought first should be enacted under Mr. Brown that one might wonder which of them was the representative of the Crown and which the minister to be responsible for formulating policy. But the heart of the document, as Brown and Dorion closely examined it, was clearly this: "The Governor General gives no pledge or promise, express or implied, with reference to dissolving parliament. When advice is tendered to His Excellency on this subject he will make up his mind according to the circumstances then existing and the reasons then laid before him."[136]

What were they to think, what were they to do? If the government were defeated when parliament met tomorrow, their natural course would be to ask the Governor for a dissolution—but would he grant it? Why all this emphasis of Head's that he had made no promise, which they had never sought? Was it tantamount to washing his hands of them? If he did refuse a dissolution, a defeated ministry could only resign. Should they take the broad hint now, and give up the attempt to form a government? But they had formed one, and at Head's invitation. How could they back out now, solely on an assumption that his statements were an intimation of refusal? If they gave way weakly on such grounds, they would have truly proved their incapacity to their friends and made themselves a laughing-stock to their enemies. In all good faith, they had formed a government. They must see it through, whatever threat hung over them in the Governor's words.

But still the leader charged with forming a ministry had to return some answer. Plainly it was called for. Brown went home late to think out an effective reply, and it was early Monday morning before he managed to draft one.[137] It was a brief note that left the matter open, but rested on sound constitutional grounds. After preliminaries it ran: "Before receiving His Excellency's note Mr. Brown had successfully fulfilled the duty entrusted to him by the Governor-General, and will be prepared at the appointed hour this morning to submit for His Excellency's approval the names of the gentlemen whom he proposes to be associated with himself in the new government.

"Mr. Brown respectfully submits that until they have assumed the functions of constitutional advisors of the Crown he and his proposed colleagues will not be in a position to discuss the important measures and questions of public policy referred to in His Excellency's memorandum."[138]

At half past ten in the morning, he went back to Government House—much less briskly this time—to submit the names of his ministers for Head's approval. To say the least, the atmosphere was no more cordial.[139] Afterwards he met his colleagues, and they unanimously approved his action.[140] They agreed not to ask for a pledge, nor to make or accept any conditions. Well aware of the threatening possibilities, they equally recognized that an attempt to bind the Governor to a dissolution would allow their enemies to raise the old "loyal" cry that had beaten Baldwin and his Reform cabinet in 1843-4—"the Crown's prerogative in danger". They would rather put the onus on Head of denying support to his constituted ministers, if that should come to pass.[141]

At noon, on that cheerless Monday, August 2, they soberly took their oaths of office. At three in the afternoon, parliament reassembled. The Brown-Dorion ministers were there, as the members expectantly filed in to the Assembly chamber, yet they were not there; that is, under the rules of the day they had officially vacated their seats until returned at by-elections. They all sat on a bench to the right of the Speaker, under the cool, appraising eye of John A. Macdonald, who appeared to be enjoying the whole set of manoeuvres.[142] Then, while they had to sit there silently, their trial by parliament began.

Patrick, a western supporter of the new government, spoke first on their behalf to say that the Brown-Dorion cabinet would announce their policy as soon as they occupied their seats again, and in the meantime wished to see the necessary business of the country closed and parliament prorogued at the earliest possible date.[143] Following this announcement, two eastern supporters of the government, Bureau and Piché, moved in regular fashion for a writ for the by-election of Dorion in Montreal. Immediately Hector Langevin, a young *Bleu* member ambitiously making his name in the House, jumped up to move a want-of-confidence amendment, which was seconded by Brown's Toronto rival, John Beverley Robinson.[144] There was to be no time allowed even for the ministers to be seated. The fight for a quick kill was on.

The Coalition forces rushed in upon the ministry. They denounced its evident lack of policy (not matured in forty-eight hours), the shameless coalition of French Canadians with the worst enemy of their people, together with the equally shameful fact that George Brown should sit in a ministry with a majority of Roman Catholics—which was shrewdly playing both ends at once.[145] They recalled the sectional vehemences of the past and deluged the ministry with them. In vain supporters of the Brown-Dorion government argued that previous cabinets had not necessarily set forth their policies on the very day they took office: they could note that the Coalition itself, formed in September, 1854, did not announce its programme for more than a month. In vain they contended that neither side, East or West, had sold out, but that agreement had been reached on principle to end the very vehemence of past sectionalism. The opposition simply was not interested in believing it; besides, they had the numbers to say they need not. With several supporters absent, nine ministers not seated, and hence most of their leaders in debate kept silent, the Reform government forces had no chance at all. They battled on until midnight; but when the vote was taken, it went overwhelmingly against the ministry: 71 to 31.[146] Now there was nothing left but dissolution.

Tuesday morning, then, August 3, Brown took the path to Government House once more. The heat had broken; it was pouring with rain. He asked Head to dissolve parliament, and was told to put his request in writing.[147] (Did a ring of angry demand, on the one side, and a note of self-satisfaction on the other, come through the formalities of the interview?) Brown withdrew, to meet with his cabinet in the Executive Council chambers nearby on King Street.[148] There they composed a memorandum setting forth their reasons for seeking a dissolution.

"When His Excellency's present advisors accepted office," they urged, "they did not conceal from themselves the probability that they would be unable to carry on the government with the present House of Assembly. The House, they believe, does not possess the confidence of the country; and the public dissatisfaction has been greatly increased by the numerous and glaring acts of corruption and fraud by which many seats were obtained at the last general election, and for which acts, the House, though earnestly petitioned so to do, has failed to afford a remedy."[149]

They went on to note the growth of "strong sectional feelings" in the country during the past several years, which especially during the present session had seriously impeded the carrying on of government. The late administration, they argued, had made no attempt to meet these difficulties, nor to suggest a remedy for them, and thereby the evil had been greatly aggravated. "His Excellency's present advisors have entered the government with a fixed determination to propose constitutional measures for the establishment of that harmony between Upper and Lower Canada which is essential to the prosperity of the Province. They respectfully submit that they have a right to claim all the support which His Excellency can constitutionally extend to them in the prosecution of this all-important object."[150]

Then they settled down to wait anxiously but none too hopefully for the Governor-General's reply. Any optimism had passed away even before their parliamentary defeat; before, in fact, they had been sworn in—ever since Brown had received that premonitory message from Head on Sunday night. Still, they had a strong case in constitutional custom and simple justice. Head had invited the creation of a Reform cabinet when he knew that the House was almost surely hostile. How could he deny them the chance at least to put their case before the people—whether or not he had promised them anything in advance?

At two o'clock the following afternoon they had their answer: refusal. Refusal argued out in a memorandum three times the length of their own, as the Governor-General sought carefully to justify his grave responsibility in thus exercising his prerogative power.[151] He noted the inadvisability of a new election. One had taken place only last winter. "This fact," he admitted, "is not conclusive against a second election now, but the cost and inconvenience of such a proceeding are so great that they ought not to be incurred a second time without very strong grounds." A valid statement of the obvious, but he went on to elaborate arguments against a new election that seemed to carry far less weight.

The business before parliament, he said, was not yet finished (although "it is perhaps true that very little which is absolutely essential for the country remains to be done"). Two bills of importance were before the Assembly, Head averred, and the resolutions respecting the Hudson's Bay territory had not been considered. (But Brown and the country might recall that in 1854 the Hincks government had readily obtained a dissolution just after parliament had met, that had left the public business, including small matters of the reserves and seigneurial tenure, very much up in the air.) Then the harvest season and the state of affairs would make an election at this time "peculiarly inconvenient and burdensome"—although again one might recall that the elections of 1854 had run on into August, and that 1844 had given the example of holding them back until October, when the harvest was over. As for the corruption and bribery that was claimed to distort the composition of the present House, this, Head contended, was all the more reason for keeping it in being until it had passed laws to prevent these abuses—though, if the premise of corruption were correct (and there were no less than thirty-two cases of alleged election fraud), such an achievement might not seem very probable.

Next the Governor-General turned to the problem of sectional discord. He conceded that, "the ultimate danger of such feelings to the union is one of a very grave kind" that "would furnish to His Excellency the strongest possible motive for a dissolution of parliament and for the retention of the present government at all hazards"—if two points were only first conclusively established. In short, if it could be shown that the measures likely to be adopted by the Brown-Dorion cabinet were a cure, and the sole cure, for sectional evils; and that they were the only men able to allay the existing jealousies. This was a tall order, indeed. Brown and his colleagues were being asked to prove in advance that they had the remedy for the union, and that they alone could bring a settlement. How could they prove it—without the chance of trying it? Why were they faced with the necessity of being the only men who could allay discord? Had such conditions been set for any other ministers?

"It may be that both these propositions are true" went on Head's memorandum, with a certain note of laying down the ace of trumps, "but unless they are established to His Excellency's complete satisfaction, the mere existence of the mischief is not in itself decisive as to the propriety of resorting to a general election at the present moment."[152] And so on. The Governor-General had a constitutional right to his course, and some grounds for his decision. Yet the nature of Head's arguments, and the impossible conditions he set upon his ministers, showed that his conscious or unconscious prejudice against them had given them virtually no chance from the start. What a contrast was there here from his treatment of his other ministers, of the Macdonald-Cartier variety—thoroughly flexible, cordial and amiable! And the contrast was shortly to be heightened, until it was positively glaring.

7

It was final, it was over. Brown went to Government House to submit his resignation before the Assembly should meet again at four o'clock. Then, before an eagerly expectant House and crowded gallery, T. C. Wallbridge, the Liberal member for Hastings, announced the government's fall. There was an outburst of Coalition cheers and jeers mixed with Reform howls of protest. The ex-ministers were still excluded, but they found fiercely indignant defenders, outstanding among them McDougall and McGee. "The whole thing is a plot" charged an impassioned D'Arcy McGee: the Macdonald-Cartier ministers had arranged the whole affair with Head's connivance to discredit the Reform leaders.[153] "How else is it that some people have of late been so confident, how is it that they knew before hand that His Excellency would not take the course the advisors recommended whom he had sworn in but a few hours previously?"[154] And as he went on to denounce the "lawyer-like cunning", the "cabal", the "back-stairs work", it was the Tories' turn for howls and protests. John A. Macdonald shot up to answer quite as fiercely, to brand McGee's charges "false as hell",[155] to deny that he had written the Governor's memorandum on dissolution (though McGee no less denied making that accusation), and to raise a standard countercharge against his Irish foe: "The honourable member is carrying out in this country the disloyalty he has displayed at home. He plotted there to deprive Her Majesty of a Crown. He makes a dastardly attempt here to deprive her representative of his character."[156]

Macdonald turned to launch into an attack on the absent Brown. He had sought to "bully" Head into a dissolution; he had accepted office under false pretences—he had given up his principles in a desperate gamble for power.[157] These were recriminations to be heard for years after, whenever the Brown-Dorion affair was raised, as raised it would repeatedly be to taunt George Brown. And on the other side, this Wednesday, August 4, had produced an accusation quite as extreme, that would be played up by the outraged *Globe* and its Reform contemporaries: that of a conspiracy by the Liberal-Conservative leaders, with Head as an accomplice, to trap George Brown and bury him, and thus save their hold on government. The real charges were something else again; but both sides preferred their far more lurid versions.

In any event, the country needed a ministry. On Thursday, Sir Edmund Head tried again. He opened fruitless negotiations with Alexander Galt, an able man and a distinguished member of the House, but leader of a party of one. The outcome now was obvious, and it surprised no one. On Friday, August 6, the old firm reopened business at the old stand, under a slightly different name: it was the Cartier-Macdonald ministry, not the Macdonald-Cartier, and it now included Alexander Galt. But there was a problem. The Cartier-Macdonald ministers had no desire to face by-elections, as the Brown-Dorion cabinet had been compelled to do. Casting around, they hit upon a wonderful way to avoid them. The Independence of Parliament Act of 1857 had among other things provided that a minister who had resigned one cabinet office and taken another one within a month did not have to go again to his constituents.[158] This made the shifting of departments within a government much easier; but the mere fact that such an exception had to be made by law showed how firmly the by-election rule was upheld.

The Cartier-Macdonald ministers, however, seized on this Act to facilitate changes within an existing government, and distorted it to a very different purpose—namely, to allow a cabinet to take office without going to the electors at all. Most of the Cartier-Macdonald ministers had held and resigned cabinet posts within a month. They now sought calmly to resume them by virtue of the Act of 1857. Still, it did seem to specify a minister taking a *different* office from that which he had held before. To be quite safe, therefore, they had themselves first sworn in to one set of offices which they did not intend to keep, then at once relinquished them, and were sworn into those which they had held previously. Now they were secure. They had the jobs they wanted, yet they had avoided elections by taking other cabinet offices within a month. By their fast footwork, their "double shuffle" (as the *Globe* at once termed it), they had conformed to the letter of the law while wholly perverting its spirit.

The half unscrupulous, half ludicrous episode even had the proper air of midnight intrigue. To make the sudden shift of offices at least appear to represent the somewhat more decent interval of two days, Cartier, Macdonald and their colleagues assembled in the Council chamber at fifteen minutes before midnight on August 6, and there swore with all due reverence to execute faithfully the duties of offices they had no intention of filling. At fifteen minutes after midnight on August 7 they swore themselves back into their original holdings.[159] Governor-General Head, of course, was a necessary partner to these proceedings. He found no difficulty in issuing one set of cabinet appointments for one day and a whole new set for the day after—no warning and stipulating memoranda here. The pugnacious rabble-rouser was out; the friendly double-shufflers were back in. The contrast in Head's treatment of Brown and his cabinet and Macdonald and his colleagues could scarcely have been more acute.

Not that Head had been unconstitutional in his conduct towards Brown, despite furious *Globe* arguments to the contrary. He had the discretionary power to grant a dissolution; he refused for reasons that to him seemed valid. But there was strong reason also for allowing an appeal to the people, even if there had been elections some seven months previous. For the first time a ministry had taken office committed to ending the undeniable sectional problems by positive action, not cabinet reshuffles. The electorate might well have deserved an opportunity to pronounce judgement. At any rate, it is hard to escape the conclusion that the position Head took was influenced considerably by his personal leanings; just as it is hard to avoid concluding that they were equally displayed in his correct but rigorously strict dealings with Brown and his helpfully easy attitude towards Cartier and Macdonald.

Head's antipathy to Brown was real enough: it was not just his natural preference for the moderate, Liberal-Conservative school of politics. In his strong concern for the growth of British North American union, he saw Brown only as an obstructive or even a disruptive influence.[160] And he could not have appreciated the lectures of the *Globe*, which for months past had been commenting on the Governor's too-ready willingness to be accommodating to John A. Macdonald. But in particular, and most immediately, there was the seat-of-government question.

If Brown and his newspaper had denounced referring the question of the capital to the Queen as in reality a return to colonialism, Head had suggested an appeal to the Crown as early as May of 1856.[161] It was Brown, moreover, who had come to office on the strength of parliament's rejection of Ottawa;

yet that had been Head's own choice as capital, carefully argued in a confidential memorandum he sent to the Colonial Office in the year 1857.[162] Finally, Head had been particularly shaken by the Canadian legislature's rejection of the Queen's decision, since he was painfully aware of the responsibility for having advised that the monarch should make the selection in the first place. It became a "point of honour" with him to see her decision made effective.[163] Brown stood in the way. Whether or not Macdonald had warmly felt the "insult" to the Crown in the rejection of Ottawa, Head assuredly had done so. The Brown-Dorion ministry was the veritable embodiment of that insult. It would go too far to say he sought to make it fail. It was only necessary that he should do nothing that might permit it to succeed.

For the present, things were much as they had been: the old order was back in power. Yet if Brown had suffered worst from the Brown-Dorion episode, his opponents had shown their own unreadiness to face the people, and had taken refuge in a much-condemned device that even their defenders found difficult to champion. And the Governor-General had added no laurels to impartial British constitutional rule.

Brown would be derided for years to come because of his "Short Administration". His enemies took unholy delight in contrasting his magnificent leap to power and sad sprawl out of it. The Conservative press made much besides of "Brown's Clear Grit Reversible Coat": orange on one side and green on the other, of course.[164] The rashness, the greed for office he had shown, became regular texts preached by Macdonald and his associates on all possible occasions. Yet Brown had not shown greed for office, but for his cause—if rashness and lack of foresight were more likely charges. Again, however, one might argue that at the end of July, 1858, he could not have done otherwise than try to form a government, lest he lose the whole position of leadership he had built up. The greater lack of foresight really came earlier, when he had failed to recognize sufficiently the need of preparing for a viable Reform administration to take office after Macdonald and Cartier had been laid low. The mind of parliament was simply not ready for the Brown-Dorion regime, especially after six more months of sectional bitterness. Brown, in short, was still a victim of his own political impatience, and his inability to conciliate effectively.

Nevertheless, the Brown-Dorion misadventure, hard blow as it was, was not unalloyed disaster. For one thing, George Brown had effectively disproved the oft-repeated Coalition charge that he was a "governmental impossibility". He had not only formed a government, he had built a strong and able one that brought together the most prominent Reformers of both sections of the union. He had shown besides that Reformers could lay the basis for a programme of constructive action acceptable to both the eastern and western party groups, and had revealed that he could move a good distance himself from the role of purely sectional leader. He had agreed to stand on a compromise on the schools question and on the seigneurial issue. Most important of all, he had agreed to link representation by population with constitutional guarantees for Lower Canada, and had based his government on that combination of principles.

What else was this but a foreshadowing of the bargain that underlay Confederation? What else was that bargain but due recognition of the majority's power of numbers, coupled with due protection for the rights of the minority? Here in 1858, in a year that in many ways anticipated the events that brought on Confederation—the rapid governmental changes, the hot sectional partisanry, the discussion of new forms of union— George Brown had taken a position which pointed to the statesmanship he would display in the final, greater crisis of the union in the next decade. His Upper Canada sectionalism was there still; and it would always be. His defeat, while severe, was only one of more to follow. His statesmanship in the Brown-Dorion attempt might seem much outweighed by his characteristic impetuosity and lack of proper preparation. And yet in the party leader who failed in 1858—this two-day premier—one might discern the bare outlines of an architect of the modern Canadian nation.

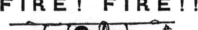

Withdrawal and Return

I

Brown was plunged back in election meetings that August, while the *Globe* railed violently against the Double Shuffle, the "embryo dictator", Sir Edmund Head, and his villainous pack of "closet councillors".[1] The ex-premier himself had little time for any reflections. He was addressing one Reform gathering after another in Toronto, in preparation for the by-election which his briefest of brief terms in office had forced upon him. The contrast here between the Brown-Dorion ex-ministers, forced to beat their way back into parliament, and the Cartier-Macdonald crew, snugly sheltering behind their technicality, was bitingly ironic. Reformers were in a frenzy of moral indignation, though Coalitionists defended the Shuffle as legal and downright clever. A Detroit paper remarked judiciously that it was sharp enough for Yankee politics.[2] On the other hand, old William Lyon Mackenzie announced himself so disgusted with the degradation of Canadian public life that he was going to retire from parliament at the end of the session.[3]

Liberal moral fervour of course filled Brown's own campaign for re-election. But he did not make a merely negative appeal, denouncing the enormities of the restored Coalition. Instead, he stressed the positive achievement of the Brown-Dorion ministry in bringing East and West effectively together behind a programme to end the sectional problems of the union. In fact, he made his Toronto by-election virtually an appeal for a public vote of confidence in the late administration. This was his chance to answer, as he could not in parliament, the Coalition's *tu quoque* arguments that his ministry had been far worse than the Double Shuffle, that it had sold out the West to the East or the East to the West—depending usually on which branch of the Coalition was pressing the charge.

These accusations could be made quite easily in the House, in the absence of the leaders who had worked out the agreements underlying the Brown-Dorion government; but Brown could set its policies squarely before the people in Toronto. His most powerful effort came in his speech at the city's Royal Exchange on August 6, wherein he graphically described the course of his discussions with Dorion, and how they had come to an accord. "I hold all as repaid," he ended strongly, "all as justified by this one fact: that in five years I have been able to construct the strongest administration ever offered to the country—and that administration pledged to settle finally the great questions of sectional strife, for the removal of which alone I entered parliament."[4]

His opponent was John Hillyard Cameron, Macdonald's erstwhile rival for the control of the Conservative party, who now was attempting to re-enter politics: his financial affairs somewhat improved, although his wealth was gone. Cameron had earlier professed some degree of sympathy for George Brown in his defence of the rights of Protestant Upper Canada; but now he declared himself revolted by Brown's surrender to Lower Canada and the Roman Catholics, his alliance with D'Arcy McGee, and his gratuitous insult to the Queen over the seat of government. The ministerial press in the city backed Cameron warmly. The *Leader* and *Colonist*, in fact, rode the "High Protestant horse" with a fervour that recalled the *Globe*'s old no-popery effusions, which they had once condemned with shocked disdain.[5]

It did not work too well, however. The selfsame election committee that had served Brown back in December was ready to function for him again. If he lost any support through his opponent's use of the Protestant cry, he lost very little at all, while at the same time he gained a substantial number of Catholic votes. It seemed also that Toronto did approve his government, and that popular feeling against the Double Shuffle played a part as well. At all events, the final count on a rainy, rowdy Saturday, August 28, revealed that the crowded polls had given Brown nearly three times the majority over Cameron that he had obtained over John Beverley Robinson in the general election of December.[6] It was reported that Governor-General Head had been seen driving fast for Government House through the noisy streets in a hired hack, on the back of which some wag had scrawled "Hurrah for Brown!"[7] Just before five, when the results were announced, the victorious candidate climbed out on the window ledge of the second floor of the *Globe* office and addressed a cheering crowd of some four thousand below. "I cannot conceal the joy I feel that at last the mists of prejudice are rising," he thankfully declared. "The capital city has set a noble example to the rest of the province in defence of constitutional rights. I will never forget what I owe to the citizens of Toronto!"[8]

Meanwhile, on August 16, the long-drawn-out session of 1858 had come to a close. And in proroguing parliament, Head had made what was possibly a most significant announcement: that the government of Canada would communicate with the governments of the United Kingdom and the Maritime Provinces to invite discussion of the idea of a federal union of British North America. General federation—this would be the one new policy taken up by the restored Coalition regime. But it was a project of such bold magnitude that it might well excuse any other lack of policy; that is, if it could be taken seriously, and if anything practical could be done with it. Cartier had made a brief reference to the project of British North American confederation in the explanations he had given when his cabinet had taken office. Its adoption, however, had little to do with Cartier, Macdonald or their old colleagues in the government. It came above all from the new Inspector-General, Alexander Galt, and from Governor Head himself.

General federation had of course been the plan embodied in Galt's resolutions, and he had made it a prime consideration in accepting office. Moreover, Head for years had been toying with ideas of British North American union, whether legislative or federal. He had produced his own series of draft resolutions on the subject of British American federation, which were far fuller than those actually introduced into parliament by Galt.[9] He was eager to see general federation brought forward; and the fact that the Cartier-Macdonald regime was ready to adopt it may have made him even more amenable to a contrivance like the Double Shuffle. But, as for the old leaders of the Coalition, there seems little reason to doubt that they were chiefly interested in the immediate political advantages that would accrue from the advocacy of a policy of federal union.

In the first place, it was an answer to the charge that they had no programme to meet the sectional ills. It was a fine, safe answer, too, since it was grand in conception, but so remote that nothing very upsetting was likely to come from it. Then it allowed the harassing seat-of-government question to be left for a while longer, since a broad new union might want to reconsider where its capital should be most suitably located.[10] Finally, it could do no harm to investigate the question. For when any negotiations broke down (as they were almost sure to do, since they required the active interest of the Colonial Office and of the other British colonies that as yet had shown virtually no concern for general union), then the Canadian government could not be blamed for any failure. Indeed, it would deserve every credit for its vision. In spite of the enthusiasm of Head and Galt, in short, there was no profound or even significant conversion of the Coalition ministry to the federal principle. The shrewd surmise of Colonial Office authorities perhaps came closest to the truth: "At this moment Federation is really a question raised for the convenience of the present Canadian administration."[11]

The *Globe* would put it more acidly, as a matter of course. "It would burn a house like the Chinese to roast a pig; it would rush into new national alliances to save John A. Macdonald's salary."[12] Believing that the confederation of British America was not yet within the realm of practical consideration, Brown's paper judged that the ministry meant to use it as an excuse to hide their own failure to deal with the inherent problems of the Canadian union. Nor did events prove that judgement wrong.

Early in September, 1858, a Canadian minute-of-council suggested by Head, calling for a British North American conference on a general federation, was circulated to the Colonial Office and the Lieutenant-Governors of the Maritime Provinces.[13] At the end of the month, three ministers, Cartier, Galt and Ross, prepared to sail for England to pursue the matter directly with the imperial authorities. Sir Edward Bulwer-Lytton, Colonial Secretary in the short-lived Derby Conservative government, was far from pleased when he first heard of the Canadian administration taking the initiative on the question of British North American union. He was very dubious about Head's procedure in refusing Brown a dissolution and subsequently accepting the Double Shuffle.[14] He was also much annoyed with Canada's Governor-General and cabinet acting on a matter of high imperial importance without prior consultation or consent—a matter which affected other colonies and properly belonged to the imperial power to initiate.[15] Though his annoyance subsided into a lecture for Head, it was clear that the imperial government would not pay much attention to the Canadian proposal.

British statesmen and officials received Canada's delegation politely and lavished hospitality upon them; but despite an interest at the Colonial Office in the long-range possibility of British North American union, the Canadian proposal was deemed wholly premature, and at that, a party manoeuvre of the moment.[16] In any case, the other provinces had not responded. They all revealed pretty complete indifference, except New Brunswick—but unfortunately New Brunswick suggested quite a different scheme, a legislative union for the Maritime Provinces alone. It would be six more years before new pressures and possibilities made Confederation a practical question throughout British North America.

Accordingly, the delegation had a pleasant time of it, and then came home. The whole venture had been "half smoke, half air," observed the *Globe* when the final reports came out.[17] There had perhaps been gains. The government of Canada had carried to the heart of Empire a proposal that could be of immense importance in the future. Confederation had been changed from a series of general resolutions on principle, not even put to the vote of the Canadian legislature, to an official cabinet policy. It might go into abeyance for years; the cabinet might itself abandon it; yet it was there on the record. Even further, the Canadian delegation in presenting their proposal to the British government had placed on record an acknowledgement that "very grave difficulties now present themselves in conducting the government of Canada".[18] They had admitted the basic constitutional problem, and "the necessity of providing a remedy for a state of things that is yearly becoming worse".[19] And when Coalitionists had been constantly and earnestly denying that there was anything inherently wrong with the existing union, this was a signal admission indeed.

Nevertheless, for the moment Confederation appeared as evanescent a programme as the *Globe* had claimed. It simply evaporated. It had served the government in time of need, clothing the Double Shuffle with constructive statesmanship. It had allowed Galt and Head to make their efforts, and left a perfect answer for the other ministers to a charge that they were not attempting to grapple with the problems of the union. They had tried—and the other provinces had failed them! They had a positive policy laid up in heaven; they could invoke it in after-dinner speeches; it was there until the rest of British North America came around. They could go on much as they had been, keeping the union functioning by parliamentary manoeuvre and exploiting every division in the opposition. And as before, all real suggestions for remaking the Canadian union would have to come from the opposition side.[20]

2

That autumn, while the government was pursuing its federation project—or red herring, as Brown would have preferred to call it—the leader of the opposition was busy with activities of his own. He was sharing in a round of public demonstrations and grand Reform assemblies across the province, intended to cement the unity of the Liberal party of Upper and Lower Canada that had apparently been achieved among its leaders in the Brown-Dorion administration. The *Globe* struck the keynote when it declared that if the forming of that cabinet had "had no other good effect, it has had that of desectionalizing the platform of the opposition".[21] No doubt as well a little drum-beating was necessary to restore party spirits, and to extol the leadership after the fiasco of the Short Administration. For Brown himself, it could only have been a relief to turn from defeat in parliament and council chamber to the welcome cheers of the electorate. Here he was at his best, rousing up mass audiences and feeling the invigorating glow of their enthusiasm—not facing the astutely calculated tactics of a Macdonald within the confines of the legislature.

But however comforting or even re-inspiring these contacts with the people might be, they represented further severe physical demands on Brown, who had hardly stopped for a minute since parliament first met. He had been going full tilt in the Assembly and in the Committee on Accounts before the Macdonald-Cartier ministry had fallen; then came his all-out effort to form a ministry, then the onset of his by-election campaign, even before he had given up the seals of office. Throughout, moreover, he had faced gathering financial worries as the dull weight of the depression steadily bore down upon him.[22] On top of all this, there was the shock of his cabinet's disaster, the bitter frustration at Head's treatment of his government, the ridicule from exultant enemies which a man of his sensitive and proud spirit could never easily bear.

No wonder, therefore, that he was writing to Holton in mid-September, even before the series of Reform demonstrations had got under way, to make plain that he was virtually exhausted: "I am out of health, worn out, driven to death, and cannot bring my mind to the most ordinary exertion." "I ought to give up all business for a month at least," he said wearily, "but it is very difficult to do so."[23] He had arranged to go down to Montreal to discuss strategy with the eastern leaders, but became so ill that he took a few days at the mineral baths in St. Catharines to recuperate instead. Now, doggedly, he took up plans again for the opening party demonstration at Hamilton a few days hence, proposing that the Lower Canadians should meet with him in Toronto to settle what they should do at the Hamilton banquet. Dorion, McGee and Holton would be there, and it was hoped that Drummond and Lemieux would also be on hand.

In many ways this was the right moment for party rallies. The spirit of amity and goodwill between East and West was still running high in Reform ranks. Upper Canadians were eager to greet the Lower Canadian ex-ministers and join them in denouncing the unconstitutional conduct of Head and his Coalition allies. Besides, the round of by-elections had only recently been finished, and all the Brown-Dorion cabinet members but Luther Holton had been triumphantly returned. Reform adherents would have agreed with Dorion's remark to Brown that "the success of our elections shows what would have been the result of a dissolution, had it been granted to us."[24] Thus the Hamilton banquet seemed almost a celebration, as Brown and Sandfield Macdonald, Dorion and Mowat, swore unwavering comradeship to one another in the struggle for the coming victory, and the banquet room resounded with applause.[25] So it was at Brantford and Elora—everywhere that the party leaders spoke.

Charles Clarke was the secretary of the committee that organized the Elora dinner, held at Bain's Commercial Hotel. On the evening of the great event, he was waiting a few miles out of town to welcome the visitors and escort them in with the Elora Brass Band—every man a good Reformer who had given his services free.[26] When the carriages arrived from the railway junction at Guelph, bearing the distinguished visitors, there was Holton, McGee, and Mowat among them; but no Brown. Clarke inquired, and was told that private business had forced the leader to return to Toronto from Hamilton. He began to express some regret when a petulant voice from the interior of one of the carriages asked sharply, "Can't you do without George Brown for a single night?"[27] It was Sandfield Macdonald, disclosing some of his real feeling for Brown, and disclosing, also, that in this particular quarter Reform amity was not much more than skin-deep.

After the Eastern leaders had joined in touring the West, it was time to move in the other direction. Early in November, Brown went down to Montreal to be the main speaker at one of the most magnificent political banquets yet held in Canada, and incidentally to make his first public address to a Lower Canadian audience. All the Brown-Dorion ministers were there except Morris, who was ill. They sat down in the sumptuously decorated city concert hall, its walls hidden by tapestries, flags, wreaths of evergreens, and inscriptions that varied from "Nos institutions, notre langue et nos lois" to "Honesty is the Best Policy".[28] The affair began about six and lasted until nearly four in the morning, lubricated only by cups of tea, since it was a temperance occasion. Brown's speech, while greatly applauded by his

new audience, was much as might have been expected. He repudiated the old charge that he had sought to excite religious
discord between sects and sections. He lauded the strength and
talents of the Brown-Dorion ministry. He asserted that they
had not been "outwitted" in taking office, but had felt it their
duty to proceed and put the responsibility on the Governor-
General for denying the constitutional aid due to his government—and that they had known when sworn in of an impending want-of-confidence vote.[29]

Then he scorchingly attacked the Double Shuffle, particularly
the false oaths of office taken by the Cartier-Macdonald ministers. But he went further, to strike a note that sounded altogether strange from this consistent defender of British institutions and the parliamentary system. "Our constitutional system
in this country is being tested," he announced. "The problem
has not been solved whether British constitutional government
can work well in Canada. If the Governor-General can set aside
at his mere will the most necessary constitutional requirement,
if he can become a partisan and espouse the cause of one party
against the other, if he can use his position to throw the leading
members of the House of Assembly out of their seats at the
most critical moment of an exciting session—then, I say, it is
time to look out for firmer bonds to bind down the executive
of the day and to secure good government at the hands of those
who rule us!"[30] Was he suggesting the American model of a
written constitution? Nothing came of his remarks for the time
being, but they seemed to indicate some deep disturbance in
George Brown: a swelling unrest that sprang not only from
failure and frustration, but also from the tensions he had so
long been under.

As a matter of fact, the *Globe* had momentarily expressed
much stronger discontent with institutions it had always upheld, during its first outburst of anger over the Double Shuffle.
On that occasion it had vehemently announced, "it will be
absolutely necessary to resort to the method of the States of
binding down the government by written constitutions of the
strictest kind."[31] This, however, was a sudden cry of outrage
that soon subsided; nevertheless, the *Globe*'s opinion that the
Double Shuffle was a gross offence against the constitution remained firmly fixed. And so that autumn it watched with almost
bated breath the suits that had been brought before the assizes
in the name of Allan Macdonell, the Toronto Liberal promoter
of North West development, in order to test the legality of
the Shuffle.

In September Dorion had raised the question of an appeal

to the courts.[32] In October, Adam Wilson, Q.C., Robert Baldwin's former law partner, had begun proceedings in Canada West to exact the penalty set by statute of £500 a day for each day that John A. Macdonald, Sidney Smith and Philip Vankoughnet had held a seat illegally.[33] There was a marshalling of Osgoode Hall's best legal skill for these momentous "state trials". John Hillyard Cameron shone for the defence, while the son of Chancellor William Hume Blake spoke most powerfully for the plaintiff: young Edward Blake, who promised "to take his father's place at the bar", adjudged the *Globe*.[34] The cases went on until mid-December. But then—alarming to relate—Chief Justice Draper and his associates ruled that the defendants had successfully stayed within the letter of the law, the Independence of Parliament Act of 1857.[35]

The judges, in fact, ignored the whole constitutional issue. Stressing that they could not consider the *intent* of the legislature in passing the statute, they found a loophole for the Double Shuffle through a literal interpretation of its wording. It was interesting, though, that Draper went on to explain what the legislature had meant to authorize".[36] From strict interpretation the judges readily switched to liberal, as they reasoned that if a whole ministry had been allowed to make one change of office without by-elections, "surely" it had been intended that they could make another.[37] In short, the judges fitted into an enduring pattern of interpreting Canadian constitutional questions whereby the legal mind first denied that the courts could examine what parliaments had intended, and then imagined those intentions for itself.

The *Globe* was furious. The decisions of the "political judges" (all good Conservatives, it noted) were a perversion of the constitution. "Of breadth of view there is none, of constitutional argument there is not an iota, of common sense there is not a particle. . . . The Governor General and his ministers escape from a disgraceful condemnation like criminals who have so managed their operations as to keep within the letter while violating the spirit of the law."[38] Again it raised the issue of Sir Edmund Head's "tampering with the usages of the constitution", which "has done more to Americanize our institutions than all other influences combined".[39] And again it darkly intimated a demand for sweeping changes. "We think it time either that we have a better governor, or else a change of system which would give us a ruler amenable to our laws."[40] There followed a fiery series of articles on the partisanship of judges, the corruption of ministers, that was possible under the existing system. Then once more the fierce heat passed away. But as the year ended, Brown's journal remained in a state of mind that could only be described as restive, gloomy and morose.

It was not only the approval of the Double Shuffle that caused the *Globe*'s disquiet: the Reform party was really in none too healthy a condition. The apparent and immediate success of the meetings in the autumn was not proving to be lasting. The flush of enthusiasm was wearing off. The sense of comradeship in a battle lost was being replaced, as that struggle faded into the distance, by an awareness that it had indeed been lost, and by a desire to blame someone. Some of the moderate element among Reformers tended to see George Brown's past record of intransigence as the main reason why their side had not gained wider parliamentary support after the formation of the Brown-Dorion ministry. Radicals were uneasy because that cabinet had contained so many moderates and no true Clear Grits of the old school, while voluntaryists were unhappy because it had held so many Roman Catholics. French Canadians claimed Brown had yielded to their way of thinking; Upper Canadians feared that he might have. Then just at the close of the year, the separate-school question came up once more: though in an academic fashion. It was a new conflict of letters between George Brown and Egerton Ryerson. Still, they had considerable significance.

Chief Superintendent Ryerson had stated in his annual educational report that the Irish national school system—which essentially allowed certain periods outside the ordinary "mixed" schooling to be given to religious instruction—was generally unsuitable for Canada.[41] Brown at once repudiated this assertion through the *Globe,* since much of the accommodation that he had reached with Roman Catholics was based on the belief, expressed in the Brown-Dorion agreements, that it was possible to maintain Catholic religious rights in education and a national school system at one and the same time.[42] Ryerson replied with a ready gush of public letters, that ran on into early 1859 and furnished him with a fine new pamphlet of polemics.[43] But whoever won—and it seemed that Ryerson generally had the best of the name-calling—it was a blow at Brown's relations with the Roman Catholics. For the present, it appeared to make no difference in his cordial association with McGee, nor in the alliance between eastern and western branches of the Reform. Yet it was one more sign among many that a great deal remained unsettled behind the facade of Reform unity. Indeed, as 1859 began, and George Brown once again made ready to face parliament, he did so more strained and less refreshed than ever: still more concerned about the state of Canadian political institutions following the legal approval of the Double Shuffle, much more convinced of the iniquity of the Coalition government, and deeply troubled over the state of the party that he led.

3

There was one brighter moment early in the new year, when on January 6, Adam Wilson, the principal Reform lawyer in the "state trials", won the first mayoralty election held in Toronto. To suit the needs of a modern city, an Act of 1858 had provided for direct choice of Toronto's mayor by the people, not by the members of the city council, as before. Capitalizing on the Liberal ascendancy in the capital so convincingly displayed in his own by-election, George Brown had taken the lead in organizing a Municipal Reform Association, which in late October chose Adam Wilson as its candidate.[44] A so-called "Independent Convention" then put forward an old Tory foe of Brown's, William Henry Boulton, while John G. Bowes, the illustrious ex-mayor of the Ten Thousand Pounds Job, threw his own bedraggled hat into the ring.[45] This time the Toronto election struggle turned out to be less disorderly in deeds than in words. As the *Leader*, supporting Boulton, reported with a sniff, "If the different actors in the scene are to be believed, they are almost without exception as precious a set of scoundrels as ever were collected together. Everybody accused everybody of everything, and everybody, pleading not guilty, offset the charge against him by a still more astounding one against his neighbours."[46] In any event, Wilson won handily, and Reformers went on to make a clean sweep of the civic government.[47] Toronto was Brown's city still.

This local victory could not greatly relieve his sombre view of the political scene. Nevertheless, there was still some hope of a change. The government organs now stated that the ministry meant to stand by Ottawa as capital, and if defeated upon that issue, would dissolve parliament themselves. Sicotte had just left the cabinet because he objected to holding to the choice of Ottawa: a former *Rouge* who had become a Coalition Liberal, though never really a *Bleu*, he exercised significant influence in Canada East which Reformers had earlier hoped to win back to their side.[48] His defection demonstrated that the ministry still faced a dilemma in the seat-of-government question. They had resigned in July of 1858 avowedly because the As-

sembly had rejected Ottawa; they could hardly reject it themselves. And yet, their all-important French-Canadian following
had made their discontent at that selection very plain. The
Globe even affected to believe that a desperate ministry would
try a sudden dissolution and appeal to the people.[49] It was busy
preparing Reformers for that eventuality when parliament met
on January 29.

The Speech from the Throne, however, soon revealed that
the government had found a neat way out of their difficulty
over the capital. They would go to Ottawa, yes; but only after
public buildings had been erected at the new capital—and until
then would move back to Quebec! An incensed *Globe* saw this
as another miserable Coalition deception: ministers could tell
their English-speaking followers that they honoured the
Queen's decision and would quite soon go to Ottawa; they
could tell their French that the final move would be several
years away, and that if a confederation were achieved in the
meantime, its new capital might well turn out to be Quebec.[50]
Besides being a mere dodge to get the maximum amount of
votes, the *Globe* protested, this "insane project" of a double
move would cost close to two million dollars.[51] It was done to
please Lower Canada; Upper Canada was simply to be ignored,
since the ministry could not hope to get control of that section.
And once again, the West's only portion would be to pay the
increased taxes produced by ministerial waste and trickery.

The debate that followed on the Address in Reply was not
as long as usual, but it was quite as acrimonious. For one thing,
although the documents on the proposal for a federal union
now disclosed that the ministers had admitted "very grave
difficulties" in the Canadian union, the government equally
declared that their only remedy could not be applied until the
indefinite future.[52] Here was a deplorable deficiency in policy
for the opposition to seize upon. For another thing, the government forces, perhaps aware that under the circumstances the
best defence was attack, made repeated onslaughts on the late
Brown-Dorion ministry. Their answer to assaults upon the
barrenness of their own programme was to ask what the Brown-
Dorion ministers had intended to do. They questioned, probed
and cross-examined, until, as Brown said, "any stranger would
think we were the government and they the opposition." "We
are out of office," he exclaimed. "We are in the minority. We
cannot control the legislature—and yet the hall echoes with
demands as to our principles, our policies. The honourable gentlemen opposite are in power, they have a majority of the
chamber, yet not one question is asked of them by their sub-

servient followers. Have they really nothing to propose, nothing to say for themselves? Sir, I do them an injustice; on one point they have a policy, a consistent policy, to keep the Attorney General West firmly in his seat!"[53]

Only Macdonald was still there, Brown noted caustically—alone out of the original Coalition that had taken office four short years before. In that time, twenty-six other cabinet ministers had come and gone! Yet this was the inevitable result of the system of the union. "All the scandalous extravagance and corruption, the feeble legislation, the accumulating financial difficulties, the ruin or withdrawal of so many public men, may in large measure be traced to the immense difficulties of governing two peoples, with two languages, two creeds, two systems of local institutions, under one general government. And unless we can find some common basis of legislation and administrative action just to both sections, that will banish sectional and sectarian jealousy from the public arena, we had better—a thousand times better—dissolve the connection!"[54]

He swept on, to one last counter-thrust: "Have these honourable gentlemen who ask so glibly for the details of our plan told us what is their own plan? They have committed themselves to a federal constitution, they have demanded it of the home government, they have urged it on the other colonies. Can they tell us even now one single feature of their scheme? Do they fancy that a change in the constitution can be made on any other basis than representation by population? If they have a plan, we have a right to know it. If they have not, what a picture of imbecility must they have presented at the Colonial Office! They demand from us the details of our scheme, though we were but in office for a day and had not an hour to mature them. We don't demand the details of their scheme, we simply ask for the outline. They have been months in office—and yet not one word of explanation can we extract from them!"[55]

The vote was close: the ministry squeaked through with a majority of five.[56] But the plaguing seat-of-government question had now been disposed of. And thus the House could move on to the equally vexatious problem of finance. On this, of course, the *Globe* would argue that the ever-mounting load of public debt arose mainly from the government keeping itself in power by freely buying up votes and interests. That, in particular, French Canadians had been given special aid and favour in return for their blank-cheque support of Grand Trunk legislation—until the "French Catholic domination" of earlier years had been replaced by a still more sweeping Lower Canadian hegemony, built upon the venal alliance of French Catholic

Bleus and Montreal financial interests. Upper Canadian interests had virtually no influence on this basic structure of power:
the Upper Canadian minority behind the government remained
there merely for the crumbs it was allowed from the Lower
Canadian feast, and in a debased desire for its share of offices.[57]

It was a thoroughly biased analysis, treated with that extremism common to the press of the day, and not restricted
merely to the *Globe*. Undoubtedly, however, Brown believed
that it was in the main true. Yet—was the analysis without some
element of meaning, when Grand Trunk bills no less than the
separate-school laws of previous years had been put through
essentially by French-Canadian votes? When the leader of the
government and the *Bleus* was himself still solicitor for the
Grand Trunk, and was but one of four Grand Trunk representatives in the cabinet?[58] And when, admitting all the opposition's
immoderate zeal for muck-raking, the jobbery and fraud that
appeared so often in politics indicated there was muck to rake?

Moreover, it was true that Upper Canada was much more
dependent on the import and export trade than was Lower
Canada; and since the revenues were chiefly collected from
trade through customs duties, then it was also true that Upper
Canada paid a significantly larger share of the taxes. There
might have been nothing unjust about that fact, except that
taxation and representation were not in fair proportion. If
Upper Canadians provided the greater share of the revenues,
they could not provide their full share of representatives to say
in parliament how they should be spent. In a very real way, the
cry of taxation without representation might be raised in Upper
Canada by the sizeable portion of the population which was
effectively disfranchised through the equal division of parliamentary seats. And all this, while the government that had
piled up the debt burden, and imposed mounting taxes which
bore more heavily on Upper Canada, was ruling over that section without majority support. For more than a year now, the
government had commanded only a minority in Canada West,
though back in 1856 John A. Macdonald had ostensibly resigned on the principle that a ministry should not continue to
govern half the province against its will.[59] Were, then, George
Brown's dark assessment and the *Globe*'s still more extreme
strictures so utterly unfounded?

The government's apparent indifference to western outcries
over the finances, and their willingness to rule by eastern big
battalions, seemed once more demonstrated when the important
Committee on Public Accounts was set up in the latter half of
February. Cartier brusquely moved to exclude Brown from the

Committee, alleging that he was ignorant of financial matters, had not been attentive to the Committee the year before, and had been scandalous in his behaviour there.[60] The first two reasons were astounding, considering Brown's long record as a financial critic and his major preoccupation with fiscal questions —and considering that the last thing the government had enjoyed from the opposition leader in regard to their accounts had been inattentiveness. The third reason, when regarded from the government's viewpoint, was no doubt the real one. At any rate, despite the indignant arguments of Brown's supporters, the ministerial majority flatly settled the issue when told to treat it as nothing less than a vote of confidence.[61]

Although kept off so important a committee, Brown could still do his best to deal with the problem of public debt in the House. The deficit now was greater than the ordinary expenditure had been in 1850, and the revenues could come nowhere near meeting it.[62] Thus the debt burden jumped $5,000,000 more within the fiscal year of 1858-9 alone.[63] For three successive years, Brown pointed out, the ordinary expenditure had vastly exceeded revenue, and the large annual deficits had only been met by new loans floated on the London exchange. This was heading straight for ruin—and yet what policy did the government offer, even under its new financial expert, Inspector-General Galt?[64] Galt had only one immediate answer: further increases in the tariff. From the Cayley level of 20% on many manufactured articles and 15% on unenumerated goods, he went on to 25% on certain items and 20% on all the rest.

His tariff, introduced in March, caused a new furore in Upper Canada, where it was widely greeted as a veritable "tariff of abominations". It went much further with protectionism; it threatened the reciprocity agreement with the United States; it raised taxes that were already far too high. But above all, charged the *Globe*, it was a "palpably sectional" tariff that sought to redirect western trade for the benefit of Lower Canadian business interests. "The aim is to secure to Montreal importers in a single year the command of Western markets, inflicting injury upon every merchant of Toronto, Hamilton and London."[65] The Toronto and Hamilton Boards of Trade met to announce their emphatic agreement.[66] Once again the *Globe* was standing for the business interests of the West: not "inimical to Montreal *per se*", it claimed, but refusing to "be made tributary to that trade".[67] And once again Brown's journal saw behind tariff the domineering influence of Montreal finance, backed by the "mouton vote" of the Lower Canadian majority.

Brown himself clashed sharply with Galt in the House, both over general financial policy and the tariff in particular. Malcolm Cameron joined him in vigorously condemning the tariff, for the Coon had made another of his bewildering shifts, and now was an ardent member of the opposition. Nevertheless, the predictable result was the passing of the tariff by Lower Canadian votes, while an Upper Canadian majority stood in opposition.[68]

The tariff had blown up the sectional fires, as the *Globe* had warned it would. Brown again was talking openly and strenuously of the costs of eastern domination, abandoning his previous appeals to Lower Canadians to turn from sectional differences and join in a constructive effort to settle the problems of the union. The vexations of the session were putting a severe strain on ties between eastern and western Reformers that had never really been consolidated. And now came the question of seigneurial claims, to tear at them still further.

The Act of 1854 abolishing seigneurial tenure had established a commission to assess the value of seigneurial rights, and had set aside funds from the public chest to provide for compensation. But the findings of the commission indicated that additional sums would be required to extinguish the seigneurial claims. Accordingly, in early April, Cartier brought in a set of resolutions to authorize payment of the extra costs. Because of the division and dualism in the union, however, it was provided that Upper Canada should receive an equal sum, to be applied to its Municipal Loan Fund—not to mention a grant to Lower Canada's Eastern Townships, where there were no seigneurial claims.[69] Under the circumstances, this might seem an equitable arrangement, particularly if money were in unlimited supply. But in a time of grave financial strain it would add nearly six and a half million dollars to the provincial debt. Besides, because Upper Canada provided much the larger share of the union's revenues (three-quarters, estimated Brown and his followers, while Cartier and Macdonald had already admitted to two-thirds),[70] the West would be in a position of not only raising and expending extra money for itself unnecessarily, but would actually be paying a large part of the outlay for Lower Canada.

Brown was out of town when the measure was first debated; but Sandfield Macdonald, Mowat, Foley, and McDougall fought it vigorously. When he did return, he at once became the centre of a violent storm, as he tried to urge that the extra money for seigneurial claims should be secured from purely Lower Canadian funds.[71] He pointed out that the Act of 1854, passed as a final settlement, had already provided some $1,200,000 from the province as a whole, and that any additional sums were supposed to come from local sources. He reminded parliament that Cartier himself, in describing the Act of 1854, to his own constituents, had explained that these were the best arrangements possible—since one should not forget that Lower Canada was joined with an Upper Canada that had no direct interest in the matter, and contributed two-thirds of the revenue of the entire province! And he also quoted this incisive passage from the House debates: "What in the world have the people of Upper Canada to do with this question? Two-thirds of the whole taxation of the country is paid by the people of Upper Canada and here they talk of taking a certain amount out of the consolidated funds for the benefit of Lower Canadians and then remunerating Upper Canada by paying her a similar sum out of her own resources. It is as much as saying that Upper Canada may be bribed with her own money!'"[2] This was John A. Macdonald speaking on the seigneurial question in 1853; but times had changed since then.

Brown's own proposal was to charge the additional seigneurial claims against Lower Canada's portion of the Municipal Loan Fund. From this fund, Upper Canada had already borrowed $7,000,000; yet since Lower Canada, entitled by statute to an equal amount, had only taken loans up to $1,500,000, there was plenty of room for the claims to be looked after. He admitted the need of extinguishing them; he simply did not wish to do injustice to Upper Canada in the process.[73] But here his opponents jumped at him, recalling that the Brown-Dorion ministry had promised to settle the seigneurial question to everyone's satisfaction. How, then, had they planned to do so, if he was raising difficulties now? When that ministry was formed, he replied, Dorion had told him that the money set aside to redeem seigneurial claims would not prove sufficient, and he had readily agreed that they must act, on the condition that local funds be used. There had not been time to decide the details; but then, as now, he had thought that the best way lay through the Municipal Loan Fund.[74] Significantly, Dorion rose to agree with his account, and to agree that the Loan Fund probably offered the best approach: in fact, he said, he himself had casually mentioned it to Brown during the cabinet negotiations.[75]

Hence the ministerial attempts to split the two Reform leaders on the seigneurial tenure issue failed. Unquestionably, however, there was much dissension sown in opposition ranks. For if most western Liberals felt strongly that seigneurial claims should not be paid out of the province's consolidated funds, most eastern Liberals felt quite as strongly that they were a provincial obligation, and that they should not be dealt with through a loan which would ultimately have to be repaid by Lower Canadians themselves. The liquidation of ancient seigneurial burdens, they insisted, should in no way fall on the actual inhabitants of seigneurial lands. Thus it was that Laberge, the former Solicitor-General East in the Brown-Dorion cabinet, felt impelled to make a trenchant declaration of his own. He had taken office, he asserted, on the understanding that the seigneurial issue would be satisfactorily settled; and, while not at the meeting of the cabinet heads, had definitely concluded that compensation would come from general public funds, and had so informed his friends.[76] The raw nerve-ends of sectionalism were exposed, as both sides fell to denying each other's interpretation, and to quarrelling heatedly over possible means of payment. In Brown himself, all the pent-up feelings of the last few months blazed forth as he denounced this latest measure of eastern domination. It showed how ominously far he had let himself go, when he threatened, "If such a bill is carried, I confess it ends—in my opinion—all hope of maintaining the union!"[77]

It was carried; by a sharply sectional vote in which the entire minority but one were Upper Canadians.[78] It brought an angry aftermath as well. On April 22, twelve Lower Canadian opposition members met to express their "great dissatisfaction" with the speeches of Brown and other Upper Canadian Reformers upon the seigneurial resolutions.[79] Dorion was not there; he had left town already in anticipation of the imminent closing of the session. Perhaps, had he been present, the affair might have gone differently; but at any rate the twelve Liberals from the East announced that they would seek a joint meeting of the opposition forces in order to reorganize. The obvious fact was that they were experiencing once more the embarrassment of being too closely associated with George Brown and the strength of Western sectional feeling—which could do them little good in their own half of Canada. Drummond was delegated to express to Brown the eastern Liberals' discontent. And the majority of the meeting concluded that if an understanding could not be reached with him, they should publicly declare that they could not act under his leadership.[80]

Brown tartly answered that he had not understood that the Lower Canadians had been under his leadership at any time in the past three months: he had believed that they were under Dorion, although he still hoped for a more cordial union with them.[81] The letters, however, which passed between Drummond and Brown, and then Laberge and Brown, over the end of April and into early May, showed few signs of cordiality— rather, growing coldness and asperity—as they debated whether Brown had correctly expressed the Brown-Dorion policy on seigneurial tenure.[82] The matter was not pressed further once parliament rose on May 4. There was no longer any urgent reason to continue an argument that could have no real conclusion, since neither side would be likely to yield its own opinion. The Lower Canadian members went on home after the short but painful session, the last to be held in Toronto. But plainly, the spirit of Reform amity and the East-West Reform alliance associated with the Brown-Dorion ministry had practically disappeared.

Things looked almost as they had back in 1857, with but few links left between the two separate Reform groups, and a good deal of unfriendliness on either side. They were not quite that bad: there was still the memory of the Brown-Dorion agreement as a basis for future constructive action. Brown's ties with Dorion and Holton were still secure, moreover; and in particular there was still his bond with McGee. Yet in a general sense he had lost much of the contact he had made with French-Canadian *Rouges* other than Dorion, and with more moderate eastern Liberals such as Drummond. It was the final blow of a thoroughly dispiriting session—that to the western Liberal leader had seemed to consist of one frustration after another, while the province moved steadily downward to financial ruin. And the accumulation of these latest misadventures, along with all he had experienced before, brought him to a state of deep dejection that produced a strange departure in the political career of George Brown.

4

Ardent struggles had been unavailing; firm-held ideas had proved their emptiness. He had worked to build a common front for eastern and western Reform, and it had collapsed in new outbreaks of sectional bitterness. He had urged representation by population, to win justice for the West while preserving the union, and it had failed of achievement. He had stood by the union, only to see it again become the instrument whereby Upper Canada was ruled against the will of its majority. And he had held to the British system of responsible government, only to watch unprincipled ministers abuse the broad powers it gave to the executive so that they could keep themselves in office, while a partisan governor abetted them at every turn. These were the black thoughts that filled Brown's mind at the close of the disastrous session, when rankling memories of the Brown-Dorion failure and the Double Shuffle readily returned to haunt him—when he was worn and spent by unremitting strain, and when his own nagging business problems had never left him for a moment.[83]

What else was left to him but counsels of despair? Break the union; go back to a separate little Upper Canada, that could at least run its own affairs. Turn from British institutions, which had not failed Canada so much as she had failed them. Turn, at any rate, far enough to recognize the hard fact that in North America governments had to be controlled by explicit constitutional injunctions; that here the executive could not be allowed so much licence and broad political influence, but should be separated from the legislature as in the American republic; and that only by these drastic changes could Upper Canada be saved from complete political and economic catastrophe.

That was the reasoning, that was the line of argument Brown now allowed the *Globe* to take. But he did indeed allow it, rather than shape the policy himself. His whole attitude reflected a despondent, tired mind, not a determined will to action; his course was a reaction to all that he had undergone, not a conversion to new zeals. He would let others present a new pattern of policy in the *Globe*. He would even welcome it, so far as a growing mood of lethargy would permit him. For the mood that Brown had fallen into earlier when he had overtaxed himself, again came on him: the consequence of his unceasing physical and mental exertions.

There was a man, however, already on the *Globe* staff who could present the new policy with whole-hearted enthusiasm, a man of decidedly "advanced" opinions: George Sheppard, one of the ablest journalists then in Canada. Sheppard, an English radical and democrat of about Brown's age, had had a varied career before he joined the *Globe*. He had written for a number of English papers, among them some of Chartist sympathies, and had edited the Washington *Daily Republic* after emigrating to the United States in 1850.[84] He had moved on to Canada in 1854, worked as an insurance actuary in Hamilton, and had struck up a friendship with a fellow English radical, Charles Clarke, when he began to contribute articles to the local western press.[85] Then in November, 1857, Sheppard had become chief editorial writer for the ministerial Toronto *Colonist*, a jump from radicalism to conservatism which apparently did not greatly bother a newspaperman of wide experience, particularly when he disliked the "theological antipathies" in provincial politics, with which, he felt, the Upper Canada Reformers were far too much concerned.[86]

In any event, he had been doing good service in reviving the somewhat moribund *Colonist*, when in parliament in June of 1858 occurred Powell's notorious personal attack on George Brown and his father. Sheppard's sense of fair play had been aroused. Alone in the office at 2 a.m., he had drafted a brief factual report of the incident, indicating that the verdict had seemed to go to Brown.[87] But this had brought the furious demand from government leaders that the party organ retract Sheppard's article. A refusal had carried the *Colonist* into opposition, while John A. Macdonald—to quote Sheppard— "hunted me with the malignity of a fiend".[88] The financially shaky *Colonist*, however, could not afford its new course. Within a few weeks its backers had agreed to a merger with the new *Atlas* founded by the ministry—and Sheppard had been thrown out of a job.

He approached the *Globe*. Assuredly he had no love left for the ministry, while his relationship to George Brown had changed since he had defended him. Brown was glad to employ Sheppard; and by no means merely out of gratitude. The *Globe* could use another editorial writer of his experience and talent. William McDougall had entered parliamentary life himself, and like George Brown could henceforth spend only part of his time at the *Globe* office. Gordon Brown could not fill in the gap alone. There was space for Sheppard, certainly; while as time went on a man of his ability could make himself more and more influential on the editorial page. Quite conceivably, he drafted the *Globe*'s radical response to the judgements of December, 1858, in the "state trials". For if that journal had echoed Brown's sudden surge of anger when it declared, "the decision in these cases will materially strengthen the hands of those who demand a written constitution after the American model", it had no less intimated Sheppard's own inherent intellectual conviction that American institutions were far preferable for Canada.[89]

That intimation had not been followed up immediately. In the early months of 1859, apart from dark allusions to the need of re-examining the political structure of the country, the *Globe* had been preoccupied with the practical issues of the parliamentary session—the finances, seigneurial claims, and so forth.

But on February 15 the paper ran a bold and sweeping article on the constitutional question that was a manifest of things to come. "Responsible government," it asserted, "has not realized the expectations of its promoters. Men begin to pronounce it a failure. The fault lies quite as much in the system as in the men, and if we would restore purity to the government and independence to the legislature we must begin by imposing restraint on executive influence." Of course, this declaration, too, might simply express George Brown's reaction to continued defeat: his enemies would charge that since he could not win the game, he sought to change the rules.[90] But it was also printed when Brown was far too busy in parliament to have written it himself—and furthermore, it came just two days after Sheppard had made a highly significant observation to Charles Clarke. "Politics," he said, "become more and more fuddled. There is no salvation in my opinion short of radical organic changes. I should like a chance to say what I think on that point."[91] Perhaps in the *Globe* of February 15 he found a chance.

This full opportunity came, however, after parliament had risen in early May. Then it was—with Brown virtually withdrawn into despondency, yet fully acquiescent to a campaign for "radical organic changes"—that Sheppard undertook to set the *Globe*'s new policy before the people of Upper Canada in a rapid sequence of powerfully argued editorials. Nor is there any doubt that he took the lead and forced the pace. As he frankly told Charles Clarke a few weeks later, "The movement of the *Globe* for organic changes is one for which I shall have to bear the responsibility. Brown and I had conversed on the failure of the present system, but he was not all prepared for the distinct committals that have been made, *and is still afraid to own them*."[92]

The campaign launched in the *Globe* of May 10 had two main aspects: dissolution of the union, and the curtailment of executive power according to American example. The two were closely linked; though one might infer that George Brown was primarily interested in dissolution as the last remedy for sectionalism in the union, while George Sheppard was chiefly concerned with constitutional reform. The latter subject involved basic principles of government, on which Sheppard considered himself much better informed than Brown. He summed up his employer rather condescendingly: "Take him on to the ground of abuses, financial blunders and wrongs, sectionalism and so forth, and he is the strongest public man in Canada. His capacity for facts is prodigious. But off this ground he is an ordinary man. He has never studied political principles, and knows nothing of constitutional questions, save such as those that have arisen from time to time in Canada. He is a vigorous *Colonial* politician—no less and certainly no more."[93]

The editorials poured forth through May and June, and on into July, depicting with undeniably sharp analysis the failure of cabinet government in Canada, demanding a written constitution and the separation of the executive from the legislature, denying that the changes would in any way endanger the British tie, and even looking beyond dissolution to a Canada of three states that might one day be federated within the British empire. The campaign readily aroused response. The ministerial press was horrified; it saw disloyalty and annexation yawning at the end of the *Globe*'s mad path. Some Reform papers were dubious or even hostile. But many others in the exasperated West welcomed the discussion of dissolution and constitutional changes. There were public meetings to advocate one or the other, or both, at Barrie, Guelph, Ayr, and elsewhere: a series held for McDougall in his constituency of North Oxford came out strongly for dissolution and the written constitution.[94] "The Ball Rolls", exulted Sheppard's *Globe*.[95]

As for Brown, he only stirred himself sufficiently to publish two open letters in reply to a London meeting that had voted confidence in his leadership.[96] But they made quite plain how far his thinking had gone—and that, in his own eyes, the failure of the union and of representation by population to reconstruct it now logically involved the failure of British responsible government as well. "The highest merit of British government," he wrote, "is in the admirable manner in which the popular will as expressed by the people's representatives is brought to bear on the whole administration of public affairs. But in Canada, as now governed, there are two popular wills, as antagonistic to each other as would be the opinions and demands of the peoples of Spain and England, were they forcibly united." Under these conditions, "the attempt to carry out responsible government could only end in failure."[97]

This was the depth of Brown's withdrawal, this flat statement of early June, 1859, published under his own signature: withdrawal from so much he had believed, maintained, and always fought for. He had passed his first five years in Canada struggling for the achievement of responsible government. A large part of the next five, he had devoted to defending responsible government and British parliamentary institutions from radical attacks upon them—and even from the Conservatives' own readiness to institute an elective Legislative Council. And he had spent much of the last five urging the closest possible kind of union between Upper and Lower Canada—in arguing for it earnestly against dissolutionists in his own party. Here, then, was the nadir of depression and defeat for Brown: not because repeal of the union, written constitutional restraints, and removing the executive from parliament were really desperate measures in themselves, but because they were untrue to all that he had stood for. The worries, the strains, strife and disappointments since the Brown-Dorion collapse had drastically taken their full toll.

But unless Brown could somehow prove false to his own character, this would be the bottom; and henceforth the way would lie upward. When his still strong reserves of energy had restored themselves, when the bitter feelings of the late session had subsided, and when his natural confidence and powers of decision came surging back, then a reinvigorated Brown would return to his old, consistent lines of effort. He would return to them, however, with ideas not unaffected by the dark passage through Despond.

5

There were strong signs of a return already visible in a private letter he sent to Luther Holton on July 8.[98] True, it expressed enthusiasm for a policy of constitutional changes—but its very spirit showed that vigour and hopefulness were coming back. He spoke of the "wonderful success the movement has met with", and noted that some who had "freely denounced me and the whole scheme" (chiefly moderates like Foley and Connor) were coming round remarkably well. He did worry, however, about the effects of the argument over the seigneurial tenure question in Lower Canada, hoping especially that "it did not affect Dorion injuriously, for that would indeed grieve me. He has always acted so manfully and generously that it would pain me deeply to think that I had been the means of compromising him. I could not help coming out on that unfortunate tenure business. The silly speeches of some friends from the back benches rendered it absolutely necessary—I should have been greatly damaged had I not spoken. Between ourselves, Laberge did me near the best service I ever received in attacking me as he did. People were really beginning to believe that I had sold U.C. to L.C. for the sake of party success."

It seemed that the old George Brown was speaking, as he laid out freshly optimistic plans: "My firm conviction is that we should merge all our questions in the one great issue of a change of constitution. It will elevate the tone of politics—cast aside the petty, vexatious issues—and be a tremendous card at the next election, come when it may. I cannot see that it should be less successful below than here. We propose having a Convention here in the fall, and if representatives from L.C. could attend it, the effect would be admirable."

"I vastly desire to have a long chat with you," he earnestly continued; and since he planned a brief but much-needed rest by the sea, would "take in Montreal" on the way. Quite probably he meant to go via the Grand Trunk to Portland, perhaps to some seaside spot in Maine: a regular vacation run for Upper Canadians of the day.

Before that holiday, however, a gradual but significant change in emphasis began to be revealed in the *Globe*. The campaign for fundamental reforms started to lay stress upon the idea of a federal union of the two Canadas. Admittedly, the possibility of a dual federation had been mentioned from the outset in the *Globe*'s discussion of "organic changes". But it had been very much subordinated to dissolution pure and simple, and to the remodelling of government along American lines. It had been something of an afterthought, a conceivable alternative to dissolution which would still give Upper Canada the all-important command of its own local affairs: or else it had been mentioned as a development which in time would follow dissolution—a useful answer to opponents who claimed that repeal of the union would only be a retrogression. Now the idea of federation was increasingly pushed forward in its own right.

It was the vigilantly hostile *Leader* which first perceived the shift. On July 7, the *Globe* had sought to argue, none too convincingly, that dissolution need not endanger Upper Canada's unhampered use of the St. Lawrence route since Montreal was too dependent on its trade. But it had added (and this was the important point) that a federal union of the Canadas would provide the necessary security in any case. While the present union must go, a simple form of federation would satisfy the West, and give it "free access to the ocean through the St. Lawrence". This the *Leader* hailed exultantly as an admission that "simple dissolution" had failed to make headway; that the *Globe* instead was ready to concede the great truth of the Coalition's policy of British North American federation.[99] By no means, came the firm reply: a *real* federation would achieve the aims of dissolution. The ministerial policy was a pretence, an excuse to do nothing, since it depended on the other provinces;

but the Reform proposal for a dual federation could immediately be implemented to settle Canada's problems.[100] That pronouncement marked a notable transition. From here onward, dissolution was no longer treated as a primary policy in the *Globe*, but once more as a last resort. Constitutional reforms also received far less attention, as the journal gave itself to arguments for a Canadian federal union. And in this whole development, one might see a restored George Brown reasserting his authority over the policy of his paper.

Sheppard disclosed as much to a sympathetic Clarke, while pouring out his difficulties in keeping the *Globe* up to the policy of organic changes, which until now he had shaped largely as he wished. If, as Sheppard saw it, Brown was "not at all prepared for the distinct committals that had been made", he now knew that Brown had already privately disowned some of them ("and I shall not be surprised to find the disclaimer repeated publicly").[101] His own explanation was that the ex-members of the Brown-Dorion government, having had a taste of office, could not get rid of the taste, and were eager for it again. "Expecting everlastingly to be sent for," they did not wish to compromise their position with too radical a policy. It was Sheppard's turn to be gloomy: "In consequence I am coming to the conclusion that the present leaders of the opposition will not press for the changes which you and I believe to be essential." Mowat, he conceded, did not care for office. "Brown cares less than most of those who were his colleagues, but he cares for it also a great deal too much. . . . This conclusion has not been hastily arrived at, and to me it is both mortifying and embarrassing."[102]

Everything indicated that Sheppard's free run on the *Globe* had been stopped—although it did not follow that the motive he imputed to Brown was the correct one. Possibly the latter did look to office, yet only in the sense that he had looked to it before, to achieve his essential purpose of solving the problem of Canadian union. If he had sought office for its own sake, he surely would have yielded to the criticisms of moderates who argued that his refusal to drop the sectional question was essentially responsible for keeping the Reform party out of power.[103] It was possible, in short, for Brown to want a policy of change no less than Sheppard, Clarke, or like-minded radicals, but to find it now pre-eminently in federation. That measure was not at all in conflict with his previous advocacy of representation by population to bring justice to the West while preserving the union. It was in keeping with his willingness in the Brown-Dorion negotiations to combine rep by pop with protection for the East: the federal principle had even been raised at that time. He had talked of federation to Holton before the session of 1858, and had then been ready to consider it. It thus emerged as the logical culmination of a long development—which had only briefly been upset by his falling into the despair of dissolutionism and permitting Sheppard to call the tune.

There was a further powerful reason why federation should become Brown's leading policy. It offered an effective means of bringing the North West into Canada, and his desire to gain that great territory had never wavered. Ever since the imperial Select Committee of 1857 had brought in its rather inconclusive recommendations on the future of the Hudson's Bay territory, he had repeatedly urged in parliament that Canada press her claims to the western regions. The *Globe*, as repeatedly, had run articles to keep up public interest in the North West. In the summer of 1858 it had enthusiastically supported the opening of steamship service between Georgian Bay and Fort William by the North West Transportation Company. The "North West Company", directed by Toronto associates of Brown such as Macdonell, Howland, McMurrich and McMaster, secured a contract to carry mails to the Red River: it represented Toronto's probing attempt to open a line of communication into the western territory.[104] Hence the *Globe* was loud with indignation when, in the following summer (July of 1859), the government transferred the company's mail contract to a political friend, McLeod, member for Essex—whose poor, decrepit little steamer, it appeared, was in miserable contrast to the Nor' Westers' splendid craft, the *Rescue*.[105]

There were other North Western developments of greater moment. The exciting reports of the preceding autumn that gold had been discovered on the Fraser River had turned the *Globe*'s gaze beyond the Rockies almost for the first time, and during the spring and summer of 1859 that paper ran lengthy correspondence from Vancouver Island, or from the booming gold camps on the mainland in the newly erected province of British Columbia. Far less encouraging was the way in which the Canadian government had refused to do anything effective to assert its rights in the North West. In response to veritable entreaties from the Colonial Office urging Canada to begin suit in the law courts to test the validity of the Hudson's Bay charter, the ministry in April, 1859, had passed an evasive set of resolutions through the Assembly rejecting a judicial test on the grounds that it was a matter for imperial action, and making only a vague claim to western lands that did not even reach as far as the Rockies.[106] The *Globe* condemned this pitiful defeatist policy out of hand.[107] The government's apathetic attitude, paying only lip-service to the prospect of acquiring the North West, was but one more consequence, Brown could feel, of its domination by Lower Canadians who were indifferent to the whole idea of western expansion. Undoubtedly, many French Canadians feared lest they be swamped in an ever greater preponderance of English-speaking population, and Cartier himself was said to be opposed to North-West annexation.[108]

The summer of 1859, however, produced another development to rouse Brown and the *Globe* to even greater concern. The new and fast-growing state of Minnesota was reaching northward towards the Red River Settlement. On July 9, the *Globe* published the news that an American steamboat, the *Anson Northrup*, had made its first trip down the Red to Fort Garry, taking the isolated little settlement completely by surprise. It was a mark of progress that was no less a sign of danger. If, in the existing union, Lower Canadian indifference or hostility prevented an effective move to join the North West with Canada, then the inheritance of half a continent could be lost to American interests that would grow year by year and day by day.[109]

But here, too, federation could provide an answer. Once Lower Canadians were assured of the protection of their own interests within a federal system, they need not fear the addition of new territories that would be populated by English-speaking settlers. Furthermore, the federal principle would supply the effective means of incorporating the North West in the Canadian union, and beyond that, would permit the extension of an even greater British North American union across the whole continent—which ultimately could come to pass. Obviously this was an answer suited to Brown's deepest political impulses. It would win the North West, let Upper Canada control its own affairs, save the union, and allow the merits of British responsible government to be preserved in a political system henceforth freed from the demoralizing effects of sectional cleavage. Federation was the one main thing to go for— the essential programme for the Liberal party.

This was the view that seemed to crystallize in Brown during the latter half of the summer: perhaps as he rested and reflected in August somewhere along the Atlantic coast. At any rate, there was a strange quiescence in the *Globe* that month, as if orders had gone out that nothing more of consequence was to be said on organic changes for the time being, or even on federation. After almost three months of strenuous agitation that had closed with the introduction of the federal theme, the *Globe* by contrast seemed almost lackadaisical in the drowsy

August heat. About the only real excitement was the first "aerial voyage" across Lake Ontario, achieved by one "Professor Steiner" overnight from Toronto to Oswego on the twenty-fourth, and glowingly written up in the paper from the daring balloonist's point of view.[110]

But the cooler airs of September brought a new phase of activity. Talk of a mammoth new Reform convention to redraft party policy had been in circulation since the spring, since the discussion of constitutional changes first began. It seemed evident that changes of such importance could not be adopted by the party's parliamentary forces without referring them first to the membership at large. It was true, moreover, that as the Liberal opposition lacked the helpful gift of patronage, it had to rely on direct appeals to the people to keep up party loyalty and morale; and after the defeats experienced within the year, some grand public gesture was surely necessary to rouse party energy and enthusiasm anew. This had been in Brown's mind during the summer. Now, with new assurance, he moved to take the first step to a convention—a great party gathering that would adopt federation as the basic policy of Reform.

The first step was to communicate with Dorion. Although the movement for constitutional changes had arisen within Upper Canada and expressed a resurgence of western sectional feeling, it would still require Lower Canadian assistance to achieve success. Brown was anxious not to destroy an alliance with eastern Liberals which, if badly damaged during the recent session, had not been wholly lost. On September 7, therefore, he sent a carefully drafted formal invitation to the eastern Reformers through Dorion, to hold an early meeting with the Upper Canadian opposition and discuss "the necessity of some vigorous party movement in reference to the present unsatisfactory position of public affairs".[111] He worded it dexterously, both to assure easterners of an earnest desire to find a common policy acceptable to both sections, and to imply that they need not feel called upon to attend an Upper Canada gathering at this stage. Dorion sent a friendly private answer,[112] followed by a formal reply that said very much what Brown had hoped for: that while he and his Lower Canadian friends agreed that the two opposition groups should co-operate on major questions of the union, it was not necessary now to meet together; their presence might even cause some "inconvenience" to the discussion of purely Upper Canadian problems and opinions.[113]

Dorion's response amounted to an expression of goodwill that left the Upper Canadian forces free to choose their course unhindered by the embarrassing presence of representatives from Lower Canada. That section was bound to come in for a lot of hard words, even though the eastern oppositionists might themselves be blameless. And so, with Dorion's blessing—together with a still more friendly message from McGee[114]—Brown could work to establish his policy within the West alone. After that, it would be referred to the *Rouges* for their advice and assent: but there was little reason to fear hostility there to the federal principle, should it be adopted in the West.

A new all-out drive for federation was sweeping ahead in the *Globe* when Brown and the western parliamentary opposition met in the Rossin House on September 23 to hold their own discussions. With Adam Fergusson in the chair, William McDougall and Gordon Brown as Secretaries, they talked from noon until one o'clock in the morning.[115] They reached a unanimous conclusion (already expressed by Dorion in his message to Brown) that constitutional changes were vitally necessary to redeem the party and the province.[116] Brown had prepared a series of resolutions, all satisfactorily adopted, which rejected various schemes other than federation as a remedy. All the same, Resolution Four, which repudiated the double majority as a permanent solution, was laid aside, since, as Brown said afterwards, "it might have appeared discourteous to Sandfield".[117] The latter was not present, though he was stated to be hoping that, "We will arrange to throw out the ministry."[118]

If Sandfield had been present, there might, indeed, have been more disagreement. Any there was, came from moderates who were closer to him in spirit. For example (Brown told Holton), "Connor and Foley showed fight, but Connor evaporated in the afternoon, and Foley at the close moved a vote of thanks to himself for his good service in bringing out so much information, declaring that he went cordially with the whole movement."[119] And the western leader added genially of a former foe, "Malcolm [Cameron] was there and behaved like a trump. Took capital views, and showed a workable spirit."[120]

As a result, it was agreed to proceed with a Convention. Secretaries were named, William McDougall and John Scoble of Lambton; they were to draft a circular inviting delegates to attend a general meeting of the Upper Canada Liberal party, to be held in Toronto on November 9. Within two weeks the printed circular was ready, calling for the election of delegates in every constituency and municipality, with opposition members of parliament and editors of opposition journals as additional members.[121] Brown's purpose was well forward. The principle of federation had been fully endorsed by the parliamentary Reform contingent. And under his careful sponsorship, it would soon go before one of the most significant party gatherings in Canadian history.

6

October was full of talk of the Convention, as the western Reform press discussed the merits of federation, dissolution and written constitution back and forth with the *Globe*, while the ministerial papers damned the whole project as useless, anti-British and absurd. The circulars had gone out across Upper Canada; in each constituency Liberals were electing delegates. But it was in Toronto, behind the scenes, that the most important events were taking place.

Here Brown and his Toronto associates who formed the real directing element in the Upper Canada Reform party were facing critical problems of strategy and management. The plain truth was that they meant as far as possible to direct the Convention towards the policy set forth at the preliminary Rossin House meeting, where the Reform members of parliament had adopted federation together with a most limited version of organic changes: merely some statutory restraint on the executive's power to spend money. There was no guarantee, however, that such a platform would gain acceptance when put before the representatives of the whole party at the Convention —even with this approval of the elite.

There was a good deal of ardent Reform sympathy for dissolution, plain and simple, chiefly centred west of Toronto in the agrarian democracy of the Peninsula:[122] there the farmers' lack of concern for the St. Lawrence trading system had earlier made it necessary to talk them out of dissolutionism and into support for representation by population. In this great western area, moreover, the enthusiasm of the original Clear Grits for elective institutions was still very much alive. The Reform Alliance of 1857, that had brought Grit radicals together with Brownites and moderate ex-Hincksites, had never disposed of the elective-institutions question. It had merely decided to lay it aside, while concentrating on other goals such as rep by pop and North West annexation, upon which all could agree. It was natural, therefore, that demands for organic changes along American lines should invoke response among the rank and file of western Grit democrats, not to mention some of the more radical parliamentary back-benchers. If the latter had not so far pressed these demands, it was because they lacked effective leaders of their own, and had followed Brown and his close associates for the sake of maintaining party unity. But if the mass democracy of the Convention should speak out for ideas like George Sheppard's, it could encourage them to make a stand for fundamental reform.

On the other hand, there were strong elements in the party just as fervently opposed to radicalism and the repeal of the Canadian union. They grew in strength as one moved eastward from Toronto; and from Kingston on, in areas wholly bound to the St. Lawrence trade, hardly one dissolutionist could be found.[123] Adopting repeal might thus split the party in two. Furthermore, the moderate Reformers looked askance on the prospect of organic changes; and whereas Brown and others like him now supported federation from keen conviction, there were those among the moderates in the parliamentary group—like Foley and Connor again—who had accepted it only with reluctance to avoid more sweeping measures.[124] Moderates were often chiefly concerned with showing Lower Canada that the West was not made up of mad Clear Grit revolutionaries, as they strove to win the eastern support that could put Liberals into power in the existing union. Gain power, they argued, then ministerial corruption and extravagance could be halted: an opposition unable to take office only invited the further ruin of the union under an unscrupulous Coalition that need not fear its foes.

Accordingly, if the coming Convention promised an opportunity to revivify the western Liberal party and give it new direction, it also spelled sheer danger. Could radicals, who would use the crisis of the union to create a new model Upper Canada, be kept associated with moderates who almost denied the crisis—and wanted new policies kept to the absolute minimum? In this touchy situation, federation was not only a constructive policy for Canada; it also offered the best chance of a party compromise. The radical side might be led to see in it a complete remaking of the union, a great organic change in itself, to be accompanied by a written constitution and the prospective transformation of the institutions of government. The moderate side might be brought to view it as the means of keeping ties with Lower Canada and enabling present political institutions to continue, since ruinous sectional issues would be removed to local spheres of government. Here Brown had a unifying principle, if he could virtually sell it to both sides. It offered a crucial test of his abilities of leadership. And here, beyond any question, he proved them—proved again that he was not all impetuosity and impatience, but on a difficult occasion could display the shrewdest skill in party management, together with a cool, judicious sense of timing.

Under his direction, the Toronto headquarters staff of Liberalism laid thoughtful plans for the Convention. Their purpose seemed all too evident to George Sheppard, now virtually on the side-lines although still employed at the *Globe*. He passed on his concern to Clarke, still a thoroughgoing representative of western Grittism. "There is a disposition in some quarters," wrote Sheppard anxiously, "to reduce the thing to a mere formality, ratifying certain views cooked beforehand, and going no further. I have had many battles upon the subject already. I may say that Brown and even McDougall would like to restrict both talk and action within limits by the little committee here, burking discussion on such delicate points as elective governor, paring the written constitution doctrine to the finest possible point, and ignoring the exclusion of the executive. Gordon Brown suggests that anybody going beyond may be gently 'hashed down'. Then touching the platform—the pine speaking-stand I mean—the 'cooking' gentlemen wish to cover the stand with certain great men of their own choosing. I have maintained that in a convention there should be equality, that one delegate is as good as another and that nobody should be on the platform but the chairman, the secretary and the speaker for the time being."[125]

As for the important committee on resolutions, he went on, "there is a general disposition to make the resolutions vague and harmless, and to do this it is hoped that the committee will be manageable." Thus, of course, it would appear to Sheppard, who added with warm feeling, "I hope that in principle, at any rate, there will be no backing down, certainly not without a fair fight. If the affair is to be saved from contempt, the whole constitutional question will have to be debated boldly and fearlessly, and upon the delegates from the country the doing of this will, in my opinion, depend." He himself meant to take no part in the Convention: "Notoriously pro-American, it is best that I should stand aloof."[126] Which was to say that Sheppard realized that the old emotional appeal to British ties and the suspicion of American still might play influential parts in the deliberations of the sons of Upper Canada.

By early November all preparations had been made for the Convention. Well over 500 delegates were expected, about half from the areas west of Toronto, a substantial body from York and the other central counties, and much smaller numbers from the districts east of Peterborough and Kingston.[127] It was apparent that the gathering would chiefly represent that Brownite-Clear Grit combination which George Brown had focused upon the city of Toronto: or, in other terms, would represent the broad hinterland now dominated by the western metropolis.

The eastern Upper Canadian regions of the St. Lawrence and Ottawa valleys, that remained tributary in trade to Montreal, would not be much in evidence at all. It was not surprising that the chief figure of those eastern regions, Sandfield Macdonald, did not intend to turn up.

Nevertheless, it would be the biggest political assembly yet seen in Canada, one burning with indignation at the wrongs long suffered by the West, and, whatever its variety of views, determined to commit the Reform party to some strenuous new effort to put them right. St. Lawrence Hall had been hired, Toronto's most distinguished auditorium. And as November 9 drew nigh, down from the hills of Grey, the lakes of Peterborough, the farms of Oxford, and the farthest reaches of Huron and Essex, came the militant forces of the Upper Canadian country-side, to mingle with town merchants, lawyers, journalists and Toronto party leaders—but always to voice the opinions and sense of outrage of Upper Canada's formidable agrarian majority. Not since the Calebite conventions of early 1850 had the native root-stock of Clear Grittism revealed itself so explicitly. Never had George Brown, the Toronto journalist and business man, faced a sharper task in holding Reform behind his leadership: and in bringing it to accept a policy of federation that might at once seem unwieldy, expensive, and inadequate to the root-and-branch radicals and simple dissolutionists of the farming West.

7

At noon on Wednesday, November 9, the Convention opened in a jammed St. Lawrence Hall.[128] With much cheering, the elderly and Honourable Adam Fergusson was unanimously requested to take the chair; then, as planned, a committee of twelve was set up to nominate regular committees on such matters as procedure, resolutions, and the organization of the party. This all-important nominating committee had obviously been well arranged by Sheppard's "cooking gentlemen". Although it represented western interests in the person of Malcolm Cameron and two other members from the Peninsula, Clear Grits like Christie, and moderates like Foley, the truly significant features of the committee were that Brown, Mowat and McDougall were all on it, that it had an actual preponderance of members from Toronto and eastward, and that for purposes of supporting federation Foley and Connor could be counted in with Brown, Mowat and McDougall. Even Cameron could be added here: Grit radicals such as David Christie were hopelessly outnumbered.

The great Convention then noisily adjourned. When it reassembled at 2:00 p.m., the nominating group presented their slate of committees, which were adopted in much good humour. But once more it was notable how they had been worked out. The most important committee, on resolutions, had been weighted with federationists, loyal Brownites, and a number of easterners again disproportionate to the total composition of the Convention. Brown and Mowat were members; William McDougall chaired the quite significant committee on the organization of the party; Gordon Brown sat on the committee on credentials; but George Sheppard had been shunted off to the relatively minor committee on procedure.

These matters of organization took the afternoon. After dinner, the Convention really got down to business, when the committee on resolutions made its report. It submitted a series of six resolutions, remarkably similar to those adopted at the Rossin House meeting which had been drafted by George Brown. They announced, first, that the existing legislative union of the Canadas had failed; second, that the double majority would be no permanent solution for existing ills. The third resolution had special meaning because it showed how greatly organic changes had been cut down: "Necessary as it is," it read, "that constitutional restraint on the power of the legislature and executive in regard to borrowing and expenditure of money and other matters should form part of any satisfactory change of the existing constitutional system, yet the imposition of such restraints would not alone remedy the evils under which the country now labours."

The fourth resolution rejected the solution of a federation of all the British North American colonies on the grounds of "the delay which must occur in obtaining the sanction of the Lower Provinces." It was not a remedy for present wrongs. The fifth came to the crux of the problem; it proposed federation: "That in the opinion of this assembly the best practicable remedy for the evils now encountered in the government of Canada is to be found in the formation of two or more local governments to which shall be committed the control of all matters of a local or sectional character and a general government charged with such matters as are necessarily common to both sections of the province." The sixth and last resolution was less important, but made a necessary gesture in the direction of rep by pop. While the details of a federal system would be subject to future arrangement, it observed, yet "this assembly deems it imperative to declare that no general government would be satisfactory to the people of Upper Canada which is not based on the principle of representation by population."

The debate on the resolution began. Malcolm Cameron opened with a typically exuberant yet effective speech in favour of federation, asserting breezily that he had always supported the union, and had also always held to the broad principle of representation by population. This conveniently forgot a good deal in between; but in the eyes of Brown and friends of federation the nimble Malcolm redeemed himself by stressing his own awareness as a lumber export merchant of the value of the unity of the St. Lawrence, and by painting the brilliant future prospects of the plan of federation as "the nucleus of an empire extending from the Atlantic to the Pacific". He closed to loud applause, as he affirmed that the resolutions "now before the Convention will lead to a cheap, safe and satisfactory management of the public affairs of the country".

There were one or two minor speeches; but repeated calls for George Brown brought the leader to the platform with some show of reluctance. He had hoped, he said, that he would not have been called upon to address the assembly that evening, and had meant to make his main speech the next day. It was probably true, however, that Brown felt some words of explanation on the resolutions might well be useful at this point. Certainly, he was careful to stress that federation was entirely consistent with the policy that had been adopted by the Temperance Hall Convention of 1857 and taken up by the Brown-Dorion ministry the year after. The policy was still representation by population; but with the protection embodied in it that Lower Canada demanded—and which he always had expressed his readiness to grant. The Brown-Dorion administration, he contended, had been formed on such a basis. "If it had had an opportunity to mature its policy, it would have been very much like that proposed here today, and would have proved entirely satisfactory to the people of both sections of the province."

He was no less careful to emphasize that the details of a scheme of federal union, the designing of its constitution—even the question as to how far the practices of responsible government should be maintained—should all be left to the future consideration of the people's representatives in parliament. He was clearly seeking to avoid issues that might divide the Convention, striving to keep it within the areas where general agreements might be reached. Yet he also tried to make a particular appeal to the sentiments of the dissolutionists by arguing that a federation need not be costly and cumbersome, as so many feared. The general government could be given as little to do as possible, and that clearly defined. It would settle such matters as the collection of revenues, the handling of the public debt, the management of canals and public works, and similar concerns. In this way, he hopefully predicted, they would have all the advantages of dissolution with all the advantages of union! On that happy note, the leader sat down to new rounds of applause. The adjournment was quickly moved. Brown had set the stage for the real discussions to follow, as well as it was possible to do.

Mowat began the proceedings the next morning with another long and eloquent speech in favour of federation. Lesser figures (chiefly farmers, so they stated) followed him; but almost all of them came from districts east of Toronto, and none put forth the case for dissolution. This may have been the reason why George Sheppard changed his mind. In spite of his earlier intention to remain out of the debate, he now felt impelled to take part. He rose, secured the Chairman's eye—and his interposition put a whole new complexion on the crowded meeting. "So far," he said bluntly, "the advocates of federation have had it all their own way. I appear here as the advocate of simple, unadulterated dissolution of the union. I think the time has come to say something on the other side!"

"I take it," he continued boldly, "that this Convention was not called with a view of ratifying any predetermined resolutions, and I think we are here met in friendly communion, not afraid honestly and manfully to declare our differences. . . . If we have differences, let us state them." He did so. He took the ground that federation was unattainable: "We must fight for years in parliament and out of parliament, and if after a long series of years of fighting you have been unable to attain representation by population, I want to know how you are to carry federation with the consent of Lower Canada—especially when it is based on the recognition of the principle of representation by population? But suppose Lower Canada says we won't grant you federation, what are you to do? Are you to continue under this union because Lower Canada says you shall? I put it to the advocates of federation if dissolution is not their only alternative?"

Then Sheppard put it another way, on the ground that dissolution was most desirable in itself. Federation was inevitably expensive: "If you have a federal government you must have a viceroy and all the expenses of a court. Say what you will, a federal government without federal dignity would be near moonshine." And he underlined the cost and complication of a federal union, arguing that, "you will be perpetuating in a stronger form every extravagance and source of ruin and difficulty which we have under our present system." Dissolution did not entail any of these difficulties: "We want economy of expenditure—and we may have it!" On one ground alone would he accept a federation: "If you say you desire federation because it would be a great step to nationality then I am with you—but if it is to be a federation with a view to nationality let us have a federation of all the provinces as much more favourable to that nationality." Even this, however, he really repudiated with the argument that federation was related far more to national than to colonial status. "I do not think you can find any union of colonies based on the federated principle." After all, had not that very principle emerged in the United States with independence?

It was a thoroughly powerful speech, no less than any made by leaders of the party on the other side. It was quickly, keenly, echoed from the floor by numerous dissolutionists. There were eager replies, too, in favour of federation; but what Brown had most to fear was happening: a split in the party, as easterners warned that they would never accept a repeal of the union, while westerners insisted that they would not be dictated to by parliamentary leaders. The afternoon was wearing on in mounting conflict, when Sheppard took advantage of the radicals' new ardour to offer an amendment to the resolution on federation that called instead for "totally unqualified dissolution". He made another long and telling speech that raised strenuous cheers from his supporters. Even Foley's strong argument that if Sheppard had sought to prove federation impracticable, he had by no means proved dissolution practicable, made little impression. Yet Foley sharply pointed out that if federation faced perhaps some difficulty in securing support from Lower Canada, dissolution faced a far more serious one in that it could not even obtain support from all of Upper Canada. "Everywhere from the east of Cobourg there will be an opposed majority against dissolution!" Despite the fact that the first four resolutions had been passed unanimously, the Convention threatened to be moving to a breaking-point.

But at this dangerous juncture William McDougall stepped smoothly forward to suggest a compromise—personable and persuasive as ever. One could hardly avoid presuming that his intervention had been planned beforehand: it came so opportunely, and no one could have filled the role of mediator more

suitably. He was closely linked with Brown, the *Globe*, and the
Toronto leadership; he had been one of the founders of Clear
Grit radicalism; yet he was also on good terms with the moderate element. At any rate, he now proposed an alternative amendment to Sheppard's, which would strike the words "general
government" out of the resolution on federation and substitute
a much more vague expression for it; namely, "some joint
authority". That term, McDougall could declare impressively,
"has already received the sanction of imperial usage in reference
to this very question, as I can show you in the instructions given
to the Earl of Durham when he was sent to this country." He
pointed out that even dissolutionists conceded the necessity for
a joint committee or authority of some kind to manage the property and interests which the two Canadas had acquired in common. As a result, McDougall's usefully indefinite phrase—
linked as it was with the great name of Durham—might hope
to draw considerable approval from both sides in the Convention; for delegates had now become uneasily aware that the
rift was widening to a chasm between them.

Then David Christie rose, surprisingly enough, to support
federation, since he regarded it as a step in the right direction:
toward that general British North American federation which
even Sheppard had declared that he would look upon with
favour. Though dissolutionists fought back, they were obviously
weakening. And if old James Lesslie spoke well on their behalf,
Dr. Connor spoke still better for federal union. But as evening
passed on into night, the demands for George Brown grew
steadily louder, and even more insistent. He was plainly holding fire, waiting for the right moment—in fact, the final moment—to speak.

At the very end, then, he came forward, when the main contenders had exhausted all their arguments and energies, when
the tight-packed floor and galleries were waiting tensely for a
decision, and when even the gods and goddesses disporting on
the ceiling of St. Lawrence Hall seemed to hang still and
breathless in the yellow gaslight, far over the tall figure that
now strode to the front of the platform. As ever, he began
slowly, mildly, complimenting the assembled yeomanry of Upper Canada on its masterly discussion, remarking on the might
of popular power embodied in the Convention, and expressing
his satisfaction that so much accord had been realized on many
vital matters of constitutional change. But then he went on to
the one crucial question of dissolution *versus* federation, Sheppard's amendment *versus* McDougall's compromise. His voice
rose steadily in strength and conviction, as he made one of the

most compelling and statesman-like appeals of his whole career—as he argued with powerful effect for the uniting of the party behind McDougall's amendment.

"There are many members of the legislature here tonight," he said earnestly, "who speak from the field of battle, who thoroughly understand the materials of which the legislature is composed. And there is not one of them who will not tell you that it would be cause for deep regret were this Convention to declare for entire dissolution of the union." This did not mean, he hastened to add, that dissolution might not be theoretically the best remedy. But it did mean that the members of the parliamentary opposition, who were well placed to know, had unanimously agreed that the scheme presented by the committee on resolutions was the best *practicable* position for the Liberal party to occupy—in view of every circumstance. It was this emphasis on the practicable which undercut Sheppard's whole position: Brown was too astute to attack the idea of repeal in itself. "I have no morbid terror of dissolution," he cried. "I have no fear that the people of Upper Canada would ever desire to become the fag end of the neighbouring republic!" That ringing avowal brought a peal of cheers.

He moved to another tack. "What is it that has most galled the people of Upper Canada in the working of the existing union? Has it not been the injustice done to Upper Canada in local and sectional matters? Has it not been the control exercised by Lower Canada over matters purely pertaining to Upper Canada—the framing of our school laws, the selection of our ministers, the appointment of our local officials? Now, Sir, can it be denied that the scheme of the committee strikes at the root of all these grievances? And this fact can never be lost sight of in the argument, that the scheme of the committee would secure us free access to the ocean and every facility for trading with Lower Canada—while dissolution would place us in both respects at the mercy of Lower Canada. Are you content to hand over the entire control of the St. Lawrence, to have customhouse officers stopping our railroad cars and our steamers at certain points in their downward journey and overhauling all the passengers as if entering a foreign country? [Hear, hear!] The whole valley of the Ottawa, the whole district from Glengarry to Kingston is supplied with merchandise from Montreal and sells its timber and produce in return. Do you fancy that you can satisfy the people of that vast section of country, that it would be well to cut off that trade in one day? Not one speaker in favour of dissolution has failed to recognize the necessity of some power to settle the difficulties which may hereafter arise between the two countries. Now, if there must be such a power is it not preferable that the people of Canada should themselves control?"

Practical arguments and warnings aside, there was still another kind of appeal to be made: through a vision of the future that Brown knew would stir his audience, as it stirred himself. With all the force and fire of his enthusiasm, he proclaimed, "Even Mr. Sheppard admits that if the question is placed on the ground of nationality he must go for federation, but a federation of all the British North America colonies. Now, Sir, I *do* place the question on the ground of nationality. I do hope there is not one Canadian in this assembly who does not look forward with high hopes to the day when these northern countries shall stand out among the nations of the world as one great confederation! What true Canadian can witness the tide of immigration now commencing to flow into the vast territories of the North West without longing to have a share in the first settlement of that great and fertile country, and making our own country the highway of traffic to the Pacific? But is it not true wisdom to commence the federated system with our own country, and leave it open to extension hereafter, if time and experience shall prove it to be desirable? And how can there be the slightest question, with one who longs for such nationality, between complete dissolution and the scheme of the committee? Is it not clear that the former would be a death blow to the hopes of future union, while the latter may at some future day readily furnish the machinery of a great confederation?"[129]

He had said all he needed. To roaring applause, he endorsed McDougall's amendment as affording "room for an honourable compromise by all parties". At once Sheppard rose, amid renewed cheering, to withdraw his own amendment, remarking that McDougall's did not suit him exactly; but that if dissolutionists were not to be charged with having thrown away their principle they would gladly make the concession for the sake of party unity. McDougall's amendment was immediately carried. In the whole gathering of 570 members there were only four votes recorded against it. The Convention broke up for the night in a cordial glow: a combination of pleasure and excitement over Brown's speech, public expressions of goodwill among Reformers of all shades—and heartfelt private relief that a disruption of the party had been avoided. The next day there were closing formalities, but the real work of the great Reform Convention had been accomplished.

In every way it had been a triumph for George Brown. He had brilliantly reasserted his leadership: held the moderates on the one side, avoided a revolt of the radicals on the other, and given a disappointed, discontented party a new sense of enthusiastic purpose. He had skilfully steered a huge public meeting to the policy he wanted—and it had required skilful steering, for while the vociferous Convention might be coaxed or persuaded, it could not be forced. Equally, it could not even have been persuaded, had its independent-minded members been convinced that they were being drawn along a predetermined path. It had not been, and could not have been, predetermined to that extent: the Convention was an open, honest voicing of Reform democracy. None the less, careful planning and committee work, judiciously selected resolutions, properly placed speeches, and Brown's own conclusive contribution to the debate at the right time, had won success, despite the numbers of the dissolutionist and radical Clear Grits from the Peninsula. The party had been focused anew about the Toronto leadership, and fixed upon a policy that would preserve a union of the lands of the St. Lawrence. One final point: Brown had brought his party to the principle of federation at a time when such a proposal was all but dead on the other side of politics. It was one more step, and a major one this time, towards the achievement of Confederation.

8

The next immediate task was to spread the Convention programme across Upper Canada. For that purpose the meeting in closing had established the Constitutional Reform Association, with a Central Committee in Toronto that would prepare an address to the electors, setting forth the platform and the reasons behind it. There would be a network of committees to circulate information across the West, along the lines of the Reform Alliance set up at the Convention of 1857. The Association took rooms on Melinda Street; McDougall was appointed the Secretary of its Central Committee. Soon there were four men busy writing the Association's address: Brown, Mowat, McDougall and John Scoble, who had been one of the Secretaries of the Convention.

The *Globe*, of course, played a major part in making the presentation to the public. Hailing the unity which had been achieved, it described the new party platform as composed of two main planks: federation and a written constitution.[130] This was a decided attempt to bury deeper the breach that had almost developed in the party: to claim that the concept of a written constitution had been adopted might help appease the friends of organic changes—though Sheppard would have deemed that doctrine "pared" to the finest point indeed. The *Globe* did have to concede that the words "written constitution" had not appeared in the Convention's third resolution; still, it contended, "their equivalent does". The doctrine had been "virtually affirmed" it said blandly: restrictions on the ministers and the desirability of defining their financial powers had been recommended, and "in these ideas we have to all intents and purposes a written constitution, efficacious and complete".[131]

As for federation, Brown's journal first sought to cover up any difference of opinion by describing the agreement reached at the Convention as "the dissolution of the existing union with the creation of some simple central authority to deal with subjects which have relation both to Upper and Lower Canada".[132] Yet from this statement forward it talked more and more as if federation had been definitely adopted—simple though it was to be. In actuality, McDougall's amendment had avoided the word "federation" in an effort to placate the dissolutionists, and had thus replaced the term "general government" with the phrase "some joint authority" which could be interpreted much as either side desired: it had carefully been asserted that the form of this joint authority would be left to later settlement. But now that the Convention was no longer in being, and the party delegates had gone home, the *Globe* could apply its enormous propaganda power to interpret the Convention compromise essentially as federation. It was done cautiously, with much emphasis on the limited nature of the federal scheme, with full reference to dissolution being "impliedly reserved".[133] But it was deliberate enough, and really represented a further stage in consolidating the victory of Brown and the Toronto leaders over the western agrarian rank and file.

Stress party unity, press federation: that was the plan to exploit success at the Convention—as George Sheppard at the *Globe* office now recognized to his great dismay. "A swindle", he called it angrily.[134] "Virtually, constitutional struggle is now ignored by the *Globe*," he told Charles Clarke. "At least I am not allowed to write about it. The one thing talked about is the prospect of getting office, the one thing to be written about is what you rightly call the old 'rigmarole' of party votes. The instructions are specific. 'No further recognition of different views—no further acknowledgement of compromise. Federation is only to be spoken of.' Suicidal such a course seems to be, but it is the course marked out for the *Globe*. All dissenters, all dissenting views, are to be snuffed out without ceremony."[135]

In consequence he planned to hand his resignation to George Brown on November 30, although he noted that "there has been but one open rupture on the subject, and that with Gordon not George."[136] The row with Gordon, incidentally, had occurred over a matter connected with Clarke. The latter had made a report to the Reformers of his home constituency, North Wellington, on the proceedings of the Convention, setting forth the basis of the compromise achieved there in a way that naturally stressed the dissolutionists' point of view. When Sheppard had tried to insert the report in the *Globe*, Gordon Brown had refused ("in a manner as unjust to you as insulting to myself"), and though the quarrel had passed off, it was further ground for Sheppard's determination to resign.[137]

It was Thursday, December 1, before he was able to have an interview with George Brown himself; the discussion proved considerably revealing. Sheppard found Brown, he admitted, "good-natured and not unreasonable".[138] The *Globe* proprietor explained his course in terms which to the baulked radical disclosed expediency and desire for office; but which, when surveyed more dispassionately, no less indicated political good sense and sound appreciation of realities. Once more Brown showed that he was not all heedless dogmatism and ill-considered haste; once more he showed concern for working with Lower Canadians—and for action on a wider basis than that of Upper Canadian sectionalism, pure, simple and separate, such as Sheppard and his Grit radical friends themselves would recommend.

Brown frankly stressed the ticklish nature of his own position, since so many of his parliamentary allies were still cool to constitutional changes. He defended the need to abstain from further discussion, because only the generalities already agreed upon could now provide the basis of party union. He even argued that, in order to induce Lower Canadians to accept the general principles, specific points must not be brought up at present, and that only by these cautious tactics could an altogether necessary agreement between the Liberals of both Canadas be assured.[139]

Accordingly, he sought to persuade Sheppard not to leave the *Globe* until the close of the next session of parliament, and in the meantime not to mention his departure as even contemplated. Brown coupled his request with a firm declaration that the coming session would determine his own course: that if the Lower Canadians concurred, he would content himself with the moderate platform of the Convention; but that if they did not, he would (so Sheppard reported) "feel compelled to accept our 'extreme views', as he was pleased to call them, and do battle for them 'hammer and tongs'."[140] To this proposal the other— the very different sort of Liberal—reluctantly agreed: "I go on, awaiting the events of the session; giving no clue to possible change; and without meddling with details, profiting by fair occasion to assail the present system."[141]

Hence Sheppard stayed for the time being, while generally across the West Reformers settled back to accept the doctrine of the Convention according to George Brown. All of them— Brown, Sheppard and the whole party together—would have to wait for "the events of the session". The *Globe* put out its own platform for the coming year, 1860: some of it still green wood, like federation and restraint on government borrowing, some of it well weathered by exposure, such as the voluntary principle, non-sectarian education, and the acquisition of the North West.[142] There was the inevitable political lull, however, as the holiday season and the end of 1859 approached. The *Globe* turned from defending the new Reform party against the Toronto *Leader* and the *Montreal Gazette* to describing Toronto's Christmas markets;[143] to reviewing the musical and romantic drama, *The Bottle Imp*, playing at the Royal Lyceum;[144] and to recommending lists of Christmas gifts for harried shoppers: from rocking-horses and wax dolls for the nursery to Parthian marble figurines and the "most beautiful" Landseer reproductions for the parlour.[145]

After many months of business dullness and failures, Toronto was beginning to look prosperous again—thanks largely to Upper Canada's good harvest. Indeed, it was the cheery, boisterous troops of farmers, driving in with Christmas produce and to shop in the good sleighing weather of a bright and snowy December, that did much to give the city its healthy, well-to-do appearance: town and country were still so closely linked.[146] And if it was a brighter Christmas for the West, it was a far brighter one for Brown himself. The past year had carried him far down. Yet at its end he could celebrate a thoroughly triumphant recovery. Personally he was healthy, vigorous and confident; he was back to doing everything with "vim"—one of his favourite words.[147] Financially, his troubles had eased; politically, he had re-inspired his party, preserved its unity under his direction, and led it to the profoundly significant policy of federation.

This was, of course, recovery, not victory. He had gained striking success; but in politics still, any final victory lay far off.

Whatever he had attained with Upper Canada Reform, he had yet to rebuild the alliance with Lower Canadian Liberals—and had then to strive once more against the entrenched Macdonald-Cartier Coalition. The close of 1859, in consequence, left Brown with little that had been conclusively decided; in fact, with a whole mass of unfinished business.

Nevertheless, this was a watershed in the course of his career. It was one of those virtually imperceptible heights of land that the traveller may pass over unawares; until, as he moves onward, it gradually becomes evident that the lie of the country is different, and that swelling streams are flowing in new directions. So it was with Brown. The years immediately ahead would place new demands upon him, set new conditions, open fresh possibilities: the strains to come from the great convulsion of the American Civil War; the quickening prospects of a federal solution in Canada and a new transcontinental state; his own marriage that would mark his life so deeply and so happily. He would be the same George Brown, yet somehow different: strongly influenced by the things which lay before him. A phase of his life was ending for him in 1859, although only the perspective of time would make that clear.

This far, what had he achieved that would be of lasting significance? First of all, and most obvious, the *Globe*. It would remain at the root of his power, and make him always a journalist first, a politician second. Next, there was the sweeping hold that he had won on Upper Canada; for if John A. Macdonald ruled in government, it was George Brown who ruled in the West. Then there was the Reform party he had rebuilt from shattered fragments and successfully held together, stamping it enduringly with his own political ideas. Throughout, he had kept it from left-wing control, both from the original Clear Grit movement and from the radical resurgence of 1859: the Convention would prove to have been radicalism's last chance for many years to come in Canada. The Reform party that went on to Dominion and Ontario politics with Confederation would profess the mid-Victorian parliamentary Liberalism of George Brown—not the elective democracy of the neighbouring American republic.

He had, as well, launched the powerful agitation for the acquisition of the North West, worked unceasingly to interest the Canadian people in an immense western heritage, and committed his party to gaining it. He had striven for the separation of church and state, for the rights of Upper Canada, for representation by population—and in so doing, unquestionably, he and his journal had heaped fuel on sectarian and sectional flames. But the fuel was there to hand, the fires were burning. George Brown did not light them; and perhaps they had to burn themselves out. Fair words would surely not have quenched them. Moreover, even by the end of this first phase of Brown's career, he had shown that he could leave aside religious issues to form ties across sectarian lines with men like D'Arcy McGee, and—much more significant—could seek a just and constructive settlement of sectional questions through the principle of federation.

Still, he remained thus far a sectional champion, however important might be the qualifications. He had grown with the growth of Upper Canada, had come to voice its aspirations and its grievances beyond all else. But this Upper Canada was no less a vigorous part of an incipient Canadian nation. Brown would go on representing the voice of Upper Canada—and in the power of that role, would help to form the nation as no other could have done.

"Christmas eve is spent now much as it was by our fathers. Still the roaring fire is kept, still the strong beer is drunk, still the mince pies are made, the white loaf cut, and all alike are welcomed to the house."[148] Thus wrote the *Globe*, and thus it was at the Browns' home on Church Street. Christmas eve and New Year's eve—the traditional Hogmanay of Lowland Scots —these were prime occasions when the circle of friends and family again drew close. The family at home now consisted only of George and his parents; Gordon and three girls had married; a tragic death had taken Catherine. But Gordon and his young wife Sarah,[149] Isabella and her husband Thomas Henning, lived near at hand; and Marianne could bring her children down from Woodstock for the holidays—Jane might even visit from New York. Then there were the friends: among them, Oliver Mowat and his wife; William Weir, another Scottish immigrant, editor of the *Canadian Merchant's Magazine*, who lived in the same Church Street terrace,[150] and Joseph Morrison, now a political opponent, but an old neighbour who years before had been one of four associates who had put up the money to help found the *Globe*.

There were so many others who called or came to stay at the Church Street house: Alexander Mackenzie or his brother Hope from Sarnia, Luther Holton or William Bristow from Montreal—Bristow who had served with George both as commissioner and inspector in the days of the Penitentiary inquiry. Dr. Burns, now professor of church history at Knox College, was regularly present. He and old Peter Brown loved to argue fine points of politics and theology together; loved it particularly when they ended up in heated disagreement, which was usually the case. Visitors also arrived from New York, Boston, London, Edinburgh and Glasgow, for George always hospitably promised "room for a bed", and his mother Marianne continually found it. Peter, of course, was always eager to see a new face and investigate another mind. It was seldom quiet at the Browns' house; and certainly not at Christmas time, now that family children were making their appearance as well.

It was the Browns' sixteenth Christmas in Canada. It was their home; Scottish beginnings seemed far away. George himself had not been back in Edinburgh for over twenty years and would not make his first return for two years more. Outside, in the chill streets of Toronto and across the frozen countryside of Upper Canada, where farms were snugged down to wait out the winter, was the land he had whole-heartedly accepted, as it had accepted him. But inside in the warm parlour, behind shutters and drawn curtains, where the lamplight and the firelight softly contended on the ceiling, where George Brown sat as ever, hands in pockets, legs thrust out straight before him— talking, as ever, in happy contentment with his father, his family and good friends—it seemed that the Edinburgh household had hardly changed at all.

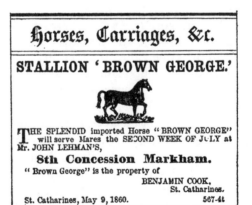

27th February, 1857

Globe Office
Toronto

My dear Sir:

It is said here that your mercantile affairs are irretrievably embarrassed, and that you are quite disheartened about it. I yet trust the case may be exaggerated, but fear there is some truth in it. You may doubt it, but I assure you nothing that has happened in a very long time has grieved me more and I have been thinking ever since I heard of it whether I could not be of service to you in your difficulty. I have had my own pecuniary trials here and in the States, but have I trust got over them; also I am vain enough to believe I have learnt that by experience which might now serve you. If you think so, I am at your services for a few weeks in any part of the country. Don't give way to despondency—from the little I know, you can retrieve matters. The only way in such cases is to look the worst right in the face and go at it with the determination to be at the bottom of it—not to cover up—and to do our duty in the sight of God. There are often circumstances which one has to regret, in looking back, by which perhaps friends suffer. Well, that can't be helped for the past, but the thought of it should only invigorate us to fresh efforts to make amends in the future.

This letter, perhaps rude, perhaps impertinent, may displease you or may produce mere contempt for the writer. I can't help that—I have done my duty and I never did a duty with more sincerity or good feeling. Had I not looked on you as we met in King Street the other day as a rich and prosperous man I would certainly have tried to make friends again. I am not going, even at this moment, to say I do not think you did very wrong in past transactions, but I will say that a knowledge of your sanguine temperament and the effect of a similar temperament on my own actions, ought to have made me at least less harsh. Politics I believe hardens men's hearts worse than anything else.

You may answer this or not, as you like—but I trust whatever you do, you will at the worst give me the benefit of doubt, and throw this letter into the flames and forget it.

Were I in Sarnia, and oppressed, I would seek first to have my mind at rest in God's sight. And as Christian fellowship strengthens one much I would seek the sympathy of my friend, Reverend MacAlister. How easy do trials become when the mind and affections are fixed on things of eternity and we feel that all here is a passing show—may end tomorrow—will end soon. Do you wonder at my writing this? I wonder myself—but thanks to a long-suffering God, I feel it somewhat.

Yours very truly,
(*Signed*) Geo. Brown

(This draft in Brown's handwriting is found in the Brown Papers. There is no indication for whom it was intended but the most likely recipient would seem to be Malcolm Cameron.)

This book is based on manuscript sources, newspapers, and public records contemporary with the period it covers. Most important in the first category are the George Brown Papers and the Alexander Mackenzie Papers. The Brown Papers are actually much fuller for the later period of Brown's life, that falls beyond this volume. They then include, in particular, a great many letters to his wife which not only illuminate his personality effectively but also provide a large amount of political information and comment. Nevertheless, although the papers that deal with the earlier half of his career are of a more scattered character, they offer indispensable aid in depicting and explaining his activities. Furthermore, they are especially useful when taken in conjunction with the Alexander Mackenzie Papers, since the two together set forth both sides of the close and long-enduring relationship between Brown and his successor in the leadership of Liberalism.

Alexander Mackenzie was also Brown's literary executor, which may explain why a number of valuable letters from Brown to another close Liberal associate, Luther Holton, are found in the Mackenzie collection. Mackenzie no doubt secured them from Holton and added them to his own Brown correspondence with a view to compiling a selection of letters for publication in his volume, *The Life and Speeches of the Hon. George Brown* (Toronto, 1882). Until the last few years, in fact, the selected letters he did publish constituted virtually the only significant body of Brown correspondence known to exist. But now that the original copies are available in the Brown and Mackenzie Papers, it is clear that the printed versions were often so cut, edited and "polished" into primness that they no longer have much importance.

The Brown Papers are now at the Public Archives of Canada, Ottawa, thanks to the generosity of Mr. G. E. Brown of Ichrachan House, Taynuilt, Argyll, who agreed to their transfer from the family home in Scotland, where the present writer had examined them in 1956. The Mackenzie Papers are in the Queen's University Archives, Kingston, although the Public Archives has a microfilm copy of the latter to complement previous holdings on Alexander Mackenzie. A number of other Brown letters of value are found in the Macdonald Papers at the Public Archives and in the Robert Baldwin Papers at the Toronto Public Reference Library. Apart from the letters they contain from Brown, these two collections also furnish much useful contemporary political material on Brown's career, as do the John Sandfield Macdonald Papers at the Public Archives and the Thomas Shenston Papers at the Toronto Reference Library. Two other collections of outstanding value for the history of the Clear Grit movement are held at the Department of Public Records and Archives of Ontario, Toronto. They are the William Lyon Mackenzie-Charles Lindsey Papers, and the Charles Clarke Papers. A number of other papers and manuscript sources consulted proved of more limited usefulness; their names appear among the chapter notes that follow.

One of the most important sources of this study lies in a different category: Brown's own newspaper, the *Globe*. There is danger, of course, in using any journal as a major historical source, especially such a thoroughly opinionated sheet as this one was. Still, if one would prepare the biography of a man whose whole life was bound up with a newspaper, it follows that his paper requires the fullest consultation. Moreover, that journal furnishes a basic record both of Brown's achievements and of his ideas and attitudes. If other public men left larger accumulations of personal documents behind them, George Brown left the piled-up issues of the *Globe*. As a source, however, it has been used chiefly to supply opinion: where a matter of fact was involved that was of real importance, the paper was checked against other sources, both manuscripts and hostile newspapers. Yet as a result it did appear that, while the *Globe* from day to day might exaggerate, suppress, or distort in some degree (and certainly most regularly made use of highly coloured language), its record of events over any length of time had an enduring core of accuracy and consistency that could be relied upon.

Other newspapers examined naturally included the *Globe*'s own predecessors, the *British Chronicle* and the *Banner*. Much use was also made throughout of the *Globe*'s Toronto Reform contemporaries, the *Examiner* and *North American*, and of its Tory, Conservative or Coalitionist Liberal enemies, the Toronto *Patriot, British Colonist* and *Leader*—not to mention the Toronto Roman Catholic organ, the *Mirror*. Other papers outside the Toronto press community were consulted on specific questions, such as the *Montreal Gazette*, the Hamilton *Spectator*, the London *Free Press* and the Quebec *Le Canadien*. These and other journals will be found mentioned in the chapter notes below.

In the category of public records, the *Journals of the Legislative Assembly of the Province of Canada* were virtually indispensable, as were certain of their Appendices, notably the *Report on the Provincial Penitentiary* of 1849; also important was *the Proceedings of the Committee of Inquiry of the House of Assembly* of 1856. Little use had to be made of state papers or official dispatches, however, since in this period, at least, Brown had practically no connection with the world of officialdom. But investigation was made both at the Public Record Office in London and the Public Archives in Ottawa into documents chiefly pertaining to Sir Edmund Head and the "Short Administration" of 1858, and mainly into the series C.O.42, for the dispatches from the Governor-General of Canada to the Secretary of State for the Colonies, and the G Series for the dispatches in the other direction.

It should be added that there was no official Hansard for the period dealt with in this volume; hence reports of parliamentary speeches are taken from the newspapers of the day, which covered the debates in great detail. On the whole they seemed quite fair in reporting the words of a political foe: testing the *Globe* on John A. Macdonald and the *Leader* on George Brown, for example, reveals as much; although it was likely that each of them would condense an enemy's speech when reasons of space demanded, while giving its own man's eloquence in full. It is for this reason that the *Globe*'s reports have mainly been used for a book on Brown. In any case, both the *Globe* and the *Leader* had among the best parliamentary reporters in the province.

As a final word, it might be noted that the newspaper files were principally consulted at the Public Archives, the Ontario Archives, the Toronto Reference Library and the Legislative Library of the Province of Ontario. The last two libraries between them provide an all-but-complete file of the *Globes* of the 1850's. A composite file of the 1840's has been microfilmed by the Canadian Library Association, though it still has some early gaps.

Chapter 1

1 Public Archives of Canada, George Brown Papers, Diary of Peter Brown, April 24 to June 30, 1837.
2 See photograph of note in "The Diary of Peter Brown", ed. by J. M. S. Careless, *Ontario History*, vol. XLII (1950), No. 3, p. 112. The original note by Peter Brown is in the possession of Miss Bessie Ball of Woodstock, Ontario, his great-grand-daughter.
3 Peter Brown's Diary.
4 *The Edinburgh Directory for 1831-2; 1834-5; 1836-7*, alphabetical (Edinburgh, n.d.).
5 Guild Register of Edinburgh, September, 1808 to September, 1817 (Edinburgh City Chambers).
6 J. C. Dent, *The Canadian Portrait Gallery*, vol. 2, p. 4 (Toronto, 1881).
7 *Ibid.*
8 *Globe* (Toronto), July 1, 1863.
9 *Edinburgh Almanack for 1835*, p. 218 (Edinburgh, 1835). Same for 1836, p. 241 (Edinburgh, 1836).
10 Speech by George Brown in defence of his father in the Legislative Assembly of Canada, reported in the *Globe*, June 28, 1858.
11 *Ibid.*
12 Peter Brown's Diary.
13 *Ibid.*
14 *Ibid.*
15 Brown Papers, Genealogical Notes of George Mackenzie Brown (George Brown's son).
16 Cup in possession of Mrs. G. M. Brown, Ichrachan House, Taynuilt, Argyll, Scotland.
17 Brown Papers, Notes of G. M. Brown.
18 *Edinburgh Directory for 1808-9* (Edinburgh, n.d.).
19 Brown Papers, Alloa Register of 1827; Notes of G. M. Brown. See also in Brown Papers a newspaper clipping commenting on the shooting of George Brown in 1880, which remarks on his family's connections with Alloa (no name, no date, but clearly originating in Alloa in 1880).
20 *Edinburgh Directory for 1825-6, 1831-2, 1834-5.*
21 Brown Papers, Notes of G. M. Brown.
22 Register of St. Cuthbert's Chapel of Ease (Buccleuch Parish Church, Edinburgh).
23 Brown Papers, Alloa clipping.
24 Sir Daniel Wilson, *William Nelson*, p. 143 (Edinburgh, 1889).
25 *Globe*, May 10, 1880.
26 These volumes, inscribed to George Brown as prizes, are in his library, kept at Ichrachan House.
27 Alexander Mackenzie, *The Life and Speeches of Hon. George Brown*, p. 9 (Toronto, 1882).

28 *Globe*, May 10, 1880.
29 J. C. Dent, *The Last Forty Years, Canada Since the Union of 1841*, vol. I, p. 363 (Toronto, 1881).
30 Dent, *Portrait Gallery*, p. 5.
31 Quoted in Michael Joyce, *Edinburgh: the Golden Age 1769-1832*, p. 155 (London, 1951).
32 *British Chronicle* (New York), October 15, 1842.
33 See speech by George Brown in the Legislative Assembly of Canada, reported in the *Globe*, April 2, 1852.
34 Joyce, *op. cit.*, p. 188.
35 Family tradition reported by the late George Brown Ball, nephew of George Brown, Richmond Hill, Ontario.
36 Speech by George Brown before Anti-Slavery Association of Canada, March 24, 1852. Mackenzie, *op. cit.*, p. 252.
37 The information regarding the Philo-Lectic Society actually comes from Peter Brown's Diary, which apparently began as George Brown's own book. George's name and Edinburgh address are inscribed inside its cover; there follows the speech on phrenology in his handwriting (noted as "delivered" on February 5, 1837). Peter Brown's Diary then starts at the other end of the book and runs back from there. Obviously the father took the volume over from the son.
38 Peter Brown's Diary.
39 *Ibid.* To avoid mere repetition of "*ibid.*", it may be stated that from here down to the next reference below the text is wholly based on Peter Brown's Diary, and all quotations are taken from there.
40 Manuscript Journal of Jane Brown, May 2 to June 28, 1838, in the possession of Miss Bessie Ball.
41 *Ibid.* In similar fashion, to avoid repetition, it may be stated that down to the next reference below the text is wholly based on Jane Brown's Journal and all quotations are taken from there.
42 *British Chronicle*, August 27, 1842.
43 Family tradition, related by G. B. Ball. *Globe*, September 1, 1847, substantiates the tradition that George Brown had visited Canada before 1842. Some sources also claim that the Browns acquired a second store in Albany. See H. J. Morgan, *Sketches of Celebrated Canadians*, p. 770 (Quebec, 1862).
44 Dent, *Portrait Gallery*, p. 5.
45 *Ibid.*, p. 6.
46 See Arthur Schlesinger Jr., *The Age of Jackson* (Boston, 1945), pp. 200-26.
47 Peter Brown's Diary.
48 E. I. Carlyle, *The Dictionary of National Biography, Supplement I*, p. 299 (London, 1901).

49 P. Brown, *The Fame and Glory of England Vindicated*, pp. 260-95 (New York, 1842).
50 *Ibid.*, p. 294.
51 Dent, *Portrait Gallery*, p. 6.
52 *Ibid.*
53 *Ibid.*
54 *British Chronicle*, December 10, 1842.
55 *Ibid.*, December 17, 1842.
56 *Ibid.*
57 *Ibid.*, March 11, 1843.
58 *Ibid.*, March 11, May 6, May 20, 1843. See also *Globe*, May 10, 1880.
59 *Globe*, May 10, 1880. Dent, *op. cit.*, p. 7.
60 Samuel Thompson, *Reminiscences of a Canadian Pioneer*, vol. I, p. 215 (Toronto, 1884).
61 Family tradition, from G. B. Ball.
62 *British Chronicle*, April 22, 1842. No definite proof exists that George Brown was the author of "A Tour in Canada". But it is asserted that he wrote "occasionally" for the *British Chronicle* (see Charles Durand, *Reminiscences of Charles Durand*, p. 436 ([Toronto, 1887]) ; and there is the known fact of his Canadian visit at the proper time, together with the style of "A Tour", to suggest his authorship fairly strongly.
63 *British Chronicle*, June 24, 1843.
64 *Ibid.*, July 22, 1843 ; *Banner* (Toronto), January 26, 1844.
65 *Banner, ibid.*; *Globe*, December 16, 1861.
66 *Banner*, November 17, December 22, 1843 ; *Globe*, December 16, 1861.
67 Thompson, *op. cit.*, p. 216.
68 *Globe*, May 10, 1880.
69 *Ibid.*
70 *Ibid.*
71 *Ibid.*
72 Dent, *Portrait Gallery*, p. 8.
73 E. R. Grace, "Canada's Century-Old Tribute to the Westminster Assembly", *The Presbyterian Record* (Toronto, monthly), April, 1944, p. 108.
74 *In Memoriam, Mrs. W. S. Ball* (Marianne Brown) (privately printed, 1903), p. 5.
75 Family tradition (from G. B. Ball) affirms that the Browns travelled to Canada via the Hudson and Niagara steamboats. Certainly this was the normal route for the time. They must have reached Toronto between July 22, 1843 (the last issue of the *British Chronicle*) and August 18, 1843 (the first issue of the *Banner*). At this time the regular Niagara steamer was the *Chief Justice Robinson*, docking in Toronto at 6 p.m. (see F. Lewis, *The Toronto Directory and Street Guide for 1843-4* [Toronto, 1843], p. 109).
76 *The Maple Leaf or Canadian Annual for 1848* (Toronto, 1847), introduction, n.p. The description of Toronto from the

Bay in 1843 is based on this account of 1847, with corrections made from the *Directory* (see above) and W. H. Pearson (see below) to establish the picture at the earlier date.
77 Charles Dickens, *American Notes for General Circulation* (New York, 1911), p. 244.
78 W. H. Pearson, *Recollections and Records of Toronto of Old* (Toronto, 1914), pp. 33-7.
79 *Ibid.*, pp. 142-3.
80 Charles Dickens to John Foster, quoted in J. E. Middleton, *The Municipality of Toronto : a History*, vol. II (Toronto, 1923), p. 679.
81 "Derry Walls and No Surrender" was an Orange slogan that recalled the desperate siege of Londonderry in Ulster in 1689, where Protestant Irish defenders held out for fifteen weeks against Catholic Irish attacks, until relieved by the forces of William of Orange that arrived from England.
82 Thompson, *op. cit.*, p. 216.
83 *British Chronicle*, July 22, 1843.
84 Peter Brown's Diary.

Chapter 2

1 *Banner*, August 18, 1843.
2 *Ibid.*, September 8, 1843.
3 *Globe*, June 15, 1896. See also C. Durand, *Reminiscences*, p. 436.
4 Elected in 1841, Buchanan had resigned his early seat in 1843, while out of Canada on a protracted business trip in Scotland.
5 H. J. Morgan, *Celebrated Canadians*, p. 558.
6 *Banner*, January 26, 1844.
7 *Ibid.*, August 18, 1843.
8 *Ibid.*
9 *Ibid.*, December 1, 1843.
10 *Ibid.*, January 26, 1844.
11 *Ibid.*, December 15, 1843.
12 *Ibid.*, December 29, 1843.
13 *Globe*, September 1, 1847.
14 See *British Colonist* (Toronto), January 5, 19, 1844 ; *Mirror* (Toronto), January 6, 1844.
15 See *Banner* of January 26, 1844, for the evidence that this as well as the critical editorial of December 15 was written by George Brown.
16 *Banner*, January 26, 1844.
17 *Ibid.*
18 *Ibid.*
19 Toronto Public Reference Library, Robert Baldwin Papers, Hincks to Baldwin, January 28, 1844.
20 Public Archives of Canada, Lafontaine Papers, Baldwin to Lafontaine, January 20, 1844.

21 Baldwin Papers, Lesslie to Baldwin, February 26, 1844.
22 Brown Papers, George Brown to Anne Brown, March 5, 1864.
23 Baldwin Papers, Peter Brown to Baldwin (enclosing £50 in repayment), July 28, 1845.
24 The earliest complete *Globe* now extant is the issue for March 26, 1844, but advertisements ran for some time. That of Wm. Henderson's was dated back to March 26. See also *Globe*, June 4, June 11, 1844.
25 *Ibid.*, June 11, August 16, 1844.
26 *North American* (Toronto), February 26, 1852.
27 *Globe*, October 6, 1847.
28 *Ibid.*, August 16, 1867.
29 The description of George Brown's mode of writing is based on the examination of rough drafts for *Globe* editorials in his hand in the Brown Papers; and on comments in both Robert Sellar, *George Brown, The Globe and Confederation*, pp. 4-5 (Toronto, 1917) and William Buckingham, "George Brown and the Globe", *Canada, an Encyclopedia of the Century*, ed. by J. Castell Hopkins, vol. 5, pp. 201-3 (Toronto, 1899).
30 Sellar, *op. cit.*, p. 6.
31 Public Archives of Canada, Alexander Mackenzie Papers (Microfilm), Brown to Mackenzie, November 4, 1877.
32 *Ibid.*; Sellar, *op. cit.*, p. 7; *Globe*, April 15, 1880.
33 *Globe*, August 6, 1844.
34 *Ibid.*, June 4, 1844.
35 *Ibid.*, June 14, 1844. Market Street became Wellington subsequently.
36 *Ibid.*, September 8, 1846.
37 *Ibid.*
38 *Ibid.*, December 9, 1846.
39 *Ibid.*, April 3, 1847.
40 *Ibid.*, July 30, 1847.
41 *Ibid.*, December 9, 1846.
42 *Ibid.*, September 8, 1846.
43 *Ibid.*, November 25, 1848.
44 *Ibid.*, June 30, 1849.
45 *Ibid.*
46 *Ibid.*, July 19, 1849.
47 *Ibid.*, August 8, 1844; *Toronto City and Home District Directory for 1846-7* (Toronto, 1846), p. 9.
48 *Globe*, June 28, 1858.
49 Sellar, *op. cit.*, p. 7; *Globe*, September 8, 1846; Baldwin Papers, Brown to Baldwin, July 10, 1845.
50 *Ibid.*, December 16, 1861. This article indicates that, in addition to the money furnished to the *Globe* at its start, in 1846 "then leaders of the Reform Party" lent some £350 more for its expansion in the party interest—quite possibly to help it to become a semi-weekly.
51 *Ibid.*
52 *Ibid.*, August 13, 1844; *In Memoriam, Mrs. W. S. Ball*, p. 7.
53 Dent, *Portrait Gallery*, p. 9.
54 *Proceedings at the First General Meeting of the Reform Association of Canada* (Toronto, 1844).
55 *Ibid.*, p. 3.
56 *Ibid.*, pp. 19-20.
57 *Ibid.*, p. 30.
58 *Ibid.*
59 *Ibid.*, p. 31.
60 *Ibid.*
61 *Ibid.*, p. 32.
62 *Ibid.*
63 Public Records and Archives of Ontario, William Lyon Mackenzie Papers, Press Clippings, *Globe*, May 21, 1844.
64 *Ibid.*
65 *British Colonist*, May 31, 1844.
66 C. B. Sissons, *Egerton Ryerson*, vol. 2 (Toronto, 1947), p. 57.
67 *Mirror*, May 31, 1844.
68 While the name "Leonidas" is often attributed to Sullivan, it was used in the *Globe* on May 28, 1844, in commenting on Ryerson's announcement of his letters, whereas Sullivan did not publish the first of his *Legion* series until mid-June (*Globe*, June 18, 1844). See the *Banner*, May 31, 1844, which reprints the *Globe* article of May 28—an issue no longer extant in itself.
69 *Globe*, June 18, 1844.
70 *Ibid.*, September 3, 1844.
71 *Ibid.*, October 1, 1844.
72 *Ibid.*, October 15, 1844.
73 *Ibid.*, October 22, 1844.
74 Baldwin Papers, Brown to Baldwin, October 13, 1844.
75 Enclosure in *ibid.*
76 Dent, *Portrait Gallery*, p. 9.
77 *Ibid.*, p. 10.
78 Quoted in John Lewis, *George Brown* (Toronto, 1910), p. 25. The original *Globes* are no longer extant for the period after the election of 1844. There is a gap from October 22 to December 10 in the files available.
79 Sissons, *op. cit.*, p. 66.
80 *British Colonist*, May 31, 1844.
81 Sissons, *op. cit.*, pp. 71-3.
82 R. F. Burns, *Life and Times of the Rev. Robert Burns, D.D.*, pp. 194-5 (Toronto, 1872).
83 *Banner*, April 10, 1844.
84 *Ibid.*, May 10, 1844.
85 *Ibid.*, July 5, 1844.
86 *Ibid.*, July 12, 1844.
87 *Ibid.*
88 Queen's University Archives, William Morris Papers, Buchanan to Morris, July 5, 1844.
89 *Globe*, July 16, 1844.
90 Burns, *op. cit.*, p. 204; Mackenzie, *op. cit.*, p. 81.
91 *Globe*, January 14, 1845.
92 Dent, *Portrait Gallery*, p. 10.
93 Baldwin Papers, Brown to Baldwin, July 10, 1845.

94 *Ibid.*, endorsation by Baldwin; Hincks to Baldwin, July 14, 1845.
95 *Ibid.*, Hincks to Baldwin, December 16, 1846, March 25, 1847; see also February 14 and April 5, 1845.
96 *Ibid.*, September 18, 1845.
97 Brown Papers, undated, unaddressed draft in Brown's handwriting, applied here by reason of the internal evidence that seems strongly convincing in itself.
98 *Western Globe* (London), October 23, 1845.
99 *Ibid.*
100 *Ibid.*

Chapter 3

1 *Globe Extra*, November 29, 1845; *Western Globe*, December 4, 1844.
2 *Globe*, December 2, 1845.
3 *Ibid.*
4 *Ibid.*
5 *Ibid.*, December 7, 1845.
6 *Ibid.*
7 *Western Globe*, March 20, 1846.
8 *Ibid.*
9 *Ibid.*, February 13, 1846.
10 See J. S. Moir, *Church and State in Canada West* (Toronto, 1959), p. 96.
11 *Western Globe*, August 28, 1846.
12 Baldwin Papers, Hincks to Baldwin, July 14, 1846.
13 *Western Globe*, February 12, 1847.
14 *Ibid.*, March 12, 1847.
15 *Ibid.*, February 26, 1847.
16 *Ibid.*, May 22, 1847.
17 Moir, *op. cit.*, pp. 98-9.
18 Baldwin Papers, Fergusson to Baldwin, November 25, 1847.
19 Public Archives of Canada, Sandfield Macdonald Papers, Baldwin to Macdonald, November 17, 1847.
20 Baldwin Papers, Brown to Baldwin, November 12, 1847.
21 Sandfield Macdonald Papers, Baldwin to Macdonald, November 25, 1847.
22 Baldwin Papers, Hincks to Baldwin, January 8, 1847.
23 Toronto Public Reference Library, Thomas Shenston Papers, W. Carroll to Shenston, November 15, 1847; J. Cameron to Shenston, November 29, 1847.
24 Baldwin Papers, Brown to Baldwin, November 12, 1847.
25 *Ibid.*, Brown to Baldwin, November 21, 1847.
26 *Ibid.*
27 *Ibid.*
28 *Ibid.*
29 *Ibid.*
30 *Ibid.*, Brown to Baldwin, November 26, 1847.
31 *Ibid.*
32 *Ibid.*, Hincks to Baldwin, January 14, 1848.

33 Shenston Papers, Hincks to Shenston, December 15, 1847.
34 *Globe*, December 29, 1847.
35 *Ibid.*, January 5, 1848.
36 *Ibid.*, December 29, 1847.
37 *Ibid.*, January 5, 1848, "Editorial Correspondence".
38 *Ibid.*
39 *Ibid.*
40 *Ibid.*, January 7, 1848.
41 Shenston Papers, Hincks to Shenston, January 10, 1848.
42 Baldwin Papers, Brown to Baldwin, December 15, 1847.
43 Shenston Papers, Baldwin to Shenston, January 24, 1848.
44 *Globe*, July 12, 1848.
45 *Journals of the Legislative Assembly of the Province of Canada* (1849). Appendix BBBBB, Report on the Provincial Penitentiary, First Report of the Commissioners, n.p.
46 *Ibid.*
47 *Ibid.*
48 *Ibid.*
49 *Ibid.*
50 *Ibid.*
51 *Ibid.*
52 *Ibid.*
53 *Ibid.*
54 *Ibid.*
55 *Ibid.*
56 *Ibid.*
57 *Western Globe*, October 23, 1846.
58 Report on the Provincial Penitentiary, First Report.
59 *Ibid.*
60 *Ibid.*
61 *Ibid.*
62 *Ibid.*
63 *Ibid.*
64 *Ibid.*
65 *Ibid.*
66 Baldwin Papers, Fergusson to Baldwin, October 10, 1848.
67 *Ibid.*, Fergusson to Baldwin, November 26, 1848.
68 *Ibid.* See also *ibid.*, December 5, 1848.
69 Report on the Provincial Penitentiary, First Report.
70 *Ibid.*
71 *Ibid.*
72 *Ibid.*
73 *Ibid.*
74 *Ibid.*
75 *Ibid.*
76 *Ibid.*, Second Report of the Commissioners, n.p.
77 *Ibid.*
78 *Ibid.*
79 *Ibid.*
80 See below, Chapter 4, p. 101.
81 Public Archives of Canada, Macdonald Papers, vol. 297, Henry Smith to Macdonald, January 23, 1849. See also *ibid.*, February 1, 1849.
82 *Globe*, January 24, 1849.

83 T. Walrond, ed., *Letters and Journals of James, Eighth Earl of Elgin* (London, 1872), p. 75.
84 *Globe*, February 21, 1849.
85 Public Records and Archives of Ontario, William Kirby Papers, Brown to Kirby, July 12, 1849.
86 *Journals of the Legislative Assembly of the Province of Canada* (1849), p. 142.
87 *Globe*, March 24, 1849.
88 *Ibid.*
89 *Ibid.*, May 5, 1849.
90 *Ibid.*
91 *Ibid.* See also *Globe*, May 2, 1849.
92 Lewis, *Brown*, p. 36. It might be added that Brown also travelled to London, C.W., during May, where on May 14 he personally defended himself in a libel suit brought against the *Western Globe's* proprietor by Col. John Prince, independent member for Essex. His paper had published reports of a civil suit in which Prince had been adjudged drunk while defending a client, and the colonel-lawyer had then sued Brown. Brown's eloquent conduct of his own defence was widely lauded; but he should not have disdained to hire a lawyer. The judge agreed that it was proved that Prince had been drunk, but for technical reasons of law, Brown's publishing the fact, with criticisms, still constituted libel. He was fined £30. The case is of interest as one of the few libel suits brought against the "sensational" *Globe*, and one of the very few lost— and, at that, lost not on a matter of fact but of law. See *Globe*, May 19, 1849.
93 Kirby Papers, Brown to Kirby, July 12, 1849.
94 C. D. Allin and G. M. Jones, *Annexation, Preferential Trade and Reciprocity* (Toronto, n.d.), pp. 54-60.
95 Baldwin Papers, Brown to Baldwin, October 9, 1848.
96 *Globe*, June 23, 1849.
97 *Ibid.*, July 7, 1849. See also *ibid.*, February 21, 1849.
98 *Ibid.*, August 4, 1849.
99 Allin and Jones, *op. cit.*, pp. 74-86; *British Colonist*, July 3, 1849.
100 Allin and Jones, *op. cit.*, p. 61; *Montreal Gazette*, July 28, 1849.
101 *Globe*, July 31, 1849.
102 *Ibid.*, August 11, 1849.
103 *Ibid.*, July 31, 1849.
104 *Ibid.*, August 2, 1849.
105 For example, see *Globe*, September 25, 1847.
106 *Ibid.*, September 6, 1849.
107 Allin and Jones, *op. cit.*, pp. 67-98.
108 See below, Chapter 4, pp. 108-11.
109 Allin and Jones, *op. cit.*, pp. 90-3.
110 *Ibid.*, pp. 134-41.
111 *Ibid.*, pp. 68-9.
112 G. M. Jones, "The Peter Perry Election and the Rise of the Clear Grit Party", *Ontario Historical Society Papers and Records*, vol. 12 (1914), p. 168.
113 *Ibid.*, pp. 168-70.
114 *Ibid.*, pp. 170-1.
115 *Globe*, October 23, 1849.
116 *Ibid.*, October 25, 1849.
117 *Ibid.*, October 20, 1849.
118 *Ibid.*
119 *Ibid.*
120 *Ibid.*, December 6, 1849.
121 Allin and Jones, *op. cit.*, p. 89.
122 *Ibid.*, passim.
123 *Examiner* (Toronto), October 10, 1849.
124 Baldwin Papers, "Poetic Pieces respectfully inscribed to the Hon. Robert Baldwin by Charley Corncobb, Tyendenaga, April 1, 1848".

Chapter 4

1 Chiefly based on Sellar, *op. cit.*, p. 3 and Buckingham, *op. cit.*, pp. 196-200.
2 Chiefly based on W. Weir, *Sixty Years in Canada* (Montreal, 1903), p. 248. See also Sellar, *op. cit.*, p. 5.
3 *Rowsell's City of Toronto and County of York Directory for 1850-1* (Toronto, 1850), p. 16.
4 *In Memoriam, Mrs. W. S. Ball*, p. 7.
5 *Globe*, June 30, 1849.
6 *Rowsell's Directory*, p. 15, p. 51.
7 *Ibid.*, March 25, 1852: Peter Brown "has had no connection whatever with the editorial department . . . for upwards of two years".
8 Family tradition related by G. B. Ball.
9 *Globe*, April 4, 1850.
10 *Ibid.*
11 *Ibid.*
12 See Chapter 5, p. 146 below. Also G. M. Rose, *A Cyclopedia of Canadian Biography* (Toronto, 1886), p. 748.
13 See note 7 above.
14 *Journals of the Legislative Assembly of the Province of Canada* (1849). Appendix RR, Report of the Penitentiary Inspectors for the fiscal year 1848-9 (March, 1850).
15 Provincial Penitentiary Letter Book, November 20, 1848 to December 31, 1856 (made available to the author through the kindness of Mr. J. A. Edmison, Kingston, Ont.), *passim*.
16 Report of the Penitentiary Inspectors for 1848-9.
17 *Ibid.*
18 *Ibid.*
19 *Ibid.*
20 Charles Clarke, *Sixty Years in Upper Canada* (Toronto, 1908), pp. 73-4.
21 *Globe*, April 19, 1850.
22 *Ibid.*, December 1, 1847.
23 Typescript history of the *Globe* (no

author, but probably M. E. Hammond), at the office of the *Globe and Mail* (Toronto), p. 122.

24 *Globe*, March 21, 1849.

25 W. H. Pease and J. H. Pease, "Opposition to the Founding of the Elgin Settlement", *Canadian Historical Review*, vol. 33, no. 3, September, 1957, pp. 203-4.

26 Pease, *op. cit.*, pp. 215-16.

27 *Globe*, March 1, April 3, 1851.

28 *First Annual Report of the Anti-Slavery Society of Canada* (Toronto, 1852), p. 2. See also *Sixth Annual Report* (Toronto, 1857), p. 2.

29 *Times* (Stratford, May —, 1880[?]), obituary article on George Brown, from a selection of press clippings on Brown compiled by the late Frank Yeigh, and kindly donated to the author by Mrs. F. Yeigh.

30 Sandfield Macdonald Papers, Baldwin to Macdonald, January 25, 1848.

31 Baldwin Papers, Brown to Baldwin, October 9, 1848.

32 Brown Papers, Price to Brown, December 28, 1848.

33 Clarke, *op. cit.*, p. 77.

34 Brown Papers, Price to Brown, December 28, 1848.

35 Baldwin Papers, Baldwin to Cameron, May 22, 1848.

36 See *Globe* and *Examiner* for January, 1849.

37 *Examiner*, January 31, 1849.

38 *Globe*, February 3, 1849.

39 *Advocate* (Long Point), *Journal and Express* (Hamilton), *Warder* (Dundas). See *Globe*, January 13, 17, 1849.

40 Moir, *op. cit.*, p. 48.

41 *Ibid.*, p. 49. Moir asserts that it was the powerful influence of Peter and George Brown and their newspapers which brought the Free Church Synod to reject any share in the reserve funds at this time. It should be borne in mind that Free Kirk *clergy* did not necessarily oppose the idea of state payments as firmly as the Free Kirk laity in general—and the Browns in particular. The clergy's stand was in keeping with initial Free Church doctrine: the break from the established Church of Scotland constituted a repudiation of temporal interference in the church, but not a denial of Christ's Headship of the nation—nor of the state's duty to maintain religion, which could follow logically therefrom. Accordingly, a Free Church ministry did not necessarily have to reject all idea of state support, as long as no "intrusion" accompanied it. But the practical fact of the Disruption cut off the Free Church from any state support in Scotland, while in Canada it had none to begin with. In the province, therefore, the actual situation, together with the fervent belief of the Free Kirk laymen, in the total separation of church and state, made this latter

principle ascendant in Free Church thinking—an ascendancy indicated when the Synod in 1848 resolved not to accept any state endowments. Thereafter Free Kirk clergy as well as laity were in the forefront in seeking the secularization of the reserves.

42 *Globe*, March 17, 1849.

43 *Ibid.*, April 7, 1849.

44 *Examiner*, September 19, 1849.

45 *Ibid.*, September 5, 1849.

46 *Ibid.*, October 10, 1849.

47 Allin and Jones, *op. cit.*, pp. 255-65.

48 *Examiner*, November 14, 1849. See also *Mirror*, October 19, 1849.

49 Jones, "Peter Perry Election", pp. 168-70.

50 *Ibid.*, p. 171.

51 *Ibid.*

52 *Examiner*, December 12, 1849.

53 *Globe*, December 4, 1849.

54 *Globe*, December 11, 13, 20, 1849; January 5, 10, 1850.

55 Dent, *Portrait Gallery*, vol. 4, pp. 147-8.

56 Dent, *Last Forty Years*, vol. 2, pp. 186-90.

57 Baldwin Papers, McDougall to Baldwin, June 9, 1847.

58 Dent, *Portrait Gallery*, vol. 4, pp. 204-6.

59 *Globe*, January 10, 1850.

60 Dent, *Last Forty Years*, vol. 2, p. 190. The *Globe* referred to "the 'true grit' party" on December 13, 1849, and on December 20 entitled an article "The 'Clear Grits' ".

61 Clarke, *op. cit.*, p. 61. Clarke's own recollection was that Perry had first used the term "Clear Grit" in a letter to a Whitby newspaper (not found). In any case, it is clear that the *Globe* very early took it up. It is true, of course, that the expression "clear grit" was fairly common parlance, and might readily be applied to a group of radical political purists. J. S. Moir has noted its use as early as 1838, when an effigy of Uncle Sam burned in Kingston along with Mackenzie, Papineau, etc., bore a scroll asserting "We are all clear grit sympathizers" ("Davy Crockett and Upper Canada", *Ontario History*, vol. 48, no. 3, 1956, n.p.).

62 *Globe*, January 10, 1850.

63 Clarke, *op. cit.*, p. 57.

64 *Ibid.*, pp. 56-7.

65 *Ibid.*, pp. 11-15, p. 29.

66 Public Records and Archives of Ontario, Charles Clarke Papers, manuscript of "Address to the Young Men of England".

67 Clarke Papers, McDougall to Clarke, August 20, 1850.

68 *Ibid.*, McDougall to Clarke, August 20, 1850. See also Public Records and Archives of Ontario, William Lyon Mackenzie-

Charles Lindsey Papers, Lesslie to Mackenzie, January 30, 1850.

69 Clarke, *op. cit.*, p. 58. See his "Tracts for the Times by *Reformator*"—sixteen published in the *Mirror* between February 1 and June 7, 1850, and widely reprinted from there. See also Clarke's Papers, McDougall to Clarke, August 20, 1850.

70 Brown Papers, Price to Brown, December 28, 1848.

71 Mackenzie-Lindsey Papers, Lesslie to Mackenzie, January 23, 1850.

72 *Ibid.*

73 *Globe*, December 23, 1849.

74 Clarke, *op. cit.*, pp. 78-9. *Globe*, March 12, 1850.

75 See Chapter 2, above, pp. 56-7.

76 *Globe*, February 14, 1850.

77 The *Examiner* of December 6, 1849 actually bears out this contention.

78 *Globe*, March 12, 1850.

79 *Ibid.*

80 Clarke, *op. cit.*, p. 78.

81 Brown Papers, Adam Fergusson to Brown, March 30, 1850.

82 *Globe*, March 21, 1850.

83 *Ibid.*, March 23, 1850.

84 For example, see *Globes* of March 23, 28; October 31, November 12, 1850.

85 *Globe*, April 9 to May 4, 1850. (The series was cut short by the meeting of parliament.)

86 Mackenzie-Lindsey Papers, Lesslie to Mackenzie, March 4, 1850.

87 Clarke Papers, Lindsey to Clarke, January 18, 1850.

88 *Globe*, January 19, 1850.

89 Clarke, *op. cit.*, pp. 58-65.

90 *North American*, October 31, 1851.

91 *Ibid.*, November 18, 1851.

92 *Ibid.*, October 31, 1851.

93 Clarke Papers, McDougall to Clarke, January 6, 1851.

94 *Globe*, July 20, 1850.

95 *Ibid.*, May 16, 1850.

96 *Ibid.*, May 11, 1850.

97 *Ibid.*

98 *Ibid.*, May 16, 1850.

99 *Ibid.*, June 22, 1850.

100 *Journals of the Legislative Assembly of Canada* (1850), p. 85.

101 *Globe*, July 25, 1850.

102 Allin and Jones, *op. cit.*, pp. 336-52.

103 Moir, *Church and State*, p. 136. The phrase was Ryerson's as Chief Superintendent of Education.

104 *Ibid.*, p. 144.

105 *Ibid.*, p. 143.

106 *Ibid.*, pp. 143-4.

107 *Globe*, July 9, 1850.

108 Moir, *op. cit.*, p. 143.

109 *Globe*, July 20, 1850.

110 *Ibid.*

111 *Ibid.*, July 31, 1850.

112 Baldwin Papers, Brown to Baldwin, October 9, 1848.

113 *Ibid.*, November 26, 1847.

114 *Ibid.*, October 9, 1848.

115 *Globe*, August 29, 1850.

116 *Ibid.*

117 *Ibid.*

118 Baldwin Papers, Brown to Baldwin, August 29, 1850.

119 Moir, *op. cit.*, p. 52.

120 *Ibid.*, pp. 52-3. See also Mackenzie-Lindsey Papers, Lesslie to Mackenzie, March 4, 1850; and *North American*, June 21, 1850.

121 Moir, *op. cit.*, p. 143.

122 *Ibid.*, p. 144; *Examiner*, July 17, 1850.

123 *North American*, June 4, December 13, 1850.

124 *Ibid.*, July 2, 1850.

125 *Mirror*, August 9, 16, September 13, 27, October 4, 1850.

126 *Globe*, October 8, 1850.

127 *Ibid.*, October 15, 1850.

128 W. Ward, *The Life and Times of Cardinal Wiseman* (London, 1912), vol. 1, pp. 542-3.

129 J. E. Collins, *The Life and Times of Sir John A. Macdonald* (Toronto, 1883), p. 139.

130 *North American*, November 29, 1850.

131 *Examiner*, December 18, 1850; *North American*, December 13, 1850.

132 Mackenzie, *Brown*, p. 33.

133 *Globe*, December 10, 1850.

134 F. A. Walker, *Catholic Education and Politics in Upper Canada* (Toronto, 1955), pp. 92-4. See also *North American*, June 18, 21, 1850; *Mirror*, January 24, 1851.

135 *Globe*, January 4, 1851.

136 *Mirror*, January 17, 1851.

137 *Globe*, January 21, 1851.

138 Walker, *op. cit.*, pp. 96-8. See also Moir, *op. cit.*, p. 145.

139 Brown Papers, Fraser to Brown, January 13, 1851.

140 *Ibid.*

141 *Ibid.*

142 *Ibid.*

143 *Globe*, February 25, 1851.

144 *Ibid.*, March 11, 1852.

145 *Ibid.*, March 20, 1851.

146 Brown Papers, Hincks to Brown, March 3, 1851.

147 Mackenzie-Lindsey Papers, 1850-1. See, for example, Mackenzie to Lafontaine, August 2, 1850; Hincks to Mackenzie, April 21, July 2, 1850; Baldwin to Mackenzie, January 4, 1851; Lafontaine to Mackenzie, January 20, 1851.

148 *Ibid.*, Hincks to Mackenzie, February 23, 1851.

149 *Globe*, April 8, 1851.

150 *Ibid.*, March 15, 1851.

151 Brown Papers, Alexander Macdonald to Brown, April 3, 1851.

152 *Ibid.*, George Brown to Peter Brown, April 13, 1851.

153 *Globe*, April 8, 1851.

154 *Ibid.*
155 Brown Papers, George Brown to Peter Brown, April 13, 1851.
156 *Globe*, April 19, 1851.
157 Mackenzie-Lindsey Papers, T. J. Wiggins to Mackenzie, March 26, 1851.
158 *Globe*, April 19, 1851.
159 *Ibid.*, June 24, 1851.
160 *Ibid.*, May 13, 1851.
161 *Ibid.*, April 26, 1851.
162 Mackenzie-Lindsey Papers, Clipping from *Advertiser* (Guelph), April 17, 1851.
163 *Globe*, May 20, 31, 1851.
164 *Journals of the Legislative Assembly of Canada* (1851), p. 117.
165 G. E. Wilson, *Life of Robert Baldwin* (Toronto, 1933), pp. 290-1.
166 Baldwin Papers, Lafontaine to Baldwin, November 6, 1851.
167 *Globe*, July 3, 1851.
168 *Ibid.*
169 *Ibid.*
170 *Ibid.*, July 17, 1851.
171 *Globe*, December 19, 1850. It might be added with reference to the *Globe*'s "No Popery" articles, which have been regularly —but almost unilaterally—condemned by historians, that there does not seem much to choose between the *Globe*'s assertions of ignorance, repression and superstition under Catholic authoritarianism and the *Mirror*'s charges of blasphemy, licence and godlessness under the Protestant "right of private judgement".
172 *Mirror*, October 31, 1851.

Chapter 5

1 *Globe*, June 26, 1851.
2 *Ibid.*
3 *Globe*, *Pictorial Supplement*, December 13, 1856.
4 *Ibid.*, July 12, 1851.
5 *Ibid.*, July 24, 1851.
6 Sir Francis Hincks, *Reminiscences of His Public Life* (Montreal, 1884), pp. 252-3.
7 See *Globe*, *Colonist* and *Patriot* (Toronto) for the latter half of July, 1851.
8 *Globe*, July 31, August 5, 7, 1851.
9 *Ibid.*, August 5, 1851.
10 *Ibid.*
11 *Ibid.*, July 31, 1851.
12 *Ibid.*
13 Mackenzie-Lindsey Papers, McDougall to Lindsey, July 17, 1851.
14 Clarke Papers, McDougall to Clarke, July 25, 1851.
15 *Ibid.*
16 *Ibid.*
17 *Ibid.* Two other radical press associates of McDougall's, George Tiffany and Robert Spence, also worked with Christie on the bargain. See *Globe*, August 22,

1851, March 10, 1854; *Examiner*, August 20, 1851, March 8, 1854.
18 *Globe*, August 7, 1851.
19 *Ibid.*, August 16, 1851.
20 *North American*, August 22, 1851.
21 *Examiner*, December 12, 1849.
22 R. S. Longley, *Sir Francis Hincks, A Study of Canadian Politics, Railways and Finance in the Nineteenth Century* (Toronto, 1943) pp. 284-5.
23 Shenston Papers, Hincks to Shenston, May 2, 1851.
24 *Globe*, August 14, 1851.
25 *Ibid.*
26 *Ibid.*, August 23, 1851.
27 *Ibid.*, August 21, 1851.
28 *Ibid.*, September 25, 1851.
29 *Ibid.*, October 16, 1851; E. C. Kyte, *Old Toronto* (Toronto, 1954), p. 296.
30 Public Records and Archives of Ontario, Crown Land Papers, Shelf 101, J. B. Williams to Commissioner of Crown Lands, March 24, 1851; J. H. Price Letter Book, J. H. P. Shirley to J. Lesslie, March 18, 1865.
31 A. Mackenzie Papers, Brown to Mackenzie, September 13, 1851; V. Lauriston, *Romantic Kent* (Chatham, 1952), p. 418.
32 *Globe*, August 18, 1857.
33 See below, Chapter 7, pp. 210-11.
34 A. Mackenzie Papers, Brown to Mackenzie, September 13, 1851.
35 *Ibid.*
36 While it has sometimes been assumed that Brown first encountered Alexander and Hope Mackenzie through his candidacy in Kent in 1851, his cordial way of writing to them through the fall of 1851, decidedly suggests prior acquaintance. The Mackenzies, furthermore, were associated with Archibald Young and George Stevenson and others active in local Sarnia business and politics (see J. M. S. Careless, "The Independent Member for Kent Reports, 1853", *Canadian Historical Review*, vol. 38, no. 1, June 1957, pp. 41-2), and Brown referred to "my friends" Stevenson and Young in his reply to Mackenzie's invitation to run. Besides, he had known the Kent-Lambton area at least since 1847 when he had reported to Baldwin on political prospects there (Baldwin Papers, Brown to Baldwin, November 12, 1847).
37 Pease, "Opposition to the Elgin Settlement", p. 209.
38 A. Mackenzie Papers, Brown to Mackenzie, September 13, 1851.
39 *Ibid.*
40 *Ibid.*
41 *Ibid.*
42 The series by Gordon Brown ran in the *Globe* through the summer of 1851.
43 A. Mackenzie Papers, Brown to Mackenzie, September 13, 1851.
44 Sir Joseph Pope, ed., *Correspondence*

of Sir John Macdonald (Toronto, n.d.), Macdonald to M. C. Cameron, January 3, 1872, p. 161.

45 *Globe*, October 4, 1851.

46 A. Mackenzie Papers, Brown to Mackenzie, October 2, 1851.

47 *Ibid.*, October 17, 1851.

48 *Ibid.* October 23, 1851.

49 *Ibid.*

50 *Ibid.*, November 7, 1851.

51 Lafontaine Papers, Hincks to Lafontaine, September 15, 1851.

52 Hincks, *Reminiscences*, pp. 254-7.

53 Clarke Papers, McDougall to Clarke, July 25, 1851; Mackenzie-Lindsey Papers, J. S. Macdonald to Lindsey, January 10, 1852.

54 Hincks, *op. cit.*, p. 254.

55 Mackenzie-Lindsey Papers, J. S. Macdonald to Lindsey, January 10, 1852.

56 *Globe*, October 23, 1851.

57 *Ibid.*, September 11, 13, October 2, 4 7, 9, 11, 1851.

58 Provincial Penitentiary Letter Book, Return of Offices for 1851. The new Board of Inspectors were appointed on November 21, 1851.

59 James Young, *Public Men and Public Life in Canada*, vol. 1 (Toronto, 1902), p. 55.

60 *Globe*, December 20, 1851, January 1, 1852.

61 Cobourg *Star*, December 3, 1851; *Globe*, December 6, 1851.

62 *North American*, November 25, 1851.

63 *Globe*, December 6, 1851.

64 *Ibid.*

65 *Ibid.*, December 20, 1851.

66 *Ibid.*, January 1, 1852.

67 *Ibid.*

68 *North American*, November 14, 1851.

69 *Globe*, December 20, 1851.

70 Mackenzie-Lindsey Papers, J. W. Moore to Mackenzie, June 28, 1851; Christie to Mackenzie, August 10, 1855.

71 *Globe*, June 1, 1852.

72 W. H. Higgins, *The Life and Times of Joseph Gould* (Toronto, 1887), p. 201.

73 *Mirror*, October 31, 1851.

74 Quoted in Moir, *Church and State*, p. 150.

75 *Globe*, August 24, 1852.

76 *Ibid.*

77 *Ibid.*, February 1, 1854.

78 Mackenzie-Lindsey Papers, Henry Smith to Charles Lindsey, April 2, 1859.

79 *Patriot*, August 24, 1852.

80 A. Mackenzie Papers, Brown to Mackenzie, December 5, 1860.

81 *Globe*, September 2, 1852.

82 *Ibid.*, September 7, 1852.

83 *Ibid.*

84 *Patriot*, September 2, 1852.

85 *News of the Week* (*Weekly Colonist*), September 4, 1852.

86 Quoted in *Globe*, October 2, 1852.

87 Brown to Mackenzie, August 23, 1852,

quoted in W. Buckingham and G. W. Ross, *The Hon. Alexander Mackenzie, His Life and Times* (Toronto, 1892), p. 109.

88 A. Mackenzie Papers, Brown to Mackenzie, September 4, 1852.

89 Lewis, *Brown*, p. 76.

90 A. Mackenzie Papers, Brown to Mackenzie, March 26, 1853; *Globe*, April 15, 1857.

91 J. Mitchell, *The Settlement of York County* (Toronto, 1952), p. 97.

92 *Globe*, October 5, 1852.

93 *Ibid.*

94 *Ibid.*, September 28, 1852.

95 *Ibid.*, September 11, 1852.

96 *Ibid.*, October 30, 1852.

97 *Ibid.*

98 G. P. Glazebrook, *A History of Transportation in Canada* (Toronto, 1938), p. 168.

99 *Globe*, October 21, 1852. See also his major speech in the Assembly on the Grand Trunk of November 2, *Globe*, November 13, 1852.

100 *Ibid.*, November 4, 1852.

101 *Ibid.*, November 9, 1852.

102 *Ibid.*, December 16, 1852.

103 *Ibid.*, January 27, 1853.

104 *Ibid.*

105 *Ibid.*, February 22, 1853.

106 *Ibid.*

107 *Ibid.*

108 Young, *op. cit.*, p. 54; *North American*, November 25, 1851.

109 *Journals of the Legislative Assembly of the Province of Canada* (1849), p. 168. L. J. Papineau was one of the three *Rouges* who supported this motion.

110 *Census of the Canadas, 1851-2.* vol. 1 (Quebec, 1853), p. xvii, p. xix.

111 *Journals of the Assembly* (1850), p. 107; (1851) p. 205.

112 Five Conservatives had supported the Clear Grit motion of 1850 by H. J. Boulton and Caleb Hopkins (lost, 10-51); ten, including John A. Macdonald, had supported that of 1851 by Boulton and Malcolm Cameron (lost, 15-46).

113 *Globe*, December 30, 1852, open letter from George Brown to the Reformers of Lobo.

114 *Ibid.*, October 9, 1852.

115 *Ibid.*, March 15, 1853.

116 *Ibid.*

117 *Journals of the Assembly* (1852-3), Part I, p. 539.

118 *North American*, July 22, 1853.

119 *Spectator* (Hamilton), August 4, 11, 1855.

120 *Globe*, March 12, 1853.

121 *Ibid.*

122 See Chapter 6 below, pp. 204-5.

123 A. Mackenzie Papers, Brown to Mackenzie, March 26, 1853.

124 Brown to Mackenzie, December 19,

1853, quoted in Buckingham and Ross, *op. cit.*, p. 111.

125 *Ibid.*, September 4, 1852.

126 Brown to Young, March 22, 1853, quoted in Careless, "Independent Member Reports", pp. 46-51.

127 Brown Papers, Macdonell to Brown, April 30, 1853.

128 *Ibid.*, Chaplin to Brown, April 1, 1853.

129 Moir, *op. cit.*, p. 112.

130 *Globe*, March 8, 1853.

131 Sissons, *Ryerson*, vol. 1, p. 273.

132 Moir, *op. cit.*, p. 153.

133 *Ibid.*, p. 154.

134 *Leader* (Toronto), June 7, 1853.

135 *Journals of the Assembly* (1852-3), Part II, pp. 1015-16.

136 *Ibid.*, Part II, p. 182: "a Bill to provide a uniform mode of incorporating Societies formed for Charitable and Educational purposes".

137 *Globe*, March 22, 1853.

138 *Ibid.*

139 D. G. Creighton, *John A. Macdonald: the Young Politician* (Toronto, 1952), p. 189.

140 *Globe*, March 24, 1853. Italics the author's.

141 *Ibid.*, February 24, April 7, 1853.

142 A. Mackenzie Papers, Brown to Mackenzie, June 18, 1853.

143 This term of reproach applied by the government press became a toast at Reform dinners to Brown.

144 Dent, *Last Forty Years*, vol. 2, p. 274.

145 *Globe*, June 4, 1853.

146 *Ibid.*, June 9, 1853.

147 *Ibid.*, June 14, 1853.

148 *Ibid.*, June 9, 1853.

149 *Ibid.*, June 9, 16, 1853.

150 Dent, *op. cit.*, p. 277.

151 *Globe*, June 14, 1853.

152 Brown Papers, William Workman to Brown, July 26, 1853.

153 *Globe*, July 5, 1853.

154 *Ibid.*, December 23, 1851.

Chapter 6

1 *Globe*, August 2, 1853.

2 *Ibid.*, September 8, 1853.

3 *Leader* (Toronto), July 11, 1853. The two Toronto Conservative papers (the *Herald* had died), the *Patriot* and *Colonist*, had also established dailies by this time. The name *Colonist* was applied to the daily; the older title, *British Colonist*, being continued for a semi-weekly edition. The *Patriot* was purchased by the *Leader* at the end of 1854, leaving the *Globe*, *Colonist* and *Leader* as the chief Toronto journals.

4 Manuscript history of the *Globe*, pp. 42-3.

5 *Ibid.*; *Globe*, September 8, 1853. The *Globe* was also big enough now to meet labour troubles—a printer's strike in July of 1853. This, however, and another similar brief episode the following June, will be left to Volume 2 of this work to discuss in relation to the *Globe*'s far larger strike of 1872.

6 *Ibid.*

7 J. R. Robertson, *Landmarks of Toronto*, vol. 1 (Toronto, 1894), pp. 37-8.

8 *Globe*, December 21, 1853.

9 Robertson, *op. cit.*, p. 37.

10 *Ibid.*, p. 38.

11 Manuscript history of *Globe*, p. 48.

12 *Ibid.*, p. 47.

13 *Ibid.* It was also true that assertions by Gordon Brown, "Junior Editor", against John White, ministerial member for Halton, involved George Brown as *Globe* "Senior Editor" in a new libel suit. The case went to the courts in April, 1854. Brown again defended himself—successfully enough that the jury could not agree on a verdict and the case was dismissed. (See *Globe*, March 1, April 24, 25, May 2, 3, 1854.)

14 T. H. Preston, "Reform Journalism", *Globe*, March 19, 1892.

15 Sellar, *Brown and the Globe*, p. 7; *Globe*, June 15, 1896.

16 Mackenzie, *Brown*, p. 293.

17 Recollections of G. B. Ball.

18 Preston, *op. cit.*; Sellar, *op. cit.*, p. 7; G. M. Rose, *A Cyclopedia of Canadian Biography* (Toronto, 1886), p. 748.

19 Sellar, *op. cit.*, p. 7.

20 See *Globe*, July, August, 1853, and especially September 6, 1853. At about this time, apparently, Brown also made an approach for such an alliance to the conductors of the *Montreal Gazette*, John Lowe and Brown Chamberlin. The reference is too vague to place precisely, or to emphasize strongly, since it comes in a letter written forty years later—but quite probably Brown made the overture in the summer of 1853. (Public Archives of Canada, Letter Book of John Lowe, Department of Agriculture, Record Group 17, 1-5, vol. 1, pp. 209-12.)

21 The pro-French majority group was led by the Grand Master, Ogle Gowan, the "Protestant union" minority by George Benjamin.

22 *Montreal Gazette*, August 18, 1853.

23 *Globe*, April 2, 1853.

24 *Leader*, August 26, 1853.

25 *Globe*, August 27, September 6, 1853. Also see *Leader*, September 1, 1853.

26 *Globe*, January 6, 1853.

27 *Ibid.*, May 10, 1853.

28 *Ibid.*

29 Longley, *Hincks*, pp. 238-9.

30 Clarke Papers, McDougall to Clarke, September 17, 1853.
31 *Ibid.*
32 *Ibid.*
33 Cobourg *Star*, September 21, 1853.
34 *Ibid.*
35 *Globe*, October 20, 1853.
36 *Ibid.*, December 26, 1853.
37 *Ibid.*, May 14, 1853.
38 *Ibid.*, April 2, 1852. See also *ibid.*, December 23, 1851, July 14, 1853.
39 *Ibid.*, September 24, October 20, 1853.
40 *Ibid.*, May 10, 1853.
41 *Ibid.*, January 26, 1854.
42 *Semi-Weekly Globe*, February 16, 1854. See *United Empire* (Toronto), February 14, 17, 1854—the semi-weekly edition of the *Patriot*.
43 *Ibid.*, February 13, 1854.
44 *Globe*, May 12, 1853.
45 *Semi-Weekly Globe*, June 22, 1854.
46 *Ibid.*, June 19, 1854.
47 *Globe*, June 24, 1854.
48 *Ibid.*
49 *Montreal Gazette*, June 21, 1854; *Advertiser* (Guelph), June 28, 1854.
50 *Globe*, June 30, 1854.
51 *Journals of the Legislative Assembly of the Province of Canada* (1854), pp. 24, 28.
52 *Ibid.*, p. 28.
53 *Ibid.*, pp. 29-30.
54 *Globe*, June 22, 1854.
55 *Ibid.*, June 24, 1854.
56 *Ibid.*, June 27, 1854.
57 *Ibid.*, June 24, 1854.
58 *Ibid.*, June 28, 1854.
59 A. Mackenzie Papers, Brown to Mackenzie, June 18, 1853.
60 Brown Papers, Mackenzie to Brown, June 29, 1854.
61 *Globe*, July 20, 1854.
62 *Examiner*, July 12, 1854.
63 *Globe*, July 14, 1854.
64 *Ibid.*, August 9, 1854.
65 Creighton, *op. cit.*, p. 206.
66 *Globe*, August 4, 1854.
67 *Ibid.*, July 19, 1854.
68 *Ibid.*, August 25, 1854.
69 A. Mackenzie Papers, Brown to J. S. Macdonald, August 16, 1854.
70 Mackenzie-Lindsey Papers, quoted in W. Spink to Mackenzie, November 18, 1854.
71 Shenston Papers, Hincks to Shenston, August 24, 1854.
72 *Globe*, September 11, 1854.
73 *Ibid.*
74 *Journals of the Assembly* (1854-5), Part I, pp. 2-3.
75 *Ibid.*, p. 3. *Globe*, September 11, 1854.
76 *Globe, ibid.*
77 *Ibid.*, September 12, 1854.
78 *Ibid.*, September 16, 1854.
79 *Ibid.*, September 15, 1854.
80 Clarke Papers, McDougall to Clarke, April 4, 1854; Mackenzie-Lindsey Papers, ——? (indecipherable) to Mackenzie,

June 28, 1854: "you have killed off Rolph, and richly he deserved it".
81 Dent, *Portrait Gallery*, vol. 4, pp. 30-1.
82 J. S. Macdonald Papers, see letters of A. Mackenzie to Macdonald from 1851 to 1855.
83 *Journals of the Assembly* (1854-5) Part I, p. 75.
84 *Globe*, June 9, 1854.
85 Mackenzie-Lindsey Papers, McDougall to Mackenzie, October 23, 1854.
86 *Globe*, October 23, November 2, 3, 24, December 4, 1854.
87 *Ibid.*, November 25, 1854.
88 *Ibid.*
89 *Ibid.*, November 11, 1854.
90 J. S. Macdonald Papers, A. McBean to Macdonald, March 8, 1855.
91 Mackenzie-Lindsey Papers, McDougall to Mackenzie, October 23, 1854.
92 *Globe*, October 11, 1854.
93 *Ibid.*
94 *North American*, October 18, 1854
95 *Ibid.*
96 *Ibid.*
97 Clarke Papers, McDougall to Clarke, April 4, 1854.
98 Mackenzie-Lindsey Papers, Lesslie to Mackenzie, November 15, 1854.
99 *Ibid.*, January 20, 1855.
100 *Globe*, February 17, 1855.
101 *Weekly Globe*, August 29, 1855. The *Examiner*'s last issue was September 5, 1855.
102 *North American*, February 14, 1855.
103 *Globe*, June 15, 1896.
104 Clarke Papers, Gordon Brown to Clarke, March 24, 1855.
105 *Globe*, October 17, 1854.
106 *Journals of the Assembly* (1854-5), Part II, p. 1093.
107 Creighton, *op. cit.*, p. 221.
108 Walker, *Catholic Education and Politics*, pp. 153-70.
109 Sissons, *Ryerson*, vol. 2, p. 328.
110 *Journals of the Assembly* (1854-5), Part II, pp. 1179-80.
111 *Globe*, June 6, 1855.
112 *Ibid.*, June 11, 1855.
113 *Journals of the Assembly* (1854-5), Part II, pp. 1286-7.
114 Repeal of the union was advocated in the *North American* in 1850. (See August 16, 1850.)
115 Mackenzie had even included repeal in his by-election campaign in Haldimand in 1850 (Mackenzie-Lindsey Papers, Haldimand Scrapbook), and thereafter raised it both in parliament and in his *Message* repeatedly.
116 *Globe*, May 10, 1853. See also *ibid.*, October 25, 1853.
117 *Ibid.*, March 6, 1855.
118 *Ibid.*
119 *Examiner*, August 8, 1855. *Globe*, July 23, 1855.

120 *Globe*, June 28, 1855. See also June 13, and *Weekly Globe*, August 24, 1855.
121 *Globe*, July 23, 1855.
122 *Ibid.*
123 *Ibid.*
124 *Ibid.*
125 *Ibid.*, August 14, 1855.
126 *Ibid.*, August 6, 1855.
127 *Ibid.*
128 *Ibid.*
129 *Ibid.*
130 *Ibid.*, August 24, 1855.

Chapter 7

1 *Globe*, October 19, 1855.
2 F. Yeigh, *Ontario's Parliament Buildings, 1792-1892* (Toronto, 1893), pp. 49-50.
3 *Globe*, October 19, 1855.
4 *Ibid.*
5 *Weekly Globe*, October 19, 1855.
6 Public Archives of Canada, Macdonald Papers, vol. 336, F. J. Cheshire to Macdonald, February 18, 1858.
7 D. G. G. Kerr, *Sir Edmund Head, A Scholarly Governor* (Toronto, 1954), pp. 146-7.
8 Cheshire to Macdonald, *loc. cit.*
9 Kerr, *op. cit.*, pp. 146-7.
10 Cheshire to Macdonald, *loc. cit.*
11 *Globe*, November 18, 1854.
12 *Ibid.*, August 18, 1857.
13 Brown Papers, C. J. Brydges to Brown, February 3, 1855.
14 Lauriston, *Romantic Kent*, p. 420.
15 *Globe*, December 28, 1856.
16 *Ibid.*
17 Lauriston, *op. cit.*, p. 420.
18 *Ibid.*
19 *Kentiana*, n.a. (Chatham, 1939), pp. 99-100.
20 Sellar, *Brown and the Globe*, p. 6.
21 *Globe*, December 1, 1854.
22 *Ibid.*
23 *Weekly Globe*, September 14, 1855.
24 *Ibid.*, August 24, 1855. The *Leader*, more cynically, accused Brown of prostrating himself to gain the Northern's patronage for the *Globe* (*Leader*, August 20, 1855).
25 *Ibid.*, October 11, 26, 1855.
26 *Globe*, December 4, 1855.
27 *Weekly Globe*, December 14, 1855.
28 *Ibid.*
29 *Globe*, December 21, 1855.
30 *Weekly Globe*, December 14, 1855.
31 *Globe*, December 21, 1855.
32 *Ibid.*
33 *Ibid.*
34 *Ibid.*
35 *Ibid.*
36 *Ibid.*
37 *Mirror*, January 25, 1856.
38 *Globe*, January 28, 1856.

39 *Ibid.*, February 19, 1855; Moir, *op. cit.*, pp. 18-19.
40 Macdonald Papers, vol. 36, Ross to Macdonald, August 23, 1853; Dent, *Last Forty Years*, vol. 2, p. 336.
41 *Globe*, December 31, 1855.
42 *Ibid.*, January 18, 1856.
43 Public Archives of Canada, Brown Chamberlin Papers, Macdonald to Chamberlin, January 21, 1856.
44 Macdonald Papers, vol. 336, Gowan to Macdonald, October 17, 1859.
45 *Globe*, February 22, 1856.
46 *Ibid.*, May 21, 1856.
47 *Ibid.*, February 27, 1856.
48 *Ibid.*
49 *Ibid.*, February 27, 1856.
50 *Ibid.*
51 *Ibid.*
52 *Ibid.*
53 *Ibid.*
54 *Ibid.*
55 *Ibid.*
56 *Ibid.*, February 28, 1856.
57 *Ibid.*
58 *Journals of the Legislative Assembly of the Province of Canada* (1856), p. 133.
59 *Ibid.*, p. 142.
60 *Globe*, April 19, 1856.
61 *Ibid.*, May 27, 1856; Thompson, *Reminiscences of a Pioneer*, p. 294. Thompson was then editor of the *Colonist*. In his reminiscences (written over a quarter of a century later) he recalled his surprise at finding Brown in confidential discussion with MacNab at the latter's home, just as J. H. Cameron ("I think") had arrived with the news that John A. Macdonald had been chosen leader—"which report broke up the conference and defeated the coalitionists". This memory, however, seems too confused and unsubstantiated to treat as definite fact. To begin with, Thompson dates it as occurring in 1855—but Macdonald did not replace MacNab until 1856. He also dates the *Globe*'s rep by pop agitation as *following* Macdonald's replacement of MacNab—whereas it had begun over a year previous. On the other hand, Brown in annotating proof sheets of a brief biographical sketch of his own life (see Brown Papers, no author, no date) *did* write that he was "offered seat in government", when the Coalition of 1854 was formed. It seems more likely that he was then in communication with MacNab, when he was still hoping to form a party alliance with Conservative forces to replace Hincks's ministry—and when politics were far more in flux than they were by 1856. Thompson, conceivably, in his recollection confused and combined events of 1854 and 1856. Taking the earlier date would also make his statement on the *Globe*'s rep by pop agitation valid. At any rate, because the evidence both from

Brown and Thompson is so thin, the matter
has been omitted from the text and
reserved for discussion here in the notes.
62 *Proceedings of the Committee of Inquiry of the House of Assembly appointed
to investigate the charges made by the Hon.
John A. Macdonald against George Brown
Esq., M.P.P.* (Toronto, 1856)), p. 4.
63 *Ibid., passim.*
64 *Ibid.,* p. 21.
65 *Ibid.,* pp. 48-9.
66 *Ibid.,* p. 51.
67 *Ibid.,* p. 97.
68 *Ibid.,* p. 146.
69 *Ibid.*
70 *Journals of the Assembly* (1856),
p. 514, p. 522.
71 *Ibid.,* p. 538.
72 *Ibid.,* p. 539.
73 *Globe,* May 27, 1856.
74 *Journals of the Assembly* (1856),
p. 555.
75 *Globe,* May 30, 1856.
76 *Proceedings of the Committee of
Inquiry,* p. 227.
77 *Ibid.,* p. 280.
78 *Ibid.,* pp. 286-90.
79 *Globe,* May 12, 1856.
80 Mackenzie-Lindsey Papers, J. Malcolm
to Mackenzie, September 13, 1856. See also
Christie to Mackenzie, September 21, 1856.
81 Walker, *Catholic Education and
Politics,* p. 185, p. 196.
82 *Ibid.,* p. 197.
83 *Globe,* December 27, 1856.
84 Lauriston, *op. cit.,* p. 420.
85 *Globe,* March 21, 1856. Even at the
end of 1854, the *Globe* had claimed
(December 19) that its total circulation
was the largest in the British Empire, "the
London Times and one or two cheap
weeklies alone excluded".
86 *Ibid.*
87 *Globe, Pictorial Supplement,* December
13, 1856.
88 *Globe,* November 10, 1856.
89 *Weekly Globe,* September 14, 1855.
90 *Ibid.,* August 24, 1855.
91 *Globe,* December 21, 1855.
92 *Ibid.,* March 24, 1847; Lewis, *Brown,*
p. 211.
93 *Globe,* March 2, 1857; June 14, 1848;
A. S. Morton, *A History of the Canadian
West to 1870-71* (London, n.d.), p. 825.
94 J. S. Galbraith, *The Hudson's Bay
Company as an Imperial Factor, 1821-1869*
(Toronto, 1957), p. 359.
95 *Globe,* November 12, 1850.
96 Galbraith, *op. cit.,* p. 334.
97 Brown Papers, McLean to Brown,
November 27, 1850.
98 *Ibid.*
99 *Ibid.,* McLean to Brown, October 26,
1853.
100 *Globe,* August 1, 1856.
101 *Ibid.,* August 13, 1856.
102 *Ibid.,* September 1, 1856.

103 *Ibid.,* August 28, 1856.
104 *Ibid.*
105 *Ibid.,* August 19, 1856.
106 *Ibid.,* October 31, 1856.
107 *Ibid.,* October 18, 1856.
108 *Ibid.,* August 19, 1856.
109 Morton, *op. cit.,* p. 827.
110 *Globe,* December 4, 1856.
111 *Ibid.,* December 10, 1856.
112 *Ibid.*
113 Brown Papers, Circular of December
15, 1856.
114 *Ibid.*
115 *Ibid.*
116 *Globe,* November 8, 1856.
117 *Ibid.,* January 9, 1857.
118 *Leader,* January 5, 6, 1857.
119 *Globe Supplement,* Proceedings of
The Reform Alliance, January 16, 1857.
120 *Ibid.*
121 *Ibid.*
122 *Ibid.*
123 *Ibid.*
124 *Ibid.*
125 *Ibid.*
126 *Ibid.*
127 *Ibid.*
128 *Ibid.*
129 *Ibid.*

Chapter 8

1 Clarke Papers, McDougall to Clarke,
January 2, 1857.
2 *Ibid.*
3 *Ibid.*
4 Mackenzie-Lindsey Papers,
A. Mackenzie to W. L. Mackenzie,
January 22, 1857.
5 *Journals of the Legislative Assembly of
the Province of Canada* (1857), Appendix
17, Order-in-Council, February 16, 1857.
6 *Globe,* March 2, 1857.
7 Morton, *History of the Canadian West,*
p. 828.
8 Alexander Fraser, *A History of Ontario,*
vol. 1 (Toronto, 1907), p. 442; *Globe,*
January 22, 1857.
9 *Globe,* March 25, 1857.
10 Kerr, *Head,* p. 172.
11 *Globe,* April 16, 1857.
12 Brown Papers, Mowat to Brown, May
20, 1857.
13 *Journals of the Assembly* (1857),
Appendix 6, *Report of the Special
Committee of Inquiry on the Grand Trunk
Railway.*
14 *Globe,* May 13, 1857.
15 *Ibid.,* May 7, 13, 1857.
16 *Ibid.,* August 18, 1857.
17 *Ibid.,* August 15, 1857.
18 *Ibid.*
19 *Ibid.,* July 21, 1857.
20 *Ibid.,* October 20, 1857.
21 A. Mackenzie Papers, Brown to
Mackenzie, Private and Confidential,
November 25, 1857.

22 Brown Papers, Circular of November 25, 1857.
23 A. Mackenzie Papers, Brown to Mackenzie as "Secretary, Central Reform Association, County of Lambton", November 25, 1857.
24 *Globe*, January 24, 1857.
25 A. Mackenzie Papers, Brown to Mackenzie in the two letters cited in notes 21 and 23 above.
26 *Ibid.*, Brown to Mackenzie, Private and Confidential, November 25, 1857.
27 *Ibid.*
28 Brown Papers, A. McKellar, J. Scoble, A. Knapp to Brown, November 26, 1857, enclosing copy of their letter to M. Cameron of the same date.
29 *Globe*, December 4, 5, 10, 1857.
30 *Ibid.*, December 15, 1857.
31 *Ibid.*, December 9, 1857.
32 *Ibid.*
33 *Ibid.*, December 15, 1857.
34 *Ibid.*, December 12, 15, 1857.
35 *Ibid.*, December 22, 1857.
36 *Ibid.*, December 23, 1857.
37 *Ibid.*
38 *Le Canadien* (Quebec), September 18, 1857, January 13, 27, 1858.
39 Young, *Public Men and Public Life*, vol. 1, pp. 111-12.
40 Buckingham, *George Brown and the Globe*, pp. 190-6.
41 Brown to Archibald Young, March 22, 1853, quoted in Careless, "Independent Member Reports", *Canadian Historical Review*, vol. 38, p. 46.
42 *Globe*, January 14, 1858.
43 A. Mackenzie Papers, Brown to Mackenzie, September 4, 1852.
44 *Ibid.*
45 *Ibid.*, March 26, 1853.
46 *Ibid.*, Brown to Holton, July 8, 1859.
47 Brown Papers, annotations by Brown on a printed sketch of his own life.
48 *Ibid.* See also Brown's speech in the Assembly of February 9, 1859 (*Globe*, February 16, 1859).
49 For example, see Brown's speech at Brampton of July 20, 1855 (*Globe*, July 27, 1855).
50 Debates of the Legislative Assembly of the Province of Canada, Canadian Library Association microfilm of Scrapbook of Press Reports, August 24, 1856.
51 *Colonist*, February 25, 1858.
52 A. Mackenzie Papers, Brown to Holton, January 29, 1858.
53 *Ibid.*
54 *Ibid.*
55 *Ibid.*
56 *Globe*, January 23, 1858.
57 A. Mackenzie Papers, Brown to Holton, January 29, 1858.
58 *Ibid.*
59 *Ibid.*
60 *Ibid.*

61 Brown Papers, Doutre to Brown, February 11, 1858.
62 *Ibid.*
63 *Globe*, February 12, 1858.
64 Brown Papers, James Morris to Brown, January 30, 1858.
65 *Ibid.*, "He has discovered that Mattice alone would follow him".
66 *Ibid.*, D. A. Macdonald to Brown, January 27, 1858.
67 A. Mackenzie Papers, Brown to Holton, January 29, 1858.
68 Mackenzie-Lindsey Papers, Macdonald to Lindsey, January 21, 1858.
69 *Ibid.*, Circular of February 13, 1858.
70 *Globe*, March 11, 1858.
71 *Journals of the Assembly* (1858), Part I, pp. 123-6.
72 Clarke Papers, Sheppard to Clarke, March 17, 1858.
73 *Globe*, May 21, 1858.
74 *Journals of the Assembly* (1858), Part II, p. 835.
75 *Globe*, July 8, 1858.
76 *Ibid.*
77 *Ibid.*
78 *Ibid.*
79 *Ibid.*
80 O. Skelton, *The Life and Times of Sir Alexander Tilloch Galt* (Toronto, 1920), p. 261.
81 *Globe*, June 21, 26, 1858.
82 *Ibid.*
83 Skelton, *op. cit.*, p. 267.
84 *Ibid.*, p. 269.
85 *Globe*, April 15, 1858.
86 Skelton, *op. cit.*, p. 270.
87 *Globe*, July 2, 1858.
88 *Ibid.*
89 *Ibid.*, July 16, 1858.
90 *Ibid.*, June 28, 1858.
91 *Ibid.*
92 *Ibid.*
93 *Ibid.*
94 *Ibid.*
95 *Ibid.*
96 *Colonist*, June 26, 1858.
97 Clarke Papers, Sheppard to Clarke, July 18, 1858.
98 *Ibid.*
99 *Colonist*, June 29, 1858.
100 *Ibid.*, July 19, 1858.
101 *Journals of the Assembly* (1858), Part II, p. 893.
102 *Globe*, July 23, 1858.
103 *Ibid.*
104 *Journals of the Assembly* (1858) Part II, pp. 842-3.
105 Walker, *Catholic Education and Politics*, pp. 218-22; A. Brady, *Thomas D'Arcy McGee* (Toronto, 1925), p. 53.
106 *Globe*, March 3, 1858.
107 *Ibid.*, June 24, 1858.
108 Skelton, *op. cit.*, p. 232.
109 *Globe*, July 17, 1858.
110 *Journals of the Assembly* (1858) Part II, p. 863.

111 *Ibid.*, p. 931.
112 *Ibid.*, p. 932.
113 Creighton, *op. cit.*, p. 266.
114 *Globe*, July 29, 1858.
115 *Ibid.*, July 30, 1858.
116 The official correspondence between Head and Brown concerning the latter's brief administration was read in the Assembly on August 4, and copies laid before the House. The documents were reprinted in the *Globe* of August 5, 1858, which is the source used here.
117 *Ibid.*
118 Brown's fullest explanation of his course of action was set forth in his public speech at the Royal Exchange, Toronto, of August 6, and printed in the *Globe* on August 9, 1858—the source used here.
119 *Ibid.*
120 *Ibid.*
121 Mackenzie, *Brown*, p. 60.
122 Brown Papers, Morris to Brown, January 30, 1858.
123 A. Mackenzie Papers, Brown to Mackenzie.
124 *Ibid.*
125 *Ibid.*
126 Speech at Royal Exchange.
127 *Ibid.*
128 *Ibid.*
129 Head-Brown Correspondence.
130 Kerr, *Head*, p. 188.
131 Speech at Royal Exchange.
132 Assembly Debates Microfilm, August 4, 1858.
133 *Ibid.*
134 Speech at Royal Exchange.
135 Head-Brown Correspondence.
136 *Ibid.* The original copy of this memorandum is in the Brown Papers.
137 *Globe*, August 5, 1858.
138 Head-Brown Correspondence. Brown's handwritten copy of the original is in the Brown Papers.
139 Mackenzie, *op. cit.*, p. 61.
140 Speech at Royal Exchange.
141 *Ibid.*
142 *Globe*, August 5, 1858.
143 *Ibid.*
144 *Ibid.*
145 *Ibid.*, August 3, 4, 1858.
146 *Journals of the Assembly* (1858), Part II, pp. 936-7.
147 Mackenzie, *op. cit.*, p. 61.
148 *Ibid.*
149 Head-Brown Correspondence. The original copy is in the Brown Papers.
150 *Ibid.*
151 *Ibid.*
152 *Ibid.*
153 *Weekly Colonist*, August 6, 1858.
154 *Ibid.*
155 *Ibid.*
156 *Ibid.*
157 *Ibid.*
158 *Statutes of the Province of Canada, 20 Victoria, 1857* (Toronto, 1857), p. 67.

159 Young, *Public Men and Public Life*, vol. 1, pp. 120-1.
160 Kerr, *op. cit.*, p. 193; C. Martin, *Foundations of Canadian Nationhood* (Toronto, 1955), pp. 262-4.
161 Kerr, *op. cit.*, p. 171.
162 *Ibid.*, pp. 172-3.
163 *Ibid.*, p. 201.
164 *Weekly Colonist*, September 3, 1858.

Chapter 9

1 *Globe*, August 6, 7, 1858.
2 Quoted in *Free Press* (London), August 10, 1858.
3 *Weekly Colonist*, August 13, 1858.
4 *Globe*, August 9, 1856.
5 *Weekly Colonist*, August 13, 1858; *Leader*, August 11, 24, 1858.
6 *Globe*, August 30, 1858.
7 *Ibid.*
8 *Ibid.*
9 Martin, *Foundations of Nationhood*, pp. 265-6.
10 Skelton, *Galt*, p. 238. Cartier in his explanations on assuming office specifically tied the seat-of-government question with the project of confederation, when he declared that the ministry would not yet seek to obtain a vote of funds for a new capital.
11 Public Record Office, 30/6, vol. 69. Covering note by Sir Edward Lytton to Cabinet, November 10, 1858; T. F. Elliot, *Memorandum on the Question of the Federation of the British Provinces in North America*; R. G. Trotter, "The British Government and the Proposal of Federation in 1858", *Canadian Historical Review*, vol. 14 (September, 1933), pp. 287-92.
12 *Globe*, March 2, 1858. This remark was actually directed at the *Colonist*, which on February 25, 1858 had written on the idea of British American confederation. But since it succinctly expresses what the *Globe* thought about the actual plan adopted by the Cartier-Macdonald ministry in August of 1858, it is applied here.
13 Martin, *op. cit.*, pp. 267-8.
14 Public Archives of Canada, pamphlet No. 2673, *Question of Federation of the British Provinces in America* (Colonial Office, November, 1858), Lytton to Head, September 24, 1858.
15 P.R.O., C.O. 42, vol. 614, Head to Lytton, August 16, 1858, minute by Lytton.
16 T. F. Elliot, *Memorandum on the Question of Federation.*
17 *Globe*, February 11, 1859.
18 *Journals of the Legislative Assembly of the Province of Canada* (1859), Appendix No. 3, G. E. Cartier, J. Ross,

A. T. Galt to the Secretary of State for the Colonies, October 23, 1858.
19 *Ibid.*
20 Martin, *op. cit.*, p. 270.
21 *Globe*, August 11, 1858.
22 *Ibid.*, December 16, 1861.
23 A. Mackenzie Papers, Brown to Holton, September 17, 1858.
24 Brown Papers, Dorion to Brown, September 14, 1858. Drummond was actually defeated at first, but won another constituency. Holton had not been re-seated in the House since his defeat in the general election of 1857-8, but he subsequently was elected to the Legislative Council.
25 *Globe*, September 25, 1858.
26 Clarke Papers, C. Kirkendall to Clarke, September 6, 1858.
27 Clarke, *Sixty Years in Upper Canada* pp. 138-9.
28 *Globe*, November 9, 1858.
29 *Ibid.*
30 *Ibid.*
31 *Ibid.*, August 9, 1858.
32 Brown Papers, Dorion to Brown, September 14, 1858.
33 *Leader*, October 18, 1858.
34 *Globe*, November 20, 1858.
35 *Leader*, December 20, 1858.
36 *Ibid.*
37 *Ibid.*
38 *Ibid.*
39 *Ibid.*
40 *Ibid.*
41 Sissons, *Ryerson*, vol. 2, p. 357.
42 *Globe*, December 8, 1858.
43 *Dr. Ryerson's Letters in Reply to the Attacks of the Hon. George Brown, M.P.* (Toronto, 1859). Ryerson asserted one of his main purposes was to expose the "traitorous alliance" of Brown and McGee (p. 16).
44 *Globe*, October 28, 1858.
45 *Ibid.*, November 1, 5, 12, 19, 1858.
46 *Leader*, December 24, 1858.
47 *Globe*, January 5, 1859.
48 See Chapter 8, p. 252 above. See also P. G. Cornell, *Political Alignments in the Province of Canada* (Toronto, in press) *passim.*
49 *Globe*, January 5, 25, 1859.
50 *Ibid.*, January 31, 1859.
51 *Ibid.*
52 *Leader*, February 4, 1859.
53 *Globe*, February 14, 1859.
54 *Ibid.*
55 *Ibid.*
56 *Journals of the Assembly* (1859), p. 40.
57 *Globe*, March 23, 30, 1859.
58 John Ross was President of the line, Rose had been active as a government director, Sherwood had close connections—also Galt had had them; while former government members, Taché and Cayley,

still sat on the Grand Trunk Board, as did James Beaty, owner of the *Leader*.
59 See Chapter 7, p. 224 above.
60 *Globe*, February 19, 1859.
61 *Ibid.*
62 Skelton, *op. cit.*, p. 261.
63 *Ibid.*
64 *Globe*, March 15, 1859.
65 *Ibid.*, March 11, 1859.
66 *Globe*, March 9, 14, 1859. Among the leading "business Liberals" at the Toronto Board of Trade meeting were W. P. Howland (President of the Board), John McMurrich, William McMaster, John Macdonald—and George Brown. But prominent Conservatives like George Gooderham and J. G. Worts, showed it was no purely party gathering.
67 *Globe*, March 11, 1859.
68 *Journals of the Assembly* (1859), pp. 216-17.
69 *Ibid.*, "Resolutions relative to the abolition of Feudal Rights and Duties in Lower Canada", pp. 383-5.
70 For Brown's estimate, see *Globe*, April 8, 18; for Cartier's and Macdonald's see following paragraph.
71 *Globe*, April 18, 1859.
72 *Ibid.*
73 *Ibid.*
74 *Ibid.*
75 *Ibid.*
76 *Ibid.*
77 *Ibid.*
78 *Journals of the Assembly* (1859), p. 426.
79 *Leader*, April 30, May 6, 1859.
80 L. T. Drummond to Brown, April 30, 1859, published in *Globe*, May 5, 1859.
81 Brown to Drummond, May 2, 1859, published in *ibid.*
82 Drummond to Brown, May 2; Brown to C. J. Laberge, May 2; Laberge to Brown, May 3, 1859, published in *ibid.*
83 Just at this time, for example, he had to meet one sizeable suit and judgement against him: for £340, together with court costs and interest. Such an amount of cash could not have been easy to find in a colony normally short of hard money and operating largely on credit—and in a depression when there was virtually no cash to realize from his own creditors. See Brown Papers, Patterson and Harrison, solicitors, to Brown, May 23, 1859.
84 J. J. Talman, ed. "A Canadian View of Parties and Issues on the Eve of the Civil War", *The Journal of Southern History*, vol. 5, no. 2 (May, 1939), p. 245; *Globe*, December 16, 17, 1861.
85 Clarke Papers, Sheppard to Clarke, November 4, 1856; October 6, 1857.
86 *Ibid.*, November 4, 1856; November 17, 1857.
87 *Ibid.*, July 18, 1858.
88 *Ibid.*
89 *Globe*, December 20, 1858.

90 Macdonald Papers, vol. 336, R. Spence to Macdonald, October 14, 1859.
91 Clarke Papers, Sheppard to Clarke, February 14, 1859.
92 *Ibid.*, July 5, 1859.
93 *Ibid.*
94 *Globe*, June 11, July 1, 9, 13, 1859.
95 *Ibid.*, June 11, 1859.
96 *Ibid.*, May 30, June 6, 1859.
97 *Ibid.*, June 6, 1859.
98 A. Mackenzie Papers, Brown to Holton, July 8, 1859.
99 *Leader*, July 8, 1859.
100 *Globe*, July 11, 1859.
101 Clarke Papers, Sheppard to Clarke, July 5, 1859.
102 *Ibid.*
103 See, for example, the views of W. D. Mattice, member for Stormont, a moderate follower of Sandfield Macdonald: "George Brown is, in fact, the great marplot which prevents the Opposition from getting the reins of power" (Public Records and Archives of Ontario, William Colquhoun Papers, Mattice to Colquhoun, February 18, 1859). The charge that Brown's insistence on the problem of union kept Reform from office appears repeatedly in the correspondence of moderate Liberals in the earlier half of 1859, and in the press can, for example, be seen in some Reform journals such as the London *Free Press* and Hamilton *Times* (see *Globe*, May 14, May 26, 1859).
104 *Globe*, July 21, 1858; A. Macdonell, *The North West Transportation, Navigation and Railway Company, Its Objects* (pamphlet, Toronto, 1858).
105 *Ibid.*, July 18, 1859.
106 *Leader*, April 16, 1859.
107 *Globe*, April 15, 1859.
108 *Ibid.*, July 9, 1859. For evidence of Cartier's actual opposition to North West annexation, see W. L. Morton, *Manitoba, a History* (Toronto, 1957), p. 107.
109 *Globe*, July 9, 1859.
110 *Ibid.*, August 29, 1859.
111 Brown Papers, Brown to Dorion (draft), September 7, 1859.
112 *Ibid.*, Dorion to Brown, September 12, 1859.
113 *Ibid.*, September 14, 1859.
114 *Ibid.*, McGee to Brown, September 20, 1859. Late in October, moreover, a committee composed of Dorion, McGee, Drummond and Dessaulles presented a report to a Lower Canadian opposition caucus advocating a dual federation as Reform policy—but it was not then voted upon (*Globe*, October 31, 1859).
115 *Globe*, September 24, 1859. See Brown Papers for the resolutions discussed (drafted in Brown's handwriting).
116 A. Mackenzie Papers, Brown to Holton, September 24, 1859.
117 *Ibid.*, October 11, 1859.

118 *Ibid.*, September 24, 1859.
119 *Ibid.*
120 *Ibid.*
121 A. Mackenzie Papers, Circular of October 3, 1859.
122 G. W. Brown, "The Grit Party and the Great Reform Convention of 1859", *Canadian Historical Review*, vol. 16, no. 3 (September, 1935), p. 252.
123 *Ibid.*, p. 259.
124 A. Mackenzie Papers, Brown to Holton, September 24, 1859.
125 Clarke Papers, Sheppard to Clarke, October 27, 1859.
126 *Ibid.*
127 G. W. Brown, *loc. cit.*, p. 252.
128 *Globe*, November 10, 1859. The following section (7) of this chapter is based on the *Globe* reports of the proceedings of the Convention, which ran through six consecutive issues beginning with November 10, 1859.
129 Brown's few brief notes for his major Convention address (jotted on one sheet of paper folded into a strip) are preserved in the Brown Papers. They include, "Not one in L.C. for dissolution—Will British go for it?—Cut off from the Atlantic—Say go for a nationality at once".
130 *Globe*, November 11, 24, 1859.
131 *Ibid.*, November 11, 1859.
132 *Ibid.*
133 *Ibid.*
134 Clarke Papers, Sheppard to Clarke, November 27, 1859.
135 *Ibid.*
136 *Ibid.*
137 *Ibid.*
138 *Ibid.*, December 4, 1859.
139 *Ibid.*
140 *Ibid.*
141 *Ibid.*
142 *Globe*, December 1, 1859. The same issue also announced that the *Globe* office now had "five power printing machines". In fact, even in the bad times of the early part of the year, the *Globe* of January 22 had claimed its circulation "has increased 2,000 within the last few weeks".
143 *Ibid.*, December 24, 1859.
144 *Ibid.*
145 *Ibid.*
146 *Ibid.*
147 *Ibid.*, March 19, 1892.
148 *Ibid.*, December 25, 1859.
149 Sarah Brown was the daughter of Daniel Morrison, a talented editorial writer who served on the *Globe*, and had previously been Sheppard's colleague on the *Colonist* in 1858, when he had agreed with the revolt the latter had briefly staged in that journal against the Macdonald-Cartier regime.
150 W. Weir, *Sixty Years in Canada* (Montreal, 1903), pp. 247-8.